KING ARTHUR

The Mystery Unravelled

To my friend David Pykitt
without whose support and invaluable research
this book would not have been possible

This book is also dedicated to the fond
memory of the late Ruth R. Ingall, our
kindred spirit across the Atlantic –
David and myself are eternally grateful to
Ruth for her wisdom and generosity

KING ARTHUR

The Mystery Unravelled

Chris Barber

PEN & SWORD
HISTORY

First published in Great Britain in 2016 by
PEN AND SWORD HISTORY
an imprint of
Pen and Sword Books Ltd
47 Church Street
Barnsley
South Yorkshire S70 2AS

ISBN 978 1 47386 182 4

Printed and bound in Malta
by Gutenberg Press Ltd

Typeset in Times New Roman by
CHIC GRAPHICS

Pen & Sword Books Ltd incorporates the imprints of Pen & Sword
Archaeology, Atlas, Aviation, Battleground, Discovery,
Family History, History, Maritime, Military, Naval, Politics, Railways,
Select, Social History, Transport, True Crime, Claymore Press,
Frontline Books, Leo Cooper, Praetorian Press, Remember When,
Seaforth Publishing and Wharncliffe.

For a complete list of Pen and Sword titles please contact
Pen and Sword Books Limited
47 Church Street, Barnsley, South Yorkshire, S70 2AS, England
E-mail: enquiries@pen-and-sword.co.uk
Website: www.pen-and-sword.co.uk

Contents

Acknowledgements

I am particularly grateful to David Pykitt whose research over many years has made a substantial contribution to this book, which also contains material from our previous publication *Journey to Avalon*. This was first published by Blorenge Books in 1993, and republished by Samuel Weiser in 1997.

The following institutions, historians and individuals have been indispensable during the research for both books and particular thanks are given to the following:

Dr Rachel Bromwich of Aberystwyth; Dr Brynley F. Roberts, Librarian, National Library of Wales; D.B. Lloyd, Secretary of the National Library of Wales; Richard H. Lewis, Assistant Librarian, National Library of Wales; Carol Edwards and Emyr Evans, the National Library of Wales, John Kenyon, Librarian, National Museum of Wales; Anna Skarseyriska, Royal Commission on the Ancient and Historical Monuments of Wales; Helen Turner and Oliver Davis of Cadw, Cardiff; Enid Nixon, Assistant Librarian, Westminster Abbey; R.J.H. Hill, Reference Librarian, Hereford City Library; Mrs Dowdle, Assistant Librarian, Gloucester City Library; P.J. Phillips and J.B. Jones, Cardiff Central Library; Ann Gallagher, University College of Wales Library, Swansea; Mrs Barber, Truro County Reference Library; Pauline Thomson, Assistant Librarian, The William Salt Library, Stafford; Jennifer Smallman, Assistant Librarian, Ludlow Library; Elizabeth Berry, University of Reading; the staff of University of Birmingham Library, Birmingham City Library, Cambridge University Library, Cardiff City Library, Burton-on-Trent Library, Lichfield Library and Derby Local Studies; Mr Walrond, Curator, Stroud Museum; Michael Williams, Bossiney Books, St Teath, Bodmin, Cornwall; Glenys Cooper and staff at Waterstone's Bookshop, Burton-on-Trent; Chris Shepard of Needwood Bookshop, Burton-on-Trent; the staff of Byrkley Books, Burton-on-Trent; Bookstall Services, Derby; Fagin's Bookshop, Derby; Laura's Bookshop, Derby; Hornby's

Bookshop, Birmingham; Dillon's Bookshop, Birmingham; John D. Austin of Arden House, Atherstone; the Revd A. Caldwell, Atherstone; Ray Tarr, St David's Cathedral; the Revd Edwin Thomas Richards of Llangammarch Wells; Canon Raymond Lockwood Ravenscroft, Probus, Truro, Cornwall; the Revd Russen William Thomas, Stratton, Cornwall; the Revd Michael Mountney, Whitchurch, Herefordshire; Norman Stubbs of Alrewas; Chris Lovegrove, Kate Pollard, Eddie Tooke and Fred Steadman-Jones of the Pendragon Society; Charles Evans-Gunther of the Dragon Society; Derek Bryce, Llanerch Press; Elizabeth Leader, Patrick Graucob, Robert Cowley, Brian and Joyce Hargreaves of the Research into Lost Knowledge Organisation; Major George M. Williams, Owain A.M. Williams, Robert M. Williams, Murray A. Mclaggan, L.V. Kelly, Selwyn Williams, University of Wales, Lampeter College; Michael Wilcox, Glamorgan Archives Service; John Vivian Hughes, Swansea Reference Library; Claire Smith, Neath Reference Library; Mike Hill, Mold Library; Graham Thomas, National Library of Wales; J. Bryn Jones, Cardiff Central Library; Richard Abbott and Margaret Donnison, Birmingham Central Library; Dawn Birkinshaw, Manchester Central Library; Anthony Beeston, Bristol City Library; Ms Nicholls, Cardiff Castle; the Revd J.J. Williams, St Basil's Church, Bassaleg; Arthur Stelfox; Robert Hardwick; Dave Pauley; George Perrell. Special thanks goes to Pat Walton and Paul Parry for their immeasuarable contributions to the research programme.

Preface

To provide a convincing solution to the matter of Arthur is an extremely difficult task for it is very difficult to unravel the truth behind the legend. One has to deal with both a mythical Arthur and a literary Arthur, while somewhere lurking in the background there is a historical Arthur. Unfortunately, there is no reference to Arthur from his own time and even Gildas, his contemporary, fails to mention him.

Stories of Arthur used to be related by the Celts of Wales, Cornwall and Brittany, and fact mingled with fiction made him the hero of some ancient tales that existed even before he was born. The deeds of Arthur are celebrated in French songs and German legends, while the Celtic stories of the *Mabinogion* provide glimpses of heroic events that happened long before they were written down.

It is accepted that the time of Arthur straddles the fifth and sixth centuries, which are often referred to as the Dark Ages, but it must be stressed that this term is not an accurate description of the years following the withdrawal of the Roman legions for it was one of the most interesting periods in the history of Britain. In many respects it was a time of enlightenment and renaissance achieved by the activities of men of vision operating in a well-organised society. It was a formative period that saw the birth of most of the languages, the ideals and traditions that still today predominate in the greater part of the British Isles.

Britain at that time was divided and sub-divided into petty kingdoms which were governed by independent sovereigns and were often at war with each other. There was no Wales, England or Scotland, just the Island of Britain, which had been governed by the Romans for about four centuries. In this book we reveal that the story of Arthurian Britain is one of a titanic struggle for supremacy between two rival factions led by members of two opposing British dynasties.

Geoffrey of Monmouth was a monk posing as a historian and in his famous book *History of the Kings of Britain* he presented Arthur as an epic hero who has been treated with disbelief. Yet it is possible to identify an authentic figure who provided the basis for the story.

It was the medieval writers who brought Arthur into their own period so that he could be more easily identified, and between 1250 and 1450 stories of this heroic king and his 'knights of the Round Table' appeared in almost every western European language. A fairy tale kingdom was invented for Arthur and accounts of his daring deeds recounted by bards in Cumbria, Wales, Cornwall and Brittany.

The identity of Arthur as a historical figure was the theme of my previous book *Journey to Avalon*, co-authored with David Pykitt and first published by Blorenge Books in 1993. During the following two decades we continued an intensive programme of research to reinforce our theories. By using a wide variety of sources and re-examining various manuscripts it is possible to show that a misinterpretation of early Welsh genealogies has obscured the identity of the Celtic prince who can be identified as 'Arthur'.

A time slot was needed in which to place Arthur and if one considers that the Battle of Badon most likely took place between 490 and 520 then it is reasonable to assume that he would have been around in that period. Next it was necessary to identify his most likely area of operation and it very soon became evident that Gwent and Glamorgan, the ancient land of the Silures, was the true realm of a historical King Arthur.

Following the time of Arthur, the Cymry were forced to retreat to the hills and valleys of the west which became their only refuge. Wales, as it was later known, was to prove the natural stronghold for the survival of the Britons. Here flourished a people who retained their language through the passing centuries to become the Welsh nation of today.

English publishers who looked at the manuscript of *Journey to Avalon* turned it down because it was packed with Welsh personal and place names, and it was even suggested that we should try anglicising them. We pointed out that it is only by giving Welsh names that the truth of the matter can be revealed. The anglicisation, suppression and corruption of Welsh history are the very reasons why the story and identity of Arthur has been obscured.

Three-hundred years after Geoffrey of Monmouth wrote his *Historia Regum Britanniae*, Henry Tudor sailed with an army from Brittany to land in Wales. Marching under the Red Dragon of Cadwaladr, he won for the true line of the Britons the Crown of England on Bosworth Field. Then using Geoffrey's work to boost his claim to the throne, he called his first born son Arthur, who had he outlived his father would have succeeded to the throne as Arthur the Second.

PREFACE

The idea that the famous Arthur of history and legend was in fact a 'Welshman' is hard for many people to accept. Confusion and brainwashing through the passing centuries has made this Dark Age Celtic warrior a legendary hero of England. This is largely due to the romantic writings of Sir Thomas Malory, who transformed him into a fifteenth-century hero leading a band of knights clad in shining armour. Likewise, the Poet Laureate Alfred Lord Tennyson made him a symbol of England's greatness. It seems remarkable that his enemies, the very people against whom he waged an unrelenting war, have turned him into their own national hero. Arthur the battle leader has become in legend King Arthur of England!

Welsh history continues to be ignored by the majority of Arthurian scholars and it is only by getting to grips with the complex matter of ancient Welsh names, titles and geography that the answers to many previously unanswered questions can be provided.

Chris Barber
Llanfoist, 2016

CHAPTER 1

Who was King Arthur?

It was the early bards who first mentioned a man named Arthur in their epic war poems which were composed in Rheged, an area of Britain now known as Cumberland. These verses celebrated the military prowess of a man named Arthur and it would seem that in the beginning he was more famous in the north than he was in the south. This has led some historians to locate his story in the border region of Scotland, while on the other hand there are others who firmly believe that his realm was in the West Country. However, the object of this book is to provide proof that the truth of the matter can only be found in Wales.

I will endeavour to explain why so much confusion has arisen and to locate Arthur in his correct place, but first of all it is necessary to sort out the identity of the various Arthurs who have been suggested as the basis for the King Arthur of legend and history.

Arthur of Dalriada
It was in the seventh-century Latin manuscript relating to the *Life of St Columbanus* (543–615) that the name of Artur (Arthur) was first mentioned.[1] It was written by Adomnan, a successor of St Columba, at the monastery of Iona.[2] This Artur (born c.570) was the son of Aedan mac Gabrain, King of Dalriada (now Argyll and Kintyre), the area on the north-west coast of Scotland, colonised by the Irish Gaels.[3]

Artur died fighting the Picts at the Battle of the Miathi, which was fought near the River Forth in Manau Guotodin in about 590–6.[4] Miathi appears to be the Irish form of the tribal name Maeatae, described by the Roman writer Dio Cassius as a tribe hostile to Rome, living next to the Antonine Wall.

While Artur mac Aedan is the earliest verifiable personage with the name 'Arthur', he is much too late to be the historical King Arthur.[5] To identify this Artur of Dalriada with the Arthur of legend is to disregard the evidence contained in Nennius's *Historia Brittonum* and the *Welsh Annals*, and to deny him his most famous victory at the Battle of Badon, fought in c.516. Aedan was well known to the British and he has never been represented in the Arthurian legend.[6]

Arthurian place names were once common in Strathclyde, a good example being Ben Arthur, near Loch Long, which may be named after Artur mac Aedan.

The Arthur Mentioned by Aneurin

The bard Aneurin in his epic poem *Y Gododdin*, written in about 595, describes the feats of a certain British hero, called Gwawrddur, by saying that his valour was remarkable, 'although he was no Arthur'.[7] This statement suggests that everyone at that time would have known who Arthur was. Roman names had by then gone out of use in Britain and the Latin name Arturius or Arthurius became shortened to Arthur through changes in speech.

The Votadini were a tribe living in the Edinburgh area and they were fighting the Angles of Deira. The Arthur referred to in this poem was most likely Artur, the son of Aedan mac Gabrain of Dalriada.

Although presumed to be written in the sixth century by the bard Aneurin, the poem may in fact date from the tenth century, or perhaps the ninth, but no earlier. Too much weight has been attached to one line: 'gochore brein du ar uur/caer ceni bei ef arthur' – 'fed black ravens on the rampart of a fort, although he was no Arthur'. This line only appears in one of two versions of the text which casts doubt on its being part of the presumed original sixth-century poem.

There were at least three men named Artur living in south-western Scotland at the time that *Y Gododdin* was compiled. These were Artur mac Aedan, Artur mac Conaing (probably named after his uncle Artur mac Aedan) and Artur mac Bicoir, who slew Morgan mac Fiachna of Ulster in 620/625.

Artorius the Roman Soldier

In 1925 the suggestion was made that the story of Arthur is based on Lucius Artorius Castus, praefectus castrum of the Sixth Legion. This Roman soldier lived in the second century (c.140–200) and served the Empire in the Middle East, Romania, Italy, Britain and Yugoslavia. He was stationed in Britain and served as praefectus (or prefect) of the VI Victrix Legion, which he led from York in AD 184 to suppress a rebellion in Armorica (Brittany).

There are two monuments near Split in old Yugoslavia which commemorate Lucius Artorius Castus, and one of the inscriptions tells us that he attained the rank of *dux* in the Roman army. It is relevant that while in Britain, Artorius, just like the Arthur of legend, commanded a band of cavalry, for this could explain why Nennius, writing in the eighth century, using a 'heap of material', referred to Arthur as a *dux bellorum* (battle-leader).

Arthur of Dyfed

A reasonably historical Arthur (c.570–615) once resided in Dyfed (south-west Wales). Of Irish descent, he was Artur mac Petuir (Arthur son of Pedr) and his great-grandfather was Vortiporius (c.470–c.545), whose memorial stone can be seen in Carmarthen Museum.[8]

Lineage of the Kings of Dyfed

Eochaid Allmuir ('from Overseas')
Corath
Aed Brosc
Triphunus Farchog ('the Knight')
Aircol Lawhir (Agricola 'the Long-handed')
Gwerthefyr (Vortiporix)
Cyngar
Pedr
Arthur
Noe (Nowy)

The Latin Name of Arthur

During the Roman occupation of Britain the name Artorius was quite common, and in post-Roman times it continued to be used. In the latter part of the sixth century there were at least four or five people called Artorius who lived in the Celtic areas of the British Isles.

It is important to emphasise that no Latin sources refer to Arthur as Artorius, but instead the Latinised Welsh version of the name is used, i.e., Arthurus, Arturus or Arturius. If Arthur's name had come from Artorius we would expect to find the Latin form of the name used in Latin texts such as the *Annales Cambriae* or the *Historia Brittonum*, but in both works the name appears as Arthur.

The *Historia Brittonum* (attributed to Nennius) refers to Arthur as Arturus and this name can be found in the earliest of the surviving manuscripts dating from the tenth or eleventh centuries. In the ancient *Book of Llandaff* the name Athruis appears and is most likely derived from Arturus.

The normal ending for an individual's name in Latin is *us* and such an ending was often added by the Britons to non-Latin names to give them a

Latin appearance (hence Arthurus). In the earliest Latin of Nennius and the *Welsh Annals* the form Arturus is found.

Legend of St Goeznovius (1019) Arturo
Lifric of Llancarfan (c.1073) Arthurus/Arthurius
Vita Carantoci (c.1100) Arthur
Vita Illtuti (c.1100) Arthurii
William of Malmesbury (c.1125) Arturis
Henry of Huntingdon (c.1129) Arthurus/Arturus
Geoffrey of Monmouth (c.1136) Arturus
Caradoc of Llancarfan (c.1150) Arthuro
Giraldus Cambrensis (c.1191) Arthuri
Ralph of Coggleshall (c.1200) Arturi

Seventh–Ninth-Century Arthurs

An entry in the *Annals of Tigernach* for 620–5 records that 'Mongon mac Fiachna Lwgan was struck with a stone by Artuir son of Bicoir the Briton and died'.

Athrwys ap Fferfael was the descendant of Athrwys ap Meurig and he ruled Gwent in the time of King Offa of Mercia, who came to power in 757.

Arthgen, King of Ceredigion, is noted in the *Welsh Annals* as having died in 807. He was the son of Scissil and grandson of Clitauc.

Arthgal or Artgal, one of the last British kings of Strathclyde, died in 872.

Arthur the Soldier

The ninth-century manuscript attributed to Nennius tells us that Arthur was a *miles*, a soldier, and he states that many men were more nobly born. He also tells us that Arthur fought 'Cum regibus Brittonium sed ipse dux erat bellorum' – 'with the Kings of the Britons, although he was the leader in battle'.

This has resulted in doubt being cast upon Arthur being an actual king and some writers have downgraded him to the role of mere battle-leader. This statement has been much debated and needs careful consideration, for while Nennius states that Arthur led the other kings in battle, he does not definitely say that he was **not** a king himself. It suggests that by fighting with the British kings he was of equal status. Perhaps, just like William the Conqueror, Arthur was a *dux* (duke) who became a king.

The words *dux bellorum* may have been intended as a descriptive term meaning 'Commander in Battle'. It implies that Arthur held a military title similar to the *Comes Britaniae* (Count of Britain) or *Dux Britaniarum* (Duke of the Britons) which were appointed in Britain during the latter years of the Roman administration.[9]

As a *dux bellorum* Arthur was something apart and distinctive, and the formal title quite literally means 'leader of wars' in the tradition of the Count of Britain. He was the leader of the British resistance against all invaders whose role was to protect Britannia and this he did alongside the rulers of petty kingdoms, he himself being the generalissimo of the Romano-Britons. In this capacity, he commanded a formidable cavalry force, the mobility of which enabled it to move rapidly from one area of Britain to another, opposing external invaders wherever the need was greatest.

It is likely that the medieval romances of Arthur's knights of the Round Table represent a genuine folk memory of a mounted war band led by Arthur. The Romans had certainly made use of cavalry and two units served in Britain during the fourth century. It would appear that Arthur established a similar mobile force a century later. The best description we have of a sixth-century war-band riding to battle is contained in Aneurin's epic poem *Y Gododdin*.

Arthur the Emperor

In a poem called 'Geraint son of Erbin', contained in the *Black Book of Carmarthen*, Arthur is described as 'Arthur amherawdyr' – Arthur the Emperor. The Welsh have borrowed the Latin title *imperator*, 'emperor', and made it into 'amherawdyr' and it was probably used in its original meaning – that of Commander-in-Chief. This may be explained by the fact that when the Roman *imperator* no longer had any interest in Britain, the title was given to the highest officer in the island, namely the *Comes Britanniae* and in this way arose the title 'yr Amherawdyr Arthur' – the 'Emperor Arthur'.

This officer had a roving commission to defend the province wherever his presence might be required. The other military captains were the *Dux Britanniarum*, who had charge of the forces in the north, especially on Hadrian's Wall, and the *Comes Litoris Saxonici*, who was entrusted with the defences of the island's south-eastern coast.

The successors of both of these captains seem to have been called 'gweldigs' (rulers), so Arthur's suggested position as *Comes Britanniae* would be in a sense superior to theirs, which fits in with his being called emperor (*imperator*) and not *gwledig*.

How the Name Changed from Artur to Arthur

In the sixth century the name was written as Artur or in Latin Arturus or Arturius. The name Artur was Latinised to Arturius and the 'h' was added by medieval writers and Artur thus became Arthur. The spelling of Arthur with 'h' did not develop until the twelfth century.

Artur – Arturius – Arthurius – Arthur

A good comparison is the Latin name Antoninus – Antony – Anthony. Latin names were also sometimes abbreviated, such as Marcus to Marc. Thus Arthurius may have been shortened to Arthur. It is significant that Latin writers refer to Arthur as Arturus or Arturis but never Artorius.

The Celtic Origin of the Name Arthur

It is necessary to understand that the name Arthur is derived from a number of similar sources which through the passing centuries became very confused. In the Welsh language 'Arth Fawr' means the 'Great Bear' and in ancient times this was the name given to the polar god who symbolised all the forces that came to us from the region of the seven main stars of the constellation called Ursa Major, which is Latin for Great Bear. The word Arctus comes from the two celestial constellations which are commonly called Ursa Major and Minor and Arcturus is a star near the tail of the Great Bear. Accordingly, Arcturus seems a more likely Latin root for Arthur than Artorius for it dates back to pre-Roman times and it is derived from the early Celtic form Artorix, meaning 'Bear King'.

Arthur was undoubtedly known as 'the Bear' and it is relevant that Celtic personal names and nicknames that referred to animals were popular during the fifth–sixth century period: Bran (crow), March (horse), Morvran (sea crow), etc. Gildas in his *De Excidio et Conquesta Britanniae* names five British kings and speaks of them as animals: Aurelius Caninus – 'the Dog', whose father is the 'Lion Whelp'; Vortipor is 'the Leopard'; Maglocunus (Maelgwyn) is referred to as 'the Dragon'; and Cuneglasus 'the Bear'.

Was the Name Arthur Derived From a Title?

The word 'Arthwyr' is a title given to someone of importance, indicating that he was strong and powerful just like a bear. In times of national crisis the Britons elected such a leader who was given this title as a token of respect. It meant 'the Bear Exalted' and was a reference to the Celtic Bear deity.

In 506 an 'Arthwyr' was elected by the Council of Britain to exercise sovereign authority, just like previous princes had been chosen as 'Pendragons' or 'battle commanders' in times of danger. He was to become the historical King Arthur who became a legend in his own lifetime. Other examples of Dark Age figures who are remembered by their titles are Vortigern and Emyr Llydaw.

The name Arthur may even be a copyist's error for Arthwyr, an epithet that in time became a name. When copies of manuscripts were made, one monk would read aloud while another did the writing, and this obviously led to names being spelt in different ways.

So Who was the King Arthur of History and Legend?
The King Arthur of history and legend was identified by writers in the eighteenth and nineteenth centuries as Athrwys ap Meurig, the hereditary King of the Silures, the Celtic tribe that inhabited south-east Wales.[10]

Lewis's *Dictionary of Wales*, published in 1759, comments: 'Meurig ap Tewdrig, a man of great valour and wisdom, was the father of that Arthur who is now regarded by Welsh writers as that hero whose exploits form so distinguished a feature of the British annals and who succeeded Meurig in his domain.'

The Revd John Whitaker, in his book *The History of Manchester* (1775), observes: 'Arthur was the Arth-uir, great man or sovereign of the proper Silures and therefore the denominated King of Gwent, the Venta Silurum of the Romans and the British metropolis of the nation.'

David Williams, in his *History of Monmouthshire*, published in 1796, also appeared to have no doubts that this was the person who can be identified with King Arthur:

> The celebrated Arthur had an actual existence; though the place of his birth is uncertain, his family, like that of other princes, combined against the strategums of Vortigern and the ferocity of the Saxons, frequently varying their residence in Siluria, in Damonium and in Armorica. He was the son of Meurig, Prince of Siluria or Gwent; succeeded his father in the Principality . . .

David Williams was also aware that Arthwyr was a title:

> Athrwys or Athruis, the son of Meurig ap Tewdrig, King of Gwent, assumed the appellation of Arthwyr, or the Bear Exalted. In 506 Arthwyr was elected by the states of Britain to exercise sovereign authority, as eminence in consequence of superior abilities and bravery; having been until then only a chieftain of the Silurian Britons.

David Williams also realised that Arthur was known by various names:

Meurig son of Tewdric, or Theodric; who is celebrated for his wisdom owes his celebrity principally to his son . . . Arthyr; who is variously called Arthwys, Arthras, Adras, Adros, Arthwy, Arthur, Uthur, and is probably the great Arthur of the British History.

William Owen Pughe, in his *Cambrian Biography*, published in 1803, made a similar statement, but disagreed slightly with the date of Arthur's election: 'About the year 517, Arthur was elected by the states of Britain to exercise sovereign authority . . . having been from 510 till then only a chieftain of the Silurian Britons, being the son of Meurig ap Tewdrig'.

John H. Parry states, in *The Cambrian Plutarch* (1834) that: 'Arthur was the son of Meurig ap Tewdrig, a prince of the Silurian Britons at the commencement of the sixth century, and who is in all probability, Uthyr or Uther of legendary celebrity.'

Copying errors by monks confused names, and Arthwyr in the *Llandaff Charters* became Athrwys. This was the way it looked or sounded to the scribes who copied and re-copied the documents through the centuries. The name is variously spelt in different documents as Arthwys, Arthwyr, Athwys, Athwyr, Arthmael, Arthmail and Arthur.[11]

Athrwys first appears in the grant of Cilcinhinn, Conuoy and Llangenni made by King Meurig, accompanied by Queen Onbrawst to Bishop Oudoceus. His brother Idnerth is also among the witnesses to this grant which commemorates his grandfather King Tewdrig.

Athrwys is also mentioned several times in the charter grants of his son Morgan who is styled as King Morgan, for example: 'Be it known that Morgan son of Athrwys gave the church of Ystrat-hafren, with an uncia of land, to God, and to St Dubricius, and St Teilo, and in the hand of Bishop Berthgwyn, and to all his successor in the Church of Llandaff.'

Arthur, Hereditary King of the Silures
Of all the heroic people of Britain encountered by the legions of Imperial Rome, the Silures, inhabiting what is now designated south Wales, were the most valiant and cultured. Tacitus, writing of them in the first century of the Christian era, bears the following testimony: '*Silurum gens non atrocitate, clementia mutibatur; validamque et pugnaccem Silurum gentem*' – 'Neither violence nor clemency could subdue the valiant Silurian'.

The Silures were a branch of the Veneti who left Armorica in western Gaul during the second century BC and entered south Wales by way of Cornwall. They probably landed on the bank of the Severn, at Sudbrook, where a camp was constructed. They later established their main fort at Caermelin (Llanmelin), just to the north of present-day Caerwent.

In due course, the bulk of the Silures occupied the lowland coastal areas of Glamorgan and Gwent and the valleys of the Black Mountains with the River Wye forming their eastern boundary with the Dobunni tribe. The cluster of small defended settlements centred on the upper reaches of the River Usk, in the heart of the Brecon Beacons, can also be regarded as part of the Silures's territory.

In AD 43 the Emperor Claudius sent his general Aulus Plautius with 4 legions (Second, Ninth, Fourteenth and Twentieth), with their accompanying auxiliaries, making in all a force of probably 50,000 troops, to conquer Britain and to make it the northern frontier province of the Empire. A particular attraction was the rich corn lands of the south and the mineral wealth of the country. The Roman army landed on the coast of Kent and advanced inland to cross the Thames west of London. They succeeded in capturing the Belgic capital of Camulodunum and within three years all south-east Britain as far as the Fosse Way had been captured.

When in AD 43, Caratacus, the last of the eastern kings, led an army of Belgic and Cantian warriors against the Roman invaders, he was defeated in a two-day battle on the River Medway. He then fled westwards to the land of the Silures and set about organising further resistance. This tribe, together with the Ordovices, was one of the most formidable opponents of the Romans, and they appointed Caratacus as their battle leader. For the next nine years he became a thorn in the side of the Roman legions trying to conquer the Silures. Of all the heroic people of Britain who the Roman soldiers encountered, the Silures were by far the most valiant and they were not amenable to negotiation or threat.

Tacitus, writing in the first century of the Christian era, described them as 'exceptionally stubborn' and commented that Caratacus, who fought the Romans for nine years, 'had in many battles, both indecisive and successful, raised himself above all other generals in Britain'.

In AD 51, Caratacus and his tribesmen were heavily defeated by Ostorius Scapula in a battle fought on the border of mid-Wales. Numerous sites for this battle have been suggested, but the most likely one is Caer Caradog near Church Stretton in Shropshire, since it is known that the battle was joined 'in the territory of the Ordovices'.

Caratacus managed to escape and headed north to seek refuge among the Briganti tribe, which inhabited what is modern Yorkshire. It was an unfortunate choice, for Queen Cartimandua, fearing reprisals upon her people if she aided the fugitive, betrayed Caratacus to the Romans. He was taken to Rome as a much-prized prisoner and led through the streets of the capital in a great triumphal procession.

Tacitus provides a record of the speech made by Caratacus to the Emperor Claudius which ended with the words, 'Spare me, and your clemency will be remembered forever.' The dignified bearing of the captive British king impressed the Emperor so deeply that he ordered that Caractacus and his wife and daughter should be set free, though they were not allowed to return to Britain.

The Silures are Finally Subdued

After the capture of Caratacus, the struggle continued with the Silures keeping up their resistance to Roman attempts to penetrate their territory. In AD 50 the Roman General Aulus Plautius was succeeded in command by Publius Ostorius Scapula, and it is recorded by Tacitus that the Silures managed to defeat a legion in a hard-fought battle. It is believed that this incident took place at Clyro near Hay-on-Wye.

When Ostorius Scapula died in AD 52 he was replaced by Aulus Didius Gallus, who had accompanied Claudius to Britain as the General of Cavalry and had been promoted to high command. By constructing an intricate system of forts and roads, he managed to contain the Silures, but it was not until AD 71–4 that the Silures were finally subjugated by Julius Frontinus.

In AD 75 Frontinus founded the Roman legionary fortress of Isca Silurum (Caerleon-on-Usk). Tacitus tells us that he used this fort as a base 'from which he conquered the powerful and beligerent tribe of the Silures, managing with difficulty to master not only courageous enemies, but a treacherous terrain'.

The Romans converted the old Celtic tribal name of Syllwg to Siluria and referred to the natives as Silures. The military fort that had been constructed a short distance from the old landing point at Sudbrook on the Severn Estuary was developed into an impressive stone walled fortress town. It became known as Venta Silurum when some of the Silures were persuaded to leave their hill-top fort at Caer Melin, a mile to the north, and sample the Roman way of life in this new town.

There is no doubt that the Romans never succeeded in fully subjugating the Silures and eventually a compromise had to be reached which resulted in the Roman Republic of the Silures. Disarmed, the tribe was allowed to flourish and their territory expanded to Pencraig in the east and Moccas in the north, reaching within a few kilometres of Hereford. Their territory also included large parts of Gwent and extended west into Glamorgan and east into Gloucestershire.

By now all the traditional tribal centres had been converted into capital towns by the Roman architects. The development of such towns as CALLEVA (Silchester), DURNOVANIA (Dorchester), VERULAMIUM (St Albans), DUROVERNUM (Canterbury), CORINIUM (Cirencester), RATAE (Leicester), ISCA (Exeter), VENTA BELGARUM (Winchester), URICONIUM (Wroxeter) and VENTA SILURUM (Caerwent) were the results.

These new Romanised towns were called *civitates* and the name came to mean not only the towns themselves but the whole tribal areas. They all had a council which was the local version of the senate in Rome with elected officers and magistrates. It was the equivalent in today's terms of a county council. Delegates from each tribal senate were sent to an annual Provincial Council which met at Camulodunum (Colchester) and it is quite likely that for a time this procedure still took place after the Romans had departed.

Venta Silurum (Caerwent) continued to function as the administrative centre of the *civitas* up to the fourth century, if not beyond. In total the Romans governed Siluria for a period of 365 years and on their departure in about 407 the native princes resumed the government of the area.

In 410 the Emperor Honorius informed the *civitates* of Britain that they could no longer rely on the Imperial armies to defend them. It was from that time that the period generally referred to as the Dark Ages began, symbolised by the mystery shrouded story of Arthur.

The Silurian commonwealth re-emerged when Glywysing, named after its founder-king Glywys, became united with Gwent. The first ruler of the united kingdom was Tewdrig Fendigaid (the Blessed). His son and successor Meurig married Onbrawst, daughter of Gwrgant Mawr (the Great), King of Erging, and as a result of this marriage alliance Meurig was able to extend his domain into present-day Herefordshire. It was their son Athrwys who was the hereditary King of the Silures.

The Identification has been Obscured by an Academic Muddle
Unfortunately, present-day historians claim that the reign of Athrwys ap Meurig was of little consequence and that he lived a century later than the time of Arthur. Such a mistaken belief has caused an academic muddle with the result that the true identity of Arthur is ignored and appears to be impossible to ascertain. This academic muddle was explained in my earlier publication *Journey to Avalon*, and this present book sets out to strengthen the case for identifying Athrwys ap Meurig as 'The Real Arthur'.

WHO WAS KING ARTHUR?

Reviewers of *Journey to Avalon* commented that we had been influenced by the writings of Iolo Morganwg (Edward Williams), who is regarded by many as a forger. However, this was not the case for the identification of Arthur with Athrwys ap Meurig had already been made by Llywelyn ap Rhisiart (Lewys Morgannwg), who flourished 1520–65, and Llewelyn Sion of Llangewydd (1540–1615) long before the time of Iolo Morganwg (1757–1826).

Was Arthur a King?

It has been argued by many writers that Arthur was not a king but merely a battle-leader and this belief is due to the fact that Nennius (*Historia Brittonum*) does not claim royal birth for Arthur. He refers to him as *miles*, a soldier, and states that many men were more nobly born than he was. However, by referring to Arthur as a *dux bellorum* (leader of battles) Nennius implies that Arthur was something apart and distinctive.

At the time when he was fighting his series of battles, Athrwys ap Meurig (Arthur) was probably only a sub-king of Erging. His father Meurig ap Tewdrig was still alive and Arthur was acting on his behalf as a warrior prince and battle-leader.

Geoffrey of Monmouth tells us that Arthur was crowned king at Caerleon after defeating his enemies at the Battle of Badon. It is significant that when Cunobelinus, after annexing the territory of the Catuvelauni (Middlesex and Hertfordshire and later that of Kent), made himself ruler of south-eastern Britain, he was referred to by the Romans as *Rex Britonnorium*, King of the Britons.

Athrwys ap Meurig appears frequently in the *Book of Llandaff* as a witness to charters and grants but he is never identified as a king. This can be explained by his father Meurig probably living to a great age and during his reign Athrwys was just a sub-king of Erging.

Arthur was also Known as Arthmael and Armel

It is not unusual for important Celtic characters of this period to be known by more than one name, and confusion is often caused by part of their name incorporating a title as an indication of their status. So it is not surprising that Athrwys ap Meurig was also known as Arthmael (Bear Prince) and the key to the real identity of King Arthur is to understand that his story is based on the man who was known by both of these names.

In the search for proof that Arthmael, Athruis and Athrwys are alternative names for the same person, we can find a significant statement in the *Life of St Cadoc*, compiled in the eleventh century by Lifris or Lifricus, son of Bishop

23

Herewald, Archdeacon of Glamorgan. He mentions that a grant of land, now known as Cadoxton-juxta-Neath, was made to St Cadoc by a certain King Arthmael. This was where our identification really started to make sense, for, according to the genealogy contained in the *Book of Llandaff*, the ruler of Morgannwg and Gwent at this time was Athrwys ap Meurig.

It also became possible to sort out why Arthur has such strong connections with Brittany. There is an interesting statement in a book entitled *Early History of the Cymry or Ancient Britons from 700 BC to AD 500*, by the Revd Peter Roberts (published in 1803). He refers to Arthur as an Armorican prince. Such a prince can be none other than Arthmael, the Messiah of Brittany. This great soldier-saint was known to the Bretons as Armel. During his life he founded churches in Brittany at Plouarzel, St Armel-des-Boschaux and Ploërmel. The name of Arthmael, like all Celtic names of that period, has taken many variants: Armel, Ermel, Ermin, Armail, Arzel, Armahel, Hermel and Thiamail. In Latin it is written as Armagillus.

The earliest record of King Arthur originated in Brittany and this was the country where he spent his last days, so it is quite naturally the place where legends concerning his life are particularly strong.

Armel (Arthmael) is remembered for the part that he played in liberating the Bretons from the tyranny of Marcus Conomorus (otherwise known as King March and Hound of the Sea), and he established a persistent legend of a King Arthur operating in Brittany which is remembered to this day. In Breton, a bear is 'arz' and Arth (Arz) mael, means bear prince. The key to the identity of King Arthur is to understand that Athrwys ap Meurig and Arthmael (known by the Breton name of Armel) were in fact the same person.

It is most unlikely that there would have been two leaders with the same name flourishing during exactly the same period. The Arthmael who reigned over Glamorgan and Gwent in the time of St Cadoc must have been the same man who liberated Domnonia in Brittany from the tyranny of Marcus Conomorus in 555. This important incident will be dealt with in Chapter Twenty.

Albert Le Grand, who compiled the *Life of St Arthmael* in 1636, states that Arthmael was born in 482 at the Roman station of Caput Bovium, which in later times became known as Boverton. It is situated to the south-east of Llanilltud Fawr (now anglicised to Llantwit Major) in the old cantref of Penychen, which in modern terms is in the Vale of Glamorgan.

The name of Arthmael's parents is not given in this account but they may be determined from the genealogy of the kings of Morgannwg and Gwent contained in the *Book of Llandaff*. Athrwys (Arthmael) is named as the son of Meurig and Onbrawst, the daughter of Gwrgant Mawr ('the Great)', King of Erging.

There are relevant statements in the *Life of St Efflam*, the text of which is contained in Arthur de La Borderie's *Annales de Bretagne*, written in 1892. Although ignored by the majority of Arthurian students, it is of interest that Arthur is referred to as Arturus Fortissimus ('Arthur the Mighty'). In some writings he is referred to as 'The Hammer of the Saxons' and it is interesting that other warrior kings have also been given similar nicknames. For example, Edward I was known as 'The Hammer of the Scots'.

The fact that Arthmael was not only a religious leader but also a military commander ties in extremely well with Nennius's description of one of Arthur's victories 'in which he carried the portrait of Saint Mary, the virgin, on his shoulders, and the pagans were routed on that day, and there was great slaughter of them through the power of our Lord Jesus Christ and the strength of the Holy Virgin Mary, his mother . . .'.

Dr John Morris, in *The Age of Arthur*, makes a very significant statement: 'The most important of the sixth-century immigrant leaders was probably Arthmael but little is known of him . . .'. It would seem that Dr Morris had failed to look at the writings of Albert Le Grand and the lack of interest by other Arthurian scholars in the *Life of St Arthmael* has resulted in the true identity of the historical King Arthur remaining a mystery.

The Territory of Arthur

Wales, Cornwall and Brittany all claim to be associated with the legends of King Arthur and his knights, and this book sets out to show how each claim is justified. Through his 'life' and the 'lives' of his kinsmen, St Samson and St Paul Aurelian, it is possible to follow the activities of King Arthur from Glamorgan and Gwent, across Cornwall to Brittany. In Wales he is the celebrated Arthwyr, King of the Silures; in Cornwall he appears to have been confused with his brother-in-law, Count Gwythian; and in Brittany he is remembered as the great soldier-saint Arthmael or Armel.

The area generally supposed to be Arthur's main sphere of activity is Wales, Somerset, Devon, Cornwall and the Welsh Marches. This territory fitted neatly within the Roman boundaries of Britannia Secunda and its capital was Isca, otherwise known as Caerleon-on-Usk, where Arthur, in the tradition established by Geoffrey of Monmouth, is supposed to have held court. Undoubtedly, the key to the identity of King Arthur is the fact that the Glamorgan and Gwentian princes held territory in south Wales, Cornwall and Brittany, for these lands became the main field of his influence.

CHAPTER 2

Geoffrey of Monmouth

Geoffrey of Monmouth was born in about 1090, the son of a Breton family who settled in Monmouth a short time after the Norman Conquest.[1] He was probably educated at Monmouth Priory and as a Welshman by birth and upbringing it may be assumed that he spoke Welsh. It is possible that he was of Breton blood on his father's side and of Welsh blood on his mother's. His Welsh connections would have made him sympathetic with the plight of the Celtic people still living in Britain, who had suffered at the hands of the Romans, the Anglo-Saxons and the Normans.

We are told by Caradoc of Llancarfan, who was a contemporary of Geoffrey, that 'Galfrai' (Geoffrey) was the son of Arthur, the domestic chaplain of William ap Robert (William, Earl of Gloucester). He also tells us that Galfrai 'was the foster son of Uchtryd, Archdeacon of Llandaff, being his brother's son; an archdeanery was bestowed on him on account of his learning. He was the instructor of many nobles.' This statement tells us that Geoffrey of Monmouth was the son of Arthur, the private priest to William, Earl of Gloucester, the son of Robert Consul, who became Geoffrey's patron, and that he was brought up as the foster-son of Uchtryd, his paternal uncle, who was then Archdeacon and later Bishop of Llandaff.

Geoffrey at Oxford
By 1129, Geoffrey was living in Oxford, serving as a secular canon in the small college of Augustinian Canons of St George. The first authentic record we have of him is in the foundation charter of the Abbey of Osney which was granted in 1129. His name is appended as a witness to this charter, and is one of a list headed by Walter Calenius, Archdeacon of Oxford.

Geoffrey, in January 1139, witnessed a charter connected with the dedication of Godstow Abbey and he signed as 'mag Galf Arthurus'. The use of the word 'mag' (*magister*), meaning 'master' implies that Geoffrey was a graduate, presumably a Master of Arts of Paris, for the University of Oxford was not yet in existence. In total, his name appears as a witness to

26

six charters, between the years 1129 and 1151, all concerning religious houses near Oxford.

During the twenty-two years that Geoffrey spent at Oxford, he wrote three manuscripts, copies of which have survived to this day. These were his *Historia Regum Britanniae*, the *Prophetiae Merlini*, which he later incorporated into it, and the *Vita Merlini*, which first appeared in 1151 as a Latin poem of over 1,500 lines, purporting to represent the life and prophecies of Merlin.[2]

Historia Regum Britanniae (*History of the Kings of Britain*)

Geoffrey claimed this work to be a history of the Island of Britain from about 1170 BC down to the death of King Cadwaladr in AD 689. The section relating to Arthur occupies about one-fifth of the entire work and it is here for the first time in literary history that Arthur is portrayed as a great conqueror.

He tells of Arthur's conquests, not only in his own country, against the Saxons, the Irish, the Scots and the Picts, but over all Western Europe. We see Arthur, after annexing Ireland, Iceland, Gothland and the Orkneys, following up these victories by subduing Norway, Dacia (presumably meaning modern Romania), Aquitaine and Gaul. After such triumphs there was nothing left for him but the overthrow of the Roman Empire. This he practically achieved, but the rebellion of Mordred (Medraut) brought him back home to deal with an uprising, which resulted in the end of his reign at the Battle of Camlann.

Geoffrey compiled his book by assembling a complex jigsaw puzzle with badly fitting pieces. By blending legend with glimpses of history he has given us a riddle story in which the very existence of Arthur has been doubted. Yet, soon after Geoffrey wrote his *Historia*, Arthur was also mentioned by both William of Malmesbury (*De Regibus Anglia*, which appeared in 1143) and Henry of Huntingdon (*Historia Anglorum*, c.1129). All three chronicles were sponsored by Robert, Earl of Gloucester, and Alexander, Bishop of Lincoln.

It is certainly necessary to reject much of Geoffrey's *Historia*, yet it is possible at the same time to identify statements that are seen to be supported by other sources. Names have been given Latin terminations and these, with errors of transcriptions, have much disguised them, but divested of their Latin endings they are found to be perfectly Celtic.

Geoffrey continued to work on revisions of his *Historia* after its first appearance in 1136 and the final version was completed by 1147. By the end of the twelfth century, thanks to Geoffrey of Monmouth, the story of Arthur was known in France, Spain, Italy, Poland and Byzantium.

For six centuries after it was written, Geoffrey's *Historia* was accepted by the majority of readers as accurate history; while the medieval poets found in its content a wealth of material for the basis of their poetry.

The *Historia Regum Britanniae* survives in 191 manuscripts in 49 libraries situated in 11 countries. In the British Museum alone there are no less than 35 copies.

There is no doubt that Geoffrey based his *Historia* on strands of oral tradition, existing manuscripts, historical fact and his own fertile imagination. Yet, at the same time there is a kernel of truth in his book which when carefully examined and compared with other sources can be explained.

Geoffrey's Source Book

Geoffrey refers to his source book as the 'Liber Vetustissimus' (the 'very ancient book').[3] He tells us in the first chapter of his *Historia* that:

> Walter, Archdeacon of Oxford, a person, pre-eminent both in eloquence, and his knowledge of foreign history, offered me a very ancient book in the British tongue ('quendom Britannici sermonsis librum vetustissimum'), which in a continued regular story and elegant style related the actions of all the British kings, from Brutus down to Cadwallader, the son of Cadwallon. At his request, therefore, I undertook the translation of that book into Latin.

This statement has provided much debate among historians as to whether Britannici refers to Brittany or to Wales. It certainly does not refer to England for the name Britannia had ceased to be used in the time of Geoffrey of Monmouth, having been replaced by Anglia. However, the name Britannia (meaning Cymry – Wales) significantly occurs in the *Book of Llandaff*, which was possibly edited by Geoffrey of Monmouth.

A further clue to the answer to this question is provided by Geoffrey of Gaimar (Chaplain to Ralph FitzGilbert), who wrote a poem titled, *L'Estoire des Englies* (*The History of the English*) in c.1140, in which he states:

> Robert the Earl of Gloucester
> Had this history translated
> According to the books of the Welsh (Waleis)
> Which he had, about the British Kings.

This statement confirms that the book used by Geoffrey of Monmouth originated in Wales. Gaimar's poem in fact refers to two books, one of which may well have been Geoffrey's original. Gaimar says that he could never have compiled his poem had he not obtained, through the assistance of his patroness, the lady Custance, 'the book of Walter Especx'. This, and 'the good book of Oxford, which belonged to Walter, the archdeacon', were both used by him in composing his poem.

Geoffrey, in his *Historia*, mentions this 'British Book' three times and if he was lying about its existence then Archdeacon Walter would certainly not have been at all pleased, as the statement was made while he was still alive.

At this time Walter, Archdeacon of Oxford, was the Provost of the College of St George, and he appears as a grantor or as a co-witness with Geoffrey to no less than five charters. Geoffrey signed a sixth charter towards the end of 1151, a few months after Walter's death.

Geoffrey's friend Walter Calenius is often confused with Walter Mapes of Llancarfan who also became an archdeacon of Oxford in the twelfth century (1197). Walter Calenius was also known as Walter of Wallingford in Berkshire, which was the place of his birth. Walter Mapes was also fascinated by the story of Arthur for he wrote a *Histoire de Roy Artur*, which was the principal source for Sir Thomas Malory's *Le Morte d'Arthur*.

Was Geoffrey's Source Book One of the Welsh Chronicles?
There exist Welsh translations or adaptations of Geoffrey's *Historia*, in widely variant forms, under such titles as *Brut Gryffydd ab Arthur*, *Brut y Brenhinedd* and *Brut Tysilio*. These manuscripts range in date from the thirteenth to the seventeenth centuries. It is possible that the original compilation of one of these works could have been the very ancient book to which Geoffrey refers.

The Brut y Brenhinedd (Chronicle of the Kings)
There are over seventy surviving manuscripts of this chronicle but the earliest dates from around 1200 and it has been generally accepted that it is merely a Welsh translation of Geoffrey's *Historia*. However, it contains material that is not in Geoffrey's book, and it is quite possible that it relates to the original ancient book that Geoffrey translated.

The Brut Tysilio – Tysilio's Chronicle
Tysilio was the son of Brochfael Ysgythrog (of the Tusks), Prince of Powys, who flourished in the sixth century and was a son of Cyngen ap Cadell Ddyrnllug. After Brochfael was defeated at the Battle of Chester in 616,

St Tysilio fled with a party of monks to Armorica. They sailed up the estuary of the Rance and landed by a little creek where they established a monastery. Tysilio died there in about 650.

No manuscript copy of *Tysilio's Chronicle* is believed to exist in Brittany now; but there is sufficient evidence that ancient chronicles were once numerous in that country. The *Prophecies of Guinclan*, written in the fifth century, were extant in the Abbey of Landevence in 1701. Furthermore, two Chronicles of Brittany: *The Brief Chronicle of the Armorican British Kings* and *The Genealogy of the Princes of Dumnonia*, by Ingomar, were both examined by the French historian Lebault, about two-and-a-half centuries ago, but are now lost.

It is possible that Walter, Archdeacon of Oxford, came across a copy of Tysilio's work while travelling in Brittany for he informs us that he possessed the *Brut* or *Chronicle of Tysilio*, and that: 'I, Walter, archdeacon of Oxford, translated this book from the Welsh into Latin and, in my old age, have again translated it from the Latin into Welsh.' Why did he do this? It may be because he had given the original Welsh copy to Geoffrey of Monmouth, or perhaps because the language of Tysilio was growing obsolete, and not easy to understand among the 'modern' Welsh.

It would not have been possible for this *Brut* to have been compiled by St Tysilio in its entirety for it ends with the death of Cadwaladr Fendigaid (the Blessed) who died in 664, some fourteen years after the death of Tysilio, but the work may have been continued by a later hand. It is possible that *Tysilio's Chronicle* was written about the year 1000. It cannot be earlier since the state of Britain is alluded to as late as the reign of Athelstan, who died in 940. Also, the state and condition of Britain are referred to in a kind of historical retrospect, which suggests a lapse of about fifty or sixty years may have taken place subsequently and this brings us down to the year 1000.

Tysilio's Chronicle was not extensively circulated as it seems to have been unknown to Geoffrey of Monmouth and his colleagues. It perhaps only became available when Walter, Archdeacon of Oxford, came across a copy, while travelling in Armorica.

The manuscript was not printed in book form till the end of the eighteenth century, when it appeared in the *Myvyrian Archaiology*. Afterwards, it was edited in a translated form by the Revd Peter Roberts, in 1811, in a quarto volume, from a transcript of the copy preserved in the *Red Book of Hergest*, formerly belonging to Margam Abbey, and now in the library of Jesus College, Oxford. It is possible that the *Red Book of Hergest* contains a unique original copy of *Tysilio's Chronicle* from its purest text. The Revd Peter

Roberts became convinced that this chronicle was in fact the 'Liber Vetustissimus' which Geoffrey of Monmouth used for his *Historia Regum Britanniae*.

The Welsh antiquary Evan Evans believed that the original of *Tysilio's Chronicle* had been lost and that the author was an Armorican who wrote c.930. His work was perhaps translated into Welsh by Walter, and Geoffrey of Monmouth turned it into Latin. Evan Evans, referring in 1785 to the Welsh version translated from the Armorican by Walter, asserts that John Jones of Gellilyfdy in the parish of Ysgifiog, 'says that he had part of the original translation by Walter in his custody in the year 1640'.

The current opinion is that the *Red Book of Hergest*, and all copies of *Tysilio's Chronicle* adopting more or less the same text, are mere translations from the Latin of Geoffrey of Monmouth, with the omission of some of the more absurd parts.

But is this correct?

Take for instance the names Asclepiodotus and Livius Gallus, in Geoffrey's *Historia*, which correspond to Alysgapitulus and Belysgalys in *Tysilio's Chronicle*. It is evident that the latter names could not have been manufactured from the two former ones; but it may be easily conceived that Geoffrey might have Latinised the two names from Tysilio.

There are obvious symptoms of editorial management in various parts of Geoffrey's work: such as introducing fresh information, giving certain references, altering various details, and, in particular going more eagerly into the marvellous than the original, which itself is not deficient in this respect. By deliberately mistranslating place names from Welsh into Latin Geoffrey no doubt was aiming to satisfy his Norman masters and the interests of his patron Robert of Gloucester.

A Possible Source from Breconshire
According to the *Brut Dingestow*, the Welsh version of Geoffrey of Monmouth's *Historia Regum Britanniae*, Meurig ap Caradog journeyed to Rome to meet Macsen (Maximus) to encourage him to visit Britain. He was well received in Rome and persuaded Maximus to return with him to Britain. They landed at Southampton but Eudaf Hen (Octavius the Old), who thought they had hostile intentions, sent Cynan Meiriadog to meet them with an army. Meurig advised Macsen to say that he had come as a messenger from the Emperor. Meurig was present when his father Caradog persuaded Eudaf Hen to marry his only daughter to Macsen and make him heir to the throne.

Although somewhat historically inaccurate, the above has an essence of truth and serves to illustrate that Geoffrey was aware of Meurig ap Caradog's correct chronological setting, so what was his source for Meurig ap Caradog?

Geoffrey had no doubt seen an early history of Brycheiniog written c.580 by the Priest of Llangasty (Tal-y-Llyyn). Passages from this early history have been preserved in 'De Situ Brecheniauc', written in c.1200 by a scribe using an older manuscript, and have also influenced the authors of the 'Lives' of saints Gwynllyw and Cadog, the latter being infinitely the most important of all the Welsh lives of the saints. All these manuscripts mention King Arthur and are contained in Cotton MS Vespasian A.xiv.

Sir John Price (1502–55), the Welsh antiquary, found an early British history at Brecon Priory. He refers to it in his *Historia Britannicae Defensio* (1573). John Leland (1506–52) found a reference to this manuscript in the library catalogue of Battle Abbey, the mother-house of Brecon, and had heard that it had been removed to Brecon; but he seems not to have realised that it was the same one that Sir John Price had discovered.

Thomas ap John (d.1616), the great-grandfather of Hugh Thomas (d.1720), is credited with having written the first history of Brecknockshire 'about the time of Queen Elizabeth I' (Harleian MS 4181, folio 68). According to Edward Owen (Catalogue of Welsh MSS in the British Museum, II, p. 460), this is the document in the Harleian Collection No. 6108, which is entitled 'The History of Brecon from the time of Meurick, King of Britain, until the year of redemption, 1606'.

It is of the utmost significance that the Meurick in question is Meuric ap Caradog (Geoffrey of Monmouth's Mauricius ap Caradocus) and the manuscript names Meuric ap Tewdric as the father of King Arthur!

Another manuscript attributed to Thomas ap John and edited by his great-grandson Hugh Thomas is 'A Geographical Description of Brecknockshire and a History of Brecknock from Meurick, King of Britain, until 1603' (Harleian MSS 7017). Significantly, this manuscript also names Meuric ap Tewdric as the father of King Arthur.

There is no doubt that his great-grandfather's manuscript stirred Hugh Thomas's imagination and prompted him to delve into Brecon's past history and improve on his great-grandfather's efforts by writing 'An Essay towards the History of Brecknockshire' (1698). The following is the relevant passage from his history:

In the time of Meurig, king of Britain, there came out of Egypt a captain called Gadelus, who was Grecian born, into parts of Albion, invaded and conquered the country called after him Gadelway or

Galloway: with whom there arrived a noble gentleman called Tathal, the son of Antonius, a peer of Greece [Antonius Donatus, son of Magnus Maximus]. This Tathal for his good qualities was so liked by King Meurig that he received him into his court. In the process of time he married Morvitha, the daughter and heiress of Gwaldreg, prince of Garth Madryn, the then name for the kingdom of Brycheiniog. Tathal by Morvitha had one son named Teithrin who succeeded to the principality of Garth Madryn.

[Teithrin died young but not before marrying a daughter of Custennin ap Macsen and siring a son named Teithfallt. Teithrin's widow then went on to marry a second time to Nynniaw ap Erb, King of Gwent, who thus became the step-father of Teithfallt. Nynniaw's brother Peibio had also married a daughter of Custennin ap Macsen].

Teithfallt had one son named Tewdrig or Tewdwr, who succeeded to the kingdoms of Gwent and Garth Madryn. Tewdrig had one daughter named Marchell who married Anlach macCormac. Anlach by right of his marriage to Tewdrig's daughter Marchell succeeded to the kingdom of Garth Madryn. They had one son named Brychan who succeeded to the kingdom of Garth Madryn after his father's death. In honour of Brychan the country was ever after called Brycheiniog.

According to the Life of St Cadog, Gwynllyw Filwr (the Warrior) had first sought the hand of Gwladys, the daughter of Brychan Brycheiniog, peaceably, but Brychan had refused, and slighted the messengers. Then Gwynllyw set out with three hundred servants, came to the court of Brychan at Talgarth, and found the young lady before the door of her residence. They took her by force and returned with speed, but were pursued by Brychan and his auxiliaries. Two hundred of his men were slain, but he arrived safely at the borders of his kingdom, still being pursued, when he was seen by Arthur and his companions, Cai and Bedwyr. They were sitting on top of Bochriw Carn. Arthur attacked Gwynllyw's pursuers and chased them back to their own land. Gwynllyw brought Gwladys to his own residence which was situated on that hill, and was thenceforward named Allt Wynllyw.

This above passage is an extract from the 'Life of St Gwynllyw' which is contained in Cotton MS Vespasian A.xiv, and so are 'De Situ Brecheniauc' and the 'Life of St Cadoc'. All three place Arthur in Glamorgan!

33

Geoffrey's Other Sources
There is no doubt that Geoffrey consulted the *Historia Brittonum* attributed to Nennius. In particular he made use of the 'De Mirabilibus Britanniae', which constitutes the seventh section of this ninth-century manuscript. Some of the remarkable wonders mentioned are strongly featured in certain parts of Geoffrey's *Historia*.

He also utilised the writings of Gildas and Bede, and he was obviously familiar with the tenth-century *Annales Cambriae* (which accounts for his dating of the Battle of Camlann at AD 542) and the stories of the *Mabinogion*. It is very likely that Geoffrey could read Welsh, while other scholars of the period, such as William of Malmesbury could not. During his lifetime, Geoffrey must have accumulated a wealth of Welsh bardic legends and traditions. William of Newburgh undoubtedly hit the nail on the head when he accused Geoffrey of having 'disguised under the respectable name of history the fables of King Arthur, which he took from the ancient fictions of the Britons and added to out of his own head'.[4]

De Excidio et Conquesta Britanniae – Concerning the Ruin and Conquest of Britain By St Gildas ap Caw (c.495–570)
This is a history of the island from the time of the Roman Conquest to Gildas's own day. It is the only account written by a Briton that has survived of Roman Britain, from the earliest times to her last overthrow. He gives a synopsis of the history of Britain in twenty-six chapters and weeps over the ruin of his country, the destruction of the Church and the slaughter and captivity of his countrymen.

In about 540 Gildas also wrote a much longer work, the *Epistle*, in which he describes the work as his 'Book of Lamentation'. It is not so much a history but more of a ranting diatribe in which he rebukes his countrymen for their sins and lack of unity in the face of danger. His comments are directed at the petty kings of his time who ruled various parts of Britain.

Writing with heavy and bitter sarcasm his document is compiled as a sermon and he is obviously greatly troubled and concerned about the future of Britain. In particular, he denounces five rulers of petty kingdoms and speaks of their constant warfare against one another: 'Britain has kings, but they are tyrants; judges, but they are impious men . . .'. These contemporary kings were Constantine of Dumnonia, Aurelius Caninus of the Lower Severn area, Vortiporix of Dyfed, Cuneglassus (Cynlas) of Rhos and Maglocanus (Maelgwyn) of Gwynedd. It is his reference to King Maglocanus (Maelgwyn

Gwynedd) that gives a date for Gildas's work for he died in 547, so the book must have been written prior to that date.

Why Did Gildas Not Refer to Arthur?

The fact that King Arthur is not mentioned by Gildas in this document has puzzled historians, for the two men were contemporaries and as a result some writers have even questioned Arthur's very existence. Giraldus Cambrensis provides an explanation which is certainly plausible. While Gildas had written a book entitled *De Gestis Arthuri*, Giraldus tells us that King Arthur killed Gildas's brother and as a result he threw the book into the sea. We do not of course know the truth of this story.

However, there would have been no need for Gildas to mention Arthur for he wrote his *Epistle* at a time when Arthur was no longer a ruler in Britain. Gildas was criticising the tyrant kings and praising the good old days (in the lifetime of Arthur) when there was peace and stability following the Battle of Badon. He is lashing out at the kings who succeeded Arthur after the Battle of Camlann.

The reason why Gildas did not mention Arthur as the victor of Badon may be that he refused to extol the virtues of the man who was responsible for the death of his brother. At the same time he did not want to risk reprisals as a result of criticising him in any way, because (as will be revealed later) Arthur was still holding sway in Armorica and had settled in an area not far from where Gildas was residing in his monastery.

It should also be pointed out that in his allusions to British history between 388 and 540 Gildas names only **one** person and **one** event! Even Ambrosius Aurelianus is mentioned only incidentally and briefly.

There is a possibility that Gildas made an oblique reference to Arthur while criticising Cuneglassus (Cynlas), one of his contemporaries and one of the five tyrants. He makes the cryptic comment: 'Why have you been rolling in the filth of your past wickedness ever since your youth, you bear, rider of many and driver of the chariot of **the Bear's Stronghold**, despiser of God and oppressor of his lot . . .'. By referring to Cuneglassus as *ursus* ('bear'), Gildas is insulting him, suggesting that he is a rough unmannerly person. This may be interpreted as him calling Cuneglassus an unmannerly bear, imitating Arthur, but he is a poor ruler compared to Arthur, the monarch of a strong Britain.

Historia Brittonum – *Attributed to Nennius (c. AD 820)*

This manuscript was written in the early part of the ninth century and much of the text is compiled from other documents which have long been lost. For convenience it is attributed to Nennius (the earliest date of compilation and in which his name is mentioned is in the introduction to the Harleian MS 3859). It would seem that he was a disciple of the holy Elvodug (Elfoddw), Bishop of Bangor, who died in 809. His Celtic name would have been Nynniaw and in the preface he apologises for producing 'a heap of all that I have found'.

The text does not follow any logical order and seems merely to be a compilation of facts and legends by a number of hands which the authors found in various ancient documents, probably written in Welsh and then translated into Latin. A cursory account is given of the history of Britain from the earliest times down to the eighth century and the following passage describes the sources to which as a monk he had access:

> I have presumed to deliver these things in the Latin tongue, not trusting to my own learning, which is little or none at all, but partly from the traditions of our ancestors, partly from the writings and monuments of the ancient inhabitants of Britain, partly from the annals of the Romans and the chronicles of the sacred fathers, Isidore, Jerome, Prosper, Eusebius and from the histories of the Scots and Saxons, although our enemies.

Nennius is the first writer (whose work has survived) to mention Arthur and provide a brief account of his military exploits. His reference to Arthur as *Dux Bellorum* implies that Arthur held a military title similar to the one established in Britain during the latter years of the Roman administration. As leader of the British resistance against the Saxons, Arthur's role was to protect Britannia and in his capacity as *Dux Bellorum* he commanded a formidable cavalry force.

Nennius also describes Arthur as *miles* (warrior) which signifies a knight and indicates that he was a cavalry leader at the head of mobile troops. Most important of all, this manuscript is the source of the famous list of twelve battles in which Arthur led the Britons to victory, and gives the ancient British names of places where they were fought. This material is believed to derive from a Welsh poem on the battles of Arthur which is no longer available to us.

In the 'De Mirabilibus Britanniae', which constitutes the seventh section of Nennius's *Historia Brittonum*, we find certain wonders mentioned which Geoffrey has inserted in different parts of his *Historia*.

Geoffrey does not mention Nennius by name, but does, however, mention Gildas and it is possible that he assumed the *Historia Brittonum* (now attributed to Nennius) to be the work of Gildas. It is relevant that Henry of Huntingdon, in a passage about the battlefields of Arthur, which he quotes in his chronicle as from the *Historia Brittonum*, makes the same mistake.

There are thirty-five manuscripts of the work in existence. Five of them, written in the thirteenth and fourteenth centuries, are prefaced by a short piece which is said to have been written by Nennius and is entitled 'The Apologies of Nennius, Historian of the British People'.

The Annals Cambriae – Annals of Wales *(Tenth Century)*
The ancient annals of Wales were compiled from the eighth century onwards at St David's in west Wales. There are three copies in existence and the earliest, which is known as Manuscript A, is in the Harleian Collection in the British Museum. It is written on parchment and the Latin script is of late tenth- or early eleventh-century style, set out in three columns. Commencing in 444, it continues to 954 and is then followed by a gap of twenty-three years to conclude in 977.

The Anno Domini system of dating is not used, but the entries can be dated from the one in year nine, which states: 'Easter is changed on the Lord's day by Pope Leo, Bishop of Rome.' It is known from other sources that this occurred in AD 455, so the ninth year was AD 455 and this means that the first year is 446.

The entries are all very brief, with one sentence often describing the events of one whole year. Against many of the years there are no entries at all. Generally, the content deals with the deeds and battles of kings and the deaths of saints and bishops.

Arthur is mentioned twice. First as the victor of the Battle of Badon and secondly as falling in the Battle of Camlann. These two entries are inserted against the years 72 and 93 and therefore relate to 518 and 539.

The Llancarfan Charters
Three of the charters written at Llancarfan Monastery in the Vale of Glamorgan were witnessed by Bishop Herewald of Llandaff and therefore date from between 1056, when he was consecrated, and 1099, when he was suspended.

The first charter is for an estate given by Iestin filius Gurcant, the last Welsh ruler of Morgannwg (a direct descendant of Athrwys ap Meurig), from 1081. The second charter is of Caratocus rex Morcannuc, his predecessor as king, who fell in 1081. It was witnessed by Caratauc filius Riugallaun, who died in 1081, and by the above-mentioned Iestin filius Gurcant. The third charter is of the above Caratauc filius Riugallaun, and approved by Roger fitz Osbern, Earl of Hereford and Lord of Gwent; offices held by Roger, the son of William fitz Osbern, only from 1071 to 1075.

Lifris, the son of Bishop Herewald and the author of *Vita Cadoci* (*Life of St Cadoc*), was magister of Llancarfan between 1071 and 1075, as well as earlier and later, in circumstances to make compiling a 'life' of its founder St Cadoc appropriate. The probability is therefore strong that the *Vita Cadoci* was written between 1073 and 1086. It seems certain that it predates Geoffrey of Monmouth's *Historia* by nearly two generations.

It was also at Llancarfan Monastery that all the 'lives' of the Celtic saints that mention Arthur were written.

Trioedd Ynys Prydein – Triads of the Island of Britain
The triad is a mnemonic device that was devised by the bards. It comprises summaries of Welsh bardic lore, grouped in sets of three, and known in full as the *Triads of the Island of Britain*. It is in effect a kind of catalogue of the names of the traditional heroes, classified in groups of three. It originated as a mnemonic device to help the young bardic noviciates remember a substantial repertoire of early history, legend and traditional stories. Arthur is mentioned in more than a dozen of these triads.

The oldest, although far from being a complete collection, goes back only to the thirteenth-century manuscript Peniarth MS 16, while the remainder are fragments in the *Black Book of Carmarthen*, the *White Book of Rhydderch* and the *Red Book of Hergest*.

In 1801 the most complete collection, the *Triads of the Island of Britain* (*Trioedd Ynys Prydein*), was first published in the *Myvrian Archaiology of Wales*. It was translated by W. Probert in 1823 but is treated with suspicion having been assembled towards the end of the eighteenth century by Iolo Morganwg (Edward Williams), who was believed to be a forger.

The **Mabinogion**
Geoffrey would no doubt have had opportunities to hear the oral stories that were told at the fireside to wile away the time. They were handed down from one generation to another and were subject to modifications.

These ancient tales were probably written down between 1373 and 1425 and preserved in two manuscripts known as the *White Book of Rhydderch* and the *Red Book of Hergest*. The first probably derives its name from

Rhydderch ab Ieuan Llwyd (c.1324–98), who appears to have been its original owner and may even have commissioned the work. It is bound in two volumes contained in the National Library of Wales (Peniarth MSS 4 and 5). The *Red Book of Hergest* is the work of three scribes working in collaboration sometime between 1382 and c.1410. It is now contained in the library of Jesus College, Cambridge (MS 111).

Between 1838 and 1848 these eleven medieval Welsh tales were translated into English to be published by Lady Charlotte Guest under the title the *Mabinogion*. This name is the plural of Mabinogi which can be translated as 'childhood'. They were stories describing the conception, birth and early life of a Celtic hero. The centenary of the first translation of these stories was marked in 1948 by a definitive version by Gwyn and Thomas Jones.

Of particular interest to Geoffrey would have been the five stories in which Arthur is mentioned, and in particular 'The Dream of Rhonabwy' and 'Culhwch and Olwen' which both feature the exploits of King Arthur and provide names of his many associates. The latter story contains the names of Arthur's weapons which were doubtless current in popular tradition in Geoffrey's time. His shield is there called 'Wynelgwrthucher', his sword 'Caledfwlch' and his lance 'Rhongomyant'.

Dedications in Copies of the *Historia Regum Brittaniae*
In the surviving manuscripts of Geoffrey's *Historia*, the dedications are mainly to Robert, Earl of Gloucester, the illegitimate son of Henry I by Nest, the daughter of Rhys ap Tewdwr, Prince of Glamorgan. Not only was Robert the Earl of Gloucester, but through his marriage to Mabel, the daughter and heiress of Robert Fitzhamon, he was also Lord of Glamorgan where Caerleon-on-Usk was situated. It was his close connections with both south Wales and Normandy that resulted in his considerable interest in the history of Wales and Brittany and it was possibly on his request that Geoffrey embarked on his quest for source material relating to Arthur.

To you, therefore, Robert Earl of Gloucester, this work humbly sues for the favour of being so corrected by your advice that it may be considered not the poor offspring of Geoffrey of Monmouth, but, when polished by your refined wit and judgement, the production of him who had Henry, the glorious King of England, for his father, and whom we see an accomplished scholar and philosopher, as well as a brave soldier and tried commander.

39

The dedication changed after the death of Robert in 1147, to include Count Waleron de Beaumont of Worcester, Alexander, Bishop of Lincoln and King Stephen.[5] It is significant that Oxford lay within the diocese of Lincoln and Bishop Alexander was also the patron of Henry of Huntingdon (who had also been sponsored by Robert, Earl of Gloucester).

Bishop Alexander died in 1148 and from that time Geoffrey dedicated his later versions of the manuscript to King Stephen. He is extolled as a scholar and a patron of letters in much the same words as Robert of Gloucester is praised in other manuscripts. It is significant that Geoffrey witnessed a charter during Stephen's reign. This was issued from Westminster in 1153, confirming the requirements of the Treaty of Wallingford.

Robert of Chesney, the grantor of the charter that Geoffrey had witnessed in 1151, had also been a canon of St George and in 1148 he became Bishop of Lincoln. Geoffrey dedicated his *Vita Merlini* to him.

Geoffrey and the *Book of Llandaff*

A strong case can be made for Geoffrey leaving Monmouth as a young man and spending time during the next twenty-four years under the care of his uncle Uchtryd, Archdeacon of Llandaff. Arthur, the father of Geoffrey, became the family priest of William, the son of Robert of Gloucester, and Geoffrey was brought up as a foster son by his paternal uncle Uchtryd, Archdeacon and subsequently Bishop of Llandaff. It is significant that Geoffrey's contemporary Caradoc of Llancarfan states that Geoffrey was the nephew of Uchtryd, Bishop of Llandaff. The previous bishop was Urban, who had died in 1134. The see was left vacant for six years until 1140 when Uchtryd, then archdeacon, was consecrated bishop. Soon afterwards his nephew, Geoffrey, succeeded the archdeaconate.

Uchtryd died in 1148 and the *Gwentian Chronicle* tells us that Geoffrey was appointed Bishop of Llandaff in 1152, but died at Mass in the cathedral before being consecrated.

Geoffrey would have had an opportunity to study the ancient records of the cathedral and may even have played a major role in the compilation of the *Liber Landavensis* (*Book of Llandaff*).[6] He may have seen the name Arthurus or Athruis, King of Gwent, mentioned in a charter as a grantor of land, and it provided the inspiration for his subsequent work on the story of King Arthur.

There can be no doubt that there is a link between the *Book of Llandaff* and Geoffrey of Monmouth's *Historia Regum Britanniae*. In both works, St Dubricius (Dyfrig) is made archbishop and he was undeniably a historical character. He figures in the earliest surviving 'life' of a Celtic saint, the seventh-century *Vita Samsonis*, as the bishop who ordained St Samson deacon and consecrated him bishop on the Festival of St Peter's Chair, 22 February 521. Even more remarkable is Geoffrey's reference to St Teilo, 'an illustrious priest of Llandaff', as St Samson's successor as Archbishop of Dol in Brittany. It can hardly be a coincidence that both Geoffrey of Monmouth and the *Book of Llandaff* associate Teilo with Llandaff as well as Dol.

The natural conclusion is that Geoffrey was familiar with the *Book of Llandaff* or at least the material from which it was composed. Since Geoffrey's *Historia* was certainly completed by 1139, we can probably date the later stages in the compilation of the *Book of Llandaff* as 1134–8; but we must allow for the possibility that what Geoffrey used was not the final article. The *Book of Llandaff* preceded Geoffrey's *Historia* and it is wholly free from the legends about King Arthur, with which a few years later it would inevitably have been filled. There is certainly a very strong case for attributing the composition of the *Historia Regum Britanniae* to the time of Geoffrey of Monmouth's residence at Llandaff.

Assuming Geoffrey of Monmouth was the editor of the *Book of Llandaff*, he must have found the Llandaff documents in disorder, and may also have had to copy many of his memoranda of gifts from entries written on the margins of ancient copies of the Gospels, such as we find in the *Book of Chad*.[7] He accordingly wrote down his records under the names of the bishops to whose age they belonged, but he had no data to determine the order of many of these bishops.

Working from a mass of notes, he tried to compile a list of the bishops of Llandaff, but made many blunders in doing so, for he took the names of those bishops who had foundations previous to Teilo scattered around Gwent and Erging. Teilo had taken hold of them after the cessation of the Yellow Plague, when they had been abandoned and lay desolate. He arranged them in his catalogue as though they had been prelates reigning in Llandaff.

A great part of the materials was so ancient that he was evidently at quite a loss as to how to handle it, and his mistakes are unintentional, for no forger could have been so bewildered by figments of his own imagination.

The latest opinion is that the *Book of Llandaff* was drafted between 1120 and 1129 and certainly before 1140. If so, it is likely that before going to Oxford Geoffrey was at the very least connected with the writers of the *Book of Llandaff* and familiar with its contents.

The Sequence of Events in Geoffrey's Life

c.1090	Born at Monmouth and educated at the priory
c.1105	Living at Llandaff under the care of his uncle Uchtryd
c.1129–39	At Oxford
1136–8	The *Historia Regum Britanniae* is completed
1140	A revised edition of the *Historia* is written
1147	Death of Geoffrey's patron, Robert, Earl of Gloucester
1148	Death of Uchtryd, Bishop of Llandaff
1151	Elected Bishop of St Asaph?
1152	Ordained priest at Westminster
1153	He was one of the bishops who witnessed the important Treaty of Westminster between King Stephen and the Empress Matilda
1155	According to the Welsh chronicles, Geoffrey died at Llandaff:

In the year 1155, Galfrai ab Arthur, the domestic chaplain of William ap Robert [Earl of Gloucester], was made Bishop [of Llandaff], but before he entered into his office he died at his house in Llandaff, and was buried in the church there. He was a man whose equal was not to be found for learning and science and every godly quality. He was the foster son of Uchtryd, Archbishop of Llandaff, and his nephew, being his brother's son; and on account of his learning and science an archdeaconry was bestowed upon him in the church of Teilo, at Llandaff, where he was the instructor of many learned men and nobles.

Chronology of the Early Charters in the *Book of Llandaff*

It has been shown by E.D. Jones, in 'The Book of Llandaff' (*National Library of Wales Journal*, IV (1945–6)), that if we arrange the kings of Morgannwg in the order suggested by the charters in the *Book of Llandaff* they coincide almost exactly with the relevant genealogy in the Harleian pedigrees. From this one might deduce one of two things: either the names of the kings are derived from genuine charters, or the editor had in front of him a copy of the genealogy. The truth may well be a mixture of the two.

There was a mass of charters and at least three genealogies to work from: two for Morgannwg, which we know from the Harleian and Jesus collections, and a genealogy (not otherwise known) of the kings of Erging. From these documents (and some attributed to St Dubricius) a pedigree of the kings of Erging can be deduced, which is otherwise unknown, but probably authentic – Morcant vab Gurcant vab Cinuin vab Peipau vab Erb.

The editor also had some annals, local traditions and his own knowledge from which to reconstruct the more recent history. From the charters he deduced which bishop should be associated with which king in the genealogies, and was so able to group his bishops roughly in three blocks, corresponding (1) to the Erging genealogy, (2) to the Morgannwg genealogies and (3) to the known facts of recent history. These three blocks he placed end to end in that order, and put a few unidentifiable bishops in where he had space. Then he set to work to expand and assimilate the charters, and to compose elaborate witness lists out of the names he had before him. These witness lists were so skillfully and plausibly devised that it has proved possible for a modern scholar to reconstruct the chronology of the abbots of the three leading monasteries of Glamorgan from them.

He made one King Morcant out of two, bearing the same name – Morcant filius Athruis, of c.600, and Morcant 'pater Iudhail', c.706–36. He also assumed that the bishop during that period (whose name may well have been omitted in the original memoranda) was likewise one and the same man, Oudoceus, and that Bertguin succeeded him. Such an episcopate, extending from Mouric filius Teudric to Iudhail filius Morcant and his sons, from c.570 to c.750, seemed to E.D. Jones, in *'The Book of Llandaff'* (*National Library of Wales Journal*, IV (1945–6)), to approach 'patharachal longevity', and to J.W. James, *'Chronology in the Book of Llan Dav 500–900* (*National Library of Wales Journal*, XVI (1969–70)), to reach a 'preposterous length'. The same error, making one Morcant out of two, appears in both the Harleian pedigree 28 and the Jesus College pedigree 9, which are both derived from the same source, and can be as old as 954; but the archetypal source was a Deheubarth document, and not a Glamorgan document.

The gap between the two kings Morcant may be due to the loss of a document, possibly a book of the Gospels, which contained memoranda covering the entire seventh century, and which disappeared in a series of calamities such as are hinted at by the *Book of Llandaff* on p. 192. However, once the two Morcants are separated in time by a century, the chronological difficulty disappears, and from 730 onwards the history of the region is unbroken.

The Welsh Version of the King List in *Brut y Brenhinedd*
The names in brackets are the Latin versions of the names contained in Geoffrey of Monmouth's *Historia Regum Britanniae*.

51. Morudd ap Dan (Morvidus son of Danius)
52. Gorbonion ap Morudd (Gorbonianus son of Morvidus)

53. Arthal ap Morudd (Arthgallo son of Morvidus)
54. Elidir War ap Morudd (Elidurus Pius son of Morvidus)
55. **Arthal ap Morudd (Arthgallo son of Morvidus) SECOND TIME**
56. Rhys ap Gorbonian (Regin son of Gorbonianus)
57. **Margan ap Arthal (Marganus son of Arthgallo)**
58. Einion ap Arthal (Ennianus son of Arthgallo)
59. Idwal ap Owain (Iduallo son of Iugenius)
60. Rhun ap Peredur (Runo son of Peredurus)

Comments

It seems obvious that Geoffrey of Monmouth had access to the charter of Llandaff and from the names of genuine kings of Glywysing he compiled his fictitious king list. We may thus draw the following interesting parallels:

Brut y Brenhinedd	*Book of Llandaff*
Arthal ap Morudd	Athrwys ap Meurig
Rhys ap Gorbonion	Rhys ap Ithel ap Morgan
Margan ap Arthal	Morgan ap Athrwys
Einion ap Arthal	Einion
Idwal ap Owain	Idwal (lon)

It is also significant that both the *Brut y Brenhinedd* and the *Historia Regum Britanniae* name Archmael as the fifty-fifth king of Britain after Brutus. Arthal (Arthgallo), the father of Margan (Marganus), became the fifty-fifth king of Britain and thirty-second from Brutus, when he ascended the throne for the second time. Thus we have Arthmael as the fifty-fifth king of Britain. He was eventually succeeded by his son Margan (Morgan).

We may compare Arthgallo with Arthegal, who appears in Edmund Spenser's *The Faerie Queene*. He was the uterine brother of Prince Arthur and he married Britomart, a warrior maiden who was the daughter of Arthur's foe, Ryence, King of Deheubarth. She became the progenitress of a line of kings that superseded both the Saxons and the Normans – the Tudors. Arthegal ruled Guerinus so he may be identical to Artgualchar, Earl of Guerensis, who attended the plenary court held by Arthur in the City of the Legions in Geoffrey of Monmouth's *Historia Regum Britanniae*. We may also compare Geoffrey's King Margan ap Maglawn, who was slain at Maes Mawr (now Maes Margan) and was buried in a place where the Abbey of Margan (Margam) now stands, with Mar ap Glywys, who received Margan (now Margam) as his patrimony. There is a distinct possibility that the inscription on the so-called 'Paulinus' stone found at Merthyr Mawr should read Paulinus fili Mar and was erected in memory of Paul ap Mar ap Glywys.

The Importance of the *Book of Llandaff*

The *Liber Landavensis* (*Book of Llandaff*) is so called because it is the ancient cartulary or Register Book of the Cathedral of Llandaff. It has also been called the *Llyfr Teilo* (*Book of Teilo*) after one of the greatest of the early bishops of Llandaff. Although generally confused and lacking in chronological arrangement, it is of immense importance for it contains clues to the solution of the identity of King Arthur.

It contains a genealogy that is of vital importance for it gives the pedigree of the kings of Gwent and Erging. Most of the kings mentioned in the Llandaff Charters belong to the dynasties of Gwent and Morgannwg, while the dynasties of Dyfed and Brycheiniog make occasional appearances.

Geoffrey of Monmouth no doubt saw the name Arthurus or Athruis, King of Gwent, mentioned in a charter as a grantor of land and thus began the legend of King Arthur with his court at Caerleon-on-Usk in Gwent.

CHAPTER 3

Arthur's Illustrious Ancestors

The fourth-century founder of the dynasty of which Arthur was a member was Magnus Maximus, who through his son Owain can be identified as the ancestor of the kings of Glywysing, the kingdom that once stretched from the Usk to the Tywi and beyond. He also finds his way into the genealogies of Gwent, Powys, Gwynedd and Deheubarth. In addition, royal families in Cornwall, the Isle of Man and Strathclyde could also claim descent from Magnus Maximus.

Magnus Maximus

Magnus Maximus was the great, great, great, great, great-grandfather of Arthur and he was a Spanish officer who came to Britain in 368 as an official in the household of Count Theodosius the Elder. While stationed on Hadrian's Wall, Maximus was successful in driving back the Picts which meant that the northern Britons were able to live in peace within the new provinces of Strathclyde and Manau Guotodin.

In Welsh tradition, Magnus Maximus was known as Macsen Wledig and a story in the *Mabinogion* entitled 'The Dream of Maxen' relates how he came to the Roman fort of Segontium in Arfon, later Gwynedd.[1] His dream involved a journey across the sea to a land where he crossed a mountain range to reach the mouth of a river. He then came upon a castle where he observed a ceiling covered with gold and walls decorated with stones. In the great hall, he found a beautiful maiden, finely dressed and sitting in a golden chair. As in all fairy tales, he fell in love with her at first sight. Taking her in his arms, he sat down with her in the golden chair. At this point, just as the dream was getting interesting, Maximus woke up, but he could not get the girl out of his mind and he became obsessed with her memory. In due course, he set out to find her and arrived at Aberseint, in Arfon. Here he met the Princess Elen, who was exactly like the girl in his dreams, and they of course fell in love and married.[2]

This ancient tale tells us that Magnus Maximus took command of the abandoned Roman fortress of Segontium, which had been built by Agricola in AD 78, prior to his invasion of Anglesey. Overlooking the present-day town of Caernarfon, it is included as 'Caer Segeint' in the list of twenty-eight cities detailed by Nennius in the *Historia Brittonum*. It is named after the old British settlement of Caer Seint yn Arfon, which was the seat of Eudaf Hen, otherwise known as Octavius the Old.[3] Coins found at Segontium indicate that it was garrisoned until about 394 and no other Roman fort was held for so long.

The *Mabinogion* story certainly contains some historical fact and it has been used by Geoffrey of Monmouth, who comments that Maximus married a royal heiress and thus came into possession of her father's kingdom. It was thus a political marriage and it is significant that the inscription on the Pillar of Eliseg (see p. 158) records that Cyngen, King of Powys, was descended from Sevira, daughter of Magnus Maximus.

In 383, towards the end of the Roman occupation, Magnus Maximus seized power and was elected emperor by his troops. He promoted the Segontium garrison to the palatine army and led them under his personal ensign of the Red Dragon on an expedition to Gaul to overthrow Gratian, the legitimate Roman Emperor.[4]

Gildas, writing in the sixth century, criticises Magnus Maximus for depriving Britain of its soldiers, leaving the country denuded of its military sources, 'to be trodden underfoot by two very cruel and fierce foreign nations'. These were the Scots (from Ireland) and the Picts from the north; the Saxons were a later threat.

Elen and her brother Cynan accompanied Maximus in his conquest of Gaul, and it was as a result of having marched with her husband's legions that she earned the epithet of Luyddog, meaning 'of the Hosts'. At Tréves she has been confounded with Helena, mother of Constantine, who was never there at all. This misconception has been made to serve as a basis for the myth of the 'Holy Coat', the seamless robe of Christ, which she is supposed to have brought from Jerusalem and to have given to the Church of Tréves, where it is preserved as a holy relic.

Gratian's legions in Gaul deserted to join Maximus, and Gratian escaped to beyond the Alps. He was captured at Lyons and murdered by Maximus's commanding officer, Count Andrathagius, on 25 August 383.

Maximus established his court at Tréves in France and afterwards at Trier, a town that at that time was a Celtic centre, where the Celtic language was spoken. For five years Maximus was recognised as co-Emperor with Theodosius and Valentinian II. From Trier in Gaul he ruled over five western provinces of the Empire.

Maximus conquered Spain and then invaded Italy where he had to deal with the forces of the Eastern Roman Emperor Theodosius I. The latter's navy slipped past Maximus's fleet, while his land armies met Maximus at Illyra and 3 miles from Aquileia, near Trieste, Maximus was finally caught and killed on 28 August 388.

Nennius comments that the armies Maximus took to Gaul never returned to Britain but settled in the area that became known as Armorica (Brittany). His widow Elen, however, returned to Britain as the heiress of substantial estates.[5] She became known as Elen Lluyddog (Helen of the Hosts), patroness of the highways along which the troops marched. The road south from Caernarfon came to be known as Sarn Helen, Helen's Causeway.

The Offspring of Magnus Maximus
In the Welsh pedigrees we are told that the first wife of Magnus Maximus was Ceindrech, daughter of Rheiden, by whom he had at least three sons, Owain, Anhun and Victor.

Owain Finddu (Owain of the Black Border), the eldest son of Maximus, by his first wife Ceindrech, moved down to south Wales, where he became ruler of the area later known as Glywysing, which stretched from the River Usk to the River Tywi. When news of the death of his father Maximus reached Britain, he was elected to be Pendragon over the native princes. In 394 he was slain by the Irish while defending Dinas Ffaraon Dandde (Fortress of the Fiery Pharoah) in Arfon. The area around Segontium had by then become threatened with constant attacks by the Irish, who quickly took possession of Mona (Anglesey) and the greater part of Gwynedd.

Antonius Donatus, the second son of Maximus and Ceindrech, was the ancestor of the Celtic kings of Gwent and the Isle of Man. When Maximus left for Gaul, Antonius (known in Welsh as Anhun Dunawd) declared himself King of Strathclyde and Galloway and founded a dynasty. St Ninian was in Galloway within fourteen years of Maximus's departure so Anhun may have been the ruler from which he obtained permission to settle. Anhun's son was Ednyfed and his grandson was Tudwal. (Aildred's *Life of St Ninian* tells us of his meeting with Tudwal.) Antonius Donatus later settled on the Isle of Man where St Germanus anointed him king.

Victor accompanied his father Magnus Maximus to the Continent and commanded troops in Spain. He was captured and killed in 388.

Magnus Maximus's subsequent marriage to Elen, the daughter of Eudaf Hen, produced two sons, Constantine and Peblig, and a daughter, Sevira.

Constantine (Cystennin ap Macsen), the eldest son of Maximus and Elen, was just an infant when his father was killed in 388, so he spent many years in exile in Armorica under the protection of his kinsman Aldwr, ruler of British settlements in the west of the peninsula. Some years later, Constantine, accompanied by St Germanus (the brother of Aldwr) and a large body of troops, returned to his homeland to reclaim his patrimony, but the Irish occupation was by now so extensive that Constantine found it necessary to request military assistance from Cunedda Wledig, a chieftain of the Votadini tribe from the area north-east of Hadrian's Wall.[6] Cunedda Wledig was a post-Roman officer who occupied the position of *Dux Britanniarum* in command of forces protecting Hadrian's Wall.

Cunedda complied by sending a formidable band of warriors led by his nine sons to deal with the Irish problem. They succeeded in expelling the Goidels from the greater part of north Wales and were all rewarded by being allowed to take possession of the areas of land that they had won back from the Irish settlers, which lay on either side of a diagonal line from Rhuddlan on the Irish Sea to Cardigan on Cardigan Bay, forming a wedge through Wales from the north-east to the south-west.

The remainder of Wales on either side of that wedge was retained by the family of Magnus Maximus. Constantine the Blessed ruled over Arfon in north west Wales; Antonius Donatus ruled in the Isle of Man, while their brother-in-law, Vortigern the Thin, subsequently ruled from Powys to Gwent.

Constantine now re-established himself at his old family seat at Segontium, which then became known as Caer Gystennin and he was elected Pendragon by the confederated states of Britain.[7] He became known as Constantine Fendigaid (the Blessed) in consequence of being considered a saint of the British Church. In conjunction with Tewdrig, King of Garth Madryn, he founded Cor Tewdws (Choir of Theodosius) near the Severn Sea, Llangystennin (the Church of Constantine) in Gwynedd, and also Lann Custenhin Garth Benni (the monastic enclosure and Church of Constantine), now Welsh Bicknor in Herefordshire.

On his death he was initially buried with due ceremonial pomp at Segontium, but in 1283 (about 840 years later), on the orders of Edward I, his tomb was transferred to Llanbeblig, the mother church of Caernarfon. We are told by Nennius that an inscription on a stone at Segontium commemorated Constantine, 'son of the great, the very great'.

This statement led to the belief that this was a memorial to the son of Constantine the Great. However, in Latin, 'the great, the very great' is Magnus Maximus, so the tomb was obviously that of Constantine the son of Magnus Maximus. Matthew of Westminster states that the body of the

Constantine was excavated and by the orders of Edward I honourably transferred to Llanbeblig Church.

Sevira, the daughter of Maximus and Elen, married Vortigern.[8] This marriage was undoubtedly calculated to gain political advantage, for when Maximus's widow, Elen, died, Sevira by right of female succession, was heiress. Vortigern thus gained control of the territory of Gwent, Erging and Ewyas and became one of the most powerful rulers in southern Britain. Their son Brydw was blessed by St Germanus of Auxerre during his visit to Britain.

Peblig (known in Latin as Publicius), the son of Maximus and Elen, was a disciple of St Ninian and he founded the Church of Llanbeblig, which stands close to the old Roman cemetery of Segontium.

Constantine the Blessed may have died of the plague in AD 443, but it is also possible that he was assassinated on the instigation of his ambitious brother-in-law, Vortigern. For a brief time the Emperor's eldest son, Constantine the Younger, became ruler, and he trustingly handed over the Council of Britain to his uncle Vortigern, who then plotted to procure the crown for himself.

Vortigern treacherously murdered Constantine the Younger and forced the prince's brothers Ambrosius and Uthyr to seek exile in Armorica, just like their father had done years before.[9] Vortigern then took the crown and kingdom into his possession.

Ambrosius Aurelianus
Known in Welsh tradition by the title Emrys Wledig, Ambrosius was one of the greatest figures of early British history.[10] He and his father Constantine were connecting links between the Roman Empire and an independent Britain. Gildas refers to Ambrosius as 'a man of unassuming character, who alone of the Roman race chanced to survive in the shock of such a storm (as his parents, people undoubtedly clad in the purple had been killed in it), whose offspring in our days have greatly degenerated from their ancestral nobleness'.

Ambrosius was a member of the Aurelii, and being Romano-British he certainly seems to have represented a return to the Roman ideas, for he demonstrated the Imperial sense of cohesion when dealing with his country's aggressors.[11] His immediate relations, with the exception of a younger brother, Uther, were presumably killed in civil wars stirred up by the tyrant Vortigern.

The latin name Ambrosius is probably linked with the family of St Ambrose, Bishop of Milan, who was born of a Roman family at Trier in 339 and was made Bishop of Milan on 7 December 374. He died in 397. Ambrose means divine or immortal and it may have been Hellenic in extraction. The father of St Ambrose was Aurelius Ambrosius and his name implies a connection with the Aurellii family. He held the illustrious office of Praetorian Praefect of the Gauls from September 337 to April 340.

It is relevant that the wife of Custennin Fendigaid (father of Ambrosius) belonged to a noble family of Rome and it is possible that Ambrosius Aurelianus was connected through his mother with St Ambrose, Bishop of Milan, and the Aurellii. This explains the statement by Gildas that Ambrosius was 'of the Roman race'.

In the *Historia Brittonum*, Ambrosius is reported to have said that his father was a Roman Consul and this obviously refers to the Romano-British Emperor Custennin Fendigaid.

Ambrosius in Glywysing

We are told by Nennius that Ambrosius as a child lived in Glywysing in a neighbourhood called Campus Elleti, which means the Maes or Plain of Elletus. This name survives as Llanmaes and it is near Llanilltud Fawr (Llantwit Major) in the Vale of Glamorgan. Nearby was also Palus Elleti, 'the Marsh of Elletus', mentioned in the *Book of Llandaff*.[12]

According to Nennius, the emissaries of the tyrant Vortigern found the child Ambrosius at 'Campus Elleti' and took him to their leader who was residing in a hill fort in north Wales (later called Dinas Emrys). Geoffrey of Monmouth repeats this story, but manages to confuse matters. He has Vortigern asking the boy for his name and Ambrosius replying, 'My name is Myrddin Emrys (Merlin Ambrosius)'. Geoffrey thus translated Ambrosius Aurelianus into Merlinus Ambrosius and then shortened it to Merlin. This was the beginning of the legend of Merlin the Magician!

The Defeat of Vortigern

Ambrosius, when just a young man, was forced to flee to Armorica, with his brother Uthyr (Victor), when their eldest brother, Constantine the Younger (named after his father), was murdered and his crown usurped by Vortigern. The two brothers remained in exile for many years and were brought up as princes by their cousin Budic (Emyr Llydaw), Emperor of Armorica.

In due course, Ambrosius returned to Britain, with St Germanus the soldier-saint, to organise a determined campaign to overthrow the usurper Vortigern, who by now had been branded a traitor.[13] When Ambrosius arrived with a strong force to claim his rightful inheritance, the Britons no doubt gave him enthusiastic support.

Tradition provides three possible locations where Vortigern was defeated.

51

He is said to have perished when his wooden fortress in Nant Gwrtheyrn (Vortigern's Valley) on the Llyyn Peninsula was set on fire. Alternatively, he was killed in a similar fashion at Craig Gwrtheyrn (Vortigern's Rock), which overlooks the River Teifi at Llanfihangel-ar-arth in Ceredigion.

The third possible location for his defeat is described by Geoffrey of Monmouth: 'Vortigern fled to the town of Gornoreu, in Erging, upon the Gania in the mountains of Cloartius'. *Tysilio's Chronicle* states: 'He [Ambrosius] marched into Kambria and made for the castle of Genoreu, for it was there that Vortigern had fled in his search for a safe refuge. This castle, which belonged to Erging country, was beside the river Wye, on a hill called Cloartius.' This location was an Iron Age fortress on Little Doward near Ganarew which was undoubtedly part of the ancient kingdom of Erging and Geoffrey's Gania is probably a copyist's misinterpretation of Gwy, the old British name for the Wye in a Romanised form. Geoffrey tells us that Ambrosius and his strong force: 'lost no time, but moved into position with their siege-machines and did their utmost to break down the walls. When everything else had failed, they tried fire; and this, once it took hold, went on blazing until it burned up the tower and Vortigern with it.'

Ambrosius the War Leader

The poor remnants of our nation, to save themselves from complete destruction took arms under the command of Ambrosius Aurelianus, a modest man, who of all the Roman nation was the only one left by chance in the confusion of these troubled times.

Gildas

Following the overthrow of Vortigern in 465, Ambrosius became the first warlord of Britain and his dominion was in modern terms the lands adjoining the Severn Estuary in the area of Gwent, Gloucestershire, Somerset, Herefordshire, Worcestershire, part of Warwickshire and the district between the Wye and the Severn, including the Forest of Dean.

He set up his headquarters at Caer Vudei (Woodchester), the former residence of a Roman governor. The place name of Amberley near Rodborough confirms his connection with this locality and he established his court at Ambrosii Aula, near Woodchester.

He restored the army of Britain as a fighting force using Roman methods, bringing strength and hope back to his countrymen. The Britons desperately needed strong leadership at this time for the Saxons were becoming a serious problem.

Bede comments that under the leadership of Ambrosius 'the Britons, scattered and defeated by the Angles, slowly began to take heart and recover their strength, emerging from their dens where they had hidden themselves'. He also tells us that Ambrosius was a skilled commander, 'brave afoot, he was braver on horse-back'.

These statements indicate that Ambrosius revived the old office of *dux bellorum* (Leader of Battles) as part of his campaign to restore the old ways established by the Romans in Gwent.

To improve his defences, Ambrosius probably ordered the construction of the extensive earthwork, now known as Wansdyke, which extends for 60 miles from Savernake Forest in Wiltshire, across the Marlborough Downs and the Avon Valley to end at a hill fort above Bristol. It consists of a mound of earth running east–west with a deep ditch on the north side, and was probably built to protect Domnonia from a Saxon army marching up the Thames Valley. The name Wansdyke comes from 'Wodensdu' – Woden's Dyke and it would appear that the Saxons named it after their god Woden.

The *Anglo-Saxon Chronicle* indicates that Ambrosius succeeded in holding back the English from 473 until 490, with only one victory for the Saxons claimed during this period. In 477, Aelle arrived from Germany with his three sons, and landing in Sussex, fought a successful battle against the Britons and drove them into the Weald of Kent.

Matthew of Westminster tells us that in 487 Ambrosius fought a battle at a plain known as Maes Beli and defeated a large force of Saxons which had hoped to take the British army by surprise.

Geoffrey of Monmouth recalls that when Ambrosius defeated Hengist he was buried in Saxon fashion under a mound of earth: 'Aurelius, who was moderate in all that he did, ordered Hengist to be buried and a barrow of earth to be raised over his body, that being the pagan custom.' The death of Hengist is mentioned in the *Anglo-Saxon Chronicle* with the statement that in 488 'Aesc succeeded to the kingdom and was king of the men of Kent twenty-four years.'

Nennius calls Ambrosius 'Rex inter omnos reges', 'King among all kings' of the British people, implying that he was leader of all the regional kings.

Ambrosius appeased the family of Gwrtheyrn (Vortigern) by allowing his son Pascent to rule over his father's old domain of Gwrthcyrnion and Buellt, and his grandson Cadell Ddyrnllug to rule over the Vale of Clwyd and Powys.

The Death of Ambrosius Aurelianus
Geoffrey of Monmouth states that Ambrosius died after being given poison

at Winchester by Eopa, a Saxon disguised as a physician and hired for the purpose by Pascentius, one of the sons of Vortigern. We are also told by Geoffrey that the death of Ambrosius was marked by the appearance of a comet:

> there appeared a star of great magnitude and brilliance, with a single beam shining from it. At the end of this beam was a ball of fire, spread out in the shape of a dragon. From the dragon's mouth stretched forth two rays of light, one of which seemed to extend beyond the latitude of Gaul, while the second turned towards the Irish Sea and split up into seven smaller shafts of light. This star appeared three times, and all who saw it were struck with fear and wonder . . .

The same comet was recorded in the *Anglo-Saxon Chronicle* as appearing in 497, which therefore gives us a date for the death of Ambrosius. It would appear that although Ambrosius nominated Arthur as his successor, the more experienced leaders held sway for a time. They were Uthyr (brother of Ambrosius) and Geraint, the son of Erbin, who was subsequently killed at the Battle of Llongborth in 508.

The Brief Reign of Uthyr Pendragon

The reign of Uthyr, the brother of Ambrosius, appears to have lasted just nine years. This is revealed by an entry in the *Anglo-Saxon Chronicle* which tells us that Cerdic of the Gewissei defeated and slew a British Pendragon with 5,000 of his men on Dragon Hill, near Uffington Camp in Berkshire. It is possible that the name of this hill commemorates the battle and the death of Uthyr Pendragon in 506.

CHAPTER 4

Arthur's Immediate Family

After the Roman legions left Britain in about 410, the Roman republic of the Silures was displaced by a monarchy and Teithfallt became the ruler of the area which in later years was known as Gwent and Glamorgan. Teithfallt was the son of Nynniaw and his name is derived from the 'Path of Mallt', the Druidic goddess of War, and virtually means 'Path of the Thunderbolt'. In his declining years he became a monk, having abdicated in favour of his son Tewdrig.

Arthur's Paternal Grandfather
Tewdrig was initially the ruler of an area known as Garth Madryn which was centred around present-day Talgarth in Powys. The name Talgarth means 'the brow of the garth' and it is situated beneath the dominating hill of Mynydd Troed.

It is likely that Tewdrig, whose alternative name is Tewdws (from which the name Tudor originates), was named after the Roman Emperor Theodosius and that he was a contemporary of King Theodoric (493–526) of the Ostrogoths. If this is the case, then the Glamorgan ruler Meirchion Vesanus (Marcianus the Mad) was named after Marcianus, Eastern Roman Emperor 450–7, and Ynyr (Honorius) I and II of Gwent were named after Honorius, Western Roman Emperor 395–423.

Tewdrig, in conjunction with the Romano-British Emperor Constantine, is credited with having co-founded the monastic college of Cor Tewdws, which was previously named Cor Worgan after Eurgain, the sister of Eudaf Hen. It was later called Llanilltud Fawr after its principal, St Illtud.

In his old age, just as his father had done before him, Tewdrig abdicated, and the government of his kingdom passed into the hands of his son Meurig. He then went into retirement to lead a monastic life in the solitude of the Wye Valley at a place that is now called Tintern. This name is derived from two old Brythonic words, *din* meaning 'fort' and *teyrn* meaning 'king', – thus 'the fort of the king.'

There have been settlements in the lower Wye Valley since prehistoric times and excavations have revealed the site of a small Roman building within the foundations of Tintern Abbey. This may have been occupied by Tewdrig but there is also a tradition that he lived as a hermit 'among the rocks at Tintern' and it is possible that he occupied a nearby Iron Age hill fort.

The Battle at Tintern

According to an account in the *Book of Llandaff*, Tewdrig was not able to enjoy the peace of his beautiful surroundings for very long. It came to an abrupt end one day when an enemy force crossed the Wye and entered Gwent. The old king, who had been victorious in all his battles, bravely took up arms, and mounted on horseback led his household troops to deal with the enemy. It is possible that the battle took place in the nearby Angidy Valley, where a stone bridge bears the name Pont y Saeson – 'Bridge of the Saxons'. The invaders were put to flight, but one of them hurled a lance which struck the old king and he fell to the ground. By now his son Meurig had arrived on the scene, and the mortally wounded Tewdrig was taken from the battlefield in a cart drawn by two stags towards the Severn Estuary. The intention was probably to bury him on the island of Flat Holm on the Severn Sea but he died at a spot on the Gwent side of the estuary, where a clear and strong spring started to flow from the ground.[1]

It would seem that Tewdrig had requested that a church should be raised on the spot where he died, and his son Meurig obeyed his father's last wishes by having an oratory erected over the grave. In due course it was blessed by St Oudoceus (whose church is at Llandogo in the Wye Valley), and it became known as Merthyr Teyrn (the church of the martyred king).[2] Mathern is the anglicised version of this name. The land around the church was granted to St Oudoceus for the monastery of Llandaff and in later times the bishops established a palace here.

The Tomb of King Tewdrig

Confirmation that a Dark Age period burial did indeed take place on the site of this church was established by Bishop Francis Godwin in 1610.[3] This Bishop of Llandaff, who had been fascinated by the story of Tewdrig contained in the ancient *Book of Llandaff*, recorded his discovery as follows:

> Whilst the work of restoration was in progress, a stone coffin was found at the base of the south wall, containing some dry mould and bones, supposed to be the remains of the king [Tewdrig].

The whole of the skull was there, although in a much injured condition, the upper jaw, containing four teeth was perfect. The coffin measured 5ft 7in long outside, and 5ft 3in inside; its widths were 20 inches outside, and 16 inches inside and depths 11in and 6 in. The sides appeared to have been broken by their jagged appearance, and there was no lid. A little to the east of the coffin an earthen urn was found measuring 8 inches in diameter by 6 inches deep, supposed to contain the viscerae of Bishop Miles Sally. This urn was unfortunately injured by the workmens' picks, a piece being broken off it. Both coffin and urn with their contents were carefully re-interred.

Bishop Godwin had a lid made for the coffin and Tewdrig's remains were reburied. A simple service was conducted and a stone plaque inscribed to commemorate the martyred king. It can be seen on the north wall of the chancel and the inscription tells the story of the last days of King Tewdrig:

Here lyeth entombed the body of Theoderick, King of Morganuck, or Glamorgan, commonly called St. Tewdrick, and accounted a martyr because he was slain in battle against the Saxons, being then pagans, and in defence of the Christian religion. The battle was fought at Tintern, where he obtained a great victory. He died here, being on his way homeward, three days after the battle, having taken order with Maurice, his son who succeeded him in his kingdom, that in the same place he should happen to decease a church should be built and his body buried in ye same, which was accordingly performed in the year 600.

Godwin was just over one-hundred years out in his dating of the event, but the wording of his inscription is based on the account given in the *Book of Llandaff*. It is of interest that the book also records three separate grants of land and rights given by Meurig and Brochmael – son and grandson of Tewdrig respectively, in honour of the late king. There is a pool in the River Wye, near Tintern, named after Brochmael, which again helps to confirm the family connection with this locality. The *Book of Llandaff* gives a list of grants reputed to have been given by Tewdrig's son Meurig and his son Brochmael to Bishop Oudoceus of Llandaff in commemoration of Tewdrig.

KING ARTHUR

In 1881, William White of Abergavenny was contracted to carry out restoration work at Mathern Church and he too was able to see King Tewdrig's stone sarcophagus and remains. The following description appeared in the *Abergavenny Chronicle*:

> Upon excavating at the base of this wall (south wall of the chancel) under the tablet of King Theoderick, a stone coffin was found, partly filled with dry mould, and some bones of the king. The whole of the skull was there, though broken in several pieces. The upper jaw, in which there are four teeth, quite perfect, and most of the other bones were in a fair state of preservation. These were carefully collected and placed in a box, in the care of the rector, the Rev Watkin Davies. The stone coffin was removed to a place of safety for reinternment. Its dimensions are 5ft 7in long exterior and 5 ft 3 1/2 in interior; its width 20 in exterior and 16 in interior; the depth 11 in exterior and 6 in interior. There is no doubt that the sides, at some former period, were broken away as the edges present a broken and jagged appearance.

Mathern is one of the few villages in Britain that can boast a palace and for three-hundred years it was the principal home of the bishops of Llandaff. In 1406 their grand palace at Llandaff had been destroyed by Owain Glyndwr and the decision was made to move to Mathern, where the see already owned land. The first palace was built there by Bishop John de Zouch (1401–23). It was later improved and extended by Bishop Marshall (1478–96) and Bishop Miles Sally (1499–1510).[4]

Several Llandaff bishops are buried in Mathern Church and one of them is Miles Sally, who left instructions in his will that his heart should be buried before the high altar near the grave of 'King Theoderick'.

Academic Disputes
1. The Date of Tewdrig's Battle at Tintern

Present-day historians have placed the Tintern battle in the seventh century, insisting that the Saxons had not penetrated so far inland during the fifth century. However , in *The British Museum Guide to Anglo-Saxon Antiquities* (1823), Reginald Smith states that the archaeological evidence, based partly on the existence of early settlements in the Thames Valley, and further, on the distribution and dating of different types of the saucer brooch, proves that in about 470 a Saxon host advanced along the south bank and up the Thames Valley, and beyond, reaching and occupying Gloucestershire. It is thus feasible that a Saxon raiding party crossed the River Severn into Gwent and was responsible for the death of Tewdrig Fendigaid.

2. The Confusion of Two Tewdrigs and Two Meurigs

An academic muddle has been caused by P.C. Bartrum and H.M. Chadwick who have confused two Tewdrigs and two Meurigs. Bartrum is quite correct when he states that Tewdrig ap Teithfallt, King of Garth Madryn, was the father of Marchell, the mother of Brychan Brycheiniog ('De Situ Brecheniauc' pedigree 10), but mistaken in his assumption that Tewdrig ap Llywarch ap Nynniaw ap Erb (Jesus College pedigree 9) was the martyr of Merthyr Tewdrig (Mathern). The issue is further confused by Hector Chadwick, who makes Nynniaw's father Erb the son of Erbig the son of Meurig the son of Caradog Freichfras.

The mistake continues to be repeated that Tewdrig was the son of King Nynniaw's son Llywarch and that he was King of Gwent in the early seventh century, with the Battle of Tintern placed at around 630 and the dates of his life are given as c.580–c.630.

Sorting Out the Muddle

Jesus College Pedigree 9	'De Situ Brecheniauc' 10
Meuric	Macsen
Erbic	Anhun
Erb	Tathal
Nynniaw	Teithrin
Llywarch	Teithfallt
Tewdric	Tewdrig
Meuric	Meurig

These two genealogies appear separate due to a misunderstanding. which makes it seem that there were two Tewdrigs. It would appear that Gwraldreg, King of Garth Madryn, had an only daughter and heiress named Morvitha (Morfudd), who married Tathal ap Annun Ddu. Their son Teithrin died young but not before marrying a daughter of Custennin ap Macsen and siring a son, who was named Teithfallt. The widow then went on to marry a second time to Nynniaw ap Erb, King of Gwent, who thus became the step-father of Teithfallt.

In his declining years Teithfallt resigned his throne to his son Tewdrig, who held court at Llanfaes just outside Brecon. It is reputed to have been on a site called Bryn Gwyn, a part of Newton Farm in Llanfaes. Upon the marriage of Tewdrig's daughter Marchell to Anlach, he granted Garth Madryn to his son-in-law Brychan so that he could concentrate on ruling his wider realm of Gwent, which in later life he granted to his son Meurig.

It is relevant that the Hanesyn Hen genealogies agree with the *Book of Llandaff* in making Tewdrig the son of Teithfallt ap Nynniaw ap Erb. Also in the *Life of St Catwg*, Tewdrig is referred to as the son of Teithfallt and as having been martyred in Gwent. The Revd Sabine Baring-Gould names Tewdrig ap Teithfallt as King of Morgannwg and Garth Madryn.

Where was Garth Madryn?
This was the original name of a region to the east of Brecon, with its eastern boundary at the town now called Talgarth, which means 'Place at the end of the garth'. Garth means hill or enclosure and it relates to the dominating hill of Mynydd Troed. Anlach was an incoming Demetian nobleman of the Deisi tribe and belonged to the dynasty of the kings of Dyfed. The son of Anlach and Marchell was Brychan, who succeeded to the kingdom on the death of his father, and it then became known as Brycheiniog.

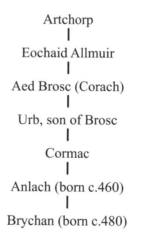

Artchorp
|
Eochaid Allmuir
|
Aed Brosc (Corach)
|
Urb, son of Brosc
|
Cormac
|
Anlach (born c.460)
|
Brychan (born c.480)

Brychan's maternal grandfather was Tewdrig, King of Garth Madryn and Gwent. Thus Brychan and Athrwys (Arthur) shared the same grandfather and were therefore cousins.

The Nynniaw ap Erb Confusion
Erb is mentioned in the *Book of Llandaff* as the father of Peibio, King of

Erging. His wife is said to have been the daughter of Custennin Fendigaid. A charter in the *Book of Llandaff* mentions Erb, King of Gwent and Erging, as the donor of Cil Hal to St Dubricius. He occurs again in a pedigree of the kings of Glywysing as the father of Nynnio: Nynniaw ap Erb ap Erbic (Jesus College pedigree 9).

Nynniaw ap Erb appears in the pedigrees of Gwent and Glywysing as the ancestor of Tewdrig, the martyred King of Gwent: Teithfallt ap Nynniaw ap Erb (ABT 5), but as Teithfallt ap Idnerth ap Erb in the *Life of St Cadoc*. Another son of Erb was Peibio, King of Erging. Nothing is known historically of Nynniaw, but he appears with his brother Peibio in the legend of Rhita Gawr, who is said to have conquered the two kings. The fact that Nynniaw and Peibio appear in the genealogies as brothers, sons of Erb, may also be connected with this part of Wales. In keeping with this is the fact that there was a place called Tref Rita mentioned in the *Book of Llandaff* which was stated by the compiler to have been near Llandegfedd, Gwent.

The Key to the Correct Dating of Tewdrig, Meurig and Athrwys

King Meurig's daughter Anna gave birth to St Samson, who can be positively dated for he signed his name at the Council of Paris in 557. This means that both Athrwys (Arthur) and his nephew Samson both belong to the sixth century, as does Meurig. Athrwys's grandfather Tewdrig thus lived in the latter part of the fifth century. When they are brought back into their correct time period everything fits together perfectly.

Another key to the dating is the fact that Tewdrig's great-grandson Catwg (Cadog) certainly lived in the sixth century and not the seventh. This simple fact is widely accepted.

When King Tewdrig, ruler of Garth Madryn and Gwent, is placed in his correct century it follows that his son Meurig and his grandson Athrwys belonged to the sixth century, the very time when the King Arthur of legend and history is supposed to have lived.[5]

King Arthur's Maternal Grandfather

Arthur's grandfather on his mother's side of the family was Gwrgant Mawr, King of Erging, who had been expelled from his kingdom by the usurper Vortigern. He established himself on the Gower Peninsula, which he liberated from the Irish.

Emrys Wledig reinstated Gwrgant Mawr as King of Erging, but he still retained Gower with his court at Aber Llychwr (Leucarum). One of the sons of Gwrgant Mawr was Caradog Freichfras, who took over the reigns of government while Arthur was away fighting battles. It was Caradog's grandson Medraut who tried to seize power during Arthur's absence and the outcome was the Battle of Camlann, which is dealt with later in the book.

King Arthur's Father

Meurig succeeded his father Tewdrig Fendigaid as King of Morgannwg and Gwent and he would have held paramount authority over a tract forming the principal part of Glamorgan, the whole of Gwent and the portion of Herefordshire that lies to the south-west of the River Wye.[6] He married Onbrawst, daughter of Gwrgant Mawr, King of Erging. They had four sons, Athrwys, Idnerth, Frioc and Comereg. Their daughters were Anna, who married Amwn Ddu, Gwenonwy, who married Gwyndaf Hen, and Afrella, who married Umbrafel. Thus all three of Meurig's daughters married sons of Emyr Llydaw (Budic, Emperor of Armorica) and created an important alliance between the two royal families. The relationship between these two important families is an integral part of the story of King Arthur and the colonisation of Brittany.

The Patrilinear Descent

Macsen Wledig (Maximus the Imperator)

|

Anhun Dunaws (Antonius Donatus) b. c.368

|

Tathal

|

Teithrin

|

Teithfallt

|

Tewdrig Fendigaid (the Blessed)

|

Meurig

|

Athrwys (Arthur)

ARTHUR'S IMMEDIATE FAMILY

The Matrilinear Descent

Maesen Wledig

|

Custennin Fendigaid

|

Daughter of Custennin Fendigaid

|

Pepiau Clavorauc (King of Erging)

|

Cynfyn

|

Gwrgant Mawr

|

Onbrawst = Meurig ap Tewdrig

|

Athrwys (Arthur)

Why Did Geoffrey of Monmouth Refer to Arthur as the Son of Uther Pendragon?

It is necessary to understand why it is possible for Arthur to be the son of both Uther Pendragon and Meurig ap Tewdrig. The simple explanation is that Meurig bore the title Uther Pendragon which means 'Wonderful Head Dragon', indicating that he was an important war leader. Geoffrey of Monmouth was the first writer to refer to Arthur as the son of Uther Pendragon and he obviously confused the title with the personal name of Uthyr, the brother of Emrys (Ambrosius). Geoffrey may also have misinterpreted the writings of Nennius who described Arthur as 'mab uter, id est filius horribilis'. The fact that *uter* means marvellous and as *mab uter* Arthur becomes 'marvellous son' may have led to Geoffrey's statement that Arthur was the son of Uther Pendragon.

Confusion may have also been caused because Arthur (Arthmael) married the daughter of Count Gwythyr. This is the same name as Uthyr, which in Latin is Victor. In other words Uthyr was the father-in-law of Arthur and not his father, as stated by Geoffrey of Monmouth. These explanations all provide sound reasons why such a puzzling statement was made.

The title Pendragon, which meant 'Dragon's Head', is of ancient origin and it signifies an important war leader. Such a title stems from a tradition established in ancient Britain. The Welsh word *draig* for dragon, takes us back to the Latin *draco* and *draconis*. These words relate to the Augustan era of the Roman Empire, when dragons coloured purple began to figure on the standards of some of the legions in about AD 175. Such a custom then extended itself to the emperors in times of peace and the Welsh word 'Pendragon' makes it highly probable that the practice was one of the Roman traditions cherished by the leaders or over-kings of the Britons.

It is significant that Ammianus Marcellinus describes how Caesar was recognised in battle by the purple standard of the dragon, which, ragged with age, fluttered from the top of a long spear.

When the Romans departed from Britain it would have been quite natural for the Britons to continue using the dragon battle standard during their resistance to the Saxons. The word *draig* (dragon) undoubtedly signified a warrior and the greatest warriors were referred to as *pendraig* (pendragon) – in other words chief commander.

It is interesting that *Y Gododdin*, written by Aneurin, refers to Gwenabwy ab Gwen as a dragon at the Battle of Catraeth. A poem attributed to Taliesin refers to Owain ap Urien as 'Owain ben draic', the 'chief dragon'.

The Saxons also used a dragon standard in battle and it is relevant that the Bayeux Tapestry shows King Harold falling at Hastings beside a dragon standard. Dragons are also to be seen on the famous Sutton Hoo shield (AD c.650).

Geoffrey of Monmouth tells us that King Arthur bore a dragon as his emblem ('aureum dracon infixit quem pro vexillo habebat') on his shield. There was also a dragon insignia on his helmet. This symbol of Roman imperialism thus lived on in Wales in the post-Roman age, and survives today as Y Ddraig Goch, 'the Red Dragon', which can be seen on the Welsh flag.

A Summary of Arthur's Relations
It would appear that Arthur's grandfather **Tewdrig** had two daughters, Gweryla and Marchell and a son Meurig:

Gweryla married Bicanys, an Armorican nobleman who was the brother of Emyr Llydaw. Gweryla and Bicanys were the parents of St Illtud (Arthur's cousin). It is relevant that Bicanys was the nephew of St Germanus, who appointed St Illtud as principal of Cor Tewdws (later called Llanilltud Fawr).

Marchell married Anlach and their son was Brychan (Arthur's cousin).

Meurig married Onbrawst and three of their daughters married sons of Emyr Llydaw, thus achieving an important alliance between these two royal families:

Gwyar married Riwal Mawr who gave Arthur assistance in some of his early battles.

Anna married Amwn Ddu and one of their sons was St Samson. Another son was St Tathan, who educated St Catwg at Caerwent. (It is of interest that Geoffrey of Monmouth states that Anna was the younger sister of Arthur.)

Afrella married Umbrafel, son of Emyr Llydaw and their son was St Maglorius.

Gwenonwy married Gwyndaf Hen and their son Henwyn founded a church at Aberdaron in Llyyn. Another son:

Meugant was made Bishop of Caer Vudei (now called Woodchester), where Ambrosius had his military headquarters and Arthur was crowned, according to the *Welsh Chronicles Brut*.

Tewdrig Mawr, who was killed in Dumnonia by a band of Irishmen.

Arthur's mother, **Onbrawst**, was the daughter of Gwrgant Mawr, King of Erging, who had been expelled from his kingdom by the usurper Vortigern. He was later reinstated by his uncle Ambrosius. It was Gwrgant Mawr's grandson Arthur who Ambrosius chose to be his successor as battle leader of the Britons.

The Grand Alliance

King Tewdrig was the father of Princess Marchell, who married the Irish Prince Anlach and their son was Brychan, who became ruler of Brycheiniog. King Tewdrig's son Meurig married Onbrawst, the daughter of Gwrgant Mawr, King of Erging.

Meurig II, the son of Caradog Freichfras and his wife Enhinti, married Dibunn, the daughter of King Glywys of Glywysing. Gwynllyw Filwr, the son of Glywys of Glywysing, married Gwladys, the daughter of Brychan Brycheniog.

The Importance of the Armorican Connections

A very important union was formed between two powerful royal familes who originated from Arfon (in north Wales), when Elen, the widow of Magnus Maximus, married Rhedyw, the prince of the British establishments in Armorica. Their son was Aldwr who became the step-brother of Constantine the Blessed.

Aldwr (Aldroen) was the brother of St Germanus, the soldier-saint who helped Ambrosius to defeat Vortigern. On becoming ruler of the British settlements in Armorica, Aldwr set up his court at Castelaudren, to the east of La Meaugon in the neighbourhood of Vannes.

Emyr Llydaw (also known as Budic II of Armorica) was the son of Aldroen, the brother of Custennin Fendigaid. Emyr Llydaw gave asylum to Ambrosius and his brother Uthyr after the assassination of their brother Constantine the Younger by the usurper Vortigern in 446. The title Emyr was used in Armorica to signify a sovereign prince and Emyr Llydaw was no doubt intended as a description – 'King of Armorica'.

Vannes was usurped by **Weroc I**, who named the area Bro Weroc, and Emyr Llydaw was forced to flee with his family to Wales, where they settled in Erging. It is possible that the locality where he resided also became known as Llydaw as a result. Emyr Llydaw and his wife Anaumed had a large family and it was their sons and daughters who are important in the story of Arthur.

The Sons of Emyr Llydaw
Riwal Mawr, who was also known as Hoel Farchog, is referred to in the Welsh Triads as one of 'The Three Royal Knights in the Court of King Arthur'. He became prominent in Arthur's reign as King of Breton Domnonia and is remembered in Brittany as Hoel Le Grand. He was succeeded as king by his son Deroch. Another son of Riwal was Derfel Gadarn, who distinguished himself at the Battle of Camlann.

Alan Fyrgan entered the college of St Illtud. He became a soldier-saint and his army is described in the Welsh Triads as one of 'The Three Disloyal Hosts of the Island of Britain' who turned back from King Arthur on the night before the Battle of Camlann. He was the father of Lleuddad, Llonio and Llynfab.

It is of particular significance that during the time that he spent in south Wales, some of Emyr Llydaw's sons married daughters of Meurig ap Tewdrig, King of Morgannwg, and strengthened the family ties which were later upheld by Arthur.

Amwn Ddu married Anna, daughter of Meurig ap Tewdrig. Their sons were St Samson and St Tathan.

Gwyndaf Hen married Gwenonwy (Arthur's sister) and their children were St Meugant and St Henwyn.

Umbrafel married Afrella, the sister of Arthur.

The Daughters of Emyr Llydaw
Gwen Teirbron married Eneas Ledewig and their son was St Cadfan who became abbot of the monastery on Bardsey Island.

Derwella married Caradog, the son of Ynyr of Gwent.

ARTHUR'S IMMEDIATE FAMILY

Alienor married Count Gwythyr of Léon, whose daughter Gwenhwyfar married Arthur.

Arthur's Brothers
Idnerth is named as grantor of a charter in the *Book of Llandaff* and also named in the Llancarfan Charters and *Vitae Cadoci*.

Frioc fell victim to his nephew Morgan. It is recorded in the *Monasticon Anglicanum* that Morcant, a king in Wales, having treacherously killed his uncle Frioc, after he had in most solemn manner sworn an inviolable peace with him before the altar, was by Oudoceus, Bishop of Llandaff and nephew of Teilo, excommunicated.

Comereg (who became Bishop of Erging) appears in the *Book of Llandaff* in a grant made by 'King Athrwys [Arthur] of Gwent to his brother Comereg, abbot of Mochros' (Moccas in Herefordshire).

Arthur's Sisters
Anna, who married Amwn Ddu, King of Graweg in Armorica.

Gwenonwy, who married Gwyndaf Hen, King of Erging.

Afrella, who married Umbrafel, was also known as Aurelia.

Meurig ap Tewdrig achieved an important alliance by marrying his three daughters to sons of Emyr Llydaw. Through the ages alliances have been made in this way and the significance of these unions is of considerable importance. For example, Meurig himself, by marrying Onbrawst, the daughter of Gwrgant Mawr, King of Erging, was able to extend his domain into present-day Herefordshire.

Arthur's Uncles
Caradoc Freichfras (Brawny Arm), the brother of Onbrawst, was based at Caerwent in Gwent but he is also said to have held sway over the district of Brychciniog. He first conquered all the land between the rivers Wye and Severn (then called Ferregs), which contained the equivalent areas of Herefordshire and Radnorshire. He then marched into Brycheiniog and expelled the family of Brychan. They vacated their holdings and crossed the Severn to settle in parts of Devon and Cornwall. Their presence in this area is confirmed by the large number of churches dedicated to Brychan's offspring. The expulsion of the Brychanites suggests a family feud, a dynastic dispute, perhaps arising from a quarrel between Brychan and Arthur.

In the *Life of St Padarn* we are told that Caradoc Freichfras extended his kingdom across the boundaries even of Britannia, and took Letavia (Llydaw) under his rule. The compiler of this 'life' mistakenly identified Padarn with Paternus, who was Bishop of Vannes in the fifth century. Looking for a reason why St Padarn should have gone to Brittany, the writer found some statement that Caradoc Freichfras had conquered Llydaw. He took Llydaw to mean Brittany, but it is almost certain that this name also applies to a district near the border of England and Wales. Tradition associates Caradoc Freichfras with Radnorshire and Brycheiniog and it is in this vicinity that the British Llydaw probably lay.

Illtud Farchog (the Knight) was the son of Bicanys, a nobleman of Llydaw (Armorica). He married Gweryla, the daughter of Tewdrig Fendigaid. He was ordained as a priest by his great-uncle St Germanus, who also appointed him principal of a monastic college at the place that became known as Llanilltud Fawr. St Illtud's students included Gildas the historian, Maelgwyn Hir (the Tall), Prince of Gwynedd, Samson, who became Bishop of Dol in Brittany, Paul Aurelian, who became Bishop of Léon, and Arthmael (Arthur).

Arthur's Cousins

Paul Aurelianus, the son of Count Porphyrius Aurelianus, a Romano-Briton of high rank, was born in 487 at the Roman station of Caput Bovium (Boverton), near Llanilltud Fawr in the centre of Penychen, Glywysing. He studied at St Illtud's monastic school, founded churches at Llanddeusant and Llangorse and then emigrated to Armorica, where he died in 573 and is buried in the Cathedral of St Pol-de-Léon. His bones are kept there in a gilded bronze shrine.

Riwal Mawr (the Great), was also known as Hoel Farchog (the Knight). He was the son of Emyr Llydaw, the benefactor of Emrys Wledig, who sprang from the line of Macsen Wledig (Magnus Maximus). Riwal bore the Roman name of Pompeius Regalis.

In 509, in the reign of the Frankish King Clovis I (482–511), he sailed to Armorica with a large number of colonists and established himself at Champ de Rouire on the north-east coast. They named the area where they settled Domnonia after the Dumnonian Peninsula of Devon and Cornwall, and in due course it was to cover almost all of northern Brittany, including (after 530) the province of Léon in the north-west.

However, after a few years, Riwal was overpowered by the soldiers of King Childebert and he returned to Wales with his second wife Alma Pompeia and their large family.

In 513 Riwal sailed to Armorica at the head of a large army and drove off the forces of Childebert to recover his provinces. His cousin Arthur gave him support by taking a force to Domnonia to deal with an invasion of the Visigoths. The combined forces of Arthur and Riwal gained an overwhelming victory over the Visigoths at Baden, situated south-west of Vannes.

Riwal later returned to Britain to assist Arthur in his wars and he died in 524. He is said to be buried at Llanilltud Fawr in the Vale of Glamorgan. His son Deroch succeeded him as the ruler of Breton Domnonia.

Brychan, the son of Anlach and Marchell (daughter of King Tewdrig), was born in about 480. He would have been a contemporary of Athrwys ap Meurig (born in 482) and as they shared the same grandfather (Tewdrig Fendigaid) they were cousins. Brychan became ruler of Garth Madryn after his father's death and his realm thereafter was known as Brycheiniog, which gave rise to the county name of Breconshire.

The name Brychan is derived from Brych, which means spotted, and it suggests that he had many freckles. He is also credited with having numerous offspring produced from his three marriages to Rhybrawst, Ambrost and Roistri.

According to the Welsh Triads, Brychan brought up his 'children and grandchildren in learning and the liberal arts, that they might be able to show the faith in Christ to the nation of the Cymry'. Churches dedicated to his offsprings are to be found in Wales, south-east Ireland, Cornwall and Brittany.

It would seem that Brychan in his later years abdicated in favour of his son Rhain and became a 'Miles Dei' ('Soldier of God'). He adopted the name Nectan and retired to 'Enys Brachen' (Island of Brychan), thought to be Lundy Island. It is feasible that Brychan's memorial stone may have been one that once existed at Capel Mair, near Llandysul. It is said to have been inscribed with the name Brocagni which is an early form of Brychan.

Arthur's Wives

Arthur's famous wife is known in the romance stories as Guinevere, which stems from the Welsh Gwenhwyfar, but it would seem that he was first married to Cenedlon. In two manuscripts (Harleian MS 4181, folio 39 and Mostyn MS 212b, p. 39) the wife of Athrwys ap Meurig is given as Cenedlon, whose father was Briafael Frydig ap Llywarch who witnessed charters in the time of Meurig ap Tewdrig (*Book of Llandaff*, pp. 143–51). He also appears as witness to one of the Llancarfan Charters.

The memorial stone of Briafael, the father of Cenedlon, may be the Cross of Brimail which can be seen inside the Church of Llandefaelog Fach, which lies 3 miles to the north of Brecon in Powys. It is a tall, narrow Celtic cross slab which formerly stood in the churchyard but some years ago was taken inside the church to protect it from the elements. It depicts a male figure wearing a long tunic, holding a spear across his right shoulder with his right hand, and a dagger in his left hand. The inscription in two lines reading horizontally is 'BRIAMAIL/FLOU' '[The Cross of] Briamail Flou'.

Gwenhwyfar (Guinevere) was referred to by Geoffrey of Monmouth as 'Guennuera'.[7] Her Celtic name Gwenhwyfar means 'White Phantom' or 'Fay', and it is based on the root word *gwen* which appears variously as *wen*, *win* or *guin* and means in each case white, suggesting purity and beauty.

She was the daughter of Count Gwythyr or Withur of Léon, and a variation of his name is Uther, which confused Geoffrey of Monmouth who identified Uther as the father of Arthur. He failed to realise that in this instance Uthyr (Gwythyr) was Arthur's father-in-law. According to the 'Bonedd yr Arwyr' pedigree 22, Gwenhwyfar was the daughter of Gwythyr ap Greidol Galofydd.

Arthur's Father-in-law, Count Gwythyr
Gwythyr, whose name stands for Uthyr (Victor), was Lord of Caerleon in Gwent and became First Count of Léon in Brittany.[8] He married Alienor, the daughter of Emyr Llydaw.

It would seem that Count Gwythyr sailed with a large army of immigrants from Caerleon in Gwent and landed on the north-west coast of Armorica. He took possession of the land from Aber Ildut to Morlaix, founded two religious settlements and formed an organised state which he called Léon or Lyonesse after Caerleon, and governed from Ile de Batz.[9]

Count Gwythyr is described in Wrmonoc's *Life of St Pol de Léon* as a pious Christian who ruled his principality of Léon by the authority of the Frankish King Childebert, who reigned from 511 to 558. A copy of the Gospels made by Count Gwythyr was kept in the Cathedral of St Pol-de-Léon until the French Revolution, when it was destroyed.

On the death of Count Gwythyr's son Gwythian, Gwenhwyfar became the principal heir to the family estates. When Count Gwythyr died in 530, Arthur gained access to his wife's inheritance and overall control of the principality of Léon. Subsequently, Léon was absorbed into the Breton kingdom of Domnonia, which Arthur ruled jointly with his cousin Deroch, son of Riwal Mawr.

Arthur's Sons
Llacheu is mentioned in the Welsh Triads as one of the 'three Fearless Men

of the Island of Britain'. We are also told that Llacheu ('the Gleaming or Glittering One') wore a circle of gold to distinguish him as the son of the Amherawdyr (Emperor). He is described as a man of most accomplished character, and no less renowned for his warlike prowess than for his deep knowledge.

In the *Black Book of Carmarthen* there is a reference to a battle between Cai Wyn and Llacheu, and Gwyddno Garanhir claims that he was present at the place where Llacheu was killed. The *Mabinogion* story of 'Culhwch and Olwen' tells us how a feud developed between Arthur and his seneschel Cai. This feud attains its climax in the episode narrated in *Perlesvaus* in which Cai is said to have treacherously slain Arthur's son Llacheu.

Amhyr, another son, is reputed to have been killed by Arthur and this idea stems from a strange story recorded by Nennius in his *Historia Brittonum*.[10] In his list of 'Wonders of Britain' he describes a tomb by a spring called Llygad Amir (the Eye of the Emperor) and suggests that the man whose body lies buried in the tomb was the son of Arthur the Amherawdyr (Emperor). Llygad Amir has been identified with Gamber Head, the source of the River Gamber near Wormelow Tump in Herefordshire. It would appear that Arthur considered himself responsible for the tragic death of his son and built a magnificent tomb in his memory (see p. 107).

The alternative explanation is that Nennius confused Emyr with Amir and that Llygad Amir is derived from Llygatrudd Emys (the Red Eyed Emys). In this case the man who is buried there could be none other than Arthur's uncle Emyr Llydaw. Unfortunately, the large mound that may have contained such a tomb was destroyed by road widening in the nineteenth century.

Gwydre, according to the *Mabinogion* tale 'Culhwch and Olwen', was killed in the Presely Mountains in Pembrokeshire.

Arthur's Brothers-in-Law

Arthur's sisters married three sons of Emyr Llydaw: Amwn Ddu, Umbrafel and Gwyndaf Hen. The latter, who married Gwenonwy, is also known as Gwrfoddw Hen (the Old) and he is mentioned in the *Book of Llandaff* as ruling Erging.

Arthur's Nephews

St Henwyn, the son of Gwyndaf Hen and Gwenonwy.

Medraut, the son of Cawrdaf, the son of Caradoc Freichfras (which makes him Arthur's great-nephew).

St Samson, the son of Anna and Amwn Ddu (the Black), Prince of

71

Graweg, the country around Vannes in Armorica (Brittany) which had earlier been colonised by British settlers. Following a family feud, Amwn fled to Gwent where he married Anna, the daughter of Meurig ap Tewdrig. Their son St Samson became Bishop of Dol in Armorica.

Maternal and Paternal Descent of Arthur

Maternal Descent of Athrwys (Arthur)		Paternal Descent of Athrwys (Arthur)
Bran Fendigaid		
Caradog		
Meurig		Macsen Wledig
Erbig		Anhun Dunawd
Erb		Tathal
Peibio Clavorauc		Teithrin
Cynfyn		Teithfallt
Gwrgant Mawr		Tewdrig Fendigaid
Onbrawst	—— married ——	Meurig
Athrwys		Athrwys
Morgan Mwynfawr		Morgan Mwynfawr

The unification of these two families can be demonstrated as follows:

(1) Macsen Wledig married Elen Luyddog, who was the daughter of Eudaf Hen, Prince of Arfon and Lord of Gwent, Erging and Ewyas. Eudaf Hen was the brother of Meurig ap Caradog, King of Siluria (Morgannwg).
(2) Pebiau Clavorauc married the daughter of Custennin ap Macsen.
(3) Onbrawst ferch Gwrgant Mawr married Meurig ap Tewdrig who thus united Erging with Gwent.

Important evidence for the strong family ties between the royal houses of Arfon and Siluria may be found in the churches founded by Elen Luyddog and her son Custennin Fendigaid in Gwent and Erging respectively.

CHAPTER 5

Red Herrings at Tintagel, Camelford and Glastonbury

One of the most exciting and best known places that has been linked with the legend of King Arthur is Tintagel Castle on the north coast of Cornwall. This connection was entirely due to Geoffrey of Monmouth, who identified Tintagel as the castle of Gorlois, Duke of Cornwall, and claimed that Arthur was conceived here.[1] He tells us that the duke's wife Ygraine was seduced by Uther Pendragon and that Arthur was the result of their union. However, it should be pointed out that Geoffrey does not claim that Arthur was born at Tintagel. It was William of Worcester, writing in 1478, who first introduced this idea.

When Geoffrey was writing his 'history' the only castle near Tintagel was a simple Norman motte and bailey erected at Bossiney in about 1086.[2] In 1141 Reginald de Dunstanville, an illegitimate son of Henry I, was created Earl of Cornwall and Lord of the Manor of Bossiney, which includes Tintagel.[3] It was at about this time that the castle on the headland at Tintagel was begun. Geoffrey's *History of the Kings of Britain* in the form that has survived was the second edition of about 1145. The first edition, which dated from 1136–8, possibly did not contain mention of Arthur's conception at Tintagel. Geoffrey may have added the Tintagel story in the second edition to please his patron Robert, Earl of Gloucester, who was the half-brother of Reginald de Dunstanville, who married a Cornish heiress.

Reginald was an illegitimate son of Henry I, resulting from an affair with Sibil, daughter of Sir Robert Corbet of Alcester. Geoffrey's patron, Robert, Earl of Gloucester, was also illegitimate, being the result of an affair between Henry I and Princess Nest, daughter of Rhys ap Tewdwr, King of Deheubarth. It may thus be more than coincidence that Geoffrey gave Arthur an illegitimate background.

By linking Arthur with Tintagel Castle Geoffrey was able to give the fortress and its owner prestige, and it is significant that this is the only time Tintagel is mentioned in the stories of Arthur.[4]

The Anglo-French name of Tintagel dates from the time when the castle was built and is derived from the Cornish Tyn-tagel. This can be explained as follows. 'Tyn' or 'din' means fort and 'tagell' means constriction, which obviously relates to the neck of rock connecting the mainland with the 'island'. In Norman times a bridge would have spanned the gap between one part of the castle and the other, but in about 1300 the cliffs collapsed on either side to form a mound of debris. A bridge was installed, but this had disappeared by 1500, and access to the island involved a very dangerous scramble across a narrow neck. A new path to the island was constructed in 1852 and the rift is now spanned at a much lower point by the present bridge. An alternative explanation for the origin of the name Tintagel is that the fortress was once known as Tente d'Agel, from the Norman-French meaning 'stronghold of the Devil'.

Of the twelfth-century fortress, only the chapel-nave and the remains of the great hall survive. The castle was extended considerably from 1236 to 1272 by Earl Richard, the younger brother of Henry II, and much of the remains date from that time.

In 1337 King Edward III made his eldest son Edward (known as the Black Prince, after the colour of his armour) Duke of Cornwall. Tintagel Castle, together with all the other possessions of the Duchy of Cornwall, passed into his hands. Since that time the Duchy of Cornwall has been a possession of the eldest son of the reigning monarch and Tintagel has remained a part of the duchy.

John Leland, writing in the sixteenth century, tells us that a thirteenth-century chapel in the castle ruins was dedicated in honour of a saint whose name he gives as Uette, Uliane and Juliana. The name of this patron saint can be found at two churches in the area. The Church of St Juliot (restored by Thomas Hardy) is 1 mile north-east of Munster, and a dedication to Juliot (or Julitta) can be found at 'Lanteglos by Camelford' – the mother church of Camelford.

St Juliot is reputed to have been one of the many sons of King Brychan, and it is of interest that nearly all the foundations of churches in north-east Cornwall were made by members of this sixth-century family who were driven out of Brycheiniog to cross the Severn and settle in Dumnonia.

Excavations carried out on the headland by C.A. Raleigh Radford in the mid-1930s revealed what was thought to be the site of a sixth-century monastery. In 1980 this idea was dismissed following re-examination of the pottery fragments that had been discovered. This pottery was found to be high-quality ware imported from various places in the Mediterranean around 520. As a result it has been decided that Tintagel was in fact the site of a well-defended royal stronghold in the post-Roman period of perhaps 475–550. It would appear that it was refortified and reoccupied by a military leader of wealth and power.

A fire in the summer of 1983 on the western side of the plateau above the castle revealed the stone foundations of more than a hundred small sixth-century buildings. Of particular interest are the foundations of a hall over 80ft long which may have once been the citadel of a sixth-century ruler of Dumnonia such as Marcus Conomorus (King Mark). Considering the wealth of Mediterranean finds discovered here, Tintagel may well have been the Dark Age capital or summer residence of a king of Dumnonia.[5]

The Artognov Stone
On 4 July 1998 a broken piece of slate measuring 20cm by 5cm, bearing a Latin inscription, was found at the castle by Kevin Brady, an archaeologist working with a team from Glasgow University on an excavation being undertaken for English Heritage. The slate had been re-used as a drain cover in a cliff-edge dwelling and was found under a pile of sixth-century debris.

The slate, which is broken along the right-hand edge, shows the remainder of two inscriptions: 'Pater Coliaviticit Artognou' which Professor Charles Thomas has translated as 'Artognou, father of a descendant of Coll had (this building) made'. The style of writing is certainly sixth century and Artognou, pronounced Arthnou, is undoubtedly proof that similar names existed in the time of Arthur.

Wishful thinking Arthurian enthusiasts immediately suggested that the name Artognou is a Latin version of the British name Arthnou which can be associated with Arthur. However, only the first three letters ART are similar to the name Arthur, so it is very difficult to accept that Artognou could be the same as Arthur and he was certainly not the father of a descendant of Coll.

Geoffrey Wainwright, the Chief Archaeologist for English Heritage, commented: 'Despite the obvious temptation to link the Artognou of this stone to either the historical or the legendary figure of Arthur, it must be stressed that there is no evidence to make this connection.'

The translation by Charles Thomas was later revised following an examination of the slate by Gordon Machan. He revealed a missing 'N' after 'Pater' and translates it as 'Artognov erected this memorial of Colus, his grandfather'. Machan suggests that the lettering may have been a draft layout by a scribe for a mason to make a final version of the commemoration. Art and Arth were common prefixes to the names of Dark Age rulers and the inscription appears to indicate that Artognou was a descendant of the late fourth-century King Coel Hen (the Old), who lived in the north of Britain where his descendants ruled until the mid-seventh century.

The Supposed Sites of Camelot and Camlann

Visitors who come to Tintagel in search of King Arthur sometimes move on afterwards to Camelford, about 6 miles away, to see one of the many sites suggested for Arthur's famous court of Camelot. An ancient British camp, south-east of the town, is referred to as 'Arthur's Hall'. He is also said to have had a hunting lodge at Castle-an-Dinas, near St Columb Major, which he used as a base from which to hunt the wild deer of Tregoss Moors. Another site of interest is Castle Killibury (or Kelly Rounds), an Iron Age fort standing in a commanding position above the River Allen. This has been identified as a possible candidate for Arthur's court of Gelliwig.

Just outside Camelford is the reputed site of the Battle of Camlann, which brought about the downfall of Arthur. The supposed battlefield is near the appropriately named 'Slaughter Bridge' which spans the infant River Camel. There are in fact several River Camels in Britain, but this one was thought to be the place in question because of its close proximity to Tintagel Castle.

Leland, writing in the sixteenth century, did his best to encourage the belief that this was the site of Camlann and he related how local farmers had ploughed up bones and a harness from the spot where 'Arture fowght his last feld'. However, it would appear that in 823 a battle was fought near here between the Cornish Britons and the Saxon King Egbert of Wessex.[6] Over the course of time the memory of this battle may have been passed on in a confused form and has become mistakenly linked with King Arthur.

In recent years an Arthurian visitor centre has been established near Slaughter Bridge and tourists now come in large numbers to see the reputed site of the fateful Battle of Camlann. A trail leads from the centre, upstream for a few hundred yards to reach a hefty oblong chunk of granite which is about 3m in length, and displays a bold but largely illegible Latin inscription. Owing to a misreading, it was at one time believed to bear Arthur's name and to mark his burial place.

In 1602 Richard Carew, a one-time High Sheriff of Cornwall, commented in his book *The Survey of Cornwall* that 'the folk thereabouts will shew you a stone bearing Arthur's name . . .'. Borlase, in 1754, recorded that the last words were MAG-URI (quasi 'Magni Arthur'). Then in 1837 Adam Clarke read the inscription as: 'LATIN HIC JACET FILIUS MAGNI ARTURI' – 'Here lies Latin the son of Arthur the Great'. Macalister in 1945 recorded that it read: 'LATINI IC IACIT FILIUS MACARI' – 'Latinus lies here, the son of Macarius'. The present-day accepted reading of the inscription is: 'LATINI IACIT FILIUS MA. RI'.

There is also an Ogham inscription on the stone (represented by groups of strokes cut against one of its long edges), but unfortunately the characters are now unreadable. The existence of an Ogham inscription is evidence that the stone was inscribed in the sixth century, but the man whom it commemorates was certainly not Arthur.

The stone once served as a footbridge on the estate of Lord Falmouth at Worthyvale and was known as 'Slaughter Bridge'. When it was removed in the mid-eighteenth century and brought to its present site, the name was transferred to the nearby bridge carrying the road over the River Camel, which rises on high ground near Davidstow and gives its name to Camelford.

The great battle fought near here in the time of Egbert in 823 is mentioned in the *Anglo-Saxon Chronicle*, in *Ethelwerd's Chronicle* and by Henry of Huntingdon, as having taken place at Camelford between the Britons of Cornwall and the Saxons of Wessex. Several thousands fell on both sides, according to Henry of Huntingdon, but we are not told which side was victorious. Probably the Britons, for the Saxons do not seem to have pushed their conquests further, at least until the time of Athelstan.

Latinus was probably a Briton of Roman descent, who was presumably fighting on the British side. That his followers had time to construct a memorial on the battlefield may be accepted as an indication that they retained their position as victors.

The Supposed Grave of Arthur at Glastonbury

One of the key locations visited by tourists intrigued by the story of King Arthur is Glastonbury Abbey in Somerset. However, while the long history of this noble ruined abbey is undoubtedly fascinating, the Arthurian connection may be nothing more than a hoax contrived by the abbey monks in 1191.

On 25 May 1184, Glastonbury Abbey caught fire, leaving the monks with a smouldering ruin and a financial crisis on their hands. All the monastic buildings were destroyed with the exception of a bell tower built by Abbot Henry and a chapel constructed by Abbot Robert.

Rebuilding of the abbey was immediately commenced under the

supervision of Randolph FitzStephen, the son of King Stephen. The old wooden church was replaced by the Lady Chapel, built in stone and of approximately the same dimensions. It was dedicated to St Mary by Reginald, Bishop of Bath, on St Barnabas's Day, 11 June 1186.

Henry II claimed that he had been told by a Welsh bard that the grave of Arthur and Guinevere could be found at Glastonbury, and he duly passed on this information to the monks of Glastonbury in 1189. It would certainly be in Henry's interests if it could be shown that Arthur, the greatest of Celtic heroes, was buried in England, rather than in Wales. The superstition that Arthur would one day return to lead Wales to nationhood would then be finally extinguished.

For some reason the monks were reluctant to carry out Henry's instructions. Before the year was out, he had fallen sick and died, and the supply of money for the rebuilding programme dried up when his heir Richard I came to the throne, for he was more interested in financing the Crusades than rebuilding abbeys.

The monks no doubt decided that they urgently needed a special attraction which would make their abbey better known and draw large numbers of pilgrims who would contribute donations to boost their funds.

So, in 1191, they decided to look for the grave of Arthur in the ancient cemetery, to the south of the site of the old mud and wattle church. The spot chosen was between two tall crosses, which marked tomb shrines, referred to by William of Malmesbury as 'pyramids'(or memorial pillars) and they were inscribed with the names of long-dead abbots.

The monks erected a curtain around the excavation site and began digging between the two pyramids. About 2m down, they found a stone slab inset with a leaden cross and we are told that it was inscribed: 'HIC JACET SEPULTUS INCLYTUS REX ARTURUS IN INSULA AVALLONIA' – 'Here lies the renowned King Arthur in the Isle of Avalon'. A further 3m lower down the monks unearthed a hollowed out tree trunk containing the skeletons of a large man and a slightly built woman. The man had ten wounds in his skull. Adhering to the woman's skull were some locks of golden hair, which crumbled into dust when a monk tried to handle them.

The monks declared the bones to be the remains of King Arthur and Queen Guinevere, and they were reverently stored in two chests and re-interred in the abbey. The unusual depth of this burial may be explained by the fact that in the time of St Dunstan, Abbot of Glastonbury, the graveyard was so full that he had it covered with a substantial layer of earth, which was enclosed by a retaining wall. The slab that the monks claimed to have found would thus have been at ground level and was presumably a grave marker.

In due course the bones were enshrined in a magnificent tomb of black marble, situated in the Lady Chapel, newly built after the fire. In 1278, the tomb was moved to a position in front of the high altar in the Abbey Church. In the Easter of that year King 'Eduardus' (Edward I) and Queen Eleanor visited Glastonbury, and Adam of Domerham, who watched the royal couple remove and examine the bones, later wrote:

In two caskets, painted with their pictures and arms, were found separately the bones of the said king, which were of great size, and those of Queen Guinevere, which were of marvellous beauty. On the following day the lord king replaced the bones of the king and those of the queen, each in their own casket, having wrapped them in costly silks.

The last visitor to provide a record of the tomb was John Leland, who tells that that there were also two other tombs in the choir, which contained King Edward the Elder and King Edmund Ironside. The tomb of 'Arcturus' was in the centre and on its side was a Latin inscription which commemorated Arthur and Guinevere, 'the fortunate wife of Arthur whose virtues merit the promise of heaven'.

In 1536 Henry VIII dissolved the monasteries of Britain and the double tomb containing the reputed remains of Arthur and Guinevere was probably smashed open and the contents destroyed. The site of the tomb, in front of the high altar, was located in 1931 and a black marble stone has been set in the ground to mark its position.

Was the Inscribed Cross a Fake?
The most likely explanation for the leaden cross is that it was prepared by the monks and revealed when they carried out their excavation. It would have been created to provide proof that the bones discovered were indeed those of Arthur and Guinevere. While it is necessary to say who is buried at a particular spot it is not usual to state the location. The wording very conveniently identified Glastonbury as the Isle of Avalon. The mention of Avalon on the cross and also the use of the word 'inclitus' (renowned) indicates that whoever inscribed it was influenced by the writings of Geoffrey of Monmouth. It is significant that from about 1170 there was a copy of Geoffrey of Monmouth's *Historia Regum Brittaniae* at Glastonbury, so the wording on the cross was most likely derived from that source.[7]

79

Giraldus Cambrensis became the first writer to identify Avalon with Glastonbury. He visited Glastonbury in 1191 and Abbot de Sully showed him the excavated bones and also the leaden cross.[8] Giraldus claimed that the lettering read: 'HERE IN THE ISLE OF AVALON LIES BURIED THE RENOWNED KING ARTHUR WITH GUINEVERE HIS SECOND WIFE'. If the cross was genuine one would expect it to read 'Here lies the tomb of King Arthur'. Of all the people who saw the cross and give details of its description, it is only Giraldus who claims that it mentioned Guinevere.

Ralph de Coggeshall omits all reference to Guinevere and just states: 'Here lies the famous King Arthur; buried in the Isle of Avalon'. John Leland saw the cross on his visit in 1542 and his description agrees with that of Ralph de Coggeshall.[9] Leland tells us that he examined the cross carefully and that it was about 1ft in height. Camden tells us that the reference to Guinevere was on the other side of the cross, yet Giraldus Cambrensis says that the wording was only on one side – closest to the stone slab.

The first edition of Camden's *Britannia*, published in 1590, gave the inscription on the cross arranged in five lines:

]HIC IACET SEP
VLTUS INCLITVS
REX ARTVRIVS IN
INSVLA AVALO
NIA

'Here lies buried the famous King, Arthur, in the Avalonian Isle'

When a woodcut illustration of the cross appeared in the 1607 edition of *Britannia* the arrangement of the wording had changed. This was the first known illustration of the cross. The drawing only showed one side, so if there was a mention of Guinevere, as stated by Giraldus, it could only have been on the reverse side. All that can be said is that the lettering on it is certainly not of sixth-century style, but more like that of the tenth century.

There is little doubt that the monks added the leaden cross with its fake inscription to make their discovery more convincing and perhaps to help persuade themselves that they had indeed found the grave of Arthur and Guinevere.

What Happened to the Inscribed Cross?
After the Dissolution the inscribed cross was held in the 'Revestry' of

St John's Baptist Church, Glastonbury, for the next 100 years. It later came into the possession of Chancellor William Hughes of Wells. There is a possibility that about 200 years later it was found in 1981 by a pattern-maker named Derek Mahoney, when he discovered a small lead cross while searching through mud excavated from an Essex lake at Forty Hall, Enfield. The keeper of Medieval and Later Antiquities at the British Museum confirmed that the cross was similar in size to the one said to have been found at Glastonbury in 1191.

Mahoney refused to hand it over and claimed that he had buried the artifact deep in the ground, in a waterproof container. He was jailed for contempt of court, but released after nine months on 21 March 1983. The cross has not been found and it will probably never be known whether it was the original Glastonbury cross or a copy of it. Derek Mahoney later committed suicide at his house in Enfield.

Was Arthur Confused with Arviragus?
In 1962 the archaeologist Raleigh Radford carried out an excavation on the site of the old cemetery and found evidence that a deep hole had indeed been dug in the location where the monks claimed to have found the grave of Arthur and Guinevere. So it would seem that the Glastonbury monks did indeed exhume someone's grave in 1191.

So, the question arises just who did they dig up if it wasn't Arthur and Guinevere? Well, to start with the burial in a hollowed out log belongs to a much earlier time than the sixth century, and a possible candidate is King Arviragus. His Gaelic-Pictish name appears to be Arc-wyr-auc meaning 'the Bear-folk-Chief'. The Gaelic 'c' would become 't' in Pictish and in Welsh it would become Arthwyr meaning 'the Bear Exalted'. This is significant because in times of national crisis the Britons elected a leader who was given the title Arthwyr, which related to the Celtic Bear deity.

King Arviragus was the son of Cunobelinus and he is mentioned by the Roman satirist Juvenal, who comments: 'Have you seen the chariot-driven British King Arviragus? A mighty omen this you have received of some great and noble triumph. Some captive king you'll take, or Arviragus will be hurled from his British chariot.'

When Vespasian landed with his legions at Totnes and captured the place now called Exeter, it was Arviragus who led the British resistance against him. Subsequently, Arviragus took refuge in the hill fort of Cadbury Castle, and we are informed by Hector Boece (*History of the Chronicles of Scotland*) that Vespasian laid siege to Cadbury Castle and captured a royal crown and

81

a magnificent sword, which he used for the rest of his life. Arviragus surrendered and Claudius received his submission.

This British king then allied himself with the Roman invaders by marrying Claudius's daughter Gennissa. As a leader of the Britons and bearing the title Arthwyr he may well have been confused with King Arthur, who lived 400 years later.

It is significant that Arviragus figures in the famous legend concerning the founding of the first church at Glastonbury by St Joseph of Arimathea. The tradition is that in AD 63 Joseph arrived in Somerset with twelve companions and they were welcomed by King Arviragus, who granted them twelve hides of land (about 1,920 acres) on which to settle.[10] Here they built a wattle church and dedicated it to St Mary the Virgin. An entry in the Domesday Book refers to the twelve hides of land as follows: 'The Home of God, the great Monastery of Glastonbury is called the Secret of the Lord. This Glastonbury Church possesses its own Villa XII hides of land which has never paid tax.'[11]

The Glastonbury monks certainly had no doubts about the origin of their abbey for in the Middle Ages a bronze plaque attached to a column in the church proclaimed: 'In the year XXXI after the Lord's Passion, twelve holy men, of whom Joseph of Arimathea was the chief, came hither and built the first church of this kingdom, in this place which Christ at this time dedicated to the honour of His Mother and as a place for their burial.' Joseph of Arimathea, in whose garden tomb the body of Jesus was laid after the crucifixion, was a wealthy merchant who may have previously visited Domnonia and was perhaps known to Arviragus as a metal trader some time before his mission.

In about AD 70 a Roman police action resulted in an attack on South Cadbury hill fort. Evidence of a massacre came to light when Leslie Alcock excavated the site during 1966–70. The remains of some thirty dismembered skeletons of men, women and children, possibly pulled to pieces by wild animals after the slaughter, were found strewn under the burnt remains of the south-west gateway. It is possible that the British King Arviragus and his wife Genissa perished in this massacre and were subsequently buried near the church reputed to have been founded by St Joseph of Arimathea.

Origin of the Name Glastonbury
The oldest recorded name for the site of Glastonbury is Ynys Witherin which is the one used by the twelfth-century historian William of Malmesbury.[12] Its marshy situation and the fact that the word witrin means glass resulted in the

place name being interpreted as 'the Island of Glass'. However, the name really stems from St Gwytherin (Victorinus), who founded a community here in the fifth century, and it became known as Ynys Witherin. It was probably Gwytherin who settled on the summit of Glastonbury Tor. Excavations there between 1964 and 1966 certainly revealed evidence of Dark Age occupation around the remains of the later medieval Church of St Michael. This may well have been the site of an early monastery.

The name Glastonbury has its origins in the sixth century and it relates to Glast, a great grandson of Cunedda Wledig.[13] In 510, he fought alongside Arthur at Luitcoyt near Lichfield, when that strategic location was besieged by a Middle Angle army. The enemy was routed in the Battle of Bassas (see p. 174).

Glast and his men then travelled south, perhaps to protect the holy sanctuary established by St Joseph of Arimathea. The cavalry force would have followed the Icknield Way and the Fosse Way to Bath and then on to Ynys Witherin. Here, the name of Glast was still remembered a hundred years later when the Saxons captured the Celtic settlement in 658 and called it Glaestingaburig. The genetive plural is Glastinga so the name means 'the borough of the sons of Glaest'. Such a name occurs in the Domesday Book as 'Glaesingebria'.

The West Saxons were new converts to Christianity and King Ine granted the monastery extensive possessions and privileges.[14] In 940 St Dunstan was made Abbot of Glastonbury by King Edmund and under his direction it became the powerhouse of the monastic revival of England in the middle and later years of the tenth century. In due course Glastonbury Abbey became one of the largest and wealthiest monastic houses in England and when completed early in the sixteenth century it was one of the largest in Europe.

Why was it Believed that Arthur was Buried at Glastonbury?
Having decided that the discovery of King Arthur's grave at Glastonbury was perhaps a genuine case of mistaken identity, it is now relevant to endeavour to explain why it was believed that he should have been buried here in the first place. To start with, Arthur was possibly confused with Arviragus, who lived four centuries before his time. An additional reason for the confusion may have arisen from the tradition that Arthur was buried at Avalon, so it is first necessary to discover why Glastonbury has become identifed with this mysterious place.

To be fair to Geoffrey of Monmouth he did not bring Glastonbury into his story. He in fact referred to the island where Arthur was taken after the Battle of Camlann as 'Insula Avallonis'.

The Norman historian William of Malmesbury spent some time looking through the abbey archives specifically for any possible mention of King Arthur, and in his notes he actually stated that he had failed to find any reference that connected Arthur with Glastonbury. Furthermore, in his *History of the Kings of England*, he stated that 'the tomb of Arthur is nowhere to be seen, wherefore the ancient songs fable that he is yet to come'. A three-line stanza contained in *The Songs of the Graves* emphasises that the location of Arthur's grave is very much a mystery. Three heroes' graves are evidently known to the writer, but the grave of Arthur is another matter.

> A grave for March, a grave for Gwythyr
> A grave for Gwrgan of the Red Sword;
> The world's wonder a grave for Arthur.

In its untranslated form, the text of the last line is 'Anoeth byd bet y Arthur', which has been interpreted in various ways, but the most important word is 'anoeth', which means an 'eternal wonder' or 'unknown' suggesting that the grave of Arthur is the most difficult thing in the world to find. The use of such a word seems to suggest that Arthur is a hero who cannot die and will one day return to come to the aid of his people. Hence, the well-known legend of this 'once and future king' who is not dead but merely sleeps in a secret place.

CHAPTER 6

Arthurian Connections in the West Country

The land we know today as Devon and Cornwall was once ruled by the Brythonic tribe of Dumonii, who were later known by the Saxons as Deofnas, and the name of this tribe has been preserved in the county name of Devon. The Cornovii (promontory people), who occupied the far west of the peninsula, were referred to by the Saxons as Cornwealas, meaning 'foreigners of the promontory', and from this term is derived the name Cornwall.[1]

During the time of Arthur the south-western peninsula (Devon, Somerset and Cornwall) was known as Dumnonia from the Latin term *Dumnonii* and the tribal capital was Isca Dumnonionrum (Exeter). The name Cornwall, derived from Cornovii, did not come into existence until the 700s.

Cornwall was a Christian land long before St Augustine brought the Gospel to Kent, and the missionaries who came here in the fifth century carved crosses on the pagan standing stones and baptised the local heathens. There are over 212 ancient parishes in Cornwall and of these no less than 170 are dedicated to Welsh saints, many of whom studied under St Illtud at Llanilltud Fawr in Glamorgan.

The Royal Family of Dumnonia
In the sixth century Dumnonia was ruled by an important dynasty to which Athrwys ap Meurig (Arthur) was related. A notable ancestor of this family was Constantine the Blessed, one of the sons of Magnus Maximus. When Constantine was an infant his father was killed in 388 and he was taken to Armorica for safety. After spending many years in exile at the home of his kinsman Aldwr, he returned to Arfon with Germanus the soldier-saint and they are remembered for expelling the Irish settlers from Gwynedd, then called Venedotia after the Venedotii.

Constantine was then elected Pendragon of the Confederated States of Britain. He ruled until 443, when he either died of the plague or was

85

assassinated by Vortigern. Constantine's son Erbin, in fear of his life, then fled from Gwynedd and settled in Dumnonia, where he raised a family and died in about 480.

The eldest son of Erbin was Geraint, who gave his name to Gerrans in Roseland, 2 miles north-east of St Mawes. His palace of Dingerrin was situated on the green mound known as Dingerrin Castle, near the church that he founded. He lived there with his wife Gwyar and their children, including Cadwy, Iestyn and Selyf. The names of Iestyn and Selyf have been Latinised to Just and Selevan (Solomon).

Just to the west of Gerrans, hidden among trees above the beautiful Restranguet Creek, is a church called St Just-in-Roseland which is associated with Iestyn, the son of Geraint ap Erbin. The name Roseland comes from the old Cornish word *ros* or *roos* meaning promontory.

Iestin ap Geraint is said to be buried at Llaniestyn Church on the Isle of Anglesey. It would seem that a dynastic conflict caused Iestyn to leave Cornwall and settle in Armorica (Brittany) for a while. He later returned to Britain and founded Llaniestyn on Anglesey, where he died.

The Church of St Just-in-Penwith is located 7 miles to the west of Penzance, and is also dedicated to Iestin. When the chancel was being restored in 1824 an ancient stone was found in the wall by the high altar, and it can now be seen inside the church by the blocked north door. One face of the stone is decorated with a simple border around a Chi-Rho cross (Greek letters for Christ). An adjacent side is inscribed 'SELUS HIC IACIT' ('Selus lies here') and it is very likely the memorial stone of Selyf ap Geraint, who died in about 550.

Selyf was married to St Gwen, sister of St Non, who was the mother of Dewi (St David). Gwen (or Wenn) was born in west Wales, a daughter of Cynyr and the granddaughter of King Brychan Brycheiniog. The son of Selyf and Gwen was St Cybi. A church was founded by St Gwen at St Wenn, near Bodmin, and there is also one at Morval near Duloe, dedicated to her. She died in 544.

It was probably due to this family connection that Non and Dewi came to Cornwall and founded Altarnon (derived from Allt-ar-Non – 'Cliff of St Non'), Pelynt and Davidstow churches.

The territory ruled by Selyf lay between the rivers Tamar and Lynher in the old principality of Gelliwig. Today, Callington is a corruption of Gelliwig-ton and the town is said to occupy the site of a royal residence of the kings of Dumnonia. (It is confusing for Arthurian researchers that Gelliwig had its equivalents in Wales, Cornwall and Brittany.)

Here, Selyf resided with his wife Gwen, who gave birth to a son named Cuby.[2] He became known as St Cybi (Kebius) and as the nephew of St Non was the cousin of St David, patron saint of Wales. Cuby was the only Cornish saint definitely known to have been born in Cornwall, but he spent a good part of his life in Wales and his name is preserved at Llangybi in Gwent and Caercybi in Anglesey.

In Dumnonia he is patron saint of Tregonwy and Duloe. He also established a church at Cuby, about 2 miles south of Grampound, Cornwall. When he died his relics were carried off by Irish pirates and eventually found their way to the high altar of Holy Trinity (now Christchurch), Dublin.

The eldest son of Geraint was Cadwy, who is remembered in the name Porthscatho, and it is indeed significant that the whole district from Roseland to Grampound is rich in memories of this Dumnonian royal family.

Cadwy played an important part in the life of King Arthur for there is a tradition that he ruled the area corresponding to north-west Somerset jointly with Arthur after the death of Geraint. Three hill forts in Somerset are possibly named after him for the name Cadbury simply means Cadwy's town. These forts are Cadbury Castle, Cadbury Camp near Clevedon and Cadbury Camp on Rhadyate Hill to the east of Yatton.

In addition, the fort of Dindraithou is described in the *Life of St Carannog* as a place where Arthur held court with his ally Cadwy. Dindraithou can be identified with Bat's Castle near Dunster in Somerset. It has a strong vallum of stone and earth 3m high and heavily fossed. The re-fortification of Dindraithou in the sixth century would have been for the purpose of protecting this side of the Severn Sea from incursions by Saxon and Irish pirates. It is significant that Cair Draithou appears as one of the 'Twenty-eight cities of the Island of Britain', listed by Nennius in the *Historia Brittonum*.

In due course it will be described how Cadwy fought alongside Arthur at the important Battle of Badon, and had the satisfaction of avenging his father's death at the Battle of Llongborth by slaying Cerdic, the leader of the Gewissei.

Cadwy's son and heir was Constantine who, according to Geoffrey of Monmouth, succeeded Arthur when he abdicated after the Battle of Camlann. As Cadwy was Arthur's cousin and close ally it was appropriate that Constantine, who became King of Dumnonia following Cadwy's death at Camlann, should be selected to be the next Pendragon.

Geraint Llyngesog, the son of Erbin, was chosen as Pendragon upon the death of his uncle Ambrosius and he had three sons:

87

Cadwy, who fought with Arthur at Badon and Camlann, and his son Constantine succeeded Arthur as Pendragon after his abdication.

Iestyn, who founded a church at St Just-in-Roseland, Cornwall, but was buried at Llaniestyn, Anglesey.

Selyf, who married Gwen the sister of Non, the mother of St David, and their son was St Cybi who gave his name to the various Llangybi churches in Wales.

Connections with the Family of Gwynllyw ap Glywys

In the sixth century St Petroc, one of the sons of Glywys of Glywysing, led a migration from Glywysing to north-east Cornwall.[3] He is particularly associated with Padstow (derived from Petroc's Stow), and a church dedicated to him stands in a green hollow on the site of the monastery where he died in 543. Inside the church, above the piscina, is a figure of St Petroc with his staff and a wolf lying at his feet.

There are eighteen churches dedicated to St Petroc in Devon and there is also St Petrox in Pembrokeshire. In Brittany there are nine churches and chapels dedicated to him, mainly in the north of the peninsula. Llanbedrog on the Llyyn Peninsula is also one of his foundations, and there is a tradition that he fought with Arthur at the Battle of Camlann and was one of the few who escaped with his life. Thus, it is relevant that it was St Petroc who converted Constantine (Arthur's successor) to the Christian faith.

Petroc was buried at Bodmin (a contraction of Bod minachu – 'the habitation of monks'), but in 1177 a canon of that church stole the reliquary containing his remains and carried them over to the Abbey of St Méen in Brittany. Henry II insisted on their return and they were initially brought to Winchester, before being returned to Bodmin. The king decided to console the monks of St Méen for having lost the relics by sending back one of St Petroc's ribs in a silver reliquary. The casket containing his bones was returned to Bodmin Church in October 1957.

Connections with the Family of Brychan Brycheiniog

When the family of King Brychan were driven out of Brycheiniog, they crossed the Severn Sea to establish themselves in what is now north Devon and Cornwall. They occupied north-east Cornwall from Padstow Harbour and the north of Devon as far as Exmoor and founded many churches.

In the village of St Neot, which nestles on the southern edge of Bodmin Moor, stands the parish Church of St Anietus. The magnificent set of stained glass windows date from about 1530 and in one of them can be seen King

Brychan. He is depicted sitting on a throne and spreading out his ermine mantle, in which ten heads nestling in his lap represent his numerous children.

Connections with Gildas ap Caw

The monk Gildas had several sons and grandsons and two of them founded churches in Cornwall. Philleigh was founded by St Fili, who gave his name to Caerphilly (Caerfili) in Glamorgan. His companion was St Kea, whose church of that name stands on the side of the River Fal, opposite Philleigh. In Brittany, the name Fili is found at Ker-fily in Elven and in Tre-fily.

To the south of Lostwithel, on the east bank of the Fowey Estuary, is the Church of St Winnow, which preserves the name of Gwynno, another son of Gildas. Llanwynog Church in Wales also bears his name.

St Samson in Dumnonia

St Samson, the son of Amwn Ddu and Anna, daughter of Meurig ap Tewdrig, was educated at the monastic school of St Illtud at Llanilltud Fawr in Glamorgan. After spending time on Caldey Island and at St Germanus's Monastery at Deerhurst (Gloucestershire), Samson made his way to Domnonia.

The *Vita Sancti Samsonis* tells us that he sailed across the Severn Sea and landed at Padstow, where he was met by St Petroc. After founding a chapel on the hill near Place House, he continued on his way across the peninsula. On reaching Golant he established a church on a hill overlooking the Fowey Estuary. The fifteenth-century church, which can be seen there today, is dedicated to St Samson and no doubt stands on the site of his sixth-century foundation. Nearby is St Samson's Well, which according to local legend was created when he drove his staff into the ground. Stained glass windows in the church illustrate various events in Samson's life as well as depicting saints, apostles and Old Testament prophets.

Leaving Golant in the hands of a disciple, Samson then crossed the sea to Armorica where he founded a monastery at Dol and died there in 565. His relics are said to be held in a chapel behind the high altar. In 1919 a small part of these were sent to the monastery on Caldey Island in Pembrokeshire.

The *Vita Sancti Samsonis* was written in the seventh century by Tigernomail who succeeded Paul Aurelian as Bishop of Léon. An important link with Tigernomail can be seen at Cubert Church, where a memorial stone commemorating his son was discovered many years ago in a wall of the tower. It has been built into the western wall of the church, near its south-east corner and the inscription reads 'CONETOCI FILI TIGERNOMALLIS'

– 'Connetoc son of Tigernomail'. It is significant that Tigernomail was the nephew of St Paul Aurelian, who just like St Samson was educated by St Illtud at Llanilltud Fawr.

March ap Meirchion, the Tyrant King

King March, who is remembered in Arthurian legend as King Mark, was a son of the Glamorgan prince Meirchion Vesanus (Marcianus the Mad). Meirchion was dispossessed of his territory, centred on Boverton, by Arthur's grandfather Tewdrig, and subsequently killed by his brother Gwaednerth. March then moved to Gwent with his wife Essyllt Fyngwen (Fair-Head) and it would seem that they settled at Cinmarch (St Kinemarks) near Chepstow.

Geoffrey of Monmouth brings March into his story when he speaks of 'Kynmaroc' attending Arthur's crown-wearing ceremony at Caerleon-on-Usk.[4] His wife Essyllt Fyngwen was very likely a royal princess from Gwent.

In due course, March ap Meirchion and his wife Essyllt Fyngwen were dispossessed of their land in Gwent and the *Book of Llandaff* records the grant of 'Lann Cinmarch' made by King Athrwys of Gwent (Arthur) to his brother Comereg, Abbot of Mochros (Moccas) and Bishop of Erging.[5]

March and Essyllt then moved to Dumnonia (Cornwall) where they established a new principality for themselves. The ruler of Dumnonia at the time of their arrival was Tewdrig Mawr, a son of Emyr Llydaw. During a fight with a band of Irish settlers, Tewdrig fell from his horse and was killed. March then replaced Tewdrig as ruler of Dumnonia and, according to the twelfth-century Anglo-Norman poet Béroul, established his court at Lancien.

In his *Le Roman de Tristan et Iseut*, Béroul describes how all the people turned out to welcome Queen Iseullt (Essyllt) as she came from King Mark's palace at Lancien to present her robe as an offering to St Samson, placing it on the altar in his church at Golant. Béroul claims that the robe, which was of rich silken cloth embroidered in silver and gold thread, was subsequently re-fashioned as a chasuble (a liturgical vestment) and displayed in the church at the annual festival for all to see.

Some writers have identified King Mark's Lancien with the Cornish Lantyan, a valley that runs from Pelyn to the estuary of the Fowey. Charles Henderson, in *Essays in Cornish History* (1935), points out that the name is probably derived from Nant (a valley). He also shows that in the middle of Lantyan there is a place called Castle and that in the form 'Nantyhan Parva Castel' it was mentioned in a deed of 1395. It is quite feasible that Lantyan Farm, about a mile south of Lostwithiel, is the site of King Mark's court. The distance from there to St Samson's Church at Golant is about 2 miles.

Béroul seems to have visualised King Mark's territory as lying between the Fal and the Fowey, in what was the old hundred of Powder. According to Béroul, Mark had his chief residences at Tintagel on the northern coast, at Lancien and a hunting lodge at Blancheland.

An indication that King Mark had a court in the vicinity of Fowey is provided by an inscribed stone that used to stand in a small enclosure beside an ancient road. Some years ago it was moved to a more prominent position, about a mile outside Fowey, near the junction of the A3082 and B269. Known as the Tristan Stone and set in a circular base, it is roughly square in shape and over 2m high. On one face is a sixth-century Latin inscription cut in two vertical lines: 'DRUSTANUS HIC IACIT FILIUS CUNOMORI' – 'Here lies Drustanus son of Cunomorus'. The lettering is now so badly weathered that it is very hard to make it out, but the persons mentioned can both be identified with some degree of certainty. In Cornish the D becomes T so Drustanus is the same as Tristan, while Cunomorus refers to Marcus Cunomorus (King Mark) and Tristan was his son.[6] Cunomorus means 'horse', a sacred animal in Celtic mythology.

On the back of the stone is a Chi-Rho monogram. This ancient Christian symbol is compatible with an early sixth-century date and Celtic missionary influence.

John Leland examined the stone in the sixteenth century and gave its measurements to be about 1ft taller than it is now. He also mentions a third inscription which read: 'CUM DOMINA CLUSILLA' – 'with the Lady Clusilla'. This inscription no longer exists and it would seem that since Leland's visit a fragment bearing these missing words has broken off the stone.

The oldest surviving version of the Tristan and Iseult romance is contained in a poem by Béroul, who places King Mark's 'lofty palace' at Lancien.[7] This may well have been at Lantyan (Domesday Book – Lantien), now a farm about 1 mile north of Castle Dore.

CHAPTER 7

Arthur's Conception and Birth

Geoffrey of Monmouth seems to have become very confused by his muddled source material, but it is open to conjecture whether it was by accident or design that he weaved a series of major errors into his entangled story. For a start, we need to explain why Geoffrey told us that Arthur was conceived from the union of Uther Pendragon and Ygerna, the wife of Gorlois:

> Transformed by Merlin's potions into the likeness of the absent King Gorlois, Uther Pendragon, King of the Britons, arrives before the gates of Tintagel fortress at twilight. The guard admits whom he takes to be his royal master. That night King Uther spends with Gorlois' Queen Ygerna, whom he loves to distraction. That night she conceives Arthur, the most famous of men.

There must have been a reason for this statement and an important clue is contained in a fourteenth-century Welsh text entitled *The Birth of Arthur*, and this provides a valuable insight into the workings of the Gwentian-Cornish-Armorican alliance.[1] The following extract is of particular interest:

> After the death of Gwrleis [Gorlois], Uther caused a feast to be prepared for the nobles of the island of Britain, and at the feast he married Eigyr, the widow of Gwrleis, and made peace with the kinsman of Gwrleis and all his allies. Gwrleis had two daughters, Gwyar and Dioneta, by his wife Eigyr. Uther caused Dioneta to be sent to the Isle of Afallach, and of all her age she was most skilled in the Seven Arts. Gwyar married Emyr Llydaw (the Armorican) and after the death of her husband she dwelt at Gwrleis's court with her son Hywel Mawr. Now Uther caused Lleu ap Cynfarch to marry her, and they had two sons, Gwalchmai and Medraut, and three daughters, Gracia, Graeria and Dioneta.

If we identify Uther Pendragon (this being a title meaning 'wonderful head dragon' rather than a name) with Meurig ap Tewdrig then it all becomes clear. Meurig had already cemented an alliance with Armorica by marrying his daughters to the sons of Emyr Llydaw (the Armorican). He then defeated and killed Gwrleis (Gorlois) and married his widow, Eigyr, thus gaining a foothold in Cornwall. Then he extended the alliance by appointing Tewdrig Mawr ('the Great'), the son of Emyr Llydaw by his first wife Anaumed, as King of Cornwall. Athruis (Arthmael/Arthur) may have been the son of his second marriage, to Eigyr, the previous wife of Gwrleis (Gorlois) whom he had killed. This would explain why Geoffrey of Monmouth told us that Arthur was born from the union of Uther Pendragon and the wife of Gorlois. It must be emphasised that Uther Pendragon is a title and not a name, and in this instance refers to Meurig. Gwyar, one of the daughters of Gorlois and Eigyr, was married to Emyr Llydaw and their son was Hoel (Riwal) Mawr (the Great). When Emyr Llydaw died she married Lleu ap Cynfarch and they had two sons, Gwalchmai and Medraut (not the one who fought Arthur at Camlann, but his namesake and a contemporary).

This is a complex and confusing web of very significant personalities who, through their family connections, are an essential part of the solution to the mystery of Arthur's identity. The idea that Arthur was born at Tintagel Castle is only due to a misunderstanding as a result of Geoffrey of Monmouth's statement that he was conceived there.

The Conception of Arthur, According to Geoffrey of Monmouth

Uther Pendragon falls in love with Igerna, the wife of Gorlois, Duke of Cornwall, while she and Gorlois are guests at Uther's court.[2] When Gorlois discovers this intrigue, he leaves the court in a rage and refuses Uther's command to return. Uther then invades Cornwall. Gorlois sends Igerna to Tintagel for safety, but Uther obtains entrance to the castle of Tintagel, where he rapes Igerna and Arthur is conceived.

A Possible Interpretation of Geoffrey's Story

Geoffrey appears to have confused Gwrlais with Glywys and changed the name to Gorlois. Gwrlais and Glywys both belonged to the lineage of Solor ap Nor ap Owain ap Macsen. They married granddaughters of Cunedda Wledig and were therefore contemporaries. The wife of Glywys of Glywysing and mother of Gwynllyw was Gwawr ferch Ceredig ap Cunedda Wledig. The wife of Gwrlais was Eigr ferch Gwen ferch Cunedda Wledig.

Both Gwrlais and Glywys were associated with Cornwall. Glywys was known as Glywys Cornubiensis and there were close connections between Glywysing and Dumnonia (Cornwall). If we substitute Glywys for Gwrlais in the story of Arthur's conception, then the matter can be resolved.

Glywys's wife was Gwawr and Meurig (Uther Pendragon) fell in love with her while she and Glywys were guests at Meurig's court. When Glywys discovered this, he left the court in a rage and refused Meurig's command to return. Meurig invaded Glywysing and Glywys sent Gwawr to Caput Bovium (Boverton) for safety. Meurig obtained entrance to Glywys's court, where he made love to Gwawr, and Arthmael (Arthur) was conceived.

There is a strong tradition that Arthur was illegitimate. If this is indeed the case then his adoptive mother would be Onbrawst, the daughter of Gwrgant Mawr, King of Erging, who was married to King Meurig.

Glywys may have been killed by King Meurig and his martyrium may be at the Church of Merthyr Mawr, as suggested by Dr Peter Clement Bartrum in his *Welsh Classical Dictionary*.

Why Did Geoffrey of Monmouth Bring Tintagel into His Story?
It is possible that Tewdrig Mawr, the son of Emyr Llydaw, has been confused with Tewdrig ap Teithfallt, the grandfather of Arthur. Tewdrig Mawr was the ruler of part of Dumnonia and may have had a stronghold on the headland at Tintagel. He was killed while fighting a band of Irishmen and his successor was Marcus Conomorus.

It is possible that Geoffrey confused Tewdrig Mawr with Tewdrig Fendigaid, who had a court at Boverton and bore the title Uthyr Pendragon. Geoffrey may have managed to muddle the title and the two Tewdrigs together.

Glywys, King of Glywysing
Glywys was the eldest son of King Solor and, like Ambrosius, he was a direct descendant of the Roman Emperor Magnus Maximus. When he became king of the area between the rivers Towy and Usk in the fifth century, he was the first ruler of this territory after the departure of the Romans. His name suggests that he was 'a man of Glevum', the Roman name for Gloucester.

On his death, according to the custom of 'gavelkind,' his kingdom was equally divided between his seven sons. Meirchion Vesanus (Marcianus the Mad) ruled westward from the River Thaw, at the southernmost part of Wales, as far as Gower. Gurai ruled the Neath area. To the east Paulinus ruled the Vale of Glamorgan. Seru held the lordship of Senghenydd.

Gwynllyw took Gwynllwg (later called Wentloog) between the River Rhymni and the lower Usk, stretching from the coastline to the mountains. Etelic took Edelogan (later called Edlogan) which lay between the River Usk and Mynydd Maen.

The Pedigree of Glywys Contained in the *Life of St Catwg*

Macsen Wledig
|
Owain
|
Nor
|
Solor
|
Glywys

Arthmael (Arthur) was Born at Boverton

Albert Le Grand, who compiled the *Life of St Arthmael* in 1636, states that Arthmael was born in 482 at Caput Bovium (Boverton) in Glamorgan. The names of Arthmael's parents are not given in this account, but they may be determined from the genealogy of the kings of Morgannwg and Gwent contained in the *Book of Llandaff*. Athrwys (also known as Arthmael) is named as the son of Meurig and Onbrawst, the daughter of Gwrgant Mawr, King of Erging.

Boverton, near Llantwit Major in the Vale of Glamorgan, was once the site of a court established in the Dark Ages which had a long history of royal ownership. Known in Roman times as Caput Bovium, it was the seat of the reguli who ruled this part of the Silurian territory under Roman supervision. The ancient name for this locality is Penychen.[3] 'Pen' means head and 'ychen' is the plural of 'ych', an ox. Thus Caput Bovium (Head of the Oxen) is the Roman equivalent. This settlement would have been linked to the Roman highway known as the Via Julia by a road, which also ran down to the ancient harbour of Colhugh.

Caput Bovium became the seat of the great Romano-British family of the Aurelii after their expulsion from Arfon in north Wales by the usurper Vortigern (Gwrtheyrn Gwrtheneu). It is significant that Nennius tells us that Ambrosius Aurelianus spent his childhood at Campus Elleti, which is now known as Llanmaes and is quite close to Boverton.

95

The brother of Ambrosius was Count Porphyrius Aurelianus, whose Welsh name was Erbin and he was the father of St Paul Aurelian.[4] According to Wrmonoc's *Life of St Pol de Léon*, Paul was born at Caput Bovium and was educated at the monastic school of St Illtud at nearby Llanilltud Fawr.

The Aurelian Connection

Count Porphyrius Aurelianus was also born at Caput Bovium and, according to Wrmonoc's *Life of St Pol de Léon*, the count was a Romano-Briton of high rank who served as a military companion to a local king in Glywysing and held land in Dumnonia. The Revd Arthur Wade-Evans has identified the Welsh name of Count Porphyrius as Erb or Erbin. If this is the case then he was none other than Erbin, the younger brother of Ambrosius Aurelianus who reigned over Domnonia and was the father of Geraint Llyngesog.

It is significant that the name Porphyrius means 'of the purple', which indicates that he was a member of the immediate family of the Romano-British Emperor Ambrosius Aurelianus, whose summer residence was at Caput Bovium (Boverton).

The Revd Arthur Wade-Evans set out to show that King Arthur was allied by family ties to the Silurian reguli. It is, therefore, very fitting that Arthmael should be born at Caput Bovium (Boverton), the seat of the Silurian reguli in the Vale of Glamorgan. Through the centuries, Boverton was to continue as the summer residence of the princes of Glamorgan down to the time of the eleventh-century Iestyn ap Gwrgan. He was the last native Welsh Prince of Morgannwg and a direct descendant of Athrwys ap Meurig, alias Arthmael (King Arthur).

It is of interest that St Paul Aurelian founded a church in the confines of the ancient British city of Exeter, and it is not surprising to find it near to the Church of St Sidwell, his sister. Another sister, St Wulvella, settled in Laneast in Cornwall, and the adjoining parish is Lanteglos, dedicated to a third sister, St Jutwara or Jutwell. This all goes to prove that the family of Count Porphyrius was active in the kingdom of Dumnonia, which was ruled over at the time by Erbin.

The Palace of Meurig ap Caradog

Meurig ap Caradog was the brother of Eudaf Hen (Octavius the Old), Earl of Gwent, Erging and Ewyas, and he is undoubtedly the same personage as the Mauricius son of Caradocus, who is mentioned by Geoffrey of Monmouth as encouraging Maximus in his visit to Britain. He was present when his father Caradocus (Caradog) persuaded Octavius (Eudaf) to marry his only daughter (Elen) to Maximus and make him heir to the throne.

At least Geoffrey of Monmouth places Meurig ap Caradog in his correct dynastic and chronological setting, and he does not confuse Caradog ap Bran with Caractacus the son of Cunobelinus, as later writers certainly did. It would seem obvious from a close examination of the early Welsh genealogies that Arfon and Gwent were ruled by the same royal house. Meurig ap Caradog was a king of Gwent and his brother Eudaf Hen was Prince of Arfon and Earl of Gwent, Erging and Ewyas.

When Macsen Wledig (Magnus Maximus) married Eudaf's daughter Elen, his descendants became inextricably linked with the old British ruling family of Arfon, Gwent and Dumnonia.

In the early Welsh genealogies, Meurig ap Caradog is shown to be a contemporary of Macsen Wledig (Maximus 'the Imperator'), and his son and successor was Erbig or Erbic, who is commemorated on a stone cross inscribed with the name 'Irbic' in Llandough churchyard.[5]

Meurig ap Caradog was a warrior king who built a palace near Boverton and his sister St Eurgain founded a college for twenty-four saints at Cor Worgan (The Choir of Eurgain), now Llantwit Major.

It would appear that Meurig ap Caradog was a client ruler appointed by the Romans in the fourth century. His villa and St Eurgain's college were both destroyed in a raid by the Gwyddel Ffichti. Evidence of a massacre of men and horses was discovered in one of the wings of the Roman style villa when it was excavated in 1888.[6]

The remains of the villa were on view to the public for quite a time, but in due course the landowner had the whole ground covered over, and the site is now indistinguishable from other fields in the vicinity. Many of the finds are to be seen in the National Museum at Cardiff.

According to Stewart Williams, in *A Glamorgan Historian* (1963), there is a relationship between St Illtud's monastery and the Roman villa with its sub-Roman cemetery at Llantwit Major. The large medieval parish of Llanilltud Fawr included Llysworney, the site of the royal llys of the cantref of Gorfynydd, and it may have once been larger, including Llandow, Llandough and Llanblethian, with its chapelries of Cowbridge, Llanddunwyd (St Donat's) and Llangwyan. The connection between Llanilltud Fawr and the rulers of Glywysing is shown by the cross erected by King Hywel ap Rhys in memory of his father. This may suggest that Llanilltud Fawr had been founded on a royal estate, perhaps a multiple estate.

Where was Bovium?

The *Antonine Itinerary*, which was written in its final form in about AD 300, lists places and distances on fifteen Roman routes in Britain. It mentions the Roman outpost of BOMIO on the Via Julia and places it 15 Roman miles from Neath and 27 Roman miles from Caerleon.

It was William Camden, writing in 1576, who was responsible for making the Latin name Bovium instead of the stated Bomium and the site of this Roman fort has long been debated.

Cowbridge, which is situated on the Via Julia, is regarded as the most likely site of Bovium and the town plan is certainly rectangular like a Roman fort. Local historians such as the Revd Dr Hopkin-James, in his book *Old Cowbridge* (published in 1922), have produced scholarly argument to make the case for this to be the site of this lost fort.

It is certainly significant that an excavation by the Glamorgan-Gwent Archaeological Trust in 1977/8 uncovered a roof tile stamped 'Leg II Aug' (Second Augustan Legion'). Also, a military style bath-house (built around AD 100) was discovered under the site of the Arthur John car park.

A stone statue of a lion, thought to be part of a funerary monument of an important Roman military official, was found near a ditch at Hopyard Meadow. It dates from the second century and is now on display in the Roman Gallery of the National Museum of Wales.

This is all evidence of a strong military presence in Cowbridge, but unfortunately not solid proof that it was in fact Bovium.

The Court of King Tewdrig

Paul of Penychen and his brother Meirchion Vesanus (Marcianus the Mad) were co-rulers of Penychen and Gower. They were both sons of King Glywys and inherited this territory on his death. Meirchion ruled westwards from the River Thaw as far as Gower. To his east Paulinus ruled Penychen to the neighbourhood of Cardiff; from there Gwynllyw's territory (Gwynllwyg) extended to Newport and Etelic ruled in the Usk Valley.

In the mid-fifth century, Meirchion was expelled from his petty kingdom, along with his son March (remembered in Welsh tradition as King Mark), by King Tewdrig Fendigaid, who then established his own court at Boverton. It was possibly just a summer residence and was later used by his son Meurig and in turn by Athrwys (Arthur).

There is a tradition that the ruins of Boverton 'Castle' stand on the site of the old palace. At the time of the Norman invasion, it was one of the courts of Iestyn ap Gwrgan, the last independent Welsh Prince of Glamorgan and a direct descendant of Athrwys ap Meurig.

When Iestyn was defeated in a Battle on the Heath, near Cardiff, the Norman knight Robert Fitzhamon seized the lordship of Glamorgan and Boverton Castle became one of his favourite seats. It is interesting that the property with its adjoining farm was purchased by Prince Charles in the mid-1970s.

CHAPTER 8

The Importance of Erging

The ancient Romano-British kingdom of Erging (western Herefordshire) included all the land between the River Monnow and the River Wye, flowing from Holme Lacy to Monmouth. Its northern limit was the Guormwy or Worm-brook to its source.

Nennius, writing in Latin, refers to 'Ercing', which is usually translated as Erging and is thus named in the twelfth-century *Book of Llandaff*. The name means pear orchard and it has indeed always been a fruitful area blessed with fertile soil.

The Saxons knew Erging as Archenfeld, a name derived from that of the Roman town of Ariconium (near Weston-under-Penyard, to the east of Ross-on-Wye), where iron mined in the Forest of Dean was forged.[1]

The Traditional Story of the Birth of St Dyfrig (Dubricius)
Erb was the earliest King of Erging and his son Peibio married a daughter of Constantine, son of Magnus Maximus. There is a traditional tale concerning Peibio, who succeeded his father as King of Erging. One day after returning from an expedition against his enemies he ordered his daughter Efrddyl to wash his head. On realising that she had become pregnant he became very angry and ordered his men to place her in a sack and cast her into a river. By divine intervention she floated back to the bank each time she was cast into the river. Peibio in a state of fury then threw his daughter onto a funeral pyre.

The following morning, men were sent by Peibio to ascertain whether any bones of his despised daughter remained. To their astonishment they found her alive and holding a boy child in her lap. When they told Peibio, he ordered that his daughter with her son be brought to him. Embracing his grandson, Peibio was overcome with paternal affection. The infant by chance touched the face and mouth of his grandfather, who was immediately healed of an incurable disease which had afflicted him for some years, causing him incessantly to emit foam from his mouth.

It is said that Madley Church once displayed a picture of King Peibio Clavorauc (the Dravellor), with a servant on each side of him with napkins wiping the foam from his mouth.[2]

THE IMPORTANCE OF ERGING

Efrddyl's child was named Dyfrig and the exact spot where she gave birth to him was said to be marked by a stone which became known as Childstone. The stone has disappeared, but a short distance from Madley is a hamlet called Chilstone. There is also a thirteenth-century Chilstone Chapel in Madley Church, which incorporates a wall remnant of the very first stone church that was built here.

Madley Church is very large for such a small village and this is explained by the fact that it was once much visited by pilgrims who came here to seek a cure for their health problems from a statue of the Virgin Mary which was believed to have the power to work miracles. Money donated by these pilgrims enabled the old Norman church (of 1100) to be enlarged in about 1250 and 1320. The statue of the Virgin Mary has been destroyed but it is believed to have stood in the crypt beneath the chancel.

The Arthurian Connection with Erging

King Peibio, son of Erb, was succeeded by his son Cynfyn, who in turn was succeeded by his son Gwrgant Mawr (the Great). It was his daughter Onbrawst who married Meurig ap Tewdrig, King of Morgannwg and Gwent. Their son was Athrwys (Arthur). The marriage of Onbrawst and Meurig brought about the union of the kingdoms of Gwent and Erging. On the death of Gwrgant Mawr, Athrwys became ruler of Erging in right of his mother Onbrawst.

The pedigree of the kings of Erging and Gwent can be found in the *Book of Llandaff*:

Macsen Wledig
|
Custennin Fendigaid   Erb
| |
Daughter – married Peibio Clavorauc (the 'Dravellor')
|
Cynfyn
|
Gwrgant Mawr
|
Caradoc Freichfras   Onbrawst = Meurig ap Tewdrig
| |
Cawrdaf   Athrwys
|
Medrod

101

Misdating of these kings has helped to push Athrwys ap Meurig into the wrong century. For example, Professor Hector Munro Chadwick, in 'The Foundation of the British Kingdoms', in *Studies in Early British History* (1954), takes the lineage of the kings of Erging and Gwent from the *Book of Llandaff* and by wrongly making Erb ap Erbig ap Meurig the great-grandson of Caradog Freichfras he projects the pedigree of the kings of Erging by 100 years into the next century. Caradog Freichfras belongs to the Bonedd y Saint Pedigree 51 and not the Jesus College Pedigree 9, to which belongs Erb ap Erbig ap Meurig.

Jesus College Pedigree 9
    Caradog
    Meurig
    Erbig
    Erb

The Caradog who was the father of Meurig may well be the same Caradog who was the father of Eudaf Hen (Octavius the Old) and belonged to the Jesus College Pedigree 4. It should be remembered that Eudaf Hen was long associated with the kingdom of Erging. The revised lineage should therefore read:

    Caradog
    Meurig
    Erbig
    Erb
    Peibio
    Cynfyn
    Athrwys
    Morgan

Efrddyl the Mother of St Dyfrig
Efrddyl, the daughter of Peibio, was a woman of secular importance, being the great-granddaughter of Magnus Maximus and the inheritor of the northern part of Erging, which became known as Ynys Efrddyl. This is not an island as the name suggests, but a wooded tongue of land bounded by the Wye, the Worm and the hills that divide the plain from the Dore. She is the patron saint of Llanferddyl (Madley) and also another Llefreddyl in Llandenny, Monmouthshire.

Her brother was Cynfyn whose son Gwrgant Mawr was the great-nephew and close ally of Ambrosius Aurelianus, who re-instated him as King of Erging after he had been dispossessed of his kingdom by Vortigern. It was Gwrgant Mawr's daughter Onbrawst who married Meurig ap Tewdrig and their son was Athrwys (Arthur).

The Importance of St Dubricius (Dyfrig)

The great saint of Erging was Dubricius, the great-grandson of Constantine, son of Magnus Maximus. The name Dubricius is a Latinisation of the Welsh Dubric (later Dyfrig) meaning 'waterling', and it is associated with the strange story of his birth in about 450. In Norman-French his name became Devereux.

St Dubricius established his first monastic community at Henllan (now Hentland), about 4½ miles north-west of Ross-on-Wye. He gathered a large number of disciples around him and founded a monastic school at Llanfrawther or Llanfrother (the Church of the Brethren).[3] Excavations at Llanfrother Farm, near Hentland, have revealed traces of this college.

After seven years, St Dubricius moved his monastic community from Hentland to a new site beside the Wye at Mochros (now Moccas), the name of which means Swine Moor.[4] It is reputed to be derived from Dyfrig's encounter with a white sow and her litter when he was looking for a suitable site for his new monastery.

Moccas lies only 6 miles from Dubricius's birthplace at Madley and is just one of his many dedications that can be found in the country between the rivers Wye and Monnow, reaching westward to the Golden Valley. In total he founded twenty-four churches, though only four are still dedicated to him: Hentland, St Devereux, Ballingham and Whitchurch. They must mark the territory where St Dyfrig preached and founded his churches in the Romano-British kingdom of Erging.

Of interest, regarding Moccas, is a grant in the *Book of Llandaff* made by King Athrwys (Arthur) of Gwent to his brother Comereg, Abbot of Mochros (Moccas). Included in this grant is Campus Malochu which can be none other than Mais Mail Lochou or Llecheu ('the Plain or Field of Prince Llacheu'), also known as Ynys Efrddyl after the mother of Dubricius.[5]

Another relevant grant of land recorded in the *Book of Llandaff* reads:

Be it known that King Pepiau [Peibio], son of Erb, gave the mainaur of Garth Benni as far as the black marsh between the wood and the field, and the water and the casting net of King Constantine, his father-in-law, across the River Wye, unto God and St Dubricius, Archbishop of the see of Llan Dav, and to Iunapeius, his cousin, for the good of his soul, and for writing his name in the Book of Life, with all its liberty, without any earthly census and sovereignty smaller or greater except to God and St Dubricius and the servants of the Church of Llan Dav for ever. King Pepiau held the writing style upon the hand of St Dubricius, in order that it might be forever a house of prayer and penitence, and an episcopal habitation for the Bishops of Llan Dav, and in witness having left there his three disciples.

This grant of land made to Bishop Dubricius by King Peibio Clavorauc of Erging and his family was the estate or mainaur of Lann Custenhin Garth Benni, at what is now Welsh Bicknor in Herefordshire.[6] It is called 'Ecclesia Sancti Custenin de Biconovria' in a St Florence charter of 1144, and it is constantly mentioned in the *Book of Llandaff*. Evidently, it was a place of special importance for it bore the name of Custenhin (Constantine), who was the original founder or donor of Lann Custenhin Garth Benni (the church and monastic enclosure of Constantine the Blessed).[7]

The foundation of Llangernyw, in the same deanery, but in Flintshire, is attributed to Custennin's son Digain, who was also responsible for founding the now extinct Church of Llangernyw on the banks of the River Dore in Erging. King Peibio, the son-in-law of Custenhin, also granted Llangernyw to St Dubricius and the Church of Llandaff.

The records of the *Book of Llandaff* show that the petty kingdom of Erging extended to the Middle Wye and that it was the first region in Herefordshire to be converted to Christianity.

Dubricius is Mentioned in Geoffrey's *Historia Regum Britanniae*
Geoffrey of Monmouth claims that Dubricius was appointed Archbishop of Caerleon by Ambrosius Aurelianus. He tells us that 'Dubricius, Archbishop of the City of the Legions' crowned Arthur at Silchester (more likely Caer Vudei, now known as Woodchester). Later, he relates how Dubricius addressed Arthur's soldiers from the top of a hill and urged them to 'fight for their fatherland'.

After the Battle of Badon, Geoffrey tells how Dubricius, 'Primate of Britain and Legate of the Apostolic See', placed the crown on Arthur's head at Caerleon at the feast of Whitsuntide and celebrated the religious services in the churches of the martyr Julius and the blessed Aaron.

Dubricius then resigns the archiepiscopal see, 'piously longing after the life of a hermit'.

Dating St Dubricius (Dyfrig)

The earliest mention we have of Dubricius is in the *Vita Samsonis*, written by a monk of the monastery of Dol in Brittany, probably at the beginning of the seventh century.[8] It shows that Dyfrig was greatly revered at the monasteries of Llanilltud Fawr and Caldey Island. He is seven times called *papa* and four times *sanctus papa* or *Sanctus Dubricius papa*.

Possible confirmation of his one-time residence in the Monastery of Piro on Caldey Island can be found on a sixth-century memorial stone, inscribed in Ogham and Latin. The now imperfect Ogham inscription reads 'MAGL DUBR', which is thought to mean 'the tonsured servant of Dubricius'.

Dyfrig's time period is partly determined by the fact that he consecrated Samson, afterwards Bishop of Dol, in Brittany, who is known to have been a contemporary of Childebert (King of Paris, from 511 to 558), and to have been present at the Council of Paris in 557, where he signs as 'Samson peccator episcopus'. According to *Achau y Saint*, Dyfrig was consecrated Bishop of Llandaff by St Germanus in 470. In c.521 Dubricius consecrated Samson bishop.

The *Book of Llandaff* contains five charters that mention Dubricius. The last of the charters prefixed to the *Vita Dubrici* purports to be a grant of land at Penn Alun (now Penally), near Tenby, immediately opposite Caldey Island, 'to God and Archbishop Dubricius'. It is significant that for many centuries the island has been within the parish of Penally and that St Teilo, the disciple of Dubricius, was born in Penally.

The *Vita Dubrici* concludes with the story of how Dyfrig retired to Bardsey Island and died there:

> The blessed man, seeing that his life (or vital powers) sufficed not for himself and for the people too, oppressed by certain infirmities and by old age, resigned the labourious task of the episcopal office, and (resuming) the eremitical life, in company with several holy men and with his disciples, who lived by the labour of their hands, he dwelt alone for many years in the island of Enlli and gloriously finished his life there.

The author of this account states that Dubricius died on 14 November 612. He seems to have forgotten that he previously told us that the saint was a contemporary of St German of Auxerre, which would make him nearly 200 years old in 612!

His death would thus have occurred more than 180 years after the visit of

105

St Germanus and 55 years after St Samson attended the Council of Paris. Dubricius was a contemporary of Illtud and he ordained Samson as bishop. So he has to be alive around the year 500 and could not possibly have died in 612.

The grave of St Dubricius was identified on Bardsey Island in 1120 when Bishop Urban had his remains brought to the newly built cathedral at Llandaff.[9] There was at one time a Chapel of St Dyfrig in the cathedral, for in his will, dated 1 November 1541, John ab Iefan, Treasurer of Llandaff, desired to be buried therein. It appears to have been the present Matthew Chapel and his tomb was probably in a recess in the north aisle wall. His remains now lie against the south-east pillar of the sanctuary near the high altar.

At the Reformation, nearly all the liturgical books in Wales were destroyed and none of the special service books in use at Llandaff Cathedral survived. If they had done, it is possible that they would have provided useful information about the cult of St Dyfrig at Llandaff.

Chronology of Dubricius
450   Birth of Dubricius
470   Consecrated Bishop of Llandaff by St Germanus (according to *Achau y Saint*)[10]
490   Dubricius becomes 'Archbishop' of Caerleon upon the death of Tremorinus (according to Archbishop Ussher)[11]
519   St Dubricius attends the Synod of Llandewi Brefi
521   St Dubricius consecrates St Samson bishop
546   Death of St Dubricius on Bardsey Island
1120   Bishop Urban has Dubricius's remains removed from Bardsey to the newly built Llandaff Cathedral

After the Battle of Deorham in 577, the Hwiccas settled on the lower Severn and made raids into the kingdom of Erging. The monasteries of Dubricius and his disciples in Ewyas and Erging were attacked and the monks had to take flight, carrying their relics and books with them.

Some of them took refuge with St Teilo at Llandaff and later on the Church of Llandaff took over the abandoned sites of Dubricius's foundations. Thus, the Church of Llandaff assumed itself the legitimate inheritor of all the possessions of Dubricius. This explains why the compiler of the *Book of Llandaff* aimed at recovering possessions of Dubricius from the see of Hereford. However, Dubricius has probably never really had anything to do with Llandaff, which may not even have been founded until after his death.

The Mystery of Wormelow Tump

The *Historia Brittonum* records a collection of 'Marvels of Britain' and one in Erging is a tomb by a spring called Llygad Amir (the Eye of the Emperor):

> There is another wonder in the country called Ergyng. There is a tomb there by a spring called Llygad Amr; the name of the man who is buried in the tomb was Amr. He was a son of the warrior Arthur, and he killed him there and buried him. Men came to measure the tomb, and it is sometimes six feet long, sometimes nine, sometimes twelve, sometimes fifteen. At whatever measure you measure it on one occasion, you never find it again of the same measure, and I have tried it myself.

This strange statement relating to the tomb changing in size could be explained by the shadow cast by a memorial stone which may have once stood at the site of the grave. The shadow would quite logically vary in length according to the time of day. An alternative explanation is that if the mound was surrounded by water, then its size would vary according to the flow of the Gamber spring.

Llygad Amir has been identified with Gamber Head, the source of the River Gamber near Wormelow Tump in Llanwarne parish, Herefordshire.[12] Wormelow takes its name from the River Worme, which in the *Book of Llandaff* is called Guormui. In modern Welsh this would mean 'winding river'. The root of the word comes from the Latin *vermis* (what winds about – a worm). The other half of the place name is the Saxon 'low' which is a division of territory. The whole word signifies the territory watered by the Gwyrmwy or River Worme and its source is a round pool a few yards north of the farmhouse called Gamber Head.

The tumulus known as Wormelow Tump used to stand near crossroads, but, owing to a road-widening scheme, no trace of it remains. Its memory, however, is preserved by the sign of 'The Tump Inn', depicting King Arthur clutching a sword.

If we are to believe this account by Nennius, it would seem that Arthur considered himself responsible for the tragic death of his son Llacheu and he was buried here in an impressive tomb.

Another explanation for Llygad Amir is that the name may be derived from Llygatrudd Emys (the Red Eyed Emys) which could mean that the man buried there was Arthur's uncle Emyr Llydaw. He was the one-time ruler of British settlements in Armorica and when he later settled in Erging, his sons married daughters of Meurig ap Tewdrig.

The Bishops of Erging

Athrwys granted six churches in Erging and one in Gwent to Bishop Comereg, so that Erging, which from St Dubricius's death had its own episcopal succession, was amalgamated under one bishop, Comereg. He was the last bishop of the Dyfrig monastery of Mochros, who succeeded St Oudoceus.

Comereg was the brother of Athrwys ap Meurig (Arthur) and he is included in the list of Suffragon, or local bishops, living in the time of St Teilo, Bishop of Llandaff. He succeeded Ufelwy as Bishop of Erging during the reign of his brother Athrwys, who granted him Llan Cinmarch, near Chepstow, with its territory comprising a large part of Erging.

A clerical error in the *Book of Llandaff* has placed Comereg under his Latin name of Comergwynus in eighth position in the list of bishops of Llandaff when he was in fact Bishop of Erging only.

In the grant of Llan Cinmarch by King Athrwys ap Meurig to Bishop Comereg, one of the principal witnesses is Gwernabwy, Prior of Llangystennin Garth Benni (Welsh Bicknor). Gwernabwy also appears as a witness to the grant of Pennalun (Penally in Dyfed) by Nowy ap Arthur to St Dyfrig. The compiler of the *Book of Llandaff* has obviously made the mistake of confounding Arthur ap Pedr, King of Dyfed, with Athrwys ap Meurig, King of Gwent.

Arthur ap Pedr was the great-grandson of Gwerthefyr (Vortiporix), who flourished c.550, which means that he lived in the seventh century. Such confusion has led to a 100-year error in the dating of the charter, pushing Athrwys ap Meurig into the wrong century.

The compiler of the *Book of Llandaff* created this problem because he failed to realise that there was a gap of approximately 100 years in the sequence of the ancient charters. This gap may be due to the loss of a document, possibly a book of the Gospels, which contained memoranda covering the entire seventh century.

According to the genealogies of the Welsh saints, Comereg was the brother of Athrwys ap Meurig which gives us a way of positively dating Athrwys (Arthur) through his brother who became Bishop of Erging.

Ufelwy was Bishop of Erging during the reign of Gwrfoddw Hen, who was none other that Gwyndaf Hen, who married Gwenonwy, the sister of Athrwys ap Meurig. Gwrfoddw Hen is recorded as having granted the Church of Llansillow in Herefordshire to Ufelwy.

Dating the Charters Relating to Erging

The grants in the *Book of Llandaff* do not express the year in which they were made, but it is possible to date the early charters contained in the *Book of Llandaff* from the names of the witnesses: Inabwy, Gwrddogwy, Elhaearn, Gwernabwy and Idno, who were all disciples of St Dubricius.

St Dubricius can be positively dated as we have already demonstrated; being consecrated bishop by St Germanus in c.470 and dying in 546.

Inabwy, Bishop of Erging, was the son of the sister of Peibio Clavorauc ap Erb, King of Erging, and was therefore the cousin of St Dubricius. In the *Book of Llandaff* he is listed as a disciple of Dubricius. King Peibio of Erging granted Lann Custenhin Garth Benni (Welsh Bicknor) to Dubricius and his cousin Inabwy.

Gwrddogwy, Abbot of Llandewi (Much Dewchurch), was a disciple of St Dubricius and he witnessed a charter as a cleric in the time of King Iddon. Later, he became Abbot of Llandewi (Much Dewchurch) in Erging, and witnessed charters in the time of Bishop Inabwy and Gwrgant Mawr, King of Erging, and of Bishop Comereg and Athrwys ap Meurig, King of Gwent. Gwrddogwy witnessed the grant of Llan Cinmarch by Athrwys ap Meurig to Comereg.

Elhaearn, Abbot of Garway, is mentioned in the *Book of Llandaff* as a disciple of St Dubricius, and appears as a witness to several charters in the times of the bishops Elwystl, Inabwy and Comereg; and kings Erb, Peibio and Cynfyn of Erging, and Athrwys of Gwent. Elhaearn witnessed the grant of Llan Cinmarch by Athrwys ap Meurig to Comereg.

Gwernabwy, Prior of Llangystennin Garth Benni (Welsh Bicknor), appears as witness to charters in the *Book of Llandaff* in the times of Inabwy and Comereg. In these two charters he is named as Prior of Llan Custenhin Garth Benni (Welsh Bicknor). Gwernabwy witnessed the grant of Llan Cinmarch by King Athrwys ap Meurig to Bishop Comereg. He is listed as one of the disciples of St Dubricius.

Idno, Abbot of Bolgros, is mentioned in the *Book of Llandaff* as one of the disciples of St Dubricius. He witnessed a charter with Inabwy and Peibio, King of Erging, two charters with Bishop Comereg and Athrwys, King of Gwent. Idno witnessed the grant of Llan Cinmarch by Athrwys ap Meurig to Comereg.

Comereg is described as Abbot of Mochros in two charters contained in the *Book of Llandaff*, while the bishop is Inabwy and the king is named as Gwrgan. This is certainly Gwrgant Mawr ap Cynfyn, King of Erging. In the grant of Llan Cinmarch Comereg is named as bishop and the king is his brother Athrwys ap Meurig, King of Gwent. Comereg has mistakenly been included in eighth position in the list of the bishops of Llandaff under his Latin name of Comergwynus. This is yet another instance where a clerical error by the compilers of the *Book of Llandaff* has put a relative of Arthur out of his time.

The Post-dating of the Kings of Erging
The kings of Erging have been identified from the Llandaff Charters and they ruled from the mid-sixth century to the early seventh century, when control passed to Gwent and then to the Anglo-Saxon sub-kingdom of Mercia in the late eighth century.

Dr Wendy Davies in *The Llandaff Charters* (1979) gives the *floruits* of the kings of Erging and Gwent as:

Erb	525–55
Peibio	555–85
Cynfyn	585–615
Gwrgan	615–45
Gwrfoddw	615
Meurig	620–65
Athrwys	625–55
Morgan	665–710

Professor H.P.R. Finberg, the late Head of the Department of English Local History in the University of Leicester, gives the approximate dates of the grants made by the kings of Erging and Gwent as under:[13]

Erb	510–40
Peipiau	540–70
Cynfyn	570–600
Gurcant	600–30
Gurvodius	630–60
Meurig	630–60
Athruis	660–90
Morgan	690–720

THE IMPORTANCE OF ERGING

These kings have been post-dated by 100 years and this was caused by the compiler of the *Book of Llandaff* taking the incorrect date of 612 for the death of St Dyfrig from the *Annales Cambriae*. St Dyfrig was born c.450 and retired to Bardsey Island about twenty years before his death in 546. King Peibio of Erging was the grandfather of St Dyfrig and his grants to his grandson would have been made when Dyfrig was a young man. Peibio married a daughter of Custennin Fendigaid (r.433–43) and the correct dating for him must be c.455–85.

CHAPTER 9

Educated at Llanilltud Fawr

Llanilltud Fawr, the Great Church of St Illtud (now known as Llantwit Major), stands about 5 miles to the south-west of Cowbridge and about 1 mile from the sea coast. Its founder, St Illtud, was the son of Bicanys and it would seem that they were a military family, for Bicanys is described as 'a soldier, illustrious in race and military prowess'. Illtud was said to have been born in 425 and his name occurs under a variety of forms: Iltutus, Ildutus, Hildutus, Eldutus, Ultyd, Illtyd, Illtud and Eltyd. The Brittonic form of his name was Eltut, as preserved in the place name Llanelltud in Merionethshire.

St Illtud belonged to the same Romano-British family as that of St Patrick macCalpurnus and St Germanus. He was the great-nephew of St Germanus and the great-great-nephew of St Patrick. Under the circumstances, it is very likely that he occupied the family villa at Oystermouth during his time on the Gower Peninsula.

The name was long preserved, in the form of Illtyd, and by the nineteenth century it was still a fairly common name in the parish of Llantwit, particularly in the ancient family of Nicholls, who generally gave the name to their eldest son.

Illtud was born in about 425 and educated by St Germanus to the age of about 12, and when he was a young man he trained as a soldier and entered the military service of Paulentius, the ruler of Penychen. He was made captain of the guard and eventually rose to the position of *Magister Militum* (Master of Soldiers). This explains why he became known as Illtud Farchog (the Knight).

His days as a soldier came to an end when St Catwg, the nephew of Paul Penychen, suggested that he should become a monk and he withdrew from Paul's service. He was ordained as a priest by his great-uncle St Germanus and then, after parting from his wife Trynihid, he spent some time as a hermit in the wooded valley of the Hodnant to the west of the River Thaw. The ruler of this area at the time was Meirchion Vesanus (Marcianus the Mad), one of the sons of Glywys. At first he resented Illtud's intrusion into his domain,

112

but later relented and granted Illtud the Hodnant Valley. Without hindrance, Illtud began to cultivate the land surrounding his settlement. Before long, he had a hundred followers and many workmen. Together, they set about rebuilding the old monastery of Cor Tewdws (Choir of Theodosius).

St Illtud's Monastic College

Under the patronage of King Meirchion Vesanus (Marcianus the Mad), Illtud built his monastery along the bank of the Ogney stream, a tributary of the River Colhugh, which flows in a broad open basin, and provided shelter from the elements. Both the monasteries of Llancarfan in the Vale of Glamorgan and St David's in Pembrokeshire were built in similar situations. With the Via Julia to the north and busy sea lanes to the south, St Illtud's monastery was certainly in touch with the world.

Under Illtud's supervision, his monastic school acquired a good reputation and began to attract large numbers of scholars from important families over a wide area.[1] It became the first university in Britain and the greatest in Europe. Among Illtud's most famous pupils were Gildas the historian, Taliesin the poet, Maelgwyn who became King of Gwynedd, Samson who became Bishop of Dol, Paul Aurelian who became Bishop of St Pol-de-Léon and Arthmael who is remembered as King Arthur.

Rulers sent their sons to the monastic colleges of Llanilltud and Llancarfan to be trained in reading, writing and religion.[2] These early monasteries represented and fostered all that stood in those days for civilisation and social order. They were schools of learning where men trained for missionary work and prepared for the sacred ministry of the Church. The earliest account we have of Illtud's monastery comes from the early seventh century *Vita Sancti Samsonis* of Dol, in Brittany, and it tells us that Samson was taken by his parents to Illtud's school: 'Now this Illtud was the most learned of all the Britons in his knowledge of the Scriptures, both Old and New Testaments, and in every branch of philosophy, and rhetoric, grammar and arithmetic; and he was the most sagacious and gifted with the power of foretelling future events.'

More holy men were sent out from St Illtud's College during the fifth and sixth centuries than from any other similar monastic establishment. Even after the death of Illtud the establishment continued to operate with a good reputation right up to the end of the eleventh century, when the Normans arrived in Glamorgan.[3]

The monastery had flourished for about 700 years, but in the eleventh century it was dealt a very severe blow by Robert Fitzhamon, when he

113

transferred the ecclesiastical revenues of the property it possessed to Tewkesbury Abbey. Only a small share of the income was allowed to be used for the maintenance of the ancient church and monastic college. Subsequently, Robert, Earl of Gloucester, the son-in-law of Fitzhamon, restored some of these revenues and gave the college a new lease of life. It was then able to survive until the reign of Henry VIII, when at the Dissolution of the Monasteries its profits were bestowed upon the new Chapter of Gloucester Cathedral.

The Present-Day Church
The church that stands here today is an unusual composite building. The surviving nave of the Western or 'Old' Church possibly stands on the site of St Illtud's original building, and it dates in part from the twelfth century. The Eastern or 'New' Church, consisting of the chancel, transepts and tower, was added to the original building about 300 years later, when Llanilltud Fawr was a prosperous farming centre owned by the Lord of Glamorgan and the home of a monastic community.

The one-time importance of Llanilltud Fawr is confirmed by the number of early Christian monuments that can be seen here. Of particular interest is the collection of early Celtic pillars and cross-shafts with inscriptions and knot and interlaced work. These can be seen in the recently restored Galilee Chapel which was built as an extension to the Eastern Church during the fifteenth century.

The Cross of St Illtud
The stone known as the Cross of St Iltutus was removed from the churchyard about a century ago and placed in the restored west chapel. Only the shaft remains but it was once surmounted by a large wheel cross. It is nearly 6ft high, about 29in wide and at the top is a socket for the cross-head. The design is an elaborate pattern of ribbons, and in two small panels is the Latin inscription: 'SAMSON POSUIT HANC CRUCEM PRO ANIMA EIUS', which translated into English reads 'Samson placed this cross for the good of his [Illtud's] soul'.

Upon the other side are four small panels, surrounded by knotted ornaments. These panels bear the names of Illtud, Samson and Samuel the engraver. It would appear that this cross was erected by Samson the Abbot of Llanilltud, afterwards Bishop of Dol in Brittany, to the memory of his relative and instructor Illtud, the renowned principal of the fifth-century monastic college at Llanilltud Fawr. This is one of the most interesting memorials of the early British Church in existence, for it commemorates two holy men whose names are among the most illustrious in Wales.

There is no tradition that Illtud was buried at his monastery; the claim for his resting place comes from the little Church of Llanilltud in the parish of Defynnog near the National Park Visitor Centre on Mynydd Illtud in Powys. This church, which has a circular churchyard, was rebuilt in 1858 and demolished in 1995.

The Cross of Hywel ap Rhys

This is a ninth-century cross which was discovered in the churchyard in 1730 and is known as the 'Cross of Howell'. It has the shape of a wheel on its top and is decorated with patterns on both sides.

A Latin inscription commemorates Rhys, the father of Hywel, who was a King of Glywysing. The translation reads: 'In the name of God the Father, and the Son, and the Holy Spirit, Houelt raised this cross for the soul of his father Rhys'. Hywel (Houelt) and Rhys were direct descendants of Athrwys ap Meurig (Arthur). Hywel, who erected the cross, is mentioned in the *Book of Llandaff* for having given lands in the vicinity of Merthyr Mawr to the Church of Llandaff in 844 as atonement for crimes for which he had been excommunicated. He is supposed to have travelled to Rome in 885 to avoid the Saxon conflict, but on his arrival was taken ill with sunstroke and died three days later.

Hywel ap Rhys was the ninth and last King of Glywysing and he was succeeded by his son Owain, who in turn was followed by Morgan Mawr (the Great) who married Elen, the daughter of Rhodri Mawr. Their eleventh century descendant Iestyn ap Gwrgan, last independent Welsh Prince of Glamorgan, was killed in battle in 1092.

The Cross of Samson

This is a large inscribed stone which at one time stood against the wall of the porch on the south side of the church after it had been discovered by the bard Iolo Morganwg in 1789. He remembered being told as a boy by Richard Pruden, the village shoemaker of Llanmaes, that a stone, commemorating two Welsh kings, had been buried many years previously in the churchyard at Llanilltud Fawr. Iolo, a stonemason, was working there one day and decided to search for the buried stone. He managed to unearth it and, with the assistance of twelve men, raised it from the ground and placed it against the church wall, where it remained for the next four years. It was then taken inside the church in 1903.

Comprising siliceous freestone, it is an imposing monolith, standing 9ft high and about 2ft wide. On the top is a socket for a cross-head, which sadly has been long lost. An oblong panel occupies the whole of the front face and contains a Latin inscription consisting of twenty-one short lines.

IN NOMINE DI SUNMI INCIPIT CRUX SALVATORIS QUAE PREPARAVIT SAMSONI APATI PRO ANIMA SUA ET PRO ANIMA IUTHELO REX ET ARMALI TECANI

'In the name of God Most High begins the cross of the Saviour which Abbot Samson prepared for his soul and for the soul of King Iuthael and Arthmael and Tecani.'

Historians have dated this stone to the ninth century, basing their assumptions on the fact that there was a King of Gwent named Ithael (Iuthal), who, according to the *Annales Cambriae* and the *Brut Twysogion*, was killed in 848. However, the inscription mentions Abbot Samson who was a contemporary relative of Arthmael (Arthur). This suggests that its message relates to the sixth century. It is also significant that there was a royal person by the name of Judwal (Welsh: Ithael), who was a Breton of the sixth century and was related to Samson, the Abbot of Dol.

Arthmael's Fellow Students
St Paul Aurelian
According to Wrmonoc's *Life of St Pol de Léon*, St Paul Aurelian was born in 487 at Caput Bovium (Boverton) near Llanilltud Fawr in the centre of Penychen, Glywysing.[4] He was the son of Porphyrius Aurelianus, who was the brother of Ambrosius Aurelianus (Emrys Wledig) and married a daughter of Meurig ap Tewdrig.[5] He served as a military companion to the King of Glywysing. His Christian name may well be derived from Porphyrogenitus, meaning he was 'born of the purple'.

In Chapter I, entitled 'Of the origin of St Paul', Wrmonoc tells us: 'The same Saint Paul, surnamed Aurelian, the son of a certain count named Perphirius, who held a position of high rank in the world, came from a province which in the language of the British race is called Penn Ohen.' Wrmonoc tells us that Paul was sent to the monastic school of St Illtud at Llanilltud Fawr. In due course, Illtud arranged for Paul to go to a monastery on Ynys Pyr (Caldey Island), where he made the acquaintance of St David, St Samson and St Gildas.

Paul afterwards travelled to Dumnonia, having been invited by Marcus Conomorus, the exiled son of the Glamorgan Prince Meirchion Vesanus, to direct the spiritual affairs of his petty realm. We can find the memory of Paul preserved in this area in the place names with the prefix Pol in the vicinity of the Fowey Estuary.

After spending two years in Dumnonia and having no desire to become bishop to Marcus Conomorus, Paul sailed to Armorica. The district where he and his companions first settled is called Lampoul (Lanpaul), on the island of Ouessant, and the monastery they built became the headquarters of the colony. Paul subsequently established a settlement on the mainland at Lampoul Ploudalmezou, then moved on to build a monastery on the island of Batz, which was ruled by his cousin Gwythyr. He then established a monastic centre in the ruined town of Ocsimor.

In due course Paul became the first Bishop of Léon. In his old age he retired to his monastery of Batz and died there at the age of 86 in 573. His bones are kept in a gilded bronze shrine inside the Cathedral of St Pol-de-Léon, which is one of the finest in Brittany.

St Samson (486–565)

It was Paul Aurelian's nephew, Tigernomail (Bishop of Léon), who compiled the *Vita Sancti Samsonis* (*Life of Saint Samson*) between 610 and 615 (possibly re-edited in the ninth century).[6] We are told that Samson was born in Glamorgan in 486, the son of Amwn Ddu (Annun 'the Black'), son of Emyr Llydaw, and his wife, Anna, daughter of Meurig ap Tewdrig.[7] At the age of 5, Samson was taken to the monastic school of St Illtud. Here he remained for many years and was taught the Old and New Testaments, together with philosophy, rhetoric, grammar, geometry, arithmetic and all the arts known in Britain at that time.

St Illtud, in due course, procured Samson's ordination to the deaconate and to the priesthood. On leaving Llanilltud Fawr, Samson joined the monastery of Piro on Caldey Island (Ynys Pyr). On Piro's death, Samson was elected as the new abbot, but resigned the position after about eighteen months, having become tired of the monks' opposition to his authority He then spent some time in Ireland, and at St Germanus's Monastery at Deerhurst in Gloucestershire..

After being consecrated a bishop by St Dubricius on 22 February 521, Samson sailed for Cornwall, apparently landing at Padstow, where he met St Petroc. After founding a chapel on the hill near Place House, he continued his mission across the Cornish Peninsula. Passing through the district of Trigg or Tricorium (now Tregeare), Samson came across a large crowd of people worshipping 'an abominable image' (a prehistoric standing stone). St Samson advanced and denounced them, and by performing a miracle persuaded them to be baptised. To mark this achievement, he took an iron instrument and cut the sign of the cross on the afore-mentioned standing stone.[8] It used to stand near St Samson's Well at South Hill, but has since been moved to the rectory grounds. Standing 9ft feet high, it bears a Latin inscription commemorating Cumregnus, son of Maucus, as well as the Chi-Rho cross.

Leaving South Hill, Samson travelled overland to the south coast of Cornwall at Golant on the estuary of the River Fowey. Here he established a church which is still dedicated to him. A carving in this church depicts Samson as a bishop. The panel, once part of a rood screen, is now a section of a wooden pulpit.

From Golant Samson sailed from the mouth of the Fowey to Armorica, landing in the estuary of the Rance and made his way towards Dol, where he achieved great fame as the founder of the monastic Bishopric of Dol.

CHAPTER 10

The Crowning of Arthur

We are told in the *Life of St Dyfrig*, contained in the *Book of Llandaff*, that Arthur was crowned emperor when he was 15 years old: 'Dubricius lamented the sad state of his country. He called the other bishops to him and bestowed the crown of the kingdom upon Arthur. Arthur was a young man only fifteen years old; but he was of outstanding courage and generosity . . .' According to Geoffrey of Monmouth, the ceremony took place at Silchester: 'After the death of Uther Pendragon, the leaders of the Britons assembled from their various provinces in the town of Silchester and there suggested to Dubricius, the Archbishop of the City of the Legions (Caerleon), that as their king he should crown Arthur, son of Uther.'[1]

The *Brut Tysilio*, however, contains an interesting statement to the effect that Arthur was crowned by St Dyfrig (Dubricius) at Caer Vudei – 'the camp in the wood': 'All the principal Britons therefore, ecclesiastics and laymen assembled at Caer Vydau, and resolved to make Arthur their king.' Geoffrey's misidentification of this ancient fort helped to push it into obscurity. Silchester was known as Calleva Atrebatum while Caer Vudei is the old name for Woodchester and this site, protected by the Minchinhampton complex of earthworks, was used by Ambrosius as the headquarters of his armed forces to prevent inroads by the Saxons into his domain.[2]

Ambrosius's campaign against the Saxons culminated in a victorious battle fought in 493 at Bown Hill, overlooking the Severn Valley, and close to Woodchester. When he took control of the territory east of the Severn he established a base at Caer Vudei, which was formerly the residence of a Roman governor. The names in this locality indicate that this fortified place was the city or seat of authority of Ambrosius, who the Welsh knew as Emrys Wledig. His court was called Ambrosii Aula and it was situated at Amberley (Ambrosius's Field) near Woodchester. It would seem appropriate that Arthur, nominated by Emrys himself as the new leader of the British resistance, should be crowned at Woodchester. It is an interesting fact that Henry II was crowned just a few miles away at Gloucester in 1216.

Ambrosius was probably handing over the military leadership to Arthur rather than making him a sovereign. It is appropriate to recall that in 1404 Prince Harry of Monmouth, the 16-year-old son of Henry IV, was put in command of the king's army and sent into Wales to deal with the uprising of Owain Glyndwr.

The village of Woodchester lies in a green valley not far from Stroud and near the church is an old house known as the Priory. On this site have been discovered the foundations of one of the largest Roman villas in England. It had inner and outer courts, over sixty rooms and a corridor 33m long. On the site was also found pottery with decorations showing the old god Pan, fragments of glass and a scabbard of a sword.

This 1,700-year-old Roman palace was built between AD 300 and 325, probably for the governor of the Roman province of Britannia Prima. It was situated 20 miles from the provincial capital, Corinium (Cirencester), the second largest city in Roman Britain.

The most amazing feature of this villa, now covered by the soil of the old churchyard, is a remarkable mosaic pavement which was discovered by gravediggers at the end of the eighteenth century. It has 1 million tiny coloured cubes, each about ½ an inch across, making up a 16m square, and laid down like a carpet in the central hall of this Roman house. It has a border with a key pattern of various designs and within the great square is a circle 8m across with a border of foliage in spirals. There are inner circles with an astonishing procession of animals, borders of leaves and birds, and a central picture of Orpheus. This Roman god sits there with all these pictures encircling him.

This remarkable hidden treasure of Woodchester was last uncovered for public viewing in 1973, when it was visited by ¼ million people who came to marvel at the most magnificent Roman mosaic ever found in this country. The building was presumably abandoned when the Romans departed and would certainly have made a fine headquarters for Ambrosius in the fifth century.

Arthur was Also Said to be Crowned at Caerleon-on-Usk
Geoffrey of Monmouth brings Caerleon into his *Historia* no less than thirteen times, and it is likely that while residing at Monmouth he may well have ridden down the Roman road to Isca (Caerleon) to visit the impressive ruins of the old fortress.

His description of Arthur's court at Caerleon was most likely based on an important Christmas feast which had been held by King Stephen at Lincoln, where the king wore his crown to go to Mass. Geoffrey envisaged Arthur's feast conducted on twelfth-century lines with a feudal homaging, a banquet and tournament in honour of the ladies. It is a fact that the ancient monarchs of France and England had a custom of holding a plenary court at the three principal festivals of Easter, Whitsuntide and Christmas. In the time of William Rufus, the Easter feast was held at Winchester, the Whitsun feast took place in London and the Christmas feast at Gloucester.

Geoffrey described the situation of Caerleon as follows:

> Situated as it is in Morgannwg [as it was in Geoffrey's time], on the River Usk, not far from the Severn Sea, in a most pleasant position, and richer in material wealth than other townships, this city was eminently suitable for such a ceremony. The river which I have named flowed by it on one side, and up this the kings and princes who were to come from across the sea could be carried in a fleet of ships. On the other side, which was flanked by meadows and wooded groves, they had adorned the city with royal palaces, and by the gold-painted gables of its roofs it was a match for Rome.

In 1187, fifty years after the appearance of Geoffrey's *Historia*, Giraldus Cambrensis was accompanying Baldwin, the Archbishop of Canterbury, on a tour of Wales, preaching the Third Crusade, and they stayed one night at Casnewydd (now Newport). In his *Itinerary* Giraldus speaks of that settlement as Novus Burgas, or New Town, in order to distinguish it from Caerleon, which he describes in glowing terms:

> The city was handsomely built of masonry, with courses of bricks, by the Romans. Many vestiges of its former splendour may yet be seen, immense palaces, formerly ornamented with gilded roofs, in imitation of Roman magnificence . . . a town of prodigious size, wonderful bath-buildings, the remains of temples and theatres, all enclosed within fine walls which are yet partly standing . . .

Geoffrey tells us that Arthur's coronation was attended by the earls and barons of the kingdoms, the vassal kings of Wales, Scotland, Cornwall, Brittany, of the conquered islands and the European provinces.

The crowning ceremony was performed by St Dubricius and Geoffrey describes it as follows:

Finally, when they had all assembled in the town and the time of the feast had come, the Archbishops were led forward to the palace, so that they could place the royal crown upon the King's head. Since the plenary court was being held in his own diocese, Dubricius made ready to sing mass in celebration of the moment when the King should place the crown upon his head. As soon as the King was enrobed, he was conducted with due pomp to the church of the metropolitan see. On his right side and on his left there were two archbishops to support him. Four Kings, of Albany, Cornwall, Demetia and Venodotia, preceded him, as was their right, bearing before him four golden swords. A company of clerics of every rank advanced before him, chanting in exquisite harmony.

Geoffrey made out that Caerleon was the seat of an archbishop and that St Dubricius (Dyfrig), who crowned King Arthur, was one of those who held the archiepiscopal throne here. He invents three archbishops who head the British Church at London, York and Caerleon, but it is the Archbishop of Caerleon whom he styles 'Primate of Britain and Legate of the Papal See'. He also tells us that in due course St David succeeded Dubricius and removed the see to Menevia (West Wales). This is all fable for there was no archbishop in Britain in those times.

CHAPTER 11

Merlin, the Round Table and Excalibur

Geoffrey of Monmouth was the first writer to introduce Merlin into the story of Arthur and it would seem that he managed to combine two persons bearing the name Myrddin, who lived about a hundred years apart. He Latinised the name to Merlinus to make it easier for his Norman-French readers to cope with it. It is also possible that Geoffrey wanted to avoid the the similarity of Myrddin to *merde* (excrement) because a large part of his readership would be French-speaking.

Myrddin Emrys (Merlin Ambrosius)
Nennius's *Historia Brittonum* includes a strange story concerning an attempt by Vortigern to build a stronghold in Snowdonia. On three occasions the building materials disappeared at night and Vortigern on consulting his magicians was told that the foundations must be sprinkled with the blood of a boy without a father.

A fatherless boy called Emrys is duly discovered in the district of Glywysing (Glamorgan). He is taken to Vortigern's fort where he explains the cause of the problem and advises Vortigern to build elsewhere.

Geoffrey repeats the same story with modifications. He calls the boy Merlinus Ambrosius (but generally Merlinus for short) and says that he was found at Caerfyrddin (Carmarthen), and that he was fatherless because his mother conceived him after being seduced by a demon.

It was as a result of Geoffrey's statement that the popular idea developed that Caerfyrddin (Carmarthen) is derived from the name of Myrddin and there is even a tradition that the magician is imprisoned in a cave on Merlin's Hill, near Abergwilli.

However, the name Caerfyrddin is derived from the British 'Maridunum', meaning sea port. The prefixing of it with the word 'caer' recalled the existence of a Roman fort established there in about AD 75. The Roman version of the name is Maridunum, which comes from the Celtic *mor*, meaning sea, and *dunum* is the Celtic word for a stronghold or fortress. Thus, Caerfyrddin was derived from the Celtic words *caer*, *mor* and *din*. It was converted by popular fancy into the name of an imaginary person, presumed to have been the founder of the fortress in ancient times. Similarly, from Caerleon, the 'City of the Legions' (Castra Legionum), the personal name Leon was evolved. In this way Myrddin of Carmarthen was created by popular imagination out of a mere place name.

The Roman military camp Maridunum may well be ascribed to Sextus Julius Frontinus, who was Governor General of Britain in about 74–7 and is known to have subdued south Wales. By 120 it became a Roman walled town covering 32 acres (13 hectares) and served as the civic centre for the Demetae tribe, whose lands corresponded to the old shires of Pembroke, Cardigan and Carmarthen.

Myrddin Wyllt

The other 'Merlin' was Myrddin Wyllt (the Wild), a bard who lived in the time of Rhydderch Hael, King of the Strathclyde Cymry. Born in Scotland, he was the son of Madoc Morfran, the son of Tegid Foel and Ceridwen. The Welsh Triads name Morfran as one of the warriors who escaped from the Battle of Camlann.

Myrddin Wyllt was a gold-torqued warrior who was present at the Battle of Arfderydd in 573, in which King Rhydderch won a great victory over other Celtic rulers.[1] The site of this battle was probably near the modern village of Arthuret on the outskirts of Longtown in Cumbria.

An entry for the year 575 in the *Annales Cambriae* says: 'The battle of Arfderydd between the sons of Eliffer and Gwenddolau son of Ceidio; in which battle Gwenddolau fell and Myrddin went mad.' During the battle Myrddin is said to have killed his nephew, Gwenddydd, and full of remorse he fled from the scene and took refuge in Coed Celyddon (the Caledonian Forest), which was situated to the north of Stirlingshire.[2] Here he settled as a recluse and became variously known as Myrddin Celidonius, Myrddin Sylvester ('of the woods') and Myrddin Wyllt (the wild).[3] It is said that he went insane and wandered in this forest for many years. During this period he is supposed to have composed a number of poems, including one, in about 550, entitled *'Yr Afallenau'* ('Apple Trees'), which is contained in the *Black Book of Carmarthen*. It mentions Arthur, Gwenhwyfar, Medraut and the Battle of Camlann.

Of Medraut and Arthur, leader of hosts;
Again shall they rush to the Battle of Camlan,
And only seven escape the two days conflict.
Let Gwenhwyfar remember her crimes,
When Arthur resumes possession of his throne,
And the religious hero leads his armies.
Alas, my lamentable destiny, hope affords no refuge;
Gwenddydd's son is slain, and by my accursed hand.

There is a tradition that Myrddin Wyllt left Scotland and travelled down to the Llyyn Peninsula to sail across to Bardsey Island, which became his final resting place. He took with him the 'Thirteen Treasures of Britain' and among these priceless objects was said to be the Sword of King Rhydderch, Merlin's adversary at the Battle of Arfderydd. Also in the hoard was the Gwyddbwyll, the gold 'chess-board', with its self-moving silverpieces, which had belonged to King Gwenddoleu, his former patron.

The Fusion of Two Merlins
Geoffrey of Monmouth's Merlinus Ambrosius is a fusion of Myrddin Wyllt and Ambrosius Aurelianus (Emrys Wledig). His 'Merlinus Ambrosius' would have lived in the time of Vortigern while Myrddin Wyllt (Merlinus Caledonius or Sylvester) lived in the days of Arthur.

In *Tysilio's Chronicle*, Merlin is introduced in two characters: first as a prophetic youth, counselling Vortigern concerning the building of his fortress; and secondly as the counsellor and architect of Aurelius Ambrosius in building Stonehenge.

It would seem that when Geoffrey wrote his *Historia Regum Britannium* in 1136 there was already a Merlin legend in Welsh and he made the mistake of confusing two separate tales, and gave the name Merlinus to the child Ambrosius in the story concerning Vortigern.

In addition, Nennius incorrectly connected the Myrddin legend with the town of Caerfyrddin and had his Merlinus discovered there instead of linking him with Glywysing.

The *Brut Tysilio* states: 'Merddyn was accordingly sought for, and having been found near the well Galabes, in Ewias, a place to which he frequently resorted brought to the king who received him with great joy.' This well can be identified as a spring on Mynydd Myrddin (Merlin's Mountain), to the east of the Black Mountains in Herefordshire. In the *Book of Llandaff* there are two Latin charters in which the boundaries of two estates of the see of

125

Llandaff mention the brook or valley of the Galles or the Gall (Nant y Gall), which in turn flows into the Cwm Brook which enters the Afon Mynyw (River Monnow) near Llancillo. The source of Nant y Gall is at Arcadia. Nant Greitol (Greidol Dingle) was named after Greidiol Galofydd, the father of Gwythyr and the grandfather of Gwenhwyfar (Guinevere). It originates as a spring on Mynydd Myrddin (Merlin's Mountain).

It is significant that the *Prophecies of Merlin*, in Geoffrey of Monmouth's *Historia Regum Britanniae*, contain the statement that 'a heron from the wood of Calaterium shall exalt the valley of the Galabes [Gallaes] into a high mountain'.

When he came to write his *Vita Merlini* (*Life of Merlin*) in 1146, Geoffrey must have realised his mistake for he portrayed Merlin as the Myrddin who features in the Welsh poems and placed him in the Caledonian Forest. Geoffrey's Merlin has contact with Ambrosius Aurelianus, but he never meets or has anything to do with Arthur. This theme is developed by later writers.

The Round Table
Although there is no mention of the 'Round Table' in Geoffrey's *Historia*, his description of the assembly of chivalrous knights at Arthur's court no doubt gave inspiration to the idea. It was Robert Wace, writing in French during the twelfth century, who first introduced the Round Table into the story of Arthur. Born on the island of Jersey and educated at Caen, he completed his *Le Romans de Brut* in 1155, and it was presented to Henry II's consort, Eleanor of Aquitaine. He tells us that he obtained some of his information from the Bretons, who 'tell many a fable of the Round Table' which he describes as follows: 'This Round Table was ordained that when his [Arthur's] fair fellowship sat to meet, their chairs should be high alike, their service equal, and none before or after his comrade. Thus, no man could boast that he was exalted above his fellow . . .'

Layamon, a Worcestershire priest, in his English translation of Wace's *Brut* in the early thirteenth century tells how a Cornish carpenter created a great Round Table that could seat 1,600 and more men, yet was easily portable. A later tradition preserved in the thirteenth century ascribes the origin of the Round Table to Merlin.

According to the Merlin Continuation in the Vulgate Cycle, the Round Table was made by Merlinus Ambrosius for Uther Pendragon at Cardoel (Caerleon) in south Wales. The Knights of the Round Table who belonged to the Round Table's first foundation at Cardoel (Caerleon) migrated from there to Carohaise in Cameliard in Brittany, where they became subjects of

Leodgrance (Count Gwythyr), the father of Guinevere and the Round Table came into his possession. The Round Table then passed to Arthur as Guinevere's dowry when she married Arthur at the Church of St Stephen at Carohaise, the principal residence of Leodegrance.

In Sir Thomas Malory's story we are told that when Arthur married Guinevere her father presented him with a Round Table that had once belonged to Uther. It was large enough to seat 150 knights and Arthur had it taken to Camelot. In other versions of this tradition, the Round Table was made by Merlin for Uther Pendragon and when Uther died Merlin gave it to Arthur and his knights.

By the middle of the thirteenth century Arthur had begun to feature in the activities of the English court, where the Round Table gave its name to the tournament as a form of joust. This was fought on horseback with blunted lances and in the presence of admiring ladies. Such events are recorded as taking place at Wallingford in 1252, Kenilworth in 1279 and at Nevin in Caernarvonshire in 1284.

Arthur was now treated as a patron of England and in 1344 Edward III held a medieval tournament at Windsor Castle to celebrate two great victories against France and Scotland. After three days of jousting and feasting, Edward called a solemn assembly of all his guests. He placed his hand on the Bible and 'took a corporeal oath that he would begin a Round Table in the same manner and condition as the Lord Arthur, formerly king of England, appointed it, namely to the number of three hundred knights, a number always increasing, and he would cherish it and maintain it according to his power'.

Soon afterwards work began in the huge courtyard of the castle's upper ward to build a great stone hall for the Round Table, where the knights of the fellowship would gather. Expenditure accounts have survived providing evidence of the amount of materials transported to the castle and also details of the wages paid to the workers who constructed this huge building.

Thomas of Walsingham, in his *Chronicon Angliae* (1344), states that the structure's diameter measured 200ft and this gives a good indication of its size. A 'Feast of the Round Table' was held at Windsor in March 1345, but there is no evidence that the building was used for this nor that any work continued on it after November 1344.

During 1356–7 a number of buildings at Windsor Castle were demolished and it has been assumed that the hall of the Round Table was among them. This was confirmed in 2006 when Channel 4's *Time Team* investigated the story of Edward III's Round Table building. Their excavations over three days revealed the foundation trench of this structure in the upper bailey and it confirmed Thomas of Walsingham's stated diameter of 200ft.

On his return from fighting battles at Crecy and Calais, Edward III established in 1348 the Order of the Garter, with St George instead of Arthur as its patron. As Edwardian chivalry was centred around the Church, the choice of a saintly knight must have seemed eminently appropriate. George was the great patron of Christian knights, and not least those of England. Edward probably regarded St George as the best symbolic figure for enhancing England's growing reputation as a military power. There were twenty-six knights appointed to form the new Order and it was ordained that:

> this Order would be a Society, Fellowship, College of Knights in which all were equal to represent how they ought to be united in all Chances and various Turns of Fortune; co-partners both in Peace and War, assistant to one another in all serious and dangerous exploits, and through the course of their lives to show Fidelity and Friendliness, the one towards the other.

The famous story of St George and the Dragon became immensely popular in the West through the *Legenda Sanctorum* (*Legends of the Saints*), later known as the *Legenda Aurea* (*Golden Legend*), by Jacobus de Voragine (1230–98), an elegantly written collection of legends of the saints. In the 'Golden Legend' St George attacks the dragon, which is terrorising the whole country with its poisonous breath. He pierces it with his lance, and leads it captive with the princess's girdle, as if it was completely tame.

It has sometimes been suggested that the famous garter of the Order of the Garter with its mysterious motto '*Honi soit qui mal y pense*' may derive from the girdle by which St George's princess led away the dragon. St George is called the 'mighty warrior' of Jesus Christ, and he may have taken over some aspects of his legend from one of the other dragon-slaying saints. It is significant that St Arthmael is generally represented in armour and a chasuble, leading a dragon with a stole around its neck.

An armill is the name for one of the coronation regalia and, although the word means bracelet, it is in this case applied to a garment resembling a stole, both in the *Liber Regalis* and in the modern Coronation Service. It has been held to signify the quasi-priestly character of the annointed king and was placed on the king's shoulders by the Dean of Westminster as one of the 'garments of salvation'. It would seem likely that an armill is derived from

Armel and in this way a memory has been preserved in the coronation regalia of the illustrious King Arthur, the Defender of the Faith.

In the *Rennes Prose* (1492) and the *Breviary of Léon* (1516), St Arthmael is invoked as the *armigere* (armour-bearer) against the enemies of our salvation. The Latin version of Arthmael's name is Armagillus which may well be derived from *armigere*. In many of the churches founded by St Arthmael in Brittany he is portrayed as mailed beneath his habit, wearing gauntlets and trampling on a dragon which he holds round his neck with his stole. This is a reference to his designation as *Miles Fortissimus* ('Mighty Warrior'). It is surely more than a coincidence that Nennius, in his *Historia Brittonum*, calls Arthur 'Arturus Miles', and in the *Life of St Efflam*, the text of which is contained in Arthur de La Borderie's *Annales de Bretagne* (1892), he is called 'Arturus Fortissimus'.

When Henry VIII abolished holy days after the Reformation he made a special exception of St George. From then on St George took over the attributes of St Arthmael with those of his alter-ego King Arthur and the crossover was complete.

The Anglicisation of Arthur
It is ironic that Arthur, a great Celtic hero who is famous for fighting the ancestors of the English, should have been adopted as a one-time King of England. The anglicisation of Arthur continued to be reinforced one-hundred years later when Caxton in his preface to the first publication of Malory's *Le Morte d'Arthur*, in 1485, refers to Arthur as the head of the Nine Worthies, 'the most renowned Christian king, first and chief of the three best Christian and worthy, which ought most to be remembered amongst us Englishmen before all other Christian kings . . .'.

Caxton went on to stress that there was evidence for the existence of Arthur in various places of England:

First in the abbey of Westminster, at St Edward's shrine, remaineth the print of his seal in red wax, closed in beryl, in which is written, 'Patricius Arthurus Britanniae, Gallie, Germaniae, Dacie Imperator.' Item in the Castle of Dover ye may see Gawaine's skull, and Caradok's mantle: at Winchester the Round Table: in other places Lancelot's sword and many other things. Then all these things considered, there can be no more reasonably gainsay but there was a king of this land named Arthur.

The Winchester Round Table

It was the chronicler John Hardyng, writing in about 1450, who first mentioned the Round Table that hangs on a wall in the hall of Winchester Castle and he was convinced that it had once belonged to Arthur.

The existence of this piece of furniture at Winchester no doubt resulted in Malory identifying Winchester as the site of Camelot and further caused Henry VII to ordain that his first son should be born there in 1486.[4] On 19 September of that year, he was christened Arthur – Arthurus Secundus (Arthur the Second). Sadly, he died at the age of 16 and the return of a king named Arthur was not to be and it was his younger brother who later ruled England as Henry VIII.

It was Henry VIII who had the table redecorated to impress the emperor Charles V when he paid a visit to Winchester in 1522.[5] It is interesting that the Tudor rose in the centre and the twenty-four alternating spokes in the Tudor colours of green and white relate to the Tudor claim to descent from Arthur. Around the Tudor rose, in the centre, is written: 'Thys is the rownde table of Kyng Arthur with xxiiii of his namyde knygttes'.

Constructed of oak and measuring 6m across, the table has twelve mortice holes cut into it which indicate that it once had as many legs. Weighing 1 ton, it is fixed to the wall giving the appearance of a giant dartboard. The table was repainted without change in 1789 and an iron rim was fitted to the table in the nineteenth century to prevent it from falling apart.

Tree-ring and radio-carbon dating methods carried out in 1976 revealed that the wood used for its construction was cut just before 1250, about seven centuries after Arthur's time. It was probably made during the reign of Edward I (1239–1307), who was a great enthusiast for the Arthurian story. Several Round Table events were held during his reign and in particular one was held in 1299 to celebrate his marriage. It is possible that the Winchester Round Table was made to celebrate that occasion.

It is significant that Edward I had been present at the opening of Arthur's tomb at Glastonbury in 1278. Four years later, following the murder of Llywelyn ap Gruffydd, the last native Prince of Wales, Edward also acquired the 'crown of King Arthur', and in due course his son (the future Edward II) was given the crown to wear.

The Round Table concept has fascinated writers for centuries and it is sometimes seen as the site of an open air council chamber where Arthur and his knights could have met. Before it was excavated in 1922, the Roman amphitheatre at Caerleon-on-Usk in Gwent was just an oval grass covered hollow in a field known as King Arthur's Mead and the depression was seriously thought to be the site of King Arthur's Round Table. There are also suggested Round Table sites near Penrith in Cumbria and at Stirling Castle in Scotland, where an octagonal earthwork surrounds a flat-topped mound.

The Sword Excalibur

The earliest reference to Arthur's famous sword can be found in Geoffrey's *Historia* in which he refers to it as 'Caliburnus'. This is a Latinised version of the Welsh 'Caledwlch' by which it is referred to in the *Mabinogion*. This name is similar to the Irish 'Caladbolg', which is the name of a sword carried by heroes in Irish legend, and is derived from *calad* ('hard') and *bolg* ('lightning'). It was one of the magical objects brought to Ireland by the Tuatha De Danann. Arthur's sword was first given the name 'Excalibur' by the French. *Ex* is Latin for 'out of' or 'from' and it could mean that the weapon came 'out of' or 'from' the stone.

Geoffrey of Monmouth claims that the sword 'Caliburn' was 'forged in the Isle of Avalon' and Sir Thomas Malory adopts this statement when he describes Arthur 'girding on his Caliburn which was an excellent sword made in the Isle of Avallon'.

Malory's imaginative story of Arthur pulling a sword out of a stone may have originated from the ancient Bronze Age practice of casting a sword in a stone mould, made in two halves tightly bound together. When the metal had cooled it would be drawn out of the stone mould. The blacksmith would then have tempered the sword by alternately heating and cooling it by plunging the red-hot blade into cold water.

CHAPTER 12

The Courts of King Arthur

According to the Welsh Triads, there were in the days of Arthur three tribal thrones: Penrhyn Rhionydd in the north and Caerleon ar Wysg in the south-west, while the third at Gelliwig in Cernyw was Arthur's home and capital.

Medieval writers have made the search for Cernyw particularly difficult by identifying it as Cornwall, but Cornwall did not become known as Cernyw until the tenth century This simple fact has played a key part in wrongly locating the story of King Arthur in the West Country.

In the *Mabinogion* stories of 'Culhwch and Olwen' and 'The Dream of Rhonabwy', and also the Welsh Triads, we find frequent mention of Kernew (Cerniw) as a district with which Arthur is intimately connected. It is to Cerniw that he retires after the hunting of the boar; and it is to Cerniw that Kai, at the close of 'The Dream of Rhonabwy', bids all repair who would follow Arthur. We are told that his court there is at a place called Kelli, or Gelli Wig.

It is possible that Cerniw is not the name of an actual place but a term denoting a headland or peninsula. The word 'corn' means 'horn' and such a name can refer to a geographical feature such as a coastal horn. This would explain why the name Cerniw may refer to not only the coastal strip in Gwent, between Cardiff and Chepstow, but the whole of the old Dumnonian Peninsula (Somerset, Devon and Cornwall), and also the Llyyn Peninsula of north Wales which stretches into the Irish Sea.[1]

When one considers that Léon in Brittany was named after Caerleon-on-Usk in Gwent, it is also possible that Kerneu in Brittany was named after Arthur's principality of the same name. It is interesting that Caerleon, Cerniw and Gelliwig all have their counterparts in Cornwall and Brittany, and this has caused considerable confusion for Arthurian researchers through the ages.

In Gwent, the name Cerniw has survived on the Ordnance Survey map which shows Coed Kernew to the west of Newport. A church was established there in the sixth century by Glywys Cernyw, a son of Gwynllyw Filwr. The present-day church, built in 1853, has been converted into a private dwelling, but it stands on an ancient site.

Where is Gelliwig?

An interesting challenge for any Arthurian sleuth is to locate Arthur's court of Gelliwig, which is the name given to his base in Cerniw in early Welsh texts such as 'Culhwch and Olwen' and the Welsh Triads. The problem is that in Arthurian literature the site of Gelliwig (variously spelt Celliwig, Kelliwig, Gelliwic and Gelliwig) has been placed at many different locations, but the most appropriate one for Arthur, the hereditary King of the Silures, would be in ancient Gwent.

The word 'Gelli' means wood or grove.[2] It was possibly a sacred grove or nemeton, a sort of ritual centre, and the Welsh Triads reinforce this idea by saying that Arthur held gatherings there on the religious occasions of Christmas, Easter and Whitsuntide. Gelliwig is mentioned as one of the 'Three National Courts of the Island of Britain' and the name implies a fortress set in woodland.

One of the Welsh Triads states that when Arthur was supreme ruler, Bedwin was the chief bishop and Caradoc Freichfras was the chief elder of Gelliwig. It is interesting to surmise that perhaps the Bedwin Sands in the Severn Estuary were named after Bishop Bedwin.

Further clues are found in the *Mabinogion* story 'Culhwch and Olwen,' which tells of the pursuit of Twrch Trwyth (Irish Boar) by Arthur and his soldiers:

> The Twrch Trwyth went from Ystrad Yw to between Towy and Ewyas and Arthur summoned the men of Devon and Cornwall unto him to the estuary of the Severn and he said to the warriors of this island, 'Twrch Trwyth has slain many of my men, but by the valour of my warriors, while I live he shall not go into Cernyw. I will not follow him any longer, but I will oppose him life to life. Do as you will.' Arthur then resolved that he would send a body of knights, together with the war dogs of the island, as far as Ewyas, that they should return thence to the Severn, and that tried warriors should traverse the island and force the Twrch Trwyth into the Severn.
>
> Then Arthur, together with all the champions of Britain, fell upon the boar betwixt Llyyn Lliwan and the Aber Gwy, plunged him into the Severn and overwhelmed him in Cernyw. Then he was hunted from Cernyw and driven forward into the deep sea. Arthur then went to Gelliwig in Cernyw to anoint himself and rest from his fatigues.

This ancient story can be deciphered like a riddle and it describes how the Twrch Trwyth was hunted from west Wales to south Wales as far as the River Severn, where Arthur's seat of government, Gelliwig in Cernyw, was threatened.

Despite Arthur's desperate efforts, 'the boar', a symbolic representation of the Gewissei, his Irish enemies, succeeds in penetrating Cerniw and a desperate battle takes place 'betwixt Llyyn Lliwan and the Aber Gwy' and the enemy force is driven into the sea.

This was the Battle of Traeth Troit, 'where many a heathen fell' and it was fought between Llyyn Lliwan and the Aber Gwy, to prevent the Twrch Trwyth from breaking into Gelliwig (see p. 177–8).

After the battle Arthur retires to Gelliwig in Cernyw to bathe and rest from his fatigues. These events were a prelude to the Battle of Badon.

From this description it would seem that the most likely place to find Gelliwig is near the mouth of the River Wye, which enters the Severn near Chepstow.

The Sacred Grove of Apple Trees
On the east side of the Wye, the Beachley Peninsula ends at an ancient river crossing, which may have at one time been protected by a fortified camp. Today, this location is dominated by the massive structure of the Severn Bridge, which opened in 1967 and replaced the old car ferry operating between Beachley and Aust on the other side of the estuary.

Behind the Old Ferry Inn, above the site of the old river crossing, is an overgrown area of land, circular in form, on which a small grove of apple trees can be seen. These trees are renowned for their regeneration abilities and could quite feasibly be the descendants of a sacred grove that existed here in the Dark Ages.[3] Excavation of this site could prove very interesting.

It would seem that apple trees were once regarded as sacred and this concept is confirmed by the story in Brittany that St Teilo, aided by St Samson, planted an immense orchard, or as the legend terms it, 'a true forest of fruit trees', 3 miles in extent. This orchard existed in the twelfth century, under the name of Arboretum Teliavi et Samsonis.

The Court at Aberllychwr
We are told in the *Brut Tysilio* that Gwrgant Mawr, the son of Cynfyn, was ousted from Erging by the usurper Gwrtheyrn Gwrtheneu (Vortigern the Thin) and he established himself in Gorre (the Gower Peninsula), which he

liberated from the Irish.[4] He was later reinstated as King of Erging by his uncle, Emrys Wledig, but he still retained Gorre.

Gwrgant Mawr is also known as Urbgennius (Urianus) and is referred to by this name by Geoffrey of Monmouth.[5] It follows that he was also known as Urien of Gorre. To complicate matters even more, Urien of Gorre has been confused with Urien of Rheged, a northern chieftain, who ruled from Caer Ligualid (Carlisle) between the years 572 and 592. The heart of his kingdom was modern Cumbria which once stretched as far north as Murief (Moray). He was one of the sons of Cynfarch Gul (the Dismal) and died fighting the Angles of Bernicia in about 593.

The two Uriens have been confounded because there are also two areas known as Rheged and they both had sons named Owain. The northern Urien Rheged ruled from his court at Carlisle and his domain reached as far as the Clyde. Some writers have claimed that after defeating the Angles, he then came south and drove out the Goidels from the districts of Gower and Cidwelli (but this may have been done by Urien of Gorre). His brother Llew (Lleuddun) is known as Lleuddun Luyddog of Dinas Eiddyn, which indicates that he settled in the Edinburgh area (Dinas Eiddyn = Edinburgh). Llew is said to be buried near Dunpinder Low, in East Lothian, and he takes his place in romantic tradition as Lot while Geoffrey of Monmouth makes him King of Norway!

Owain, son of the northern Urien, married his cousin Denw, who was the daughter of his father's brother, Llew. Their son was Cynderyn or Kentigern, who established a church at Llanelwy (later called St Asaph). He subsequently went to Dalriada in Scotland at the invitation of King Rhydderch. His mother Denw joined him there, probably after the death of her husband Owain, and in Glasgow she is known as St Enoch.

In south Wales, Rheged was the district between the rivers Tywi and Tawe, comprising the territories of Gower, Kidweli, Carnwyllion, Iscennen and Cantref Brychan. The name Rheged is derived from *anrheg* – a gift – in this instance, the kingdom of Gower being bestowed upon Gwrgant Mawr who thus became known as Urien Rheged and Urien of Gorre. Confirmation that such a name existed in this area can be found on early editions of the Ordnance Survey maps of the Llandeilo area which show 'Heol Rheged'. Urien was said to have had an army of ravens in his service, by which we are probably to understand that he controlled an army of men with ravens emblazoned on their standards. This tradition is preserved in the Loughor coat of arms which features ravens.

Urien of Gorre is said to have fought a battle at Cadle, in the vicinity of

Gowerton, in which he defeated the invading Irish King Gilmore who had seized Gwyr (Gower). Taliesin tells us that Urien was slain in battle at the mouth of the River Lliw and it is relevant that the River Lliw flows into the sea at Llwchwr (Loughor).

There is also a tradition that on occasions King Arthur held court in 'Goyr' (Gower) and the most likely place would have been at the headquarters of his maternal grandfather, Gwrgant Mawr, otherwise known as Urien of Gorre. It is surely more than coincidence that Chrétien de Troyes, in his *Chevalier de la Charrete*, locates King Arthur's Camelot in the kingdom of Gorre (Gower).

A passage in the *Life of St Illtud* speaks of Arthur's court in Glamorgan, but does not name it:

> In the meantime the magnificent soldier Illtud, hearing of the magnificence of his cousin, King Arthur, desired to visit the court of so great a conqueror. He left what we call Further Britannia [Brittany], and arrived by sailing, and here he saw a great company of soldiers, being honourably received in that place, and being rewarded as regards his military desire. His desire to receive guerdons being also satisfied, he withdrew very pleased from the royal court. Journeying he came to Paulentus (Paul of Penychen), king of the Glamorgan folk, accompanied by his very honourable wife, Trinihid.

The commentary would seem to locate the court somewhere in southern Glamorgan, while in the *Life of St Cenydd*, written by John of Tynemouth, it is said to be in 'Goyr' (Gower):

> In the days of King Arthur, the prince of Letavia [Llydaw], now Brittany, was Deroch, who, by incestuous fornication, polluted his own daughter. Summoned by King Arthur, as a tributary, to come to his court to celebrate the feast of Christmas in Goyr, he took with him the woman, and she gave birth to a child, who was born a cripple and baptised Cenydd.

A place called Caer Gynydd at Waunarlwydd, a few miles from Loughor, may preserve the name of the place where St Cenydd was traditionally born.

Where was the Court of Urien of Gorre?
Over the passing centuries Loughor has been known by a variety of names

which have both Welsh and Irish origin: Aberllwchwr, Aberllyw, Cas-Llwchwr, Llwchwr, Lohot, Lurcher, Lozherne and Locharne. This settlement probably marked the western border of Silurian territory with their neighbours the Demetae. The River Severn (Sabrina Fluvius) formed a boundary between the Silures and the Dobonni.

Loughor stands on a promontory which is the remains of a glacial terminal moraine of sand and gravel formed during the final stages of the last Ice Age. The rivers Lliw and Loughor which unite and run into the Bury inlet provide natural defences to the south, west and north. In Roman times the river Loughor was known as Leuca Fluvius.

Urien of Gorre's court may have been where the Norman Castle of Loughor was built, on the crest of a natural spur, by Henry de Beaumont, Earl of Warwick, in about 1099. It was considered a very important position at that time for it commanded the ferry across the river. In 1115, the castle was attacked by Gruffydd, the son of Rhys ap Tewdwr, and razed to the ground. Before long it was rebuilt by the Normans, but captured by the Welsh again in 1150 and set on fire. In 1215 it yet again suffered the same fate.

Where was Arthur's Camelot?
Camelot is reputed to be the place where King Arthur established his main court but such a name is not mentioned in the earliest stories. It is generally assumed that its first mention is in Chrétien de Troye's *Le Chevalier de la Charrete*, written in the 1180s, and he placed it 'in the region of Caerleon'. However, the first mention of Camelot can in fact be traced back to fifty years before that time, for it is mentioned in the original version of *Y Seint Greal*, which was written in the 1130s by Bledri ap Cydifor:[6] 'Megys y doed yr amherawdyr Arthur yn y llys aelwit **Camalat** nos sadwrn sulgwynn . . .' – 'As the emperor Arthur was in the court called **Camalot**, on the eve of Whitsunday . . .'. Bledri ap Cydifor was also known as Bledri Latimer ('the Interpreter') and he gave to the world two of the most famous Arthurian stories: the tale of Tristan and Iseult and the tale of the Quest for the Holy Grail.[7] This work was undoubtedly Chrétien's principal source for the idea of a Camelot. Bledri ap Cydifor mentioned the name just once and it was later writers who provided detailed descriptions of Arthur's fabulous court.

Arthurian researchers have quite naturally attempted to link Camelot with place names containing the word cam or camel, such as Camelon, near Falkirk, and Camelford in Cornwall. Others have also endeavoured to locate it at such places as Tintagel Castle, Winchester, Carlisle, Chester, Caerleon,

Viriconium, near Wroxeter, and Camlagana, a fort on Hadrian's Wall. The latter was once thought to be at Birdoswald, but more recently it has been suggested that Camboglanna was Castlesteads (the next fort to the west) and that Birdoswald was Banna (possibly confirmed by an inscribed stone found there, recording a unit called Venetaes Banniensis).

Cadbury Castle

One of the strongest contenders for the site of Arthur's Camelot has long been Cadbury Castle which is situated near the border of the old counties of Somerset and Dorset. The hilltop site was fortified with a single rampart in the Iron Age (c.600 BC). Later, even more impressive ramparts were added and by the 1st century AD the fort was occupied by people of the Dorotriges tribe, who were slaughtered by the Roman general Vespasian in about AD 43 when he led the Second Legion in his conquest to subdue this part of Britain.

In about 1010, the fort was again re-fortified and re-occupied and even used as a Saxon mint for about seven years. Coins were being issued, up until 1020, with the mint mark CADANBYRIG in the last years of Ethelred the Unready. The mint was destroyed by King Canute.

The idea that Cadbury Castle is the site of Arthur's Camelot was first put forward in 1532 by John Leland, who served as King Henry VIII's antiquary. He observed:

> At the very south end of the church of South Cadbyri standeth Camallate, sumtyme a famouse town or castelle, upon a very torre or hille, wonderfully enstrengthened of nature. In the upper part of the coppe of the hille be four diches or trenches, and a balky waulle of yerth betwixt every one of them . . . The people can telle nothing there but they have hard say that Arture much resortid to Camalat.

Leland had no doubt been influenced by the fact that the River Cam flows past the foot of Cadbury Castle hill fort and nearby are the villages of Queen's Camel and West Camel. The little road that leads up to the fort from South Cadbury Church used to be known as Arthur's Lane.

By the nineteenth century many local stories of Arthur using this fort as his main base had been created and one must admit that it would have been well-situated as a place from which to organise campaigns against the West Saxons's advance into the Thames basin.

Has King Arviragus been Confused with Arthur?
Cadbury Castle can be shown to be connected with the first-century British King Arviragus, the son of Cunobelinus.[8] From the *Kentish Chronicles* we can learn that, upon the landing of Roman reinforcements at Portus Lemanis (Lympne) under Vespasian and Titus, the British King Arviragus abandoned Dover. It is interesting to note at this point that there is a King Arthur's Tower at Dover Castle which suggests that two personalities have become confused. Arviragus subsequently took refuge in the hillfort of Cadbury Castle in Somerset. When Vespasian landed at Totnes and took the place now called Exeter, it was Arviragus who led the British resistance against him.

Hector Boece, in his *History of the Chronicles of Scotland*, informs us that Vespasian, who was laying siege to South Cadbury, captured a royal crown and a magnificent sword, which he used for the rest of his life.

Arviragus allied himself with the Roman invaders by marrying Claudius's daughter, Gennissa, and he emerged as a client ruler, holding sway from his hill fortress at South Cadbury. He held out defiantly in the area of hill forts and the stretches of marshes, lakes and islands which lay between South Cadbury and the Bristol Channel. As a leader of the Britons and bearing the title Arthwyr he has thus become confused with the King Arthur of legend who lived 400 years later.

Discovery of the Site of a Dark Age Hall
In 1966–70 a large archaeological excavation directed by Leslie Alcock was carried out on the summit plateau of the fort and some interesting discoveries were made. It was proved that, after being abandoned for nearly 400 years, Cadbury Castle was reoccupied in the late fifth or early sixth centuries. Alcock's team uncovered the foundations of a massive gate tower at the south-west end of the site, which has been dated to this period.

Post holes revealed in a central position, indicated the site of a great hall measuring 21m by 11m. It was also found that, during the fifth and sixth centuries, the fort defences had been strengthened with the construction of a massive drystone wall some 7m thick. On the evidence of pottery found, both the hall and the stone wall had been constructed during the Arthurian period.

Such a large hall must have been erected by a person of importance, perhaps a military leader who commanded a large army, and it has been suggested that the most obvious candidate to suit the time period is King Arthur.

Was Cadbury Castle the Court of Cadwy, the Son of Geraint Llyngesog?

It is interesting that there are other Cadbury hill forts in this area, for apart from Cadbury Castle there are Cadbury Hill (Congresbury) and Cadbury Camp (Tickenham). Another Cadbury Camp stands on the ridge that rises from Failand to Clevedon, which has a camp near its eastern end. It is a hill-top fortress with double and in places triple defences. From its ramparts the view over the Severn and the Nailsea levels is very fine and this fortress would have commanded the crossing of the estuary to Gwent.

There is a northern Cadbury Camp on Rhydgate Hill, ½ mile east of Yatton. It is defended by a rocky escarpment on three sides and encloses 12 acres with a raised platform at the centre of the enclosure.

Such a name appears to be a blend of Celtic and Saxon terms. *Cad* is Celtic, meaning either army or battle and bury is from the Saxon *burb*, meaning a settlement. So the name indeed suggests that such a place was the headquarters for an army.

Alternatively, the name may be derived from a person of importance who lived at the same time as Arthur and was a ruler of Dumnonia, the ancient name for the West Country. Such a person was Cadwy, the son of Geraint Llyngesog, and he was not only related to Arthur, but was also his ally. It is therefore possible that the name Cadbury is derived from Cadwy and the timber hall that once stood on the summit of Cadbury Castle hill fort was used by him.

Cadwy (c.482–537) succeeded his father Geraint Llyngesog as King of Dumnonia and may well have utilised this hillfort as one of his strongholds. The name Cadbury may mean 'Cadwy's Fort'.

According to Geoffrey of Monmouth it was in Cadwy's household that Arthur found Guinevere. In the *Mabinogion* story entitled 'The Dream of Rhonabwy' it is Cadwy who arms the king before battle. After the Battle of Camlann, in which Cadwy was killed, Arthur passes his crown to Cadwy's son Constantine.

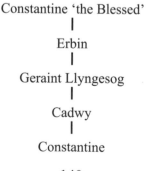

Constantine 'the Blessed'
|
Erbin
|
Geraint Llyngesog
|
Cadwy
|
Constantine

Possible Origin of the Name Camelot

It is probably unlikely that Camelot even existed as an actual place and it is just part of the traditions of the Arthurian romantic stories. It is best seen as the name of a moveable court which was established by Arthur and his followers as they moved from place to place. However, it is interesting to consider the possible origin of the name Camelot. To begin with it is perhaps significant that Camulos was the Celtic god of war. The Roman name of Colchester is Camulodunum (in full Colonia Victricensis Camulodunum) and it means 'the fortress of Camulos' who was a Celtic winged god whom the Catuvellauni tribe worshipped.[9] Colchester is said to be the 'oldest recorded town in Britain' and before the Romans came it was the capital of the British King Cunobelinus (immortalised by Shakespeare as Cymbeline).[10]

In the old British language the name of the fortress of Cunobelinus would have been Camulod-dun (the fort of Camulod). The final *um* was added by the Romans. It is possible that the romantic writers took hold of this name and altered it into Camelot.

Camulos = Celtic god of war
Camulodunum = the fortress of Camulos
Camulod-dun = the fort of Camulod
Camulod was changed to Camelot

Malory Placed Camelot at Winchester

Thomas Malory, in his *Le Morte d'Arthur*, identifies Camelot as Winchester. He was perhaps influenced by the existence of the 'Round Table' which hangs on the wall of Winchester Castle (see p. 130).

However, William Caxton, who was Malory's editor and publisher, obviously disagreed with Malory for in his preface to *Le Morte d'Arthur* he refers to 'the towne of Camelot which dyvers now lyvying hath seen in Wales'. This seems to be a reference to the Roman remains at Caerleon, which Geoffrey of Monmouth had described as the place where Arthur occasionally held court. So it would seem that Malory might have confused Winchester with a place in Wales.

Arthur as a hereditary king of the Silures is much more likely to have had his headquarters in his homeland and it is most unlikely that he would have been able to maintain a court in Winchester, which during most of the sixth century was in the possession of the Gewissei, who were his enemies. The old Roman city of Venta Belgarum (Winchester) became the capital of Wessex under Alfred the Great, whose statue can be seen in High Street, and it was the chief city in England until after the Norman Conquest.

One of the most significant forts that Arthur could have used as a base is Llanmelin, near Caerwent in Gwent. This was the headquarters of the Silures at the time of the Roman invasion and it is a very impressive site. Situated 110m above sea level, the oval camp is surrounded by a double foss with each ditch being 3–4m deep. The old name for the fort is Caer Melin which again is a possible origin for the romantic name of Camelot.

Caerleon-on-Usk

It is at Caerleon-on-Usk where, according to Geoffrey of Monmouth, Arthur is said to have held court after his series of battles and it is here that he is first portrayed in tales from the *Mabinogion* as a High King. In Geoffrey of Monmouth's time much of the Roman city would have still been standing and it would have been a very impressive place, as described in the *Historia Regum Britanniae*.

> When the feast of Whitsuntide began to draw near, Arthur, who was quite overjoyed by his great success, made up his mind to hold a plenary court at that season and place the crown of the kingdom on his head. He decided too, to summon to this feast the leaders who owed him homage, so that he could celebrate Whitsun with greater reverence and renew the closest possible pacts of peace with his chieftains. He explained to the members of his court what he was proposing to do and accepted their advice that he should carry out his plan in the City of the Legions.
>
> Situated as it is in Morgannwg [as it was in Geoffrey of Monmouth's time], on the river Usk, not far from the Severn Sea, in a most pleasant position, and being richer in material wealth than other townships, this city was eminently suitable for such a ceremony. The river which I have named flowed by it on one side, and up this the kings and princes who were to come from across the sea could be carried in a fleet of ships. On the other side, which was flanked by meadows and wooded groves, they had adorned the city with royal palaces, and by the gold-painted gables of its roofs it was a match for Rome.

Arthur would have moved his court celebrations accordingly to coincide with the important Celtic and Christian religious festivals. It is known that in the Middle Ages the king's seasonal feasts were great social occasions. Apart from making use of the grand buildings still standing in the deserted Roman city of Isca, it is possible that Arthur may have utilised the Silurian hill fort on the summit of Lodge Hill to the north-west of Caerleon. Overlooking the River Usk, it is a fine vantage point and the surviving ditches and ramparts are very impressive.

Excavations at several of the Iron Age hill forts in Wales, which had become disused following the Roman occupation, have proved that they were brought back into use during the Dark Ages and they no doubt played an important part in the story of Arthur. Yet writers in the twelfth and thirteenth centuries always described him as holding court in stone, medieval style castles.

In the summer of 2000 a small excavation, financed with a grant from the Charles Williams Trust, was carried out on Lodge Hill by a team from the University of Wales, Newport. They excavated a 106m² area within the western enclosure and exposed a group of seven post holes, which defined a small sub-rectangular building which may well relate to reoccupation of the site. Further investigation is certainly needed.

Did Arthur Hold Court on Chapel Hill Camp, Merthyr Mawr?

Another possible location for one of Arthur's courts is the site of an Iron Age fortress in the private woods to the north of Merthyr Mawr House, in the Vale of Glamorgan. The only remnant of this fort is a low bank encircling the hilltop. Within the confines of this ancient fortress, which may well have been re-occupied during the Dark Ages, stand the ruins of fifteenth-century St Roque's Chapel. It possibly occupies the site of the long lost chapel of St John which was mentioned in 1146 concerning a dispute between Llandaff and Tewkesbury

Chapter 7 explores the possibility that Geoffrey of Monmouth may have transferred the story of Uther Pendragon's attack on the court of Gorlois from Glywysing to Cornwall to fit in with his false claim that Arthur was conceived at Tintagel Castle: 'Uther Pendragon ravaged Cernyw and besieged Gorlois in the fortified camp called Dimilioc. Gorlois was killed at Dimilioc by Uther Pendragon's men at the very moment that Uther Pendragon was seducing his wife Ygerna at Tintagel. Thus Arthur was conceived.' This may be interpreted as follows: Meurig ap Tewdrig (bearing the title Uther Pendragon = 'Wonderful Head Dragon') ravaged Glywysing and besieged King Glywys in the fortified camp (on Chapel Hill) at Merthyr Mawr. Glywys was killed at the camp by Meurig's men at the very moment that Meurig was seducing his wife Gwawr at Caput Bovium (Boverton). Thus, Athrwys/Arthmael (Arthur) was conceived.

Chapel Hill Camp, as it is known today, then became one of Meurig's possessions and in due course it may have been used by his son Athrwys (Arthur) as a place to hold court. A significant statement in 'Guiron le Courteous' (edited by Lathuillere (p. 29, para. 48)) tells us that 'After his victory over the Saxons near the Severn on St John's Day [i.e., Midsummer Day, 24 June], Arthur built a chapel at Camelot and dedicated it to St John.'

St John's Day is a popular date in the Arthurian romances and it was an occasion on which courts were held, for, as well as being the Feast of John the Baptist, it symbolically marks the Summer Solstice, celebrated in the Celtic Festival of Lughnasadh.

Why is this Chapel Dedicated to St Roque?

St Roque was born in 1295 and his death is commemorated on 16 August. (It may be more than coincidence that the Feast of St Arthmael is also on 16 August.) Born at Montpellier, St Roque is known by various alternative names: Roch, Rochus (Latin), Rocco (Italian) and Rock (English) and used to be invoked by Catholics against the bubonic plague and other infectious diseases. However, in this instance the dedication to St Roque is probably due to a misunderstanding because this location was once known as the 'Chapel of the Rock'.

Merthyr Mawr means the Great Martyrium (or shrine) and seems to indicate an ancient burial site of importance. An earlier name for this church was Merthyr Glewis, recalling Glywys the fifth-century ruler of Glywysing. It is significant that his name can be found on two Dark Age inscribed stones that were erected in this locality.

In 1929 a memorial stone was found during restoration work at Ogmore Castle. It had been used as a doorstep and when it was removed an inscription was noticed on its bottom face. The stone is on display in the National Museum of Wales and a replica also stands on a plinth within the castle ruins. The inscription reads: '(SCIENDVM) EST OMNIB(VS) QUOD DED ARTHMAIL DO ET GLIGWS ET NERTAT ET FILI EPI' – 'Be it known to all that Arthmail has given this field to God to Glywys and to Nertat and to Bishop Fili.' The inscription appears to be a record of a land grant by Arthmael (King Arthur) to the Church of Glywys, at Merthyr Mawr, which is situated a short distance away on the other side of the River Ogmore. This church was no doubt founded by King Glywys, who is probably buried there, and his name is mentioned on the stone. He would not have been alive at this

A youthful King Arthur is depicted in a Victorian stained glass window in Llandaff Cathedral. It is appropriate that he should be shown here for south-east Wales is his rightful realm. His true identity was known by certain scholars in the nineteenth century, but has been rejected by present-day historians due to a misinterpretation of ancient genealogies.

Geoffrey of Monmouth is depicted in a window in St Mary's Priory Church, Monmouth in recognition that he was born in this town. It was his book *History of the Kings of Britain*, written in about 1136, that first revealed the story of King Arthur to the world.

This inscribed stone in Caerwent Church, Gwent, dates from AD 220 and confirms the importance of the Silures, who once occupied the Roman fort of Venta Silurum. Arthur was a hereditary king of the Silures, which at the time of the Roman invasion was the most powerful tribe in Britain.

Tintern Abbey in Gwent is where King Tewdrig, the grandfather of Arthur, settled in retirement during the latter part of the fifth century. The name Tintern has been corrupted from Din Teyrn which means 'Fort of the King'. Tewdrig was mortally wounded here in a battle against the Saxons.

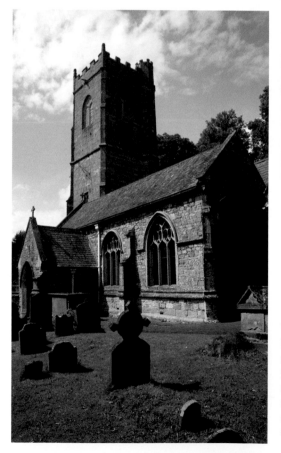

ST. TEWDRIC'S WELL
BY TRADITION AT THIS SPRING KING TEWDRIC'S WOUNDS WERE WASHED AFTER THE BATTLE NEAR TINTERN ABOUT 470 A.D. AGAINST THE PAGAN SAXONS. HE DIED A SHORT WAY OFF AND BY HIS WISHES A CHURCH WAS BUILT OVER HIS GRAVE (NOW MATHERN CHURCH).

St Tewdric's Well at Mathern is where the king died and he was buried nearby. This ancient well was mentioned by Nennius writing in about AD 822. He refers to it as one of the 'marvels' of Britain.

The original church at Mathern was built over the grave of King Tewdrig and the name Mathern is a corrupted form of 'Merthyr Teyrn', signifying 'the martyrium of the King'. Tewdrig's skeleton was found in a stone sarcophagus during the seventeeth century by Bishop Godwin.

Tintagel Castle in Cornwall, is traditionally held to be the birthplace of King Arthur and this idea established by Geoffrey of Monmouth, eight centuries ago, has been a misleading clue in the quest for the real identity of Arthur and his realm.

An inscribed stone near Slaughter Bridge in Cornwall was once believed to bear the name Artorius (Arthur). It is in fact a memorial stone to Latinus, the son of Magorus. The fact that the stone is near the River Camel gave rise to the idea that this was the site of the Battle of Camlann. Nearby Camelford was also suggested as the site of Arthur's court of Camelot.

The Tristan Stone can be seen near Fowey in Cornwall. Carved on it is a Latin inscription that commemorates Tristan, the son of Marcus Conomorus.

Glastonbury Abbey became famous in 1191 when the monks claimed to have discovered the grave of King Arthur and his wife Guinevere. The oak coffin in which the skeletons were found was shaped like a dug-out canoe and it is more likely to have been a pagan burial, for in Arthur's time a stone sarcophagus would have been used.

William Camden's drawing of the Arthur Cross (1607).

It is possible that the Glastonbury monks may have discovered the bones of King Arviragus and his wife Gennissa, a similar name to Guinevere.

King Arthur's 'Round Table' in the Guildhall, Winchester was made in about 1344. The surface of the table is divided into four segments which are painted green and white and indicate the named places of knights who are supposed to have sat around its rim. Arthur's place is at the top where the picture of a king is shown.

This nineteenth-century engraving depicts a grass-covered hollow in a field at Caerleon-upon-Usk in Gwent. It became known as King Arthur's Mead and was even marked on maps as 'King Arthur's Round Table'.

The grass-covered hollow was excavated in 1926 by Sir Mortimer Wheeler and his wife, to reveal the remains of an impressive Roman amphitheatre. It is oval in plan with stone walls, vaulted passages and entrances. Isca's entire garrison of 6,000 men could be accommodated here. It is open to conjecture that in the sixth century this abandoned arena was used by Arthur as a council chamber.

This fifteenth-century stained window in Hentland Church, Herefordshire, depicts St Dubricius (Dyfrig) who, according to Geoffrey of Monmouth, crowned Arthur king.

Llandaff Cathedral, near Cardiff, is said to be the oldest bishopric with a continuous history in the country, for a religious establishment existed here soon after the introduction of Christianity to these islands.

The tomb of St Dubricius (Dyfrig) in Llandaff Cathedral. His effigy, carved in 1720, depicts him in episcopal habits with a plain mitre. He died on Bardsey Island in 546 and in 1172 his bones were brought to Llandaff by Bishop Urban.

The ruins of Boverton 'Castle' (built about 1580) stand on the site of an ancient palace once owned by King Tewdrig, the grandfather of Athrwys ap Meurig (Arthur). This site has a long history of royal ownership and was possibly the birthplace of the Celtic prince who came to be known as Arthur.

Llanilltud Fawr (Llantwit Major) was founded in the sixth century by St Illtud. He established a monastic college here and among his most famous pupils were Arthmael (Arthur), Gildas the historian, Samson who became Bishop of Dol and Maelgwyn who became King of Gwynedd.

Drawing of an inscribed stone discovered at Ogmore Castle which translated reads: 'Be it known to all that Arthmael has given this field to God to Glywys and to Nertart and to Bishop Fili'. It is a record of a land grant made in the sixth century by Arthmael (King Arthur) to the Church of Glywys at Merthyr Mawr which is situated a short distance away.

The ancient kingdom of Gwent at one time comprised nearly the whole of Glamorgan, Erging and Ewyas. It had its origins in the administrative system established by the Romans at Caerwent and it flourished between the fifth and the eleventh centuries. The rulers of Gwent were also kings of Glywysing and from 665, the joint kingdom was known as Morgannwg. Gwent is the true land of King Arthur and of enormous significance is the Severn Estuary for this coastline provides the key to the location of his domain. Here was the land of Cernyw, where the site of Gelliwig, Arthur's main court, was situated. His grandfather Tewdrig was buried at Mathern near Chepstow and Geraint, the fleet commander who died at the Battle of Llongborth, was buried at Merthyr Geraint near Magor. Arthur gathered his army near Black Rock before crossing the Severn to follow the Via Julia, which led to the old Roman town of Aquae Sulis where the Battle of Badon was fought at Bannerdown and Solsbury Hill.

The story 'The Dream of Rhonabwy' in the *Mabinogion* decribes how Arthur gathered his army on the banks of the Severn prior to crossing the estuary to fight the Battle of Badon at Bath (Caer Baddon).

Little Solsbury hill near Bath is a possible site of the Battle of 'Mons Badonicus', as it was written in Latin. Excavation has proved that this hill fort was fortified by the Britons in the fifth or sixth centuries.

A stained glass window in Llandaff Cathedral depicting Arthur returning from the Battle of Badon.

Gushing from a source deep in the earth, the hot springs of Bath were revered by the Celts who regarded this location as a sacred site of great importance.

Porth Cadlan (Battle Place Harbour), near the tip of the Llyn Peninsula, is where Arthur may have landed his army prior to the Battle of Camlann. The detatched island known as Maen Gwenonwy was named after Arthur's sister. Her son St Henwyn founded a church at nearby Aberdaron.

Directly above Porth Cadlan, these gently sloping fields are known locally as Cadlan Uchaf (Upper Battlefield) and Cadlan Isaf (Lower Battlefield). Such names are a folk memory of a battle that took place here long ago.

The Church at Aberdaron was founded in the sixth century by Arthur's nephew St Henwyn. He was the son of Arthur's sister Gwenonwy and her husband Gwyndaf Hen.

The Battle of Camlann may have been fought near Dinas Mawddwy in mid-Wales on this mountain pass, where the name 'Camlan' is still preserved on the Ordnance Survey map of the area.

The mysterious island of Bardsey lies off the tip of the Llyn Peninsula in north Wales. Geoffrey of Monmouth tells us that after the Battle of Camlann the wounded King Arthur was taken to 'Insula Avallonis' to have his wounds tended. Welsh vesions of Geoffrey's manuscript render the name as 'Ynys Afallach' (the Island of Afallach). Glastonbury has long been misidentified as the 'Isle of Avalon' but it is Bardsey that was once occupied by an Afallach who flourished in the same period as Arthur. On the island was a monastery where Arthur's cousin St Cadfan was abbot.

Stained glass window in Cornwall depicting King Constantine, ruler of Domnonia, who was named by Geoffrey of Monmouth as Arthur's successor after his defeat at Camlann.

The Abbey du Reliqu stands on the site of the Battle of Brank Aleg in Brittany in which Marcus Conomorus (traditionally known as King Mark) was defeated and killed. As a result of this battle, Prince Judwal was restored as rightful heir to the throne of Domnonia.

This inscribed stone can be seen in the Church of St Illtyd at Llantwit Major in the Vale of Glamorgan, Wales. It appears to commemorate the victory of a battle against Marcus Conomorus in Brittany. A Latin inscription testifies that St Samson made the cross for his own soul and for those of Judwal the king and Arthmael (Arthur). It provides confirmation of a successful campaign to overthrow Marcus Conomorus. It is of great significance that the area in Brittany that was granted to Armel (Arthmael = Arthur) by King Judwal in thanks for his services is particularly associated with the Breton legends of King Arthur.

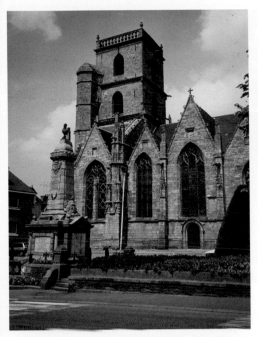

The Church of Gildas de Rhys stands on the site of a monastery founded by St Gildas, who was a contemporary of King Arthur, and he died here in 570 at the age of 94. His tomb can be seen behind the high altar and some of his bones are kept in a casket.

Plöermel Church was founded by St Armel (Arthmael = Arthur) in the sixth century. It was once known as Lann Arthmael and is situated just south of the Forest of Paimpont. The present church was built between 1511 and 1602.

St Gildas established a hermitage under a large rock beside the River Blavet and it is possible that it was here that he wrote his famous *Book of Lamentations* in which he rebukes his countrymen for their sins and lack of unity. The present stone chapel was constructed in later times.

St Armel-des-Boschaux, just south of Rennes, was founded in the sixth century by St Armel (Arthur) on land granted to him by King Judwal for services rendered. It is significant that this part of Brittany is strongly associated with the legends of King Arthur and his band of knights.

A stone sarcophagus in this church once contained the bones of St Armel, who was buried here in 562 at the age of 80. Above the decorated archway is an inscription in French, which translated reads 'The Tomb of St Armel'.

Near Loutehel Church is a shrine containing an effigy of St Armel trampling on a dragon which is a symbolic way of commemorating how he vanquished the tyrant Marcus Conomorus.

A stained glass window in St Armel-des-Boshaux depicting the funeral of St Armel (King Arthur) in 562. It would seem that he died at Plöermel and his body was taken to St Armel-des-Boschaux for burial.

A gilded casket kept in St Armel-des-Boschaux contains the jaw bone of St Armel. It is regarded as a holy relic but the Bretons have failed to realise that St Armel is the King Arthur of history and legend who abdicated after the Battle of Camlann and settled in Brittany, where he founded several churches.

Henry VII traced his descent from the ancient British kings and proudly saw himself as the successor of King Arthur. When he went into battle he marched under the standard of the Red Dragon, which he saw as the emblem of Arthur's Britain.

This window in St Laurence's Church, Ludlow, depicts Prince Arthur, the first born son of Henry VII. He had been given this name with the intention that one day he would be King Arthur the Second. Sadly, the prince died in Ludlow Castle at the age of 16.

Henry VII died in 1509 at the age of 52 and this magnificent chapel in Westminster Abbey is where he lies entombed behind the altar, with his wife Elizabeth of York. It would appear that Henry knew that King Arthur was synonymous with the great soldier saint Arthmael. During his fourteen years of exile in Brittany he would have become well acquainted with the life of St Armel (Arthmael), where he is highly venerated. There is a statuette of St Arthmael in the chapel, depicting him as a bearded man vested in a chasuble. His hands are enclosed in plated gauntlets and in one he holds a stole in which a dragon is bound. Henry Tudor believed that in freeing his country from the tyranny of Richard II he was fulfilling an ancient prophecy which foretold the return of King Arthur. Henry even ascribed his successful military campaign to the prayers of St Arthmael.

time so the inscription refers to his grandson Glywys Cernyw. Bishop Fili was the father of St Cenydd and his name also appears on a stone at Merthyr Tydfil.

Glywys in association with Nertat is also mentioned on a large stone pillar cross (known as the Conbelanus Cross), which formerly stood on the bank of the River Ogmore and was erected inside St Roque's Chapel by Sir John Nicholl in the nineteenth century. An inscription on two panels on the face of the stone reads: 'Conbelanus placed this cross for his soul and for those of Glywys and Nertat and for that of his brother and that of his father. It was prepared by me, Sciloc'. Conbelani (Conbelanu) is a variant of the name Conbelin (Cymbeline = Cynfelin in Welsh and he was the brother of King Tewdrig). The cross was obviously carved by Sciloc.

Also of interest is a stone that was discovered when the foundations of the present Merthyr Mawr Church were being excavated in Victorian times and it is on display, with other interesting stones, in an open shed on the north side of the churchyard. It is the upper fragment of a slab inscribed 'PAUL FILI MA'. The inscription is unfortunately not complete for the stone is broken, but it is reasonable to suppose that it commemorates Paul the son of Mar the son of Glywys.

Another grandson of King Glywys was Glywys Cernyw (patron of Coed Kernew in Gwent), who, after spending time in Cornwall, returned to Wales and is said to have settled at Clivis in Newton Nottage, Glamorgan (formerly Merthyr Glywys). This place appears as Merthir Gliuis in the *Book of Llandaff*.

CHAPTER 13

Enemies of the Britons

Britain remained part of the Roman Empire until 410, when Rome fell into the hands of the Visigoths and it became obvious that the Roman legions, who had been withdrawn in 407, would never return to this island. Britain was being ravaged by Saxon pirates and the *civitates* of the island appealed to Honorius, the Western Emperor, for help.

Honorius replied by informing the British *civitates* in no uncertain terms that henceforth they would have to fend for themselves. This decision ended 400 years of Roman rule in Britain and put the island at the mercy of the Irish, Picts, Angles, Jutes and Saxons. The context of Honorius's letter to the *civitates* makes it plain that there was no longer a *Dux* or *Comes Britanniarum* in the island, for otherwise it would have been his duty to organise the defence.

The Irish had begun to cause problems for the Britons during the third century. They succeeded in taking the whole of north Wales and Anglesey, and their incursions along the western seaboard (from Scotland right down to Cornwall) were to last for another 200 years.

The Romans allowed a whole Irish tribe to settle in Dyfed late in the third century. By the fifth century some of these had spread as far as the district of Kidwelly and the Gower Peninsula. These Goidelic Celts, as they were called, spoke Irish while the Brythonic Celts of Wales spoke a dialect which later became Welsh.

A Goidelic tribe, known as the Deisi, from Waterford in Ireland, having been defeated by Cormac Mac Airt crossed the sea to reach the territory of the Demetae, which roughly speaking was equivalent to the modern county of Pembrokeshire. They came in sufficient numbers to establish a kingdom of their own and implant the Irish language. Their leader was Eochaid Allmuir, son of Artchorp, and it is possible that the Romans allowed them to settle in this area in order to protect the western fringes of the Empire against further incursions of their countrymen.

By the middle of the fifth century the ruler of this area was King Triphun (a form of the Latin Tribunus) and he was succeeded by his son Aircol

146

(Agricola), followed by Vortiporix. He was referred to by Gildas as 'the tyrant of the Demetae' and was a direct descendant of the leader of the exiles from Munster who settled in Dyfed. There is a pedigree of Irish kings in this part of Wales for fourteen generations, from Eochaid down to a king reigning in the eighth century. The names of the later kings are Welsh.

Another band of Irish immigrants also penetrated the mountains of Wales to establish themselves in the district that in due course became known as Brycheiniog, after King Brychan who ruled it in the time of Arthur.

Evidence of the distribution of these Irish settlers is shown by their Ogham inscriptions on memorial stones which have been found in the old counties of Pembrokeshire, Carmarthenshire and Breconshire. This form of writing was made by cutting notches along the edges of stones and it probably originated in southern Ireland during the fourth century. In Pembrokeshire there are twenty-one such stones and seven in Powys, within the ancient kingdom of Brycheiniog, which confirms the very strong Irish connections in this area. Of the Ogham stones in Wales, twenty-six also have Latin inscriptions which makes them bilingual.

It is not generally realised by most people today, but Scotland takes its name from the **Scottis**, a tribe from northern Ireland who crossed the sea and settled along the west coast to the north of the Antonine Wall, in the area now known as Argyll.

The Picts lived in the area north of Hadrian's Wall. The Latin word *picti* means 'the painted ones' and no doubt originates from the Celtic practice of warriors painting or tattooing their naked bodies before going into battle.

The Angles came from the territory between Jutland and Holstein, which today is known as Schleswig-Holstein. They also inhabited the adjacent islands which are now the property of Denmark. Crossing the sea to Britain, they worked their way inland along river routes by following the Wash, the Trent and the Yorkshire Ouse. They must have been forced to leave their countries of origin for some definite reason. Perhaps their numbers had increased so rapidly that many of them were compelled to seek new homes. They would also have been feeling pressure from other tribes who were moving westwards. Obviously, the fertile plains of Britain were a considerable attraction.

The Jutes originally resided in Jutland but they migrated south to the area around the mouth of the Rhine and from there made raids on Britain and settled in Kent.

The Saxons came from the lands north of the River Elbe, which is now called Holstein, and from the district between the rivers Elbe and Elms which became Hanover. Saxon ships first started to raid the south-eastern coast of Britain in the third century and in 286 Aurelius Mausaeus Carausius (the Carawn of Welsh tradition) was appointed to command a Roman fleet to protect the coasts of Britain and Gaul. The Saxons came at first as pirates in search of loot, but gradually began to settle in corners of Britain and take possession of substantial areas of land.

The Roman word **Saxones** was a generic term for Germanic Angles, Jutes and Saxons who had arrived from the Continent. These three tribes seem originally to have constituted one nation, speaking the same language and ruled by monarchs who all claimed descent from the deified monarch of the Teutons, Woden or Odin.

Saxons were drafted into the Roman army as auxiliaries, while others came as mercenaries in late Roman times to such towns as Venta Silurum (Caerwent), where they helped the inhabitants to ward off other foes.

Britain was certainly no stranger to the tribesmen of Germania when the Roman forces were withdrawn in the early fifth century. From this time onwards, particularly after 450, increasing numbers of Germanic settlers entered Britain until all the most desirable fertile regions lay in their hands.

The Reign of Vortigern
There are many complex problems associated with the life of Vortigern, whose reputed dealings with the Saxons are said to have taken place in the south-east of England. He figures as a ruler in central Wales and is also connected with south Wales and Gloucester, from whose founder he was descended. He is also said to have married Sevira, the daughter of Macsen Wledig (Magnus Maximus) and Elen Luyddog.

It is important to understand that the name Vortigern is a title derived from the Latin Vertigernus meaning 'Overlord' or 'High King'. He was probably the first 'High King' acknowledged by the Britons and he was known to the Welsh as Gwrtheyrn Gwrtheneu (Vortigern the Thin). In the oldest Welsh records Vortigern's name appears as Guorthigirn and later as Gwrtheyrn. Bede, writing in Latin, gives it as Vertigernus and Uurtigernus. Gildas refers to him as the *superbus tyrannus*, the 'proud tyrant', while Nennius and the *Annales Cambriae* use the title Vortigern. Here the title Vortigern will continue to be used as it is easier to remember and to pronounce.

Of Irish descent, Vortigern was the son of Vitalis, the son of Vitalinus, the son of Gloiu Gwalltir, who established Caer Gloiu, a settlement beside the River Severn. The Saxons knew it as 'Gleucister' (Gloucester).

The epithet of Vortigern's great-grandfather, Gloiu Gwalltir (of the Long

Hair), seems to indicate that he was a Goidel, not a Romano-Briton. His descendants were called the Gwyddel Ffichti (Goidelic Picts), and may have been so named by his grandson Guitol (Vitalis in Latin), to distinguish them from the Picts of the north.

The epithet Gwrtheneu translates as 'of the Repulsive Lips', and it has been suggested by Sir John Rhys that this means Vortigern spoke a language which was unfamiliar to his subjects. He was thus a Goidelic king ruling over the Brythons of Wales and spoke Irish. Confirmation can be found in the early Welsh genealogies that his great-grandfather Gloui Gwalltir was of the same pedigree as Casanauth (Casnar Wledig) and Carawn (Carausius).

Carawn (Carausius)
Casanauth (Casnar Wledig)
Gloui Gwalltir (Long Hair)
Guoitolin (Vitalinus)
Guoitaul (Vitalis)
Gwrtheyrn Gwrtheneu (Vortigern the Thin)

Nennius tells us that Vortigern began to reign in AD 425 and he negotiated a non-aggression pact with the Irish, sealing the alliance by marrying his daughter Scothnoe to Fedelmid, the son of the Irish High King Loegaire (428–63). As a direct result of his alliance with the Irish, Vortigern was able to surround his domain with the friendly Irish buffer states of Venedotia, Llyyn, Dyfed and later Brycheiniog. He was thus in an impregnable position.

St Germanus realised that in order to restore the rightful heir Custennin Fendigaid (Constantine the Blessed), the son of Macsen Wledig and Elen Luyddog, to the throne of Britain he had to open negotiations with Vortigern. He succeeded in achieving what was thought to be virtually impossible by arranging a marriage between Vortigern and Sevira, the daughter of Macsen and Elen. Vortigern evidently decided that his best policy was one of co-operation until the time was ripe for the further advancement of his plans. By his marriage to Sevira he extended his territory into the lands of the Gewissei, which he considered his rightful heritage.

The Sons of Vortigern
Nennius tells us that Vortigern had three sons:

whose names are Vortimer, who fought against the barbarians, as I have described above, the second Cateyrn; the third Pascent, who ruled in two countries called Buellt and Gwrtheyrnion after his father's

149

death by permission of Ambrosius, who was a great king among all the kings of the British nation. A fourth son was Faustus, who was born to him by his daughter.

Vortimer, the eldest son of Vortigern, was known as Gwrthefyr Fendigaid (Vortimer the Blessed). His title comes from Vortamorix (*vor* – over, *tamo* – most, *rex* – king – thus 'over-most' or 'highest king').

Vortimer is remembered by the name Gwrthefyr at Gwrthefyrig (Vortimer's Town), the ancient name for Wonastow in Gwent. His daughter Madryn married Ynyr I of Gwent and left her name at Garth Madryn (Matriona's Enclosure), now Talgarth in Powys.

Catigern (Cateryn), the second son of Vortigern, is named by Nennius in the *Historia Brittonum* and also on the Pillar of Eliseg. He appears in Geoffrey of Monmouth's *Historia* as Katigern. Catigern translates as ' Battle Lord'. He was a warrior prince who led the British troops at the Battle of Rithergabail (Aylesford, Kent) in 455 and was killed on the battlefield.

Pascent, the third son of Vortigern, appears in the *Historia Brittonum* and is also named on the Pillar of Eliseg. In Geoffrey of Monmouth's book he is called Paschent. After Vortigern's death, Ambrosius allowed him to rule Buellt and Guerthigirnion.

The Alleged Saxon Invasion

Gildas tells us that in 446 a letter was sent by what must have been the Council of Britain to the Roman commander-in-chief in Gaul, requesting martial assistance against the Picts and the Scots, who were bent on an invasion of the island on a grand scale. It contained the statement: 'To Aetius, three times consul, the groans of the Britons. The barbarians drive us to the sea, and the sea drives us to the barbarians; between these two kinds of death we are either massacred or drowned.' No answer was received to this appeal and it became obvious that the Britons had to organise their own defence. Gildas states that in about 450 Vortigern, the 'proud tyrant', presided over a council that met to discuss the defence of the island and they decided to invite a band of Saxon mercenaries to Britain in order to repel the island's invaders.

Then all the councillors, together with the proud tyrant Guorthigern [Vortigern], the British king, were so blinded that, as a protection to their country, they sealed its doom by inviting in among them (like wolves to the sheepfold) the fierce and impious Saxons, a race hateful to God and men, to repel the invasions of the northern nations.[1]

ENEMIES OF THE BRITONS

According to Bede, the Britons 'consulted how they might obtain help to repel frequent attacks of their northern neighbours, and all agreed with the advice of their king Vortigern to call on the assistance of the Saxon peoples across the sea'. It was the Venerable Bede (*A History of the English Speaking People*), writing in 731, who adopted Gildas's account to invent his story of the *Adventus Saxonium*, the alleged Saxon invasion:

> the Angles or Saxons came to Britannia at the invitation of King Vortigern in three longships, and were granted lands in the eastern part of the realm on condition that they protected the country: nevertheless their real intention was to subdue it . . . They engaged the enemy advancing from the north, and having defeated them, sent back news of their success to their homeland, adding that the country was fertile and the Britons cowardly. Whereupon a larger fleet came over with a great body of warriors, which, when joined to the original forces, constituted an invincible army.

Bede incorrectly makes this out to be the first arrival of the Anglo-Saxons. He tells us that the leaders of the war band were the brothers Hengist and Horsa and that they arrived between 449 and 455. The *Anglo-Saxon Chronicle* says that the brothers landed at Ypwines-fleet, which has generally been identified as Ebbsfleet, on Pegwell Bay, south of Ramsgate.

It is possible that Gildas misplaced the appeal to Aetius in his narrative and Bede followed suit, misdating Vortigern's invitation to the Saxons. He introduced the date of AD 447–9 for the coming of the Saxons which is now seen to have been falsely calculated. He took the appeal of the Britons at the beginning of the story, addressed to Agitus and then followed Gildas's account from that point. The Roman commander in Gaul during the years 457–62 was Agitus (Aegidius) and as far as we know he was never consul. Bede amended the name of the Roman commander to Aetius, who is known to have been consul in 447.

Bede stated that the first Saxon war band led by the brothers Hengist and Horsa arrived in 449 and and this false date was adopted by the compilers of the *Anglo-Saxon Chronicle*.[2] 'Vortigern invited the English hither, and they came in three ships to Britain at the place Ebbsfleet. King Vortigern gave them land in the south-east of the island on condition that they should fight the Picts.' Nennius does not say that the Saxons were invited by Vortigern but states that 'three vessels, exiled from Germany, arrived in Britain. They were commanded by Horsa and Hengist, brothers, and sons of Wihtgils,' and

151

that 'Vortigern received them as friends, and delivered up to them the island which is in their language called Thanet.'

Vortigern's intention was to use the Saxons as mercenaries, just as the Romans had done during the third and fourth centuries. Some of these mercenary soldiers had even been given lands to enable them to become permanent settlers in the province in the hope that they would help to repel further newcomers. (Very much the same thing was done in 912 when the French king settled Vikings in Normandy.) Modern archaeology has proved that the Angles and the Saxons were firmly established in eastern Britain before the departure of the Roman legions.

The Angles, the Saxons and the Jutes had been settling for some time, but the three boat loads were no doubt invited as special reinforcements, hired by Vortigern as mercenaries.

It is important to realise that there were two distinct groups of 'Saxons', namely the 'English Saxons' and the Continental Saxons. The English Saxons had started settling on the island during the Roman occupation and were responsible for the internal conflicts with the Britons. The German Saxons from the Continent were responsible for the external wars.

In recent years the idea of a large-scale Saxon invasion during the fifth and sixth centuries has been reassessed. The Germanic tribes no doubt came to settle in the east part of Britain, but it was more of an infiltration than an invasion.

It was not possible for the Britons to evict the Anglo-Saxons but they did manage to hinder and restrict their advances. They certainly failed to conquer the area that is now Wales, and this was the only part of the western Roman Empire that managed to retain its identity and keep the Saxons at bay.

Vortigern is said to have strengthened his alliance with the Jutes by marrying Alis Ronwen, the daughter of Hengist.[3] The marriage agreement was cemented by a gift of territory and it represented an attempt to weld the Jutish federates under Hengist.

Nennius tells us: 'Then Hengist . . . demanded [in return for] his daughter the province, called in English Centland, in British, Ceint [Kent]. This cession was made without the knowledge of the king, Guoyrancgonus, who then reigned in Kent . . .'.

We are told by Gildas that Vortigern gave the Isle of Thanet to the Jutish leader Hengist and his warriors in return for a promise of armed resistance. These treaty troops were settled in Thanet in the territory of the Canti, which in later times became the county of Kent. Their capital town was called Cantwareburg, which became Canterbury.

ENEMIES OF THE BRITONS

The Saxon Federates' Revolt

The Saxon mercenaries were not easily won over by rewards, for the lure of greater areas of land and loot was too strong. In 455, following the murder of the Roman Consul Aetius, which removed the likelihood of any assistance from Gaul, the federates revolted and started a sharp campaign against the Britons.

It is significant that Vortigern is never represented as a military man or even called *gwledic* or *dux*, and Nennius tells us that his army was commanded by his eldest son Guorthemir (Vortimer), supported by his brother Catigern. The first battle was fought in 455 at Aylesford, a crossing point on the River Medway, and it resulted in the death of Catigern and Horsa.

Nennius tells us:

Four times did Vortimer valorously encounter the enemy; the first has been mentioned, the second was upon the river Darent, the third at the Ford, in their language called Epsford, though in ours Set thirgabail, there Horsa fell, and Catigern, the son of Vortigern; the fourth battle he fought, was near the stone on the shore of the Gallic sea, where the Saxons being defeated, fled to their ships.

One year later, Vortimer led the Britons to victory at the battles of Darenth, Stonar and Dartford, driving the federates back to their stronghold on the 'Isle of Thanet'.

Nennius tells us:

At length Vortimer valiantly fought against Hengist, Horsa, and his people; drove them to the Isle of Thanet, and thrice enclosed them within it, and beset them on the western side.[4] The Saxons now dispatched deputies to Germany to solicit large reinforcements, and an additional number of ships; having obtained these, they fought against the kings and princes of Britain, and sometimes extended their boundaries by victory, and sometimes were conquered and driven back.

In 457 the Britons were defeated by reinforced federates led by Hengist and his son Oeric Oesc in the Battle of Crayford, fought in a quiet valley near Orpington. We are told that shortly after this defeat Vortimer died from poison administered by his stepmother Alis Ronwen.

Vortigern now realised too late that matters were getting out of hand and he decided to negotiate with Hengist, the Jutish leader. A truce was agreed and

153

Vortigern accompanied by other British chieftains is said to have attended a conference and banquet arranged by Hengist at a place called 'Caer Caradoc'.

The event is remembered as 'Brad y Cyllyll Hirion', 'The Treachery of the Long Knives', and, according to Geoffrey of Monmouth, Hengist instructed each Saxon to conceal a long knife or short sword in his boot and sit beside a British chieftain at the banquet.[5] At an agreed signal each Saxon drew his knife and killed his British neighbour. We are told that 460 of the British nobles were slaughtered with the exception of Vortigern, who survived to conduct a humiliating agreement with the enemy.

Henceforth, Vortigern was branded a traitor and declared unfit to rule.[6] The Britons then supported a coalition led by Ambrosius and members of the clergy roused by St Germanus.

The Confusing Story of Cerdic and his Descendants

The *Anglo-Saxon Chronicle* tells us that in 495 two ealdormen came to Britain: 'Cerdic and Cynric his son, with five ship-loads of followers, to the place called Cerdicesora; on the same day they fought the Britons.'

The nationality of Cerdic is uncertain, for the name itself is British rather than Saxon. It would appear that he was not a Saxon invader and was more likely to have been a Celt.

Cerdic is regarded as ruler of the Winchester–Southampton area in the late fifth century; as the commander of the Saxons who landed in that area and also as a king who constantly fought with the English against the British armies. Later Wessex kings are regarded as his descendants and it is even claimed that from Cerdic is descended the Royal House of England and the present day royal family.

Possible Explanations

One might suspect that there has been a blending of two men bearing names similar to Cerdic. One was a Romano-Briton and the other a transmarine invader, whose name appears in the *Anglo-Saxon Chronicle* as Cerdic due to a copyist's error.

Alternatively, Cerdic was a Briton who had a Saxon mother and perhaps on being driven from his own territory he decided to ally himself with the Saxons. This idea begins to make sense when one considers that the name Cerdic is a variation of Ceredig. This name as Ceretic can be found in Nennius's tale in which he states that Ceretic was the name of Hengist's British interpreter during his negotiations with Vortigern. This suggests that Ceretic was bilingual, and that he was an ally of the Saxons.

Geoffrey of Monmouth names Careticus (a Latinised version of Ceretic) as undoing the work of Arthur and it would appear that he is referring to Cerdic, Ealdorman of the Gewissei. He was a Romano-Briton whose pedigree, upwards and downwards, contains British names. He was the son of Elesa, the son of Elsa, the son of Gewis.

His father Elesa, was also known as Elafius or Elasius, and it was he who welcomed St Germanus, Bishop of Auxerre, on his second visit to Britain in 447. There is a striking similarity between Elesa and the Eliseg named on the ninth-century inscription cut into the Pillar of Eliseg at Valle Crucis in the Vale of Llangollen (see p. 157) and the two names Elesa and Esla, the father and grandfather of Cerdic compare with the Eliseg and Elise of the Powysian pedigree.

The inscription on the Valle Crucis Pillar, which was erected in honour of King Eliseg, shows that this royal family of Powys traced its descent to Vortigern's son Britu by Sevira, daughter of Magnus Maximus. Bearing in mind his relationship to Vortigern, it is possible that after this tyrant's overthrow by Ambrosius in 465 Cerdic was regarded with suspicion and disposed of his inheritance. He sought refuge on the Continent and came to the mouth of the Loire, which was the territory of a Saxon chief named Odovacer. This locality became Cerdic's recruiting ground and in 494 he returned to Britain to claim his inheritance, accompanied by a mongrel contingent of Saxon federates.[7]

Cerdic, his son Creoda, and their followers, landed at a place which thereafter became known as Cerdicesora. It lies between Calshot and the River Beaulieu on the shore of Southampton Water. Here Cerdic carved out a principality for himself by asserting his rights and fighting all comers. At first his followers were small in number, for the future showed little promise and the Britons kept the Gewissei in this area firmly in check. However, Cerdic succeeded in subjugating the Teutonic settlers who passed through his neighbourhood and his followers grew significantly in number.

It was Cerdic's heirs who eventually succeeded in reaching the Thames Valley where they imposed their authority on the disorganised peasants, who formed the major West Saxon body. In the course of political re-arrangements, Cerdic was probably made overlord of the various Jutish and Saxon colonies under British domination. He sided with the Saxons in the long wars and started a lineage which was at once Celtic and Teutonic. His descendants finally emerged as the kings of Wessex.

Accordingly, it can be established that the Gewissei were now living in the territory of Venta Belgarum (Winchester) in the canton of the Belgae, which stretched from Portsmouth Harbour, including the Isle of Wight, across southern Hampshire and Wiltshire into Somerset. Under their leader Cerdic, they spread eastwards as far as Cerdicesora on the Solent and Cerdicesleaga (Netley).

In 501 a band of Jutes from Kent under leaders Bieda and Maegla landed at Portsmouth Harbour (which has been mistakenly identified as Llongborth). They pillaged Portus Adurni (Porchester) and Clausentum (Bitterne) and then formed an alliance with the Gewissei. By 508 the two factions had made themselves masters of the district between the mouth of the Itchen and Portchester Harbour. From here they made a piratical raid up the Severn Estuary but their advance was halted by the western Britons led by Geraint Llyngesog (the Fleet-owner) and a battle was fought at a place remembered as Llongborth, which is investigated in the next chapter.

The Enemy Within

The Saxons, who allied themselves with the Picts and the Scots, were not the only enemies of the Britons during the times when our island was the scene of a mighty struggle for domination. Arthur also had to deal with another set of foes who were known as the Gewissei, which is a term meaning 'allies' or 'compatriots'. John Morris, in his book *The Age of Arthur* (1973), defines them as federates or confederates and they later became known as the 'West Saxons'.

The leaders of these Irish federates claimed descent from Casnar Wledig and Carawn (Carausius). It is significant in *The Death Song of Uther Pendragon* by Taliesin the enemies of Uther are referred to as the 'Sons of Casnar'.

It was the policy of the Romans in Britain to hire federate troops to help police the province. Gradually, the power of these confederates grew and upon the departure of the Romans they became a force to be reckoned with. Their powers were temporarily broken by Eudaf Hen but re-established by Gwrtheyrn Gwrtheneu (Vortigern the Thin). What followed was a struggle between the two main forces of the Romano-British elite and the Gewissei.

The Gewissei (Confederates) were Irish federate troops employed by the Roman Empire to police the republic of the Silures and they were associated with the city of Gloiu, which is now called Gloucester. Gloiu was given the epithet Gwalltir ('of the Long Hair') and this probably stemmed from a hair plume that he wore in his helmet to signify his position as commander of the Gewissei.

Gloucester was called in Welsh Caer Loyw or Loew, which means the Castle of Gloyw. The Cair Gloui of Nennius's *Historia Brittonum* is the same as Caer Gloyw for Gloui and would be exactly the old spelling of the Welsh Gloew or Gloyw. In the Brythonic tongue the Castle of Gloyw would have

156

sounded Castra Glevi, which agrees with Glevum. The importance of Glevum to the Romans belonged to the time before they had taken possession of Isca Silurum (Caerleon-on-Usk) so Caer Loyw probably marks a boundary of much earlier importance to the Celts.

Let us now recall the story of Magnus Maximus, who took over the rule of Britain by marrying Elen, the daughter of Octavius the Old (Eudaf Hen), Prince of Arfon. Geoffrey of Monmouth gives Elen's father the title *Dux Gewissei* and significantly also attaches the same title to Vortigern, whom he clearly regarded as the subsequent ruler of the same territory.

On studying the ancient inscription displayed on the ninth-century Pillar of Eliseg at Valle Crucis in the Vale of Llangollen, I found confirmation of the association between Vortigern and Sevira, the daughter of Magnus Maximus and Elen. The statements made by Geoffrey of Monmouth and the Pillar of Eliseg may be reconciled by the fact that Vortigern derived his ostensible claim to the territory of the Gewissei through his wife, who was the heiress to Magnus Maximus.

The Pillar of Eliseg

The Pillar of Eliseg, near the ruins of Valle Crucis Abbey, Clwyd, was once part of a tall cross erected here in the Vale of Llangollen by Cyngen in honour of his great-grandfather Eliseg, who regained the kingdom of Powys from the Saxons. The valley became known as the Valley of the Cross – 'Valle Crucis', and the field where it stands used to be called Llwyn y Groes – 'The Grove of the Cross'. Long before the Cistercian abbey was founded, the first church here was called Llan Egwestl after its founder Gwestl or Egwest who lived here at the end of the fifth century.

It is possible that the cross was erected over the tomb of Eliseg, and in 1779 the mound on which it stands was investigated. It was found to contain a slab-constructed and covered grave, within which lay the bones of a single male. A large piece of silver coin was found in the coffin, implying that it was a post-Roman burial rather than a prehistoric one.

The pillar may have originally been a Roman column which Cyngen re-used as a memorial stone. It is also very similar to the Mercian crosses which can be seen in the Peak District. Cyngen was the last King of Powys of the old line and he died while he was on a pilgrimage to Rome in 854. His ancestor Brochmail Ysgythrog fell in the Battle of Bangor-is-Coed in 613 when the Welsh army was defeated by the Angles of Northumbria under Aethelfrith. There is a memorial stone to Aethelfrith at Bewcastle, a little Cumberland village north of Hadrian's Wall. Here an ancient cross bears an inscription recording that it was erected by Hwaefred and Worthgaer in honour of Aethelfrith, son of Aethelric.

There is a long Latin inscription on the Pillar of Eliseg, but it has weathered so badly that it is now impossible to read. Fortunately, it was written down in 1696 by the antiquary Edward Llwyd. There are thirty-one horizontal lines (only seven can be seen now), divided into paragraphs, each introduced by a cross. Translated into English this fascinating inscription reads as follows:

+ Concenn son of Cadell, Cadell son of Brochmail, Brochmail son of Eliseg, Eliseg son of Guaillauc
+ And so Concenn, great-grandson of Eliseg, erected this stone for his great-grandfather Eliseg
+ This is that Eliseg, who joined together the inheritance of Powys . . . out of the power of the Angles with his sword of fire
+ Whosoever repeats this writing, let him give a blessing on the soul of Eliseg
+ This is that Concenn who captured with his hand eleven hundred acres which used to belong to his kingdom of Powys
[Next two paragraphs illegible]
Maximus . . . of Britain . . .
Concenn, Pascent . . . Maun, Annan
+ Britu, moreover [was] the son of Guorthigirn [Vortigern]
Whom Germanus blessed and whom
Sevira bore to him, daughter of Maximus the king, who killed the king of the Romans
+ Conmarch painted this writing at the request of King Concenn
+ The blessing of the Lord upon Concenn and upon his entire household and upon all the region of Powys until the day of doom
Amen.

Eliseg was the tenth generation of this Powys dynasty and he lived in the middle of the eighth century. His grandson Cadell died in 808 and was succeeded by Concenn or Cyngen who erected this pillar cross in memory of his great-grandfather. This suggests that the cross was erected during the first half of the ninth century, for Concenn died about 854 during a pilgrimage to Rome, and he was the last of the line.

The inscription shows that Eliseg, who was the last in line of the dynasty of Powys, traced his ancestry to both Vortigern and Magnus Maximus. It tells us that Vortigern married Sevira, daughter of Magnus Maximus, by whom he had a son, Britu, whom St Germanus blessed.

It is significant that the Nennius manuscript indicates that all the princes of Powys are descended from Vortigern, and Germanus is mentioned on the pillar as the patron of the dynasty of Powys.

Vortigern and his son Britu are given special mention in the inscription, and also Pascent, who was Vortigern's third son. It is of interest that Nennius, writing in the early ninth century, records that the later kings of Buellt (now Builth Wells) and Gwrtheyrnion – sub-kingdoms of Powys, were descended from Pascent. It is possible that Pascent's memorial stone was found at Tywyn in the eighteenth century. It was inscribed with the name Pascentius, but this was quite a common Romano-Christian name and may not necessarily have applied to him. Unfortunately, the stone was subsequently lost or destroyed. Nennius tells us that following the death of King Guorthigirn (Vortigern), Ambrosius bestowed upon Pascent, the third son of Guorthigirn, the regions of Buellt and Guortherniaun.

The Principal Enemies of King Arthur

It is important to understand that there was a long sustained struggle for power between rival dynasties. During Arthur's time the majority of alliances were achieved by marriages, and most dynastic wars were fought over disputed territorial claims. It is only when one fully realises this situation that one can comprehend the result of Arthur's expansionist policies.

After the departure of the Roman legions, there was a struggle for power between the legitimate Romano-British chieftains, who claimed descent from Macsen Wledig, and the Gewissei, whose leaders claimed descent from Carawn (Carausius I, 287–93). The Romano-British alliance of Siluria, Dumnonia and Armorica eventually triumphed over the Gewissei, who were expelled, but the alliance fell apart with the revolt of Medraut and the fall of Arthur, and the old order changed.

The Dukes of Gewissei

When Eudaf Hen (Octavius the Old) married the daughter of Carausius II and took control of the territory of the Gewissei, he gained the right to hold the title of *Dux*. The corresponding form of Gewissei is *Iwys* and this is preserved in Ewyas Harold and Ewyas Lacey in Herefordshire. Besides Gwent, Eudaf's estate comprised that of the Hwiccas, a British and Christian people with whom the Anglo-Saxons later intermingled. It was portioned out into areas equivalent to the shires of Hereford, Gloucester, Worcester, part of Warwick and the district between the Wye and the Severn, which included the Forest of Dean.

The title *Dux* Gewissei, i.e., Prince of Gwent, Erging and Ewyas, was also held by Vortigern, who derived his claim to rule this territory through his marriage to Sevira, the daughter of Magnus Maximus and Elen. This marriage was undoubtedly calculated to gain political advantage and to pacify the border, for when Elen died, Sevira by rule of female succession was heiress. She succeeded her mother and gained control of the territory belonging to the family. Vortigern had access to his wife's inheritance and thereby became one of the most powerful rulers in southern Britain.

In the *Book of Taliesin*, which names Ynyr of Gwent, Gwrfoddw Hen of Erging and Ruduedel of Gwrtheyrn's family, appears Gwenhwys gwallt hiryon am Gaer Wyrangon, 'long-haired Gwentians about Caer Wrangon'.

The people of Gwent were called the Gwenhwys or Gwenwyssos and this name would appear to be the origin of the word Gewissei, which clearly means not the territory of the people but the people of it. The land of the Gewissei was in Erging and Ewyas, which were both small areas to the north-east of Gwent. It has also been proposed that the Gewissei were Teutonic federates who had been settled in the region and when the time was ripe rebelled under Cerdic, who was struggling to regain his patrimony.

Nennius in his *Historia Brittonum* implies that the chief opponent of Arthur and the Britons was Octha II, but he persists in confusing him with Oeric Oesc, son of Hengist (Octha I).[8] The venerable Bede, in his *Historia Ecclesiastica*, however, made him the grandson of Hengist, and this is confirmed by the Kentish king list cited by the same author.

The Kings of Kent

Ebissa (Horsa)	455
Octha I (Hengist)	455–88
Oeric Oesc	488–512
Octha II	512–34
Eomenric	534–60
Ethelbert I	560–616
Ealdbald	616–40
Earconberht	640–64
Egbert I	664–73
Hlothere	673–85
Eadric	685–6

Octha II was the grandson of Octha I (Hengist) resulting from the union of Vortigern and Alis Ronwen, the daughter of Hengist (Octha I).[9] Octha II was the step-brother of Vortimer, the eldest son of Vortigern and his first wife Sevira. In Welsh tradition he is known as Osla Gyllellfawr (of the Great or Long Knife), which with a touch of humour associates him with the Saxon short sword.

He features in the *Mabinogion* story, 'The Dream of Rhonabwy', where his name is written in the Welsh form Osla and he is the adversary of Arthur at the Battle of Badon. Under this name he also appears in the *Mabinogion* tale 'Culhwch and Olwen', where his prowess in the hunt of the Twrch Trwyth, or Porcus Troit, resulted in the loss of his marvellous knife.

Octha II (Osla Gyllelfawr) laid claim to the former territory of his step-brother Gwrthefyr Fendigaid (Vortimer the Blessed), after his death in 457, and to the territory of his father Gwrtheyrn Gwrtheneu (Vortigern the Thin), who died in 465. There is a possibility that Octha's accession was disputed because his father was the infamous King Vortigern.

Cerdic, Ealdorman of the Gewissei, laid claim to the territory of March ap Meirchion through his marriage to March's daughter Henwen.

March ap Meirchion (Marcus son of Marcianus), was known in the romance stories as King Mark, while his Latin name was Marcus Conomorus.[10] Meirchion Vesanus, the father of March, was supplanted by Arthur's grandfather Tewdrig, who dispossessed him of his territories in the Vale of Glamorgan and his seat at Boverton.

March ap Meirchion and his wife Essyllt Fyngwen were supplanted by King Arthur and dispossessed of their territories in Gwent, which were subsequently re-allocated to Arthur's family. The *Book of Llandaff* records the grant of Llan Cinmarch (near Chepstow) by Athrwys ap Meurig (Arthur) to his brother Comereg, Bishop of Erging.[11] Included in this grant is Campus Malochu, which can be none other that Mais Mail Lochou ('the Plain or Field of Prince Llacheu'). It now seems obvious that March's territory was granted by Arthur first to his son Llacheu, and, upon the death of Llacheu, to his brother Comereg.

It may be that the Battle of Castellum Guinnion mentioned by Nennius took place at Cas-Gwent (Chepstow) or Caer Gwynt (Caerwent) and it resulted in March ap Meirchion being dispossessed of his territory in Gwent. With his wife Essyllt Fyngwen he then settled in Cornwall where they carved out a principality for themselves. March no doubt bore a lifetime grudge against Arthur, after he expelled him from his territory in Gwent.

CHAPTER 14

Looking for Llongborth

Arthurian scholars have made various attempts to identify the site of the Battle of Llongborth in which Geraint of Dumnonia was said to have been killed while fighting a band of invading Saxons. This incident is described in a battle poem reputed to have been written by Llywarch Hen (the Aged). Entitled 'Gereint ap Erbin', it is contained in the *Red Book of Hergest* and the *Black Book of Carmarthen*, which were compiled in the late thirteenth century.[1]

> In Llongborth I saw a rage of slaughter,
> and biers beyond all count,
> and red-stained men from the assault of Geraint.
>
> In Llongborth I saw the edges of blades meet
> Men in terror, with blood on the pate,
> Before Geraint, the great son of his father.
>
> In Llongborth Geraint was slain,
> A brave man from the region of Dyfnaint,
> And before they were overpowered,
> they committed slaughter.

It appears that the invaders' ships entered the warship port of Llongborth and succeeded in landing. They then had to face the Britons of Dumnonia led by Geraint, who was slain during the conflict.

Suggested Sites for Llongborth
There is a popular theory that this battle was fought either at Portsmouth in Hampshire or at Langport in Somerset. The former location was probably the site of a battle fought in 501 when a war band led by the Jutish brothers Bieda and Maegla landed at Portsmouth Harbour and pillaged Portchester

and Bitterne. They then made an alliance with the Gewissei and, by 508, the two factions had made themselves masters of the district between the mouth of the Itchen and Portsmouth Harbour.

Langport on the River Parrett in the old county of Somerset used to be an important river crossing, and at one time navigation to this location from the sea would have been possible. It appears that a battle took place here in 710 between Prince Geraint of Devon and invading Saxons from the Glastonbury area. However, the Battle of Llongborth would have been fought in the early years of the sixth century, when an earlier Geraint, a kinsman of Arthur, lost his life. It is possible that these two incidents have been confused with the result that Langport has wrongly been identified as Llongborth.

In 1740 Theophilus Evans suggested that Llongborth can be found at Lanporth near Tresaith in Ceredigion:

> It is the judgement of some that the place which the bard calls Llongborth is Llamporth in the parish of Penbryn in Ceredigion. There is a place near there commonly called Maesglas, but the old name was Maes-y-llas (The Field of the Killing) or Maes Galanas (The Field of the Massacre). There is another site in the neighbourhood, in the parish of Penbryn, called Perth Geraint.

However, Llongborth means the port or harbour of ships and Lanporth means the church by the harbour. A mound near a farm has been named Beddgeraint, no doubt to support the idea that Penbryn is the site of the Battle of Llongborth.

In the old British language the words Llongu Borth meant a 'Port of Boats' or 'Haven of Ships'. According to the well-known Arthurian scholar Geoffrey Ashe, in *A Guidebook to Arthurian Britain* (1983), it means 'Warship Port'. The word *Llong*, when translated from Welsh, suggests ships of all types, but this word originally comes from the Latin *Longa Navis* – 'A Port of Warships', in other words a naval base.

Which Geraint Died at Llongborth?

During the Dark Ages, Geraint was a very popular name and this simple fact has caused considerable confusion, resulting in the Battle of Llongborth being wrongly placed and misdated. Many Arthurian writers have tended to follow the same old standard theories and failed to study the genealogies properly. It would seem that Geraint Llyngesog, who died at Llongborth, has been confused with his grandson who also bore the same name.

163

On examining the 'Life of St Teilo', contained in the *Book of Llandaff*, we found that mention is made of a certain Gerennius, King of Cornwall. We are told that when St Teilo fled from the yellow plague to Armorica in 547, he passed through Cornwall and paid a visit to King Gerennius. The king was getting on in years, and Teilo promised him that when his death was near he would be sure to visit him. On his return from Armorica in about 555, Teilo brought a stone sarcophagus as a present for the elderly king. Landing at the fort of Dingerrin, in the parish of St Gerrans, Teilo set off to visit the king. He found him alive, but very ill. After receiving the communion, Gerennius very shortly passed away and he was laid in the sarcophagus provided by Teilo.

A later Geraint appears in Aneurin's epic poem *Y Gododdin*, which tells the story of the Battle of Catraeth, fought in the Scottish Lowlands between 586 and 603. This Geraint was a Strathclyde chieftain. The name appears yet again in the West Country when in 705 St Aldhelm wrote a letter to King Geraint, urging him to abandon certain Celtic religious customs in his realm and to conform to the ways of Rome. This Geraint fought against Ine, King of the West Saxons, at Taunton in 710, when he attempted to conquer Dumnonia.

Yet another Geraint was the son of Carannog, of the family of Cadell Deyrnllwg, and was prince of Erging or Archenfeld, in Herefordshire. The Welsh pedigrees make him the father of St Eldad or Aldate, Bishop of Gloucester, who was slain by the Saxons following the Battle of Dyrham in 577. The *Life of St Meven* states that St Eldad was a son of Gerascennus, King of Orcheus, a district in Gwent. It would appear that Orcheus is a misprint for Erchens, meaning Erging, and that Gerascen is an affected form of Geraint (the son of Carannog).

Which Geraint was Living in the Time of Arthur?
We need to look for a Geraint who lived in the early part of the sixth century, came from the 'region of Dyfnaint' (Devon/Cornwall) and was responsible for protecting a harbour that served as a naval base.

The most obvious candidate is Geraint Llyngesog, a West Country prince who lived in the fifth/sixth century. He was the son of Erbin and the grandson of Constantine the Blessed.[2] According to the Peniarth MS (No. 27, Pt II) he was married to Gwyar, the daughter of the Romano-British Prince Amlawdd Wledig. Their children named Selyf, Cyngar, Iestyn, Caw and Cadwy were all cousins to Athrwys ap Meurig (Arthur). Geraint's second wife was Enid, the daughter of Ynywl, Lord of Caerleon, whom Geraint delivered from great distress when he was deprived of his lands and position by an usurping kinsman.

Geraint took Enid home to Cornwall, where his father Erbin, exhausted by old age, resigned the kingdom of Dumnonia to him.

In addition, Geraint also held territory in Armorica. He had a court in Belle Ille and portions of newly acquired land at Blavet, in Morbihan, and near Martignon, in Côtes-du-Nord. Dedications to him include St Geran, Pontivy, which was the centre of his settlement, and another St Geran in the deanery of Porhoet, while the bishopric of Vannes has him as patron. There was also a Chapel of St Geran in Dol Cathedral, and between Loudeac and Pontivy is a parish of St Gerand.

Geraint was chosen as Pendragon to head the confederacy of British kingdoms upon the death of his uncle Ambrosius and he carried on the struggle against the Saxons. In consequence of this appointment, we find traces of his name in Wales, Herefordshire, Somerset and Cornwall. He had the honour of being canonised and four of his sons, Selyf, Cyngen, Iestin and Cadwy, are also included in the list of saints.

Geraint the Naval Commander
The Welsh Triads state that Geraint was a naval commander who possessed not only an army but also a fleet of ships. Known as Geraint Llyngesog (the Fleet-owner), he kept a fleet of six score ships moored in a harbour in the Severn Estuary, with six score men on board each one. Their purpose was to patrol the coast against the Saxon pirates, who, in conjunction with the Irish, infested the coast of the Severn Sea. Some readers may find this idea somewhat hard to accept for many of us tend to have preconceived ideas of the ancient Britons having limited resources and construction abilities. However, it is important to remember that many of the Roman methods of defence were continued by the British, and the presence of Geraint's fleet would have had a precedent for the Romans kept a fleet moored at Cardiff to protect the Severn Estuary.

Supporting Evidence at Lydney Park
On a hilltop overlooking the Severn, about 9 miles north-east of Chepstow, are the remains of a Roman temple dedicated to the god Nodens. This elaborate complex of buildings was erected within the southern part of a hill fort.

The Romans no doubt visited this site when they wished to find a cure for their various ailments. Nodens, who is associated with the sun, water and healing, is a Romano-Celtic version of Nudd, who can also be identified with the Irish hunting god Nuadha Argetletam (Nuada of the Silver Hand), while in Welsh he is known as Lludd Llawereint (Ludd of the Silver Hand). He is also equated with the Roman Neptune, making him a sea deity: a god of the sea, of commerce, the owner and giver of ships. This temple overlooking the estuary of the Severn was furnished with mosaics, altars, bronzes and nautical motifs which all suggest an association with seafaring.

The earliest date for the foundation of the temple would be AD 364. It survived into the fifth century and by then was surrounded by a defensive wall to protect it from barbarian raiders.

Excavations by Sir Mortimer Wheeler in 1928–9 revealed a fourth-century mosaic bearing the inscription 'PR.REL', which quite conceivably stands for Praefectus Reliquationis Classis. He was the supplies officer for the Western Fleet, which was probably moored in the Bristol Channel for defensive purposes. This naval commander, who dedicated a mosaic floor in the temple, was probably attached to a fleet set up to patrol the Bristol Channel, with its headquarters at the fort constructed at Cardiff.

The Importance of the Severn Estuary
The Severn Estuary played a major role in the shaping of Britain's history and it can even boast the second highest tidal range in the world. The difference in height between high and low water often exceeds 17m, and is only surpassed by the Bay of Fundy in Newfoundland.

Through the passing centuries the Severn Estuary has altered considerably and since the Dark Ages the river has become very silted. For every century that has passed since Arthurian times, the sea has risen approximately ¼ metre. This means that in the sixth century the high water level would have been 4m lower than it is today. A large-scale map will reveal the original bed of the Severn which today provides the only safe navigational channel for certain craft. The land on each side of it has been washed away by the fast-flowing river.

Along the Gwent coastline between Newport and Chepstow are the sites of several harbours that would have been in use in ancient times. They were to be found at inlets, referred to as pills (from the Welsh *pwll*, meaning hollow, inlet or creek), but in some instances now seem to be no more than mere indentations in the coastline, yet at one time they would have provided safe anchorages.

There has been traffic across the Severn since Roman times and these little harbours were once of great importance, for they had considerable influence on the development of this southern part of Gwent.

St Pierre Pill

The large houses Moynes Court, St Pierre and the Bishop's Palace at Mathern stand in close proximity to one another and are sited for easy access to the harbour at St Pierre Pill. The stream to this pill and also the one to Sudbrook, further along the coast, were once substantial rivers but they are now heavily silted and much diminished.

Fifteen centuries ago the harbour must have extended over the meadows which now separate St Pierre from Mathern, and it is recorded that in 1843 the water covered an area of 22 acres. As late as 1860 70-ton barges floated on the tide up St Pierre Pill, which stretched as far as the New Inn at Pwllmeyric (Meyric's Pool). We know this from the Nennius manuscript which refers to St Tewdrig's Well at Mathern: 'When the sea is full, at high tide, Severn is spread out as far as the well and the well is filled with much of the Severn . . .'.

The Ancient Harbour of Porth-is-Coed

According to the Welsh Triads, the three great ports of the Isle of Britain in ancient times were Porth-is-Coed (on the Severn Estuary in Gwent), Porth Wygar (at Cemaes, near Llanbadrig, Anglesey) and Porth Wyddno (Borth in old Cardiganshire).

The exact location of the Gwent port of Porth-is-Coed is difficult to ascertain for there are several possible sites. In old manuscripts the name is written as Porth Yshewydd or Porth Kiwedd and Porth Yskiwed, which probably translate as the 'Harbour of the Elder Wood'. The name was later written as Porthscueth and this became Portscuett and Portscuit, from which the present-day village of Portskewett takes its name, but this is not necessarily the site of the ancient harbour of Porth-is-Coed.

The size and obvious one-time importance of St Pierre Pill suggests that it may have been the site of Porth-is-Coed, and it is significant that the land to the west of the pill used to be known as Yscuit Cyst (Iscoed Shore).

The name St Pierre Pill is comparatively modern while the older name Porth-is-Coed (the Harbour below the Wood), corrupted into Porthiscuin and Potischivet (in the Domesday Book), has come down to us in the form of Portskewett. This was transferred from the harbour to the manor lying between it and Sudbrook (or Southbrook, its south-west boundary) and also to the church and village founded in the manor, a mile or so westward of the Pill.

Sudbrook Harbour

When, in AD 75, Julius Frontinus landed at Sudbrook with his invading army the coastline would have looked very different from how it appears today. It would have stretched out to Denny Island, separating the River Severn from the Nedern to form a large natural harbour. Such a different land formation would have made the crossing of the Severn much easier at this location, for the dangerous rapids now known as 'The Shoots' would have been avoided.

Guarding the harbour was a circular British promontory camp which was no doubt immediately stormed by the Roman invaders and used as a ferrying base. Today, only half of the camp remains, which is an indication of the coastal erosion that has taken place. Adjoining the camp is a ruined Norman chapel, which stands on the site of an earlier church, once known as the Church of the Castle of Conscuit. This is not a reference to nearby Caldicot Castle but relates to another name associated with the fort. This was Castell Twyn Iscoed – 'Fortress mound of Iscoed', which suggests that the part of the camp eroded away by the sea once contained a fortified mound.

The *Book of Llandaff* refers to a relevant grant made by the kings of Gwent to the bishops of Llandaff at the beginning of the tenth century. It recorded the gift of the Church of Castle Conscuit and lands with free approach for ships at the mouth of the Taroci (Troggy or Nedern Brook) and all its weirs and fisheries. One of the boundaries mentioned was the junction of the Taroci with the Severn Sea.

In the Welsh Triads this ancient harbour is referred to as Abertwggi and, as the Troggy Brook enters the River Nedern at Llanfair Discoed village (the Church of St Mary below the Wood), there is an obvious connection between the two names. The Troggy was once known as the Twrc and the Romans knew it as Tarocus.[3] Twrc means 'Boar' and in ancient charters in the *Book of Llandaff* its source is called Pen Tyrch, 'the Head of the Boar'. On the Ordnance Survey map the anglicised name of Troggy is given.

The Troggy brook rises on the edge of Wentwood, passes Maesgwyneth (mentioned in the *Mabinogion*), rounds Caerwent and, before reaching Caldicot, changes its name to Nedern. At Deepweir in Caldicot the brook divides with the main stream entering the Severn at Sudbrook Pill. In the mid-eighteenth century a new cut was made to improve the drainage, by which the Nedern was turned directly into Caldicot Pill and Sudbrook Pill became silted up as a result. In Roman times this harbour was known as Portus Tarogi, but cannot be seen as centuries of coastal erosion have obscured the site and it no longer resembles a port or harbour.

Abergwaitha Harbour
About 4 miles further down the coast and to the south of the village of Magor

is a small inlet which is all that remains of the once important harbour and settlement of Abergwaitha. This name suggests the mouth of the River Gwaitha but *gwaitha* comes from *gweithiau* and is the plural of *gwaitha* and it means works.

The stream, which rises near Penhow and flows through Magor, was restrained by artificial banks (*gweithiau*) to prevent flooding, and then on to the Severn, where the mouth (*aber*) of this stream became known as Abergwaitha.

This watercourse is now called 'Whitewalls reen' and in a medieval charter it is referred to as 'Alba Walda' – meaning a tide bank, sea bank or other bank for keeping out the flow of water. The English name perhaps arises from a corruption in the course of which *gwaitha* (or waith) has passed into 'white' and *walda* into 'wall'.

Today, the location is shown on the Ordnance Survey map as 'Cold Harbour', which is a name generally associated with Roman roads or camps, and there are numerous examples of such a place name in Britain. For example there is also a Cold Harbour Pill on the other side of the Severn near Avonmouth. 'Harbour' (Here-bearg) signifies a 'place of refuge' for a land army, or for a collection of ships forming a naval force.

The Burial Place of Geraint

If it can be assumed that the Battle of Llongborth was fought at one of the harbours along the Gwent side of the Severn Estuary, the next step is to seek a possible place where Geraint may have been buried after he was slain by the invading force.

Such an important royal commander would have been given a hero's burial and he would have long been remembered as a martyr who died defending his countrymen. The discovery of his burial site would help to confirm the general location of the Battle of Llongborth and thus provide yet another piece in the jigsaw puzzle.

The *Book of Llandaff* provides a very significant clue. In one of the ancient charters mention is made of an ecclesiastical site called 'Merthyr Gerein' (Martyrium of Geraint).[4] This name appears on old maps, but the present-day Ordnance Survey map shows it as Chapel Tump at Lower Grange Farm, near Magor. Here on a low mound once stood a little chapel overlooking the ancient port of Abergwaitha, which became deserted after the Black Death. It is possible that the simple building known as Merthyr Gerein was erected on this site as a martyrium raised to the honour of Geraint who fell at the Battle of Llongborth.[5]

169

CHAPTER 15

Arthur's Twelve Battles

The *Historia Brittonum*, compiled in the ninth century and attributed to Nennius, provides us with a list of twelve battles, long debated by Arthurian researchers endeavouring to identify their possible locations. However, all there is to go on is a list of ancient British place names which are very difficult to identify from any map, yet over the years a wide assortment of possible locations have been suggested, with little more reasoning than the similarity of placenames. It is interesting that Henry of Huntingdon, writing in the twelfth century, could not identify the battle sites even in his day, but perhaps he was expecting to find them all in England.

Nennius tells us that:

> The first battle was at the mouth of the river called Glein; the second, third, fourth and fifth on another river, which is called Dubglas in the region of Linnius, the sixth battle on the river called Bassas. The seventh battle was in the forest of Celidon, that is the battle of Coed Celidon. The eighth battle was at Castellum Guinnion, where Arthur carried the portrait of St Mary, ever Virgin, on his shoulders; and the pagans were routed that day, and there was a great slaughter of them through the power of our Lord Jesus Christ and the strength of the Holy Virgin Mary, His mother. The ninth battle was fought in Urbs Legionis. The tenth battle was fought on the shore of the river called Tribruit. The eleventh battle was fought on the mountain called Agned. The twelfth battle was on Mons Badonis, where in one day nine hundred and sixty men were killed by one attack of Arthur, and no one save himself laid them low, and he appeared as victor in all the battles.

Some researchers have raised objections to the even number of twelve, suggesting that there is something suspicious about a neat figure of one dozen. However, one might point out that there were in fact twelve battles

170

during the Wars of Roses and no doubt other parallels can be found. It is actually possible that Arthur only fought nine battles in this list and that one of them, 'on the river Dubglas', lasted four days. It is interesting that Geoffrey of Monmouth, who obviously makes use of the Nennius manuscript, does not name all the battles and assigns one only instead of four to the River Douglas.

This campaign list will long be argued over by Arthurian sleuths for not only are the ancient British names very difficult to identify on the map but the battle list does not give us any idea of where Arthur was based or his own domain. Did he fight the battles over a wide area or in just one part of the country? Numerous suggestions have been made for the battle sites, including places in Lincolnshire, Northumberland, Cheshire, Strathclyde, Somerset, Wiltshire, Berkshire and East Anglia.

Skene, writing in 1868, identified all the battles in Scotland. He was of the opinion that they all took place beyond Hadrian's Wall, and were aimed at recovering the territories of the North Cymru and securing their defences. In support of his theory Skene pointed out that it would explain why there is no mention of Arthur's battles in the *Anglo-Saxon Chronicle*, for it refers mainly to events south of the Humber.

Anscombe, in 1904, claimed that the battles were all fought in the Midlands. In 1929, Collingwood placed all the battles in the south-east, which suited his theory that Arthur only fought the Jutes. Ronald Millar, in his tongue-in-cheek book *Will the Real King Arthur Please Stand Up?* (1978), makes a good case for the battles all taking place in Brittany.

It is interesting that most of the battles took place either at river fords or in river valleys. The following locations are suggested for these twelve battle sites.

Battle 1 – 'At the Mouth of the River called Glein'
There is a River Glen in Northumberland, mentioned by Bede as the river where Paulinus baptised the Angles in 627; and also one in Lincolnshire, where to the south-east of Grantham runs the West Glen River to the east of Ermine Street. The East Glen River runs to the west and parallel with the course of another Roman road.

Nennius says that this battle was fought at the **mouth** of the River Glein which suggests a confluence. The River Glen in Northumberland is a tributary of larger rivers, so it has no mouth. The Glen in Lincolnshire, however, converges with the River Welland about 4 miles north of Spalding.

171

Battles, 2, 3, 4 and 5 – At 'On Another River which is Called Dubglas in the Region of Linnius'

This statement indicates a River Douglas in the area of Linnius. Nennius tells us that four battles were fought on a single river. Perhaps on four occasions Arthur prevented the enemy from crossing a river without actually defeating them.[1] Dubglas is Celtic for 'black river' and the form Dulas or Dowlais is a common name for water courses in Wales. Dulais is pronounced Dill lais or Dillas and Dubglas is Dulais Latinised.

Linnius is most likely an extension of the Roman Lindum, which is now Lincoln. If Linnius is Lincoln then the name may refer to Lindsey, the central and northern part of a district of Lincolnshire, which in the sixth century became an Angle kingdom. So, assuming this is the right location, Arthur's enemies at battles 2, 3, 4 and 5 were the Angles of Lindsey, and he probably based his forces at Lincoln, which at that time was the abandoned Roman fort of Lindum Colonia.

Arthur's cavalry would have ridden there along the great Roman highways which led from the south via the city of Uriconium (Wroxeter) in Shropshire. The purpose of his expedition would have been to deal with the Anglo-Saxon settlers who had arrived in their boats along the Wash and the Humber and advanced inland. Initially, Arthur may have fought the invaders on the banks of the Lincolnshire Glen, which flows towards the Wash. The next battle was possibly fought beside the River Douglas, which is also in Lincolnshire, just a few miles from an area called Lennox (probably Nennius's 'Linnius'), before finally defeating the enemy after two long battles fought on the same river.

On the west bank of the East Glen River is Bourne, where there are earthworks and a chalybeate spring called the Blind Well, which may be derived from Black Stream. The holy wells were sacred to the Britons and at least one of Arthur's battles may have been fought to preserve the Blind Well from the pagan invaders.

There is archaeological evidence for settlements of the Angles in present-day Lincolnshire. A series of Frisian-Angle urns dating from Arthur's time was discovered on Loveden Hill, which is south-west of Hough-on-the-Hill, south-west of Caythorpe and north of Grantham. A pot, dating from the same period and matching the urns from Loveden Hill, has been found at Drakelow, near Burton-on-Trent. This archaeological discovery denotes settlements by the Middle Angles at both Loveden Hill and Drakelow during the time of Arthur. The battle at or near Loveden Hill may have been fought to repossess the Romano-British town of Ancaster from the Middle Angles. Battlestead Hill at

Tatenhill overlooks the plain of the River Trent at Drakelow and it reputedly marks the site of a battle between the Britons and the invading Angles.

According to the *Chronicle of the Kings of Britain*, Arthur's principal ally in his campaign against the Angles of Lindsey was Hoel (Riwal) Mawr, the son of Emyr Llydaw.[2] Their combined forces probably rode to Lincoln along the Roman road that later became known as the Ermine Way. This name may be derived from Erme or Ermin, which are both variants of Armel or Ermel, and the road may have been named after Arthur in memory of this sixth-century expedition.

Arthur's Cavalry Force

As a leader of cavalry, it would certainly have been possible for Arthur to have fought battles over a wide area. His guerilla band, organised in light cavalry units, would have enjoyed a mobility that could not have been matched by the Saxons or the Angles, who rarely fought on horseback.[3]

It is relevant that the epic poem *Y Gododdin*, written in about 595, speaks of Britons riding long distances into battle. Also, it may be pointed out that Ceolwulf of Wessex fought the Angles, the Britons, the Picts and the Scots during the sixth and seventh centuries.

Arthur's task force of fast-moving cavalry would have been modelled on the earlier mounted cohorts of the Romans which ensured swift action whenever needed along the frontiers of the Empire.

It is important to realise that in the sixth century it would have been easier to travel long distances in Britain than it would have been, for example, in Norman times, for the intricate network of Roman roads was still intact and in relatively good condition.

Importance of the Roman Roads

During four centuries of Roman occupation, over 5,000 miles of main roads, paved, ditched on either side and cambered, were built in Britain. These roads were about 7m wide and covered in gravel to provide an all-weather surface for cavalry, heavy chariots and waggons. Initially, their purpose was to assist the legions in their conquest of Britain.

A marching army would have only covered 10 Roman miles in a day. If it was a forced march, then the distance might be doubled, but a cavalry unit or war band would have ridden 40 to 50 miles in a day. In the sixth century it would have been easier to travel, for example, from Caerleon to York along the Roman highways than it would have been in the eighteenth century, when Britain's roads were in a deplorable state.

In 613 Aethelfrith led an army 175 miles from his base at Bamburgh to Chester in order to do battle with Selyf, son of Cynan Garwyn. Cadwallon, in 633, set off with an army from his royal seat at Aberffraw in Anglesey and travelled more than 145 miles to fight Edwin at Hatfield Chase.

Such examples demonstrate that it would have been feasible for Arthur to have fought a series of battles spread over a wide area of Britain. Riding long distances was no doubt made easier by this time by the introduction of the knee-stirrup during the fifth century. This not only gave greater control over one's mount but enabled the rider to enjoy a less tiring seat in the saddle.

The Roman roads were still being used as routes to the sites of battles in later centuries. King Harold, in September 1066, rode south along Roman roads from London to Rochester and Maidstone to his fateful battle at Hastings. In 1485, Henry Tudor and Richard III fought the Battle of Bosworth beside a Roman road leading out of Leicester.

Battle 6 – Fought 'On the River Called Bassas'
This identification is particularly difficult, for 'bass' is a very common prefix in some parts of Britain. For example, there is a Bassingthorpe on Ermine Street, a Bassingham to the north-west of Leadenham, a Baschurch in Shropshire and a Bassaleg in Gwent.[4]

The *Brut Tysilio* records how:

> Howel Mawr, in consequence of an application for auxiliaries by King Arthur and his council of chiefs, came to Northampton, with fifteen thousand men at arms, to the great joy of Arthur. From there they rode to Caer Llwyd Coed, where the Saxons were. Here a furious battle ensued, in which six thousand of the Saxons perished, either slain or drowned.[5]

In 510, Glast, a great-grandson of Cunedda Wledig, is said to have been defending a strategic intersection of two Roman roads at Luitcoyt, which is near Lichfield. Near here, Watling Street, the road leading from London to Chester, was crossed by the Icknield Way. Luitcoyt was the Roman fort of Letocetum, which is situated about 2 miles west of Lichfield.[6] The fort was being besieged by an army of Middle Angles and we can surmise that Arthur came to Glast's assistance and routed the enemy in a battle fought on the banks of the River Bassas, now known as Hammerwich Water. This flows south-west of Lichfield and traces of its former name can be found in the three Staffordshire Basfords.

ARTHUR'S TWELVE BATTLES

The Importance of a Sacred Shrine at Letocetum

The village of Wall-by-Lichfield takes its name from the remains of a first-century Roman fort, known as Letocetum, a Latinised version of the Celtic word for 'the grey wood'. It developed in the second century as a civilian settlement and nearby was an important Celtic religious site where a Druidic grove was set in dense woodland.[7] It contained a pagan temple to Minerva, the Romanised form of the Celtic goddess Brigit, whose name can be found in other parts of Britain. This was a pagan temple of the Cornovii tribe whose name means 'worshippers of the horned one'. Cernunnos, 'the horned one', fits the description of the father god who was the ancestor of the Celtic tribes.

A number of carved stones with human horned heads have been found built into the walls of the old Roman settlement just below St John's Church. It would seem that the Romans destroyed the ancient shrine, but re-used these stones as a small gesture to the Celtic gods.

Julius Caesar recorded that 'the Gauls all assert their descent from Dis Pater and say that this is their Druidic belief'. He also stated that the Gallic Druids came to Britain for religious instruction, so it is evident that the principal seat of the cult of Dis Pater was in Britain.

The capture of this shrine at Letocetum by a Continental tribe would undoubtedly have been of considerable concern to the Britons and this would help to explain why a battle was fought here in Arthur's time.

Nearby Lichfield is a name derived from 'death's field' and it is likely that this stems from the tradition that Christians were slaughtered here by the Romans on an order from the Emperor Diocletian. It was undoubtedly an area of considerable importance to the Britons and one which would have been defended at all costs. Caer Luitcoet (Wall-by-Lichfield) was also the site of another battle in 656, when Prince Morfael of Luitcoyt joined Prince Cynddylan of Powys and won a victory over the invading Angles of Mercia under their King Peada.

The so-called Staffordshire hoard could well have been the property of Peada, the son of Penda. He had been appointed sub-king of Mercia by King Oswin of Northumbria after the defeat and death of Penda in 654.

The site of the burial place of Cynddylan is very likely to be the Berth at Baschurch in Shropshire. In the 'Marwnad Cynddylan' ('Lament for Cynddylan'), a ninth-century poem set in the seventh century, it is called the Churches of Bassa. It may also be identified with Pengwern.

Battle 7 – Fought at 'Cat Coit Celidon'

This battle in the Forest of Celidon is always pinpointed in Scotland for it is

175

generally believed that the name refers to Coed Celyddon (the Forest of Celyddon), which lies to the west of Selkirk and is now known as Ettrick Forest. The ancient extensive forest of Celidon or Caledonian Wood covered Dumfries, Selkirk and the head waters of the Clyde and the Tweed.

Arthur's enemies here would have been the Picts, perhaps joined by the Irish warriors who had founded the kingdom of Dalriada and later gave the Latin name of *Scotti* to the northern kingdom of Scotland. It has been suggested that Arthur's main purpose in fighting this battle was to deal with Hueil, a British nobleman who was in league with the Picts.

An alternative suggestion for the site of this battle was made by Gunn who first translated the Nennius manuscript. He identified it with Englewood Forest between Carlisle and Penrith, which places it in a more suitable position with the possible sites for battles 2, 3, 4, 5, 6 and 8.

But the identity of this battle site will always remain a problem, for the term 'celidon' or calyddon is said to mean coverts or thickets, and there may be something in Richard of Cirencester's statement that all the woods of Britain were once called 'Caledonia'. The term 'Callyddon' was once a usual denomination for extensive tracts of forest land and 'cat coit celidon' seems to imply that it was not one of the great Caledonian forests of Scotland, but some other of minor importance.

Battle 8 – At 'Castellum Guinnion'

Castellum Guinnion suggests a Roman auxiliary fort. Nennius provides an interesting clue in which he tells us that Arthur was carrying a shield bearing a portrait of the Virgin Mary and that the pagans were routed with great slaughter.[8]

It is of interest that an ancient shield, reputed to be the one carried by Arthur in this battle, used to be preserved in the Church of St Mary at Stow (anciently called Stow in Wedale), south-west of Lauder in the Borderlands. Significantly, the name Wedale means 'the dale of woe' and it was given to this valley by the Saxons, with the obvious implication that they experienced a great defeat here. Also, it may be more than coincidence that the church is dedicated to St Mary and not far away is the site of a Roman castellum which could have been the fort of Guinnion.

F.G. Snell, in his book *King Arthur's Country*, suggests: 'There is a chance that Castle Guinnion in the neighbourhood of which Arthur fought his eighth battle, is identical with Cair Guorthegirn, the castle or city of Vortigern, previously mentioned by Nennius.'[9]

Another possibility is that Caer Guinnion is another name for Caer Gwynt

(Caerwent). Guinnion may be derived from Gwyn meaning white and the old fort of Venta Silurum (Caerwent) is certainly white for its impressive walls are constructed of limestone.

Battle 9 – Fought in the *Urbs Legionis*
This can can generally be interpreted as 'a city where Roman legions were stationed'. and could apply to Caerleon, Chester, York, Lincoln, Colchester, Wroxeter, Gloucester or London (Londinium).

It may be significant that Manuscript D of the *Historia Brittonum* has recorded in its margin '*Qui Britannice Kairluin dicitur*'. This means 'which the British call Kaerliun'.

Important clues in the *Mabinogion* indicate that this battle is most likely to have been fought in the vicinity of Caerleon. The actual site of the battle may have been at the old Roman fort, as the name suggests, but it may also have taken place on the route of the Roman road on a ridgeway above Caerleon.

The story of 'Culhwch and Olwen' tells of Arthur pursuing his enemies, led by Osla Gyllelfawr (of the Long Knife), eastwards towards the Severn Estuary. It is reasonable to suppose that Osla followed the Via Julia which crossed the Usk on a trestle bridge, passed through Ultra Pontem and crossed the Wentwood ridge at a pass known today as Cat's Ash. This name is significant for the word cat is generally derived from cad, meaning battle, and the Celtic Ash is derived from the old English 'aesc'.

Therefore, it is feasible that Cat's Ash originated from Cad Aesc and represented the Battle of Oesc (or Aesc), who was the son of Hengist, and his corrupted name may be a folk memory of that event.[10] In ancient charters the name is given as Cathonen and there was once a public house here displaying a sign depicting a cat in an ash tree, which was an attempt to explain its English name.

Remnants of an ancient chapel can be seen at Cat's Ash and the fact that it is dedicated to St Curig, who was known as Curig Farchog ('the knight'), may be of some significance.[11]

Battle number 10 – 'On the Shore of the River Called Tribruit'
Various suggestions, including the Scottish Lowlands, have been made for the site of this battle. However, if one bears in mind that it occurred after a battle fought at the City of the Legions, it would seem logical to suppose that the enemy force was chased by Arthur to the Gwent shore of the Severn Estuary, which is a nearby and significant location.

177

A useful clue can be found in Tennyson's *Idylls of the King*. In the poem concerning Lancelot and Elaine he describes Arthur's tenth battle as follows: 'and down the waste sand-shores of Traeth Troit, where many a heathen fell'. Alfred Lord Tennyson spent a great deal of time in Gwent researching the story of King Arthur and he obviously based his account of Arthur's exploits on local traditions, many of which are no longer remembered. The original Cymric form of Traeth Troit can be found in two of the poems contained in the *Black Book of Carmarthen*.[12] It features in one as Trywruid and in the other as Traetheu Trywrid, which implies a sandy shore, and in this instance can only be applicable to a river having an estuary. It suggests a tract of sand where the tide comes in, but is left bare when the tide ebbs. There are two examples of a traeth in Wales to be found in Anglesey – Traeth Dulas and Traeth Llugwy, both locations where a river flows into an estuary, as at Chepstow in Gwent.

The story of Arthur's hunt of the Porcus Troit, is first recorded in the 'De Mirabilibus Britanniae' appended to Nennius's *Historia Brittonum*. However, it is told with greater elaboration in his hunt for the Twrch Trwyth (Irish Boar)[13] in the story of 'Culhwch and Olwen', contained in the *Mabinogion*. Here we learn that the course taken by the Twrch Trwyth was across Carn Cavall (near Rhayader in mid-Wales) and the Brecon Beacons to Aber Gwy, where the Wye falls into the Severn below Chepstow. The princely monster then dashed into a flood, to appear for a short time in Cernyw, before he vanished entirely from view. This riddle story appears to be a folk memory of the expulsion of the Gewissei from Gwent. It becomes apparent that the Gewissei were collectively known by the Welsh as the Twrch Trwyth, or Irish pig.[14]

The *Brut Tysilio* mentions Arthur and Hoel viewing a lake near the Severn, called Llyyn Lliwan. Arthur says, 'There is also a lake near the Severn which ebbs as the tide fills, and does not rise to the surface, not withstanding the influx of fresh water, and throws out mountainous waves of water from which those who face them scarcely escape with life; whereas those whose backs are to it, escape however near they be.'

A description of this remarkable lake also appears in the tract entitled 'De Mirabilibus Britanniae', contained in Nennius's *Historia Brittonum*:

> There is another wonder, which is Aber Llyyn Lliwan, the mouth of which river opens into the Severn, the sea in the like manner flows into the mouth of the above-named river, and is received into a pool at its mouth, as into a gulf, and does not proceed higher up. There is a beach near the river, and when the tide is in the Severn, that beach is not covered; and when the sea and the Severn recede, then the pool

178

Lliwan disgorges all that it had swallowed from the sea and that beach is covered therewith, and it discharges and pours it out in one wave, in sight like a mountain. If there should be a whole army of all that country there, and they should turn their faces towards the wave, it would draw the army to it by force, their clothes being full of moisture, and their horses would be drawn in like manner. But should the army turn their backs towards the wave, it will not injure them. When the sea has receded, then the whole beach which the wave had covered is left bare again, and the sea retires from it.

John Nettleship, writing on behalf of the Caerwent Historic Trust, provides an explanation for the lake once known as Llyyn Lliwan. He comments:

Just east of the former Roman town of Caerwent there were two large swallow holes, blocked up 125 years ago, called the Whirley Holes. Swallow holes are a feature of limestone geology and often, as with icebergs, there's more below the surface than seen above! We gather that the water of the stream (the Nedern) made quite dramatic appearances and resurgences at these holes, such that they were regarded as one of the 'Wonders of Britain'.

Although the site is now 2 miles from the banks of the Severn Estuary, we believe that the water at high tide rose to only a short distance from Caerwent.

It is only in the last 400 years that the sea wall and drainage schemes have established a reliable coastline here. The drainage increased with the building of the Severn Tunnel and has increased again such that Llyyn Lliwan, from being a brackish or tidal lake has shrunk to a wetland which is becoming less and less wet, drained by a frequently dry stream (the Nedern or Cas Troggy Brook). However, some winters Llyyn Lliwan reasserts itself with a vengeance, attracting hundreds of migratory geese, and fortunately for motorists the M48 is carried on a viaduct above it.

This location fits in well with the 'Culhwch and Olwen' story: Twrch Trwyth probably knew his escape routes – he will have been heading for the Severn Crossing at Black Rock or the nearby one at Sudbrook. These are between the mouth of the Nedern and the mouth of the Wye. However, unless he reached there at low tide, he is unlikely to have survived.

179

The phenomenon of the Severn Bore starts when the incoming Atlantic tide is confronted by the constriction and rising bed of the Bristol Channel.[15] The tide, which is then 3–5ft high, runs into the continental shelf which increases its height. This 50-mile tidal wave is thus trapped between Cornwall and South Wales, and in the 85 miles to Avonmouth is reduced in width to 5 miles, being squeezed to a great height as it enters the funnel-like Severn Estuary.

At a particularly high tide the in-rush of the water from the sea stops the flow of river water and forces it back upstream, forming a moving wave or bore which occurs on roughly 135 days of the year. Really large bores, numbering about fifty, are seen from February to April and August to October, reaching their peak at the vernal and autumnal equinoxes.

Battle 11 – 'Fought on the Mountain Called Agned'

This has always seemed to defy all attempts at even guessing a feasible location. The brief description suggests a hill named after a person called Agned and over the years many an Arthurian sleuth has spent long hours scanning old maps in search of anything remotely resembling this name. However, there is an alternative name for this battle, for in some versions of the Nennius manuscript it is referred to as Cath Breguoin.

The Vatican manuscript states: 'The eleventh battle was on the mountain called Breguoin where they [the enemy] were put to flight, which we call Cat Bregion [Battle of Bregion].'

Quite by chance a clue to its location came to light in a book written by Joseph Ritson in 1825, entitled *The Life of King Arthur from Ancient Historians and Authentic Documents*. Ritson had examined the Cotton Nennius manuscript and noticed in the margin opposite this particular battle someone had written, 'In Somersetshire, quem nos Cath bregion'.

Just north of Bristol, at one end of Filton airfield, is a place named Catbrain and quite close to it is the site of a hill fort. As previously stated, the word 'cat' or 'cad' generally seems to indicate an old battle site and 'brain' may well be derived from Bregion. The location of this place is now in the county of Avon, but prior to local government reorganisation in 1974 it would have been in the old county of Somersetshire, which of course agrees with the comment on the manuscript.

It is certainly a feasible location for Arthur's eleventh battle, for geographically it makes sense if one accepts that the Battle of Badon, which followed, was fought at Bath, as stated by Geoffrey of Monmouth.

This most important twelfth battle will be dealt with in the next chapter.

CHAPTER 16

The Battle of Badon

The first writer to mention the Battle of Badon is Gildas who refers to it as 'Mons Badonicus' and describes it as a siege in which the Saxons were defeated and states that it was followed by forty years of peace.[1] Unfortunately, Gildas neither gives an exact date for the battle, nor provides any clues to its location, and does not say who was actually besieged. Was it the Saxons or the Britons? It is also annoying that he does not give the name of the commander of the British army, and there has been much debate whether it was Arthur or Ambrosius.[2] Nennius, writing two centuries after Gildas, says that it was Arthur and the *Annales Cambriae* confirm that Arthur was at least involved in the battle: '518 The Battle of Badon, in which Arthur wore the cross of our Lord Jesus Christ on his shoulders for three full days and in which the Britons were victorious.' Nennius on the other hand is more explicit about the part played by Arthur, for he tells us that: 'The Twelfth battle was on Mons Badonis, where in one day nine hundred and sixty men were killed by one attack of Arthur and no one save himself laid them low.'[3]

In order to accept the *Annales Cambriae* date of 518 for the Battle of Badon it is necessary to sort out a confusing statement made by Gildas. He gives the impression that the battle was fought at Mons Badonicus in the year of his own birth – forty four years before he wrote his *De Excidio et Conquesta Britanniae*. However, this would mean that if the battle took place in 518 this would bring the composition of *De Excidio* to 562. This would not make sense for Gildas verbally attacks Maelgwyn, King of Gwynedd, who died at the outbreak of yellow plague in AD 547. This is the date given in the *Annales Cambriae* for Maelgwyn's death and Gildas in his work gives the impression that Maelgwyn is still alive.

Further examination of the words of Gildas is thus necessary:

> That they might not be utterly destroyed, they [the Britons] take up
> arms and challenge their victors to battle under Ambrosius Aurelianus
> . . . To these men there came victory. From that time, the citizens were

181

sometimes victorious, sometimes the enemy . . . This continued up to the year of the siege of Mount Badon and of almost the last great slaughter inflicted upon the rascally crew. And this commences as the forty-fourth year, with one month now elapsed.

This statement of Gildas gives us two undated events, the victory of Ambrosius and the victory at Mount Badon between which there was a period of success and defeat. It is highly probable that Gildas was referring to this period in between the two battles as forty-four years' duration 'less a month'. So, if the Battle of Badon took place in 518 then the battle fought by Ambrosius and the start of the aforementioned period of forty-four years was in 474.

Furthermore, the passage 'It is also the year of my birth' refers not to the year of Mount Badon, but perhaps to that of the victory of Ambrosius. Such an explanation provides a practical solution to the frequently discussed problem of the dating of Badon which has been caused by the strange literary style of Gildas.

Bede says, in his *Ecclesiastical History of the English Nation*: 'until the year of the siege of Mons Badonicus when they inflicted not the smallest slaughter upon their enemies in about the forty-fourth year from their coming into Britain'. It is possible that Bede had an earlier copy of Gildas's manuscript than we possess today and it contained what was actually written, rather than a copyist's error. It is possible that Gildas may have written: 'the forty-fourth year from their first coming into Britain, and which, was also the year of my birth'. If Gildas was born in 517 and the *Annales Cambriae* says that he died in 570 then he would have been 53 years old when he died and about 30 years of age when he wrote his manuscript.

Matters have been further confused by a statement in the *Annales Cambriae* that a second Battle of Badon was fought in the year 665. It would appear that there was approximately 150 years between these two battles and in the second one, 'Morcantius' was slain. A possible site for this battle is on Mynydd Baedon in Glamorgan, where a number of entrenchments can be seen. The victim mentioned was most likely Morgan, the great-great-grandson of Arthur, whose court was significantly just a few miles away at Margam.

Where was the Battle of 'Mons Badonicus' Fought?
Various locations have been suggested for the site of the first Battle of Badon and they include the following:

1. Liddington Castle, an Iron Age hill fort near Swindon in Wiltshire
2. Badbury Hill, near Farringdon in Wiltshire
3. Badbury Rings, a hill fort near Wimborne Minster in Dorset
4. Baydon (first known as Beidona in 1146), a few miles east of Badbury, Wiltshire. To the north of the village is the steep hill of Baydon, the earliest spelling of which is 'Beidona'
5. Bath, where there are the hill forts of Bannerdown and Solsbury Hill

The Vital Clues

Gildas tells us that Mons Badonicus was near the mouth of the Severn. This is a reasonable description of a hill near Bath and certainly excludes such sites as Badbury Hill, near Farringdon, Badbury Rings, Liddington Castle and Baydon in Wiltshire. He also speaks of 'the siege of Mount Badon' ('Obsessionis Badonici Montis'). This gives us a picture of a hill crowned by a fort, a distinct and separate hill at or near a place known as Badon. Only Solsbury Hill is a separate mons, sharply escarped on all sides and small enough to be defended by a body of dismounted cavalry. It certainly suits the description of Gildas and the nature of the campaign.[4]

Gildas states that the Battle of Badon ushered in a period of peace which was still lasting when he wrote his *De Excidio et Conquesta Britanniae* in about 545. The *Anglo-Saxon Chronicle* appears to support this statement by not recording any serious battles between the Saxons and the Britons between the years 519 and 552.

Nennius speaks of 'the hot lake, where the baths of "Badonis" are in the country of the Hwicce.[5] It is surrounded by a wall, made of brick and stone, and men go there to bathe at any time and every man can have the kind of bath he likes. If he wants, it will be a cold bath; and if he wants a hot bath it will be hot.'

The *Annales Cambriae* refers to 'Bellum Badonis – the battle of Badon'.

The *Anglo-Saxon Chronicle* tells of the later capture of Bath in 577 and refers to the place as Badanceaster, the 'City of Bath'.

Bede mentions 'the siege of Baddesdown Hill' and this name certainly resembles Bannerdown Hill, which overlooks Bath. John Aubrey, when writing his *Monumenta Britannica* in about 1680 (it was not published until 300 years later), made the suggestion that the Battle of Badon was connected with a siege of Bath and that it took place on the hill called Banner Down which is situated at Batheaston on the outskirts of Bath, and in common with most of the neighbouring hills has remains of entrenchments. It is a large camp enclosing 30 acres, defended on three sides by steep slopes.

William of Malmesbury also describes the battle as a siege and tells us that 900 Saxons were engaged. This seems a more acceptable estimate than that of Nennius, who claims that 940 of the enemy were slaughtered by Arthur. Nennius probably mistook the figure of those engaged for the casualty list, and his statement that Arthur alone killed them means that Arthur won the battle with his own army, without the assistance of the soldiers of other British kings.

Brut y Brenhinedd calls the site of the battle Caer Faddon, a name that is used elsewhere to represent Geoffrey of Monmouth's Badon (Bath).

Geoffrey of Monmouth, no doubt influenced by Gildas, Nennius and Bede, identifies Bath as the site of the Battle of Badon, which he describes as follows:

> Then they [the Saxons] proceeded by a forced march to the neighbourhood of Bath and besieged the town . . . Arthur put on a leather jerkin worthy of so great a king. On his head he placed a golden helmet, with a crest carved in the shape of a dragon; and across his shoulders a circular shield called Pridwen, on which there was painted a likeness of the Blessed Mary, Mother of God, which forced him to be thinking perpetually of her. He girded on his peerless sword called Caliburn, which was forged in the Isle of Avalon. A spear called Ron graced his right hand: long, broad in the blade and thirsty for slaughter. Arthur drew up his men in companies and then bravely attacked the Saxons, who as usual were arrayed in wedges. All that day they resisted the Britons bravely, although the latter launched attack upon attack. Finally, towards sunset, the Saxons occupied a neighbouring hill, on which they proposed to camp. Relying on their vast numbers, they considered that the hill in itself offered sufficient protection. However, when the next day dawned, Arthur climbed to the top of the peak with his army, losing many of his men on the way. Naturally enough, the Saxons, rushing down from their high position, could inflict wounds more easily, for the impetus of their descent gave them more speed than the others who were toiling up. For all that the Britons reached the summit by a superlative effort and immediately engaged the enemy in hand-to-hand conflict. The Saxons stood shoulder to shoulder and strove their utmost to resist.
>
> When the greater part of the day had passed in this way, Arthur went beserk, for he realised that things were still going well for the enemy and that victory for his own side was not yet in sight.

He drew his sword Caliburn, called upon the Blessed Virgin and rushed forward at full speed into the thickest ranks of the enemy. Every man whom he struck, calling upon God as he did so, he killed at a single blow. He did not slacken his onslaught until he had dispatched four hundred and seventy men with his sword Caliburn. When the Britons saw this they poured after him in close formation, dealing death on every side. In this battle fell Colgrin with his brother Baldulf and many thousands of others with them. Cheldric, on the contrary, when he saw the danger threatening his men, immediately turned in flight with what troops were left to him. As soon as Arthur had gained the upper hand, he ordered Cador, the Duke of Cornwall, to pursue the Saxons . . .

Clear evidence is provided by Geoffrey that in his time Bath was known by the Britons as 'Caer Baddon'. The Welsh word for a bath is *baddon* and the hill overlooking the city was perhaps known in Welsh as Mynydd yr Baddon (Bath Mountain) – and in Latin Mons Badonicus. The double 'dd' has in Welsh the sound of 'th', as in though; thus we have Caer Baddon, pronounced Bathon. The English later abbreviated this to Bath.

In Book II, Chapter ii of Geoffrey's history, he makes Merlin prophesy that 'The baths of Badon shall grow cold and their salubrious waters engender death'. Geoffrey can only be alluding to the waters of Bath.

Who was Arthur Fighting?

In recent times, historians have tended to dismiss Bath as a site for the Battle of Badon, claiming that the Saxon invaders had not penetrated this far into the south-west by the time of this conflict. However, this argument does not stand up if we substitute the Gewissei for the Saxons. It is important to realise that Arthur's protracted campaign against the Gewissei culminated in his victory at Caer Badon and resulted in their expulsion from south Wales and Somerset.

The centre of the Gewissei activity was at Bradford-on-Avon, just 2 miles east of Bath. It was formerly known as Wirtgernesburg (Vortigern's Town) after Vortigern, *Dux* Gewissei. The statement by Nennius that 'the Hot Lake, where the baths of Badon are in the country of the Hwicce' confirms that this area was once occupied by the Gewissei.

Arthur was fighting the combined forces of Osla Gyllefawr, the leader of the Jutes, Cerdic, leader of the Gewissei, and Bardolfus, the son of Aelle of the South Saxons. Geoffrey of Monmouth confusingly refers to Cerdic as

'Cheldric' and tells us that he was slain by 'Cador' (Cadwy, the son of Geraint, who was killed at Llongborth).[6]

The Roman City of Aquae Sulis

The three hot springs that have made Bath so famous must have been a source of wonder to the Celts who first settled here, and they set up a shrine to the goddess of the remarkable water, who they named Sul or Sulis. In both Welsh and old Irish, the words *sul* and *sulis* mean an eye, gap or orifice. Such words describe the nature of the springs and conveniently provide a suitable name for the presiding goddess.

It was the presence of these hot springs that attracted the Romans to this valley for they did not build a fort or station a military garrison here, yet it certainly had some military value for it commanded the gorge of the River Avon, upon which several Roman roads converged. The Romans used the place mainly as a spa and around the ancient springs they constructed a 23-acre walled town which became an important centre of medicinal bathing.

The Romans first called their city Aquae Calidae (hot waters) but subsequently changed the name to Aquae Sulis (the waters of Sul). It was generally their policy not to suppress the native deities, but to combine them with their own gods. They no doubt reconstructed the Celtic shrine, with its druidical associations, and incorporated this sacred site into a new Roman temple, where offerings could be made to Sulis-Minerva, who was a combination of the Roman goddess of Healing and Sulis, her native counterpart.

When the legions departed in about 410, many Romans stayed behind and for a while the old city of Aquae Sulis would still have functioned as a spa for the local Romano-British population. However, by the sixth century the city would have been abandoned and in ruins, although as a sacred site it would still have been of great importance to the Britons.

Consequently, it was most desirable that it should be defended and not allowed to fall into the hands of the enemy. This was no doubt the main reason why the Battle of Badon was fought. The Celts believed that their springs and holy wells were entrances to a mystical underworld occupied by their ancestors. It is for this reason that there are many examples of lakes and springs where votive offerings have come to light.

The Later Destruction of Aquae Sulis

In 577 the old city of 'Caer Badon' fell to the Saxons when a force led by King Ceawlin defeated the Britons at the Battle of Deorham (Dyrham),

186

5 miles to the north of Bath.[7] An eighth-century English poem entitled 'The Ruin' tells how the city of Bath was stormed, its buildings overthrown and 'death destroyed all'. For a century or so afterwards the place lay desolate, until, in about 676, a Saxon monastery was founded here by Osric and the settlement that grew up around it became known by the Saxons as Acemannesceaster, a corruption of Aquae-ceaster. It was later called Bathu (hot baths) and by the time of the Domesday Book was known as 'Bade'.

The healing waters of the hot springs continued to flow and in the Middle Ages other baths were built on the spot to take advantage of the waters' curative powers. By the seventeenth century the city reached its peak of elegance under Beau Nash, but the Roman baths had silted up, the roof and walls collapsed and the ancient bathing establishment disappeared from view. Its ruins lay buried until towards the end of the nineteenth century when they were revealed as a most important discovery.

Clues in the *Mabinogion*
The composition of the ancient tale entitled 'The Dream of Rhonabwy' in its present form has been dated to the tenth century, but was written down in the second decade of the thirteenth century. It is contained in the *Red Book of Hergest* and was probably influenced by the writings of Geoffrey of Monmouth.

The story is set in 1132 at the start of the reign of Madog, son of Mareddud, Prince of Powys (d.1159). It tells how his brother Iorwerth becomes an outlaw and Madog musters his war band to seek him throughout his land.

Rhonabwy and his companions, while on this search for Iorwerth, stay at the house of Heilyn Goch (the Red). Rhonabwy goes to sleep upon a yellow ox-skin and in his dream travels back to the age of King Arthur. With his companions, Rhonabwy is led to the ford of Rhyd-y-Groes on the Severn, where a mighty host is encamped. On a flat island below the 'Ford of the Cross of the Severn', King Arthur sits in state, with all the pomp of a Roman Emperor about him. There is 'Bedwini the Bishop on one side of him, and Gwrthegydd, the son of Kaw, on the other.' Among his retainers are his cousin March (or Mark), the son of Meirchion, Edern the son of Nudd, Kai, 'the fairest horseman in Arthur's court' and a number of others, many of whose names appear in the long catalogue given in the tale of Culhwch and Olwen. Preparations are in progress for the Battle of Badon.

Arthur is engaged in a game of 'gwydbyll', which is played with gold pieces on a silver board. His opponent is Owain, who is attended by a flock of ravens. Then troop after troop come riding towards the ford and Rhonabwy travels with Iddawc and with 'Arthur and his army of mighty ones' towards Caer Badon.

But the impending battle does not take place, for Arthur's enemy Osla sends horsemen to ask for a truce. A council is held and the truce is agreed. Kai rises to urge all who follow Arthur to be with him that night in Cernyw. With the consequent noise Rhonabwy then awakes.

This story was possibly composed either during Madog ap Maredudd's lifetime or very shortly after his death. The writer is remembering another famous battle and associates it with Arthur's Battle of Badon which he transfers from Gwent to a location near Welshpool in Powys.

However, 'The Dream of Rhonabwy' does in fact provide clues to the true location of the Battle of Badon and also the site of Arthur's fort of Gelliwig.[8] In the story Arthur is gathering his army together on the banks of the Severn prior to fighting the Battle of Badon. He is described as sitting on a flat island just below a fording point on the river and he is accompanied by Bishop Bedwin.

The mention of this bishop is of particular interest for he also appears in the *Mabinogion* story of 'Culhwch and Olwen', in which we are told that he was the 'one who blessed Arthur's meat and drink'. One of the Welsh Triads states that Bedwini presided as archbishop over Arthur's court at Gelliwig in Gwent. The description of Arthur sitting with Bedwini on an island in the Severn is significant because on the Ordnance Survey map at a point just below the ancient crossing point is a strip of land called the Bedwin Sands. This connects with Denny Island, which may well have been the island in question. The *Mabinogion* story tells that Arthur's great army is gathering here to fight the Battle of Badon at noon, and it is again significant that Caer Badon (Bath) would have been just a few hours ride from here.

The Battle of Badon resulted in a fifty-year period of peace for the Britons and enabled them to become a united nation. It may be said that this was Arthur's greatest achievement but sadly on his abdication in 537 the unity quickly disintegrated.

CHAPTER 17

Arthur's Gallic Campaign

Geoffrey of Monmouth tells us that immediately after the festivities following Arthur's crown-wearing ceremony at Caerleon-on-Usk messengers from Lucius Hiberius, the Roman Emperor, arrived, demanding tribute on the grounds that Britain was once a Roman province. After much discussion, it is agreed that these outrageous demands can only be answered by marching on Rome. Arthur sails with his army to France and lands at Barfleur.

As he was likely to be detained abroad some time, Arthur left Medraut, his nephew, as regent in his absence, at the same time entrusting him with the care of his wife. Medraut, hungry for power, saw his chance and seized Arthur's realm and queen.

Geoffrey of Monmouth in fact speaks of Arthur leading two expeditions into Europe: 'Arthur sailed off to Gaul. He drew his troops up in companies and began to lay waste the countryside in all directions. The province of Gaul at that time was under the jurisdiction of Tribune Frollo, who ruled it in the name of the Emperor Leo.'

Geoffrey has Arthur fighting battles in Gaul for nine years and tells us that 'he returned to Britain just as spring was coming on'. It is possible that Geoffrey's account of this long campaign by Arthur is based on the late fourth-century invasion of Gaul by Magnus Maximus. In 383, Magnus, who was originally from Spain, having served in Britain for a number of years, led a British army into Gaul against the Roman Emperor Gratian. After Gratian was killed, Maximus ruled over the north-western part of the Roman Empire, comprising the provinces of Britain, Gaul and Spain. He then invaded Italy and took Milan but was defeated and killed in 388 on what later became the border between Italy and Yugoslavia. Geoffrey may well have taken the story of Magnus Maximus and attached it to Arthur.

Geoffrey of Monmouth refers to Arthur and Hoel Mawr mounting a joint expedition into Gallic territory and it would seem that Arthur took a force over to the Continent to help his kinsman Hoel (Riwal) Mawr against an

189

invasion of the Visigoths during the reign of the Frankish King Clovis I (482–511), whose wife was a Christian from Burgundy.

The combined forces of Hoel and Arthur succeeded in repelling a seaborne attack by the Visigoths at Baden, situated south-west of Vannes, the ancient capital of the Venetii. It had been wrested from them by the legions of Julius Caesar in 56 BC and was originally called Daritoritum. In 510 the Venetii of Vannes appointed Arthur as their *Dux*. Significantly, there is a curious custom called Armel Beniquet, the 'Blessed Hammer', in the majority of the chapels in the vicinity of Vannes. Armel is named among the Breton saints as the 'Price Bear' (Excellent Bear). According to Rapin de Thoyras (1732), Arthur signifies a 'horrible bear', or an **iron hammer**, from the British word 'arth', a bear.

The Silures were a branch of the Venetii, whose capital was Vannes, so, as a hereditary king of the Silures, Arthur's campaigns on the Continent were fought to protect his motherland.

Arthur left Riwal with part of his army and, in due course, Riwal was able to exercise sovereign jurisdiction over the kingdom of Armorican Domnonia. He continued to rule this area jointly with Arthur as *Dux Britanniarum* until his death in 524 at the memorable Battle of Langres.

In Thomas Malory's *Le Morte d'Arthur*, Arthur forms an alliance with King Bors of Gaul and King Ban of Benwick (or Bayonne) in France. To gain their support, Arthur has to help them in battle against their enemy King Claudas. This monarch is probably synonymous with Clovis I, King of the Franks (482–511) and thus a contemporary of the real King Arthur.

Clovis made Paris his capital in 486. He is reported to have defeated a British (Breton) force around 490. By 494 he had conquered all of northern Gaul and as late as 530, according to the *Life of St Dalmas, Bishop of Rodez*, a 'legio Britannica' was based at Orléans (Gallic: Cenabum; Roman: Aurelianum).

This was part of the territory of the Carnutes, who rebelled against Rome in 52 BC, murdering many Roman traders.[1] Julius Caesar retaliated by burning the town and massacring the inhabitants, but the Carnutes still had 12,000 men under arms and again made trouble for Julius Caesar in 51 BC.

What was the Reason for the Carnutes's Rebellion?
In the first century BC the Carnutes were the dependents of the Remi, who were friendly with Rome, but in 53 BC they suddenly broke off relations with Julius Caesar, who had invaded Britain in 55 and 54 BC with a view to conquest.

The high priests of the Carnutes were Druids, who were alarmed at the prospect of the Romans sacking their sacred groves and shrines. Their principal grove was at Autricum (Chartres) and there was very likely another at Cenabum (Orléans), but their instructions came from a sacred centre in Britain – Caer Llwyd Coed (the Camp in the Grey Wood) at Lichfield. If Julius Caesar had made an all-out attempt at a conquest of Britain then the 'Holy of Holies' of the high priests of the Carnutes would have been under threat. This may have been the principal reason why the Carnutes broke off relations with Julius Caesar and rebelled.

King Arthur seems also to have concerned himself with protecting the sacred groves. He may have fought a battle against the Middle Angles at Caer Llwyd Coed to protect the sacred grove there, so there is good reason to suppose that he stationed his legion at Cenabum in order to protect its sacred grove.

The only portion of Gaul not subdued by Clovis I and his Franks was Bretagne (Brittany), now ruled over by Hoel, the cousin and subject of Arthur. Reviving the claims of his predecessors to the Gallic dominions, Arthur in five years (521–6) achieved the conquest of Gaul.

There is a distinct possibility that Arthur allied himself to the Burgundians in their ongoing feud against the Merovingian Franks. Clodomir, the son and successor of Clovis, fell fighting the Burgundians in a great battle on the plain of Langres in 524. We also know that Hoel Mawr died in the same battle, fighting alongside Arthur, his kinsman and ally.

The feud had been brought about by Chrotechildis (Clotild), the widow of Clovis who was by birth a Burgundian. She urged her sons to avenge the deaths of her parents, not on the murderer, her uncle Gundobad, but his sons, Sigismund and Godomar. In other words, the Merovingian princes were required by their mother to attack their second cousins. This they then proceeded to do and defeated the Burgundian princes, imprisoning Sigismund, perhaps with the intention of obtaining a heavy ransom. Godomar escaped and managed to prevent the Frankish invasion.

It was only on a later occasion, after a second attack had become necessary, that Clodomir decided to kill the imprisoned Sigismund and his family, throwing them down a well. However, the Burgundians under the surviving brother Godomar would not submit, so Clodomir persuaded his half-brother Theuderic to join him in a fresh attack on Burgundy.

This is when Arthur and his kinsman Riwal took up the Burgundian cause, and a great battle was fought on the plain of Langres in 524. The Burgundian contingent under Godomar was defeated, but the Bretons under Arthur and

Riwal prevailed. Clodomir was reputedly killed by Arthur himself. His head was severed and raised on a spear, so publicly demonstrating the Burgundian viewpoint in the feud.

The Legend of Goeznovius

This account was written in 1019 by a Breton called William, chaplain to Bishop Eudo of Léon. He claims to have based his story on an earlier manuscript called *Ystoria Britannica* (now lost). His work has a few references to Arthur and tells us that he was 'King of the Britons', that he fought successfully against the Saxons in Britain and Gaul and 'was summoned at last from human activity'. This work preceded Geoffrey's *Historia* and states that Arthur fought in Gaul and that he disappeared in mysterious circumstances.

The *Chronicle of St Brieuc*

In Latin this chronicle is known as the *Chronicon Briocense* and in French as the *Chronique de Saint Brieuc*. Its anonymous author, who was most probably Hervé le Grant, the ducal archivist and secretary to Jean IV (1341–5) and Jean V (1365–99), said that he was moved to compose his work, which breaks off in 1416, because little mention appeared in French chronicles of Breton kings and, especially, that Arthur's deeds were ignored. In his view, the Grand Chroniques of the Capetians and Valois suppressed many laudable Breton deeds which he proposed to rescue from oblivion.

The 'Chronique Briocense' was edited by Dom Pierre Hyacinthe Morice in *Memoirs pour servir de preuves a l'histoire ecclésiastique et civile de Bretagne* (Charles Osmont, Paris, 3 vols, 1742–6). It is still of fundamental importance as it contains both narrative and record sources, although many of its contents have been re-edited. (See Patrick Galliou and Michael Jones, *The Bretons* (1991), pp. 231, 232 and 292.)

It is very significant that the *Chronique de Saint Brieuc* cites the *Legenda Sancti Goeznovii* (*Legend of St Goeznovius*), which was seen by Albert Le Grand in the seventeenth century. He describes it as being written by William, chaplain of Bishop Eudo of Léon, during the second year of his episcopacy in 1019. The Legend tells (1) how the Bretons and the insular British lived for such a long time on friendly terms; (2) of the usurpation of Vortigern; (3) the coming of the Saxons; (4) the victories of Arthur both in Britain and in Gaul; and (5) the final Saxon conquest, which led to further emigration from Britain to Brittany.

The *Legend* contains material additional to and in some respects different from the British source the *Historia Brittonum*, and the use made of the source by Geoffrey of Monmouth in the *Historia Regum Britanniae*.

What is unusual is that the legend dates Arthur's Gallic victories to the late 460s, whereas Geoffrey accepts the sixth-century dating to within a few years. The author of the *Chronique de Saint Brieuc* opted for Geoffrey's dating in the *Historia Regum Britanniae* so it seems obvious that William, the author of the *Legenda Sancti Goeznovii*, confused Arthur with Riothamus.[2] This aberration was recognised by the author of the *Chronique de Saint Brieuc*, but not by Geoffrey Ashe in *The Discovery of King Arthur* (1985).

There is evidence that knowledge of Arthur was widespread in Brittany prior to the publication of Geoffrey of Monmouth's *Historia Regum Britanniae*. In 'The English Journey of the Laon Canons' the renowned Arthurian scholar J.S.P. Tatlock draws our attention to the well-known account of a journey to Britain made in 1113 by a group of canons of Laon in northern France. Tatlock shows that this account, written in about 1145 by a monk called Herman (possibly Hermann of Tournai), was substantially compiled at about the time of the visit in 1113. Thus, the popularity of Geoffrey's *Historia* in France is due in part to previous knowledge of Arthur.

The Riothamus Theory

In 1985 Geoffrey Ashe, the well-known Arthurian scholar, published *The Discovery of King Arthur*, in which he identifies King Arthur with Riothamus, an important immigrant leader who flourished in the fifth century. His theory depends largely upon a passage in Geoffrey of Monmouth's *Historia Regum Britanniae*, which portrays Arthur as a British king campaigning in Gaul during the reign of the Eastern Roman Emperor Leo I, who reigned from 457–74. The British king who campaigned in Gaul at this time was indeed Riothamus, but he was certainly not Arthur who was victorious at the Battle of Badon in 518 and ended his reign at the Battle of Camlann which, according to the *Welsh Annals*, was fought in 537.

The shadowy figure called Riothamus, who is said to have been a king of the Britons, is briefly alluded to by the writers Gregory of Tours, Jordanes and the poet Sidonius Apollinaris, who between them testify that in the 470s he led an army of sea-borne troops from Britain to Gaul in order to assist the Emperor Anthemius (ruled 467–72) against Euric, King of the Visigoths (466–84).[3]

It would seem that Euric, seeing the frequent depositions of the Roman governors, endeavoured to possess himself of the remaining Roman part of Gaul and Anthemius solicited the assistance of the Britons.

In response to his request, Riothamus arrived with 12,000 men, and disembarking from his ships was received in the state of the Bituriges.

Euric, King of the Visigoths, however, brought a very large army against him and defeated Riothamus near Bourges, before his Roman allies would arrive. Having lost a large part of his army, he collected as many as he could of the remainder and sought refuge in the neighbouring kingdom of the Burgundians, at that time in alliance with the Romans. He then disappears from history, although the Burgundian town of Avallon (the Gallic Aballone, the 'place of apples'), is suggested as his destination.

Who was Riothamus?

Jordanes, the sixth-century historian, in his *De Rebus Gothicus*, refers to Riothamus as 'King of the Brittones' which most likely means the Britons in Armorica. The statement that he came 'by way of the Ocean, and was received as he disembarked from his ships' suggests that he sailed around the coast of Armorica and down the Loire Valley.

It is probable that the army of Riothamus included a contingent from Britain itself. Ambrosius Aurelianus was most likely involved in this 'last ditch' attempt by Britain to aid the dying Western Roman Empire. He strove to maintain the connection with the crumbling Roman Empire, and no doubt the expedition of Riothamus into central Gaul in 469 was inspired by him. Ambrosius must have had political connections with the Gallo-Roman patrician Syagrius, who until 468 maintained his sovereignty in central Gaul, and with the Merovingian Franks under their philo-Roman king Childeric, King of the Salian Franks, 457–82. The Angles and the Saxons were the enemies of all three, and Ambrosius must have exercised some kind of influence over the Britons in Armorica.

The Cartulary of Quimperlé lists four early *comes* (counts) of Cornubia (Cornouaille), one of whom was Iahan Reith who came to Armorica with a large fleet of ships in the 450s. His name has probably been confused with that of Riatham, son of Deroch, who lived four generations later.[4]

Paul Karlsson Johnstone, a consultant archaeologist who is well known for his *Consular Chronology of Dark Age Britain*, asserts that Riothamus was known as both Ian Reith and St Rhedyw (Ridicus) and that he was the father of St Germanus. If this is so, he must have fathered St Germanus when he was a very young man, lived to be a great veteran fighter and possibly survived his illustrious son. There is no doubt that St Rhedyw was the founding father of a family of soldier-saints who flourished in both Wales and Brittany, but in our opinion it is more likely that Riothamus was

194

Rhedyw's son. There is no doubt that Riothamus was a title or epithet used for an individual and in due course replaced his real name.

Arthur was first identified with Riothamas by the historian Sharon Turner in the late eighteenth century and the theory has been revived by Geoffrey Ashe. He argues that Riothamus is a title meaning 'great king' and that this fifth-century 'King' of the Britons who campaigned on the Continent is the historical prototype of Arthur used by Geoffrey of Monmouth in his *Historia*.

The story of Riothamus as it appears in the *Legend of St Goeznovius* (composed in about 1019, some time before Geoffrey's *Historia*) and the legends of Maximus in 'The Dream of Maxen Wledig' is an obvious source for Arthur's Continental activities in Geoffrey's *Historia Regum Britanniae*.

CHAPTER 18

The Battle of Camlann

Arthur's thirteenth battle fought at a place known as Camlann (or Camlan) resulted in the end of his reign as King of the Britons. The site of this battle has long been sought by Arthurian researchers and has been placed in many different locations, yet few of them are particularly convincing.

They include Camelford in Cornwall, the River Cam below Cadbury Castle in Somerset, Camelon on the River Falkirk in Stirlingshire and Camoglanna (Crookbank) on Hadrian's Wall in Northumberland. The latter site used to be identified as Birdoswald, but that place is now considered to be the settlement of Banna, while Camoglanna (curved glen) is believed to be at Castlesteads by the Cam beck. These locations all have an element of the word Camlann in the place name.

Nennius fails to mention the battle but it is possible that his battle list is based on an ancient poem which predates the Battle of Camlann. It is listed in the *Welsh Annals* under the date 537: 'The battle of Camlann, where Arthur and Medraut fell, and there was death in Britain and in Ireland'. Although the words are in Latin, the name of the actual battle is written in the old British tongue, 'Gueith Camlann' (Battle of Camlann). It would seem that such a name has been taken from an older manuscript written in the language of the Britons. The death referred to was the plague that broke out in 539. In the reference to the Battle of Badon, the *Welsh Annals* use the word *bellum* (battle), but for Camlann, the Celtic word *gueith* is used, which translates merely as 'a fight'.

In the Welsh Triads, Camlann is recorded as one of 'The Three Futile Battles of the Island of Britain'. It was referred to by the Welsh bards as a 'terrible slaughter' and the word *cadgamlan* came to mean a rout.

It is Geoffrey of Monmouth who provides a detailed account of the battle, but unfortunately gives very few clues to its location.[1] He merely tells us that it was fought near the River Camlann.

196

THE BATTLE OF CAMLANN

Why was the Battle of Camlann Fought?

In order to provide an answer to this question we must first give consideration to the identity of Arthur's adversary in the battle, who is named Mordred by Geoffrey of Monmouth and Medraut in the *Welsh Annals*.[2] It would seem that Geoffrey changed the Welsh name of Medraut to the Cornish Mordred (or Modred). He also describes him confusingly as both Arthur's illegitimate son and his nephew.

The identity of Medraut is complicated by the fact there were two British princes of this name in the sixth century. They were Medraut ap Llew ap Cynfarch and Medraut ap Cawrdaf ap Caradog Freichfras. The former Medraut was the nephew of the northern Urien of Rheged, who died in 580 and would have lived too late to have fought Arthur at the Battle of Camlann, which according to the *Welsh Annals* took place in 537. The more likely candidate to be Arthur's adversary is therefore his contemporary, Medraut, the son of Cawrdaf ap Caradog Freichfras.

Medraut's father, Cawrdaf , is recorded in the Welsh Triads as one of the 'Chief Officers of the Island of Britain'. The Welsh triads also record that Cawrdaf's father, Caradog Freichfras, was Arthur's Chief Elder at his court of Gelliwig in Cernyw, which we have located in Gwent.

According to the *Lives of the Saints*, Cawrdaf was not only an influential politician but also a leading light in the Welsh Church. He established a religious house for 300 monks at Cor Cawrdaf, above Miskin in Glamorgan. In addition, he became patron of Abererch in the Llyyn Peninsula (north Wales). It therefore becomes apparent from the evidence of the Welsh Triads and the *Lives of the Saints* that Medraut was the member of a very powerful family who held sway in Gwent and the Llyyn Peninsula.

From the evidence of early Welsh tradition contained in the *Mabinogion* and the Welsh Triads, it would appear that Arthur's expansionist policies left a power vacuum which resulted in a dynastic revolution. The Battle of Camlann was the culmination of a civil war and it is significant that Geoffrey tells us that there was a period of turmoil after Arthur's abdication.

Medraut Can be Associated with the Llyyn Peninsula

The Llyyn Peninsula is shaped like a horn and it would appear that Medraut's family had a residence on this peninsula for the following connections are relevant:

1. According to the Welsh Triads, Cawrdaf, the father of Medraut, was one of the three counsellors of Arthur. He founded a church at

Abererch, which became known as Llan Gawrda, and he is reputed to be buried there. A further memory of Cawrdaf's presence here is preserved in Cadair Cawrdaf (Cawrdaf's Seat), which is a large boulder with a flat piece seemingly cut out of it. This strange-looking rock can be found on the hillside about 1 mile to the north of the church dedicated to him.

2. Cawrdaf's brother was Cadfarch and his name is preserved in Ffynnon Gadfarch, which is near the site of a now extinct chapel called Llangedwydd, at the northern end of Abererch parish. Significantly, Cadfarch is also connected with Berach, identified with Capel Anelog under Aberdaron. There is even a possibility that Medraut was buried at his uncle's church after his death at the Battle of Camlann. It is also significant that Cynwyl, who is mentioned in the Mabinogion as one of the survivors of the Battle of Camlann, is the patron saint of Penrhos near Llannor on Llyn. Being very powerfully built, he is said to have escaped from the battle because the enemy were afraid to tackle him.

Possible Events Leading Up to the Battle of Camlann
Clues in the *Mabinogion* and the Welsh Triads can enable us to construct the following account of what may have taken place during the period immediately prior to this fateful battle.

The preliminary weaving of a plot is referred to in the *Mabinogion* story of 'Culhwch and Olwen'. This story names Gwenhwyfach as the sister of Gwenhwyfar (Guinevere in English), Arthur's queen. This is of considerable interest, for according to the early Welsh genealogies, Gwenhwyfach was the wife of Medraut ap Cawrdaf, Arthur's adversary. Furthermore, according to the Welsh Triads, it was she who contributed to the cause of the Battle of Camlann by inflicting a blow on her sister Gwenhwyfar.

The Welsh Triads state that the first of 'Three Unrestrained Ravagings of the Island of Britain' occurred when Medraut came to Arthur's court at Gelliwig in Cernyw (Gwent) and dragged Gwenhwyfar from her throne and struck her. The second one occurred when Arthur made a retaliatory assault on Medraut's court.[3]

It would appear that Arthur left the government of Britain in the hands of Medraut while he made a journey to Ireland to deal with the Irish warlord Llwch Wyddel (Lucius Hibernus), who was also known as Llwch Llawinawg, Lord of the Lakes. He in the Arthurian romance stories became Lancelot of the Lake and was made out to be one of Arthur's noble knights. Llwch had dispatched messengers to Arthur to demand payment of tribute to him and the men of Ireland. Arthur's reply to Llwch's messengers was that the men of Ireland had no greater claim to tribute from Britain than this island had from them.

Without delay, Arthur mustered the most select warriors of his kingdom and led them across the sea against Llwch and his army. The two forces met beyond the mountain of Mynneu and an untold number were slain on each side. Finally, Arthur encountered Llwch and slew him. When Medraut heard that Arthur's army was dispersed, he decided to seize the reins of power. On receiving news of this uprising, Arthur returned with all that remained of his army and succeeded in landing a force in opposition to Medraut.

Where did Arthur Land his Army?

It is interesting that Geoffrey of Monmouth tells us that Arthur fought two battles against Medraut prior to the one at Camlann. He says that the first battle took place at 'Rutupi Portus' which is obviously the harbour where Arthur landed. A more detailed description of this event can be found in the *Brut Tysilio*: 'The battle began on Arthur's part from the ships and on Medrod's from the shore; and a great slaughter ensued, in which Arawn ap Cynfarch, and Gwalchmai ap Gwyar fell . . . and with great labour and loss Arthur made good his landing, put Medrod to flight, and dispersed his army'. For a number of reasons, which will be explained in due course, it is possible that this preliminary battle took place at a small harbour on the Llyyn Peninsula, where Medraut's family had strong connections.

On the Ordnance Survey map, just to the east of Aberdaron, which is known as the 'Land's End of Wales', can be found the name Porth Cadlan, which significantly means 'Battle Place Harbour'. Adjoining this little inlet is a detached rock named 'Maen Gwenonwy'. It seems a remarkable coincidence but a lady by the name of Gwenonwy was the daughter of Meurig ap Tewdrig. In other words she was the sister of Arthur and the rock was possibly named after her through folk memory of her witnessing the battle which took place here in the sixth century.

Gwenonwy was married to Gwyndaf Hen, the son of Emyr Llydaw, and one of their children was St Henwyn, who established a church on the edge of the sea at Aberdaron, about 2 miles away.[4] Therefore, it is quite feasible that Gwenonwy was a witness to the battle while visiting her son, who was a nephew of Arthur.

It is easy to imagine the scene as Arthur's boats laden with warriors landed in this little harbour, while Medraut was waiting with his army on the sloping fields above. Names on the Ordnance Survey map are most significant, for Cadlan Uchaf means Upper Battlefield and Cadlan Isaf means Lower Battlefield, suggesting indeed that a major conflict took place here in ancient times.

In *Journey to Avalon*, Cadlan was identified as the site of the Battle of Camlann, but consideration should also be given to an alternative site. Bearing in mind that a series of battles may have been fought, the clues in Geoffrey's *History* and the *Brut Tysilio* suggest that Medraut's force took flight with Arthur's army in pursuit.

From Geoffrey of Monmouth we can assume that the Camlann battlefield was three days from the point of disembarkation.

The *Brut Tysilio* tells us that after two further engagements: 'Medrod made a stand on the river Camlann, with a force of sixty thousand six hundred and six men, resolved rather to hazard an engagement than fly from place to place.'

Geoffrey of Monmouth comments:

Arthur was filled with great mental anguish by the fact that Mordred had escaped him so often. Without losing a moment he followed him . . . reaching the River Camlan, where Mordred was awaiting his arrival . . .

Combat was joined, and they [the two armies] all strove with might and main to deal each other as many blows as possible. It is heart rendering to describe what slaughter was inflicted upon both sides, how the dying groaned, and how great was the fury of the attacking. Everywhere men were receiving wounds themselves or inflicting them, dying or dealing out death. In the end when they had passed much of the day in this way, Arthur with a single division in which he had posted six thousand, six hundred and sixty-six men, charged at the squadron where he knew Mordred was. They hacked a way through with their swords and Arthur continued to advance, inflicting terrible slaughter as he went. It was at this point that the accursed traitor was killed and many thousands of men with him.

Medraut (Mordred) and his followers appear to have been in a fixed position and Arthur and his soldiers advanced towards them, inflicting great slaughter as they went.

Perhaps the strongest contender for the site of the Battle of Camlann is a location of that very name, still shown on the Ordnance Survey map, between Dinas Mawddwy and Mallwyd, near the border of Gwynedd with Powys (SH 815163).[5] The old Roman road from Wroxeter to Brithdir crossed the River Dyfi here.

In the vicinity of Dinas Mawddwy are the names 'Maes y Camlan' 'Camlan isaf' (lower Camlan), 'Bron Camlan' (upper Camlan) and 'Bryn Cleifion' (hill of the wounded). However, the latter may have received its name from a skirmish that took place between detachments of the Parliamentarians and the Royalist forces in 1644 or 1645, in which years several incursions were made by both armies into Merionethshire and Montgomeryshire.[6]

Laurence Main, a writer living in Dinas Mawddwy, suggests that the battle started at Maes-y-Camlan, and that the wounded were laid to rest on Bryn Cleifion. The fighting moved up the valley of the River Cerist, a tributary of the Dyfi, towards the Mawddach Estuary. Laurence comments:

> Place-name evidence is strongly in favour of Camlan being fought where there is a bend in the river near Dinas Mawddwy. Maes y Camlan, the field where the battle started and finished, even has a tributary of the Afon Dyfi flowing through its southern corner. This is Nant Gamell and is the very *crooked stream* that some see at Camelford, despite the fact that Saxons and Cornish clashed there centuries after Arthur.[7]

An interesting local connection is Mallwyd Church, which was founded in the sixth century by St Tydecho, the son of Anna, a daughter of Meurig ap Tewdrig, which makes him the nephew of King Arthur.

There is another potential site for Camlann about 4 miles north of Dolgellau on the A470, where the River Gamlan, a possible distortion of Camlann, flows into the confluence of the Eden and the Mawddawch. It would actually have been a more convenient location for the wounded Arthur to have been taken away by boat.

Was Arthur Killed in the Battle of Camlann?
We are told by Geoffrey of Monmouth that 'Mordred' was killed and Arthur was 'mortally wounded' ('*letaliter ulneratus*'), and was removed to the island of Avalon 'to have his wounds healed' ('*as sananda ulnera sua insulum Avallonis euectus*').

This statement is certainly ambiguous, for 'mortally wounded' implies that death will come shortly, while 'to have his wounds healed' suggests that there is hope that Arthur will survive his injuries.

It is of interest that two of Sir Thomas Malory's sources for his novel *Le Morte d'Arthur* were *Morte Arthure* and *Le Morte Arthur*, two Middle English romances on the death of Arthur written by two unknown authors. The first mentioned was written about 1400 and follows very much the same plot as Geoffrey of Monmouth's work and it mentions Mordred's betrayal which resulted in the downfall of Arthur's kingdom. The second work, *Le Morte Arthur*, was written in about 1350 and was intended as an addition to Geoffrey's *Historia*. It actualy states that Arthur 'gave orders that he should be carried to Gwynedd for he intended to stay in the Isle of Avalon, a pleasant and delightful place, and very peaceful where the pain of his wounds would be eased'.

King Arthur Abdicates
Geoffrey of Monmouth tells us that the wounded King Arthur 'handed the crown of Britain over to his cousin Constantine, the son of Cador, Duke of Cornwall; this in the year 542 after our Lord's Incarnation'.

The *Brut Tysilio* states: 'Constantine, the son of Cador, succeeds to the throne by Arthur's choice.' It is relevant that it was a Celtic tradition that if any ruler was maimed or disfigured then he had to step down from power. This would explain why Arthur gave up his crown to Constantine.

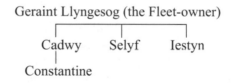

Geraint Llyngesog (the Fleet-owner)

Cadwy   Selyf   Iestyn

Constantine

CHAPTER 19

The Island of Avalon

Geoffrey of Monmouth tells us that Arthur was taken away by boat to 'Insula Avallonis' to have his wounds tended. The word Insula (island) indicates the site of a religious foundation, such as the Isle of Whithorn, where a monastery would be found. It is also reasonable to suppose that such an island must be fairly close to the site of the Battle of Camlann. An important clue to its identification is provided by James Bonwick in his book *Irish Druids and Old Irish Religions* (1894). He makes the following statement: 'The Welsh Avalon, or the Island of Apples, the everlasting source of the Elixir of Life, the home of Arthur and other mythological heroes, lay beyond Cardigan Bay, the Annwn of the old Sun, in the direction of Ireland.'[1] Support for this statement can be found in Archdruid Owen Morgan's book, *The Royal Winged Son of Stonehenge and Avebury*, in which he states that the Celtic Elysium was between Borth on Cardigan Bay and Arklow in Ireland.[2] There is only one possible island that fits this description and that is Bardsey, which lies just off the far end of the Llyyn Peninsula.

Bardsey is a Norse name, being a compound of the old Scandinavian personal name of *Bardr*, and *ey*, island, meaning Bardr's Island. The name was given by the Vikings from Denmark and Norway who carried out sea raids along the coast of Wales, and it relates to Bardr, who was a Viking leader in the tenth century.

The Glastonbury Confusion

When Geoffrey of Monmouth tells us that the wounded Arthur was taken away by boat to 'Insula Avallonis' he certainly does not identify it with Glastonbury, or with any actual place for that matter. He would certainly have known of Glastonbury for in his time it was one of the most important Christian shrines in Britain.

Glastonbury became identified as Avalon, the shortened version of Avallonis, when the monks 'discovered' the leaden funerary cross that boldly stated that Arthur was buried in the Isle of Avalon. Influenced by these words

203

on the cross, the first writers to connect Glastonbury with Avalon were Giraldus Cambrensis (*Speculum Ecclesiae*) and Ralph, Abbot of Coggeshall (*Chronicum Anglicanum*).

The Island of Afallach

In all the Welsh versions of Geoffrey's *Historia* his 'Insula Avallonis' is rendered as 'Ynys Afallach' (the Island of Afallach) and it is significant that in the sixth century there was a Celtic prince of this name. Geoffrey, in his later *Vita Merlini*, even mentions that Aballach, father of Modron, was the ruler of the island to which Arthur was taken. Other examples of islands off the coast of Wales that were named after people are Ynys Cybi (Island of St Cybi) and Ynys Tudwal (Island of St Tudwal) and Ynys Seiriol (Island of St Seiriol). The Isle of Man is named after the god Manannan and is said to have been his home.

Giraldus Cambrensis says that Avallonia may have got its name 'from a certain Avallo' (*Speculum Ecclesiae*, Ch. IX), and William of Malmesbury states that Afallach lived on the Island of Avalon with his daughters. Thus, Insula Avalonia and Ynys Afallach signified that the island belonged to a man called in Latin Avallo and in Welsh Afallon or Afallach.

In the genealogies, Afallach is the father of two daughters, Modron and Gwalltwen, who are said to be concubines of Urien of Gorre and Maelgwyn Gwynedd.[3] Rhun, the son of Maelgwyn Gwynedd, was the grandson of Afallach, according to certain texts of the 'Achau'r Manau', contained in the Peniarth MS 75.

Geographical evidence for the existence of Afallach can be found in the hamlet of Caerfallwch (a corruption of Caer Afallach), which is situated near Rhosemor in north-east Wales. This name translates as 'the fort of Afallach' and it probably refers to a large Iron Age fort known as Moel-y-Gaer, which may well have served as a base for Afallach.

The Island of Apples

In his *Vita Merlini* Geoffrey has Merlin meeting Taliesin after Arthur's passing and, in the course of the conversation, Merlin tells how Arthur was taken by boat to 'insula pomorum que Fortunata' (the Island of Apples which is Fortunate). This would appear to be yet another name for Bardsey Island.

The idea of a large number of apple trees growing on this windswept island may seem unlikely, but in 2000 an interesting discovery was made, when a single gnarled and twisted tree produced a crop of apples. They were examined by Dr Joan Morgan ,who described them as 'boldly striped in pink over cream, ribbed and crowned'. She said, 'We could not put a name to it, but who would wish it to be anything but the Bardsey apple?'

This single tree, which is evidently very hardy and resistant to disease, may be a descendant of the original orchard on this one-time 'Island of Apples'. The introduction of sheep on Bardsey in the Middle Ages may have prevented the trees from regenerating.

Who was Morgan Le Fay?
In his *Vita Merlini* Geoffrey describes how Arthur was brought to the island by Merlin and Taliesin to be cured of his wounds by Modron and her nine sisters:

> Thither after the battle of Camlan we took the wounded Arthur . . . and Morgan [Modron] received us with becoming honour. In her own chamber she placed the king on a golden bed, with her own and noble hand uncovered the wound and gazed at it long. At last she said that health would return to him if he were to stay with her a long time and wished her to make use of healing art.

Geoffrey's description of Morgan and her island kingdom corresponds with a passage in the *Gesta Regum Britanniae*, written in c.1235 by Guillaume de Rennes. It describes a mighty princess attended by nine maidens in a miraculously fertile island called Avallon and it is implied that she is the daughter of the King of Avallon.

It would seem that Sir Thomas Malory, in his *Le Morte d'Arthur*, also converts the name Modron into Morgan and extends it into Morgan Le Fay. He also is aware of the fact that she was the wife of Urien of Gorre.[4]

According to the Welsh Triads, Urien of Gorre married Modron, the daughter of Afallach. Their son Yvaine was known in Welsh tradition as Owain. If we refer to Triad No. 70 (contained in the Peniarth MS 47), we find that it states that Owain and his sister Morfudd were carried in the womb of Modron, the daughter of Afallach, and wife of Urien of Gorre.

By comparing the references to Morgan Le Fay of the Romance stories with her Welsh counterpart Modron it becomes evident that this daughter of Afallach is the very same lady whom Geoffrey of Monmouth claims cured Arthur of his wounds.

The Disappearance of Arthur
Geoffrey of Monmouth states that Arthur, mortally wounded, was taken to

'Insula Avallonis' to be healed of his wounds. This ambiguous statement can only mean that Arthur was badly wounded but did not die from his injuries.

In 1139, Henry of Huntingdon, in a letter to a certain Warinus, states that Arthur 'himself received so many wounds that he fell; although his kinsmen the Britons deny that he was mortally wounded and seriously expect he will come again'. William of Malmesbury also remarked that the grave of Arthur 'is nowhere beheld' and that ancient songs prophesy his return.

Adam of Tewkesbury, writing in 1170, observes:

His [Arthur's] departure will be obscured by doubt, which is indeed true, for there are today varying opinions as to his life and death. If you do not believe me, go to the kingdom of Armorica, that is, lesser Britain, and preach in the villages and market-places that Arthur the Briton died as other men die; and then if you escape unharmed, for you will be either cursed or stoned by your hearers, you will indeed discover that Merlin the prophet spoke truly when he said that Arthur's departure would be obscured by doubt.

The traditional story gives the impression that Arthur died soon after the Battle of Camlann, but it would appear that he was healed of his wounds and abdicated, to disappear from the scene by sailing away to Brittany, where he became known as St Armel. It should be remembered that his grandfather Tewdrig also abdicated and thereafter became known as St Tewdrig.

The Island Monastery, Where Arthur was Healed of his Wounds
In the sixth century Einion Frenhin, King of Llyyn, is reputed to have founded the monastery on Bardsey Island. He was was a cousin of Maelgwyn Gwynedd and his brother was St Seriol, who established a monastic community at Penmon in Anglesey. King Einion also founded Llanengan on Llyyn where he is buried.

The monastery on Bardsey was founded by Einion in conjunction with Emyr Llydaw, whose grandson, Cadfan, became the first abbot. St Cadfan was the son of Gwen Teirbron, daughter of Emyr Llydaw by her first husband Eneas Ledewig. Her second husband was Fragan, cousin of Cadwy.

Cadfan was driven from his homeland in Armorica by the Franks and his companions included Cynon, Padarn, Tydecho, Trinio, Gwyndaf, Dochdwy, Sulien, Tanwg, Eithrus, Sadwrn, Lleuddad, Tecwyn and Maelrys.

On settling in Wales, Cadfan first founded churches at Llangadfan and Towyn. His patron at Llangadfan in Powys was Cyngen the son of Cadell, who had succeeded his father as ruler of Powys and was distinguished for his patronage of the saints and making liberal endowments to the Church.

Cadfan probably moved from Towyn to Bardsey in about 512 and, after establishing a brotherhood, was appointed abbot of the monastery in 516.

The Companions of St Cadfan

When St Cadfan left Armorica and came to Wales, he was accompanied by numerous followers who all gave their name to various church foundations in Gwynedd and on the Llyyn Peninsula in particular. The following connections can be made.

Henwyn, the son of Gwyndaf Hen by Gwenonwy, the sister of Arthur. He trained at Llanilltud Fawr and later became the confessor of his cousin St Cadfan on Bardsey Island, where he eventually became abbot.

Lleuddad was a son of Alan Fyrgan and with his brother Llynab he became a member of the college of St Illtud in Glamorgan. He was appointed abbot of the monastery on Bardsey following the death of St Cadfan. His name survives on the island in Gerddi Lleuddad (Lleuddad's Gardens) and near Aberdaron in Ogof Lleuddad (Lleuddad's Cave). He also founded a church at Bryn Croes, where a holy well (Ffynnon Lleuddad) is associated with him.

Mael was a son of Riwal Mawr and, in conjunction with his brother Sulien, he founded churches at Corwen in Gwynedd and Cwm in Flintshire. He later joined Cadfan on Bardsey Island.

Maelrhys was a son of Gwyddno ab Emyr Llydaw and a cousin of Cadfan and Henwyn. His name is usually coupled with his cousin Sulien. On the coast opposite Bardsey is the Church of St Maelrhys. His holy well Ffynnon Faelrhys is nearby.

Sadwrn was the brother of Illtud and he married Canna, the daughter of Tewdwr Mawr, son of Emyr Llydaw. Their son was Crallo, who founded Llangrallo (Coychurch) in the Vale of Glamorgan. Sadwrn is commemorated at Llansadwrn in Anglesey, where an inscribed stone bears his Latin name 'Saturninus'. He died there in 530.

Tanwg was a son of Ithael Hael of Armorica. He is patron of Llandonwg in Gwynedd, which, situated near the coast, became a chapel of rest for corpses being taken to Bardsey.

Tydecho was a son of Amwn Ddu, the son of Emyr Llydaw by Anna, daughter of Meurig ap Tewdrig. This makes him a nephew of King Arthur and the first cousin of St Cadfan.

Buried on Bardsey Island

St Cybi, a son of Selyf and Gwen (sister of Non, mother of St David), established a church near Pwllheli. He then moved on to Caer Gybi in Anglesey where Maelgwyn Gwynedd allowed him to build a church within the ruins of a Roman fort. When he died in 555 his body was brought to Bardsey for burial.

St Dubricius (Dyfrig), who is said to have crowned Arthur, retired to Bardsey in 522 and would have been on the island in 537, when Arthur was brought there after being wounded at Camlann. When Dubricius died in 546, he was buried on the island. Six centuries later, in 1172, on the orders of Bishop Urban, his bones were removed and taken to Llandaff Cathedral in Glamorgan, where they were installed in a new tomb with much ceremony.

Gwyndaf Hen (the Aged), a son of Emyr Llydaw, was the father of Henwyn who married Gwenonwy, the sister of Arthur. In his old age he retired to Bardsey, where he is said to be buried.

Meugant, the son of Gwyndaf Hen and brother of Henwyn, became a monk at Llanilltud Fawr and then followed in his father's footsteps by going to Cor Dyfrig at Caerleon-on-Usk. He was made Bishop of Caer Vudei (Woodchester) by King Arthur and later retired to Bardsey where he died and was buried.

St Padarn, the son of Pedrwyn ab Emyr Llydaw, left Armorica in 516 and settled in Wales. He subsequently founded a monastery at Llanbadarn Fawr, near Aberystwyth, where he died in 550 and was buried on Bardsey.

St Trillo, a son of Ithael Hael, founded a church at Llandrillo and was buried on Bardsey.

St Tudno, a son of Seithenyn, founded a church at Llandudno and was buried on Bardsey.

The Final Days of the Abbey

By the Middle Ages the island had become a famous place of pilgrimage and many people were still choosing to be buried there. In the Vatican library there is even a list of indulgences specially granted to pilgrims making the journey to Bardsey.

In 1536–7, under the Reformation of Henry VIII, the monasteries of Britain were dissolved and it is recorded that the last abbot on Bardsey was John Conway of Bodnithoedd in Meyllteyrn. His isolated monastery was dissolved in 1537 and valued at just £46.

St Mary's Abbey with all its lands and property came into the hands of John Wynn, High Sheriff of Caernarfon, in 1553. The island later came into the possession of the Newborough family, and it was the 3rd Lord Newborough who established the tradition of appointing a 'King of Bardsey' to ensure that the small community living on the island had a leader. The last 'King' was Love Pritchard, who died in 1926.

The stump of a ruined tower is all that is left of the Abbey of St Mary, and a tall Celtic cross of white Anglesey marble marks the grave of the 3rd Baron Newborough. A second cross has been set up in memory of the '20,000 saints'.

Today this fascinating island is a Site of Special Scientific Interest, owned by the Bardsey Island Trust, which maintains it as a nature reserve and seabird sanctuary.

CHAPTER 20

A New World in Armorica

From the time of Julius Caesar, an area of north-west France was known as Armorica, a name derived from the Celtic words 'Ar' and 'Mor', which signify on or near the sea. In many respects this green and rugged land that we know today as Brittany is similar to Wales. The countryside is gently undulating, interspersed with woods and there are two hilly ranges – the Arée Mountains in the north and the Noires Mountains in the south. The magnificent and varied coastline is 800 miles in length and, being situated where the English Channel and the Atlantic Ocean meet, it is washed by the world's highest tides.

According to Geoffrey of Monmouth, the first British settlers in Armorica arrived when Magnus Clemens Maximus invaded Gaul in 383. The armies of the men who accompanied him on this expedition never returned to their families in Britain, but settled in the area that today can be defined as Normandy and Brittany. The leader of the British soldiers who settled in Armorica was Conan Meriadoc, the brother of Maximus's wife Elen. Maximus bestowed the land of Armorica upon Conan as a reward for the assistance given to him in the conquest of Gaul, and Conan governed Armorica until his death in about 421.

During the next two centuries there was a constant flow of settlers from Britain, seeking refuge and a new life in Armorica. Many of them came from Dumnonia (Devon and Cornwall), but most of all they sailed from south-east Wales, led by men who were largely of princely families. It is evident from the place names of present-day Brittany that the leaders were holy men, and it is significant that some of the Breton saints are traditionally descended from Gwent and Glamorgan kings.

These people brought with them their own laws, customs and organisation, both civil and ecclesiastical, as well as their own language. With considerable energy they set about clearing, cultivating and Christianising the land, which in time ceased to be called Armorica and instead became Lesser Britain (Petite Bretagne), to distinguish it from Great Britain (Grande Bretagne), and eventually it became Bretagne, 'Brittany'.

Sadly, the story of this settlement of Celtic people from western Britain in this sparsely populated land has been largely forgotten. This is mainly due to the fact that after the French Revolution Brittany became an integral part of France.

The Breton kingdom of Domnonia in the north is named after the Dumnonii of the Severn Sea, and the name survives in Britain as Devon. It was Riwal Mawr ('the Great'), a prince of Erging, who made the first settlement here. Accompanied by a large party of colonists, he sailed from Gwent in about 514 and landed in what is now known as the Bay of St Brieuc. He set up his court at Lishelion and his realm covered the whole north of the peninsula, from the mouth of the River Elorn in the west to Coueson in the east, and extended southwards to the great forest. After 530 it also enclosed the province of Léon in the north-west. This is the country north of Brest and of the Arée Mountains with St Pol-de-Léon, the ancient Occismor, as its capital.

Cornubia, or Cornouaille, in the south-west is a large peninsula shaped like a pointing hand with the thumb tucked in and the extending forefinger being the Pointe du Raz. It was colonised by immigrants from Cornwall, who gave the name of their homeland to their new territory. It extended into north Finistère, but the name is now confined to the coastal region west of Quimper, which is remarkably similar to Cornwall. Along its northern shore are many rocks and cliffs, terminating in the picturesque Pointe du Raz.

Finistére, derived from *Finis Terrae* ('the World's End'), is the most westerly part of Brittany and feels quite remote. There are two ranges of hills, the Noires Mountains, reaching from Cairhaix to the Menez Hom, near Chateaulin, and on to the sea, while the Arée Mountains stretch across the country from east to west, between Morlaix and Huelgoat. The northern part of Finistére from Morlaix to the region of the Abers (the estuaries of Aber Wrac'h, Aber Benoit and Aber Illdut), is known as Pays de Léon after the counts of Léon who once owned it. St Pol-de-Léon is the main town set in the little corner north-west of Morlaix.

Bro-Weroch or Vannes in the south and south-east is traditionally derived from Weroch, the founder of the ruling dynasty. Today, it is an area that corresponds roughly with modern Morbihan. This name is Breton for 'little sea' and the Gulfe du Morbihan is a vast and wild stretch of island dotted water linked to the Atlantic by a narrow channel to the south.

The Forest of Brocéliande

The centre of the Armorican peninsula was once an area of vast forest and barren, rock-strewn moors, untrodden by man and roamed by wild beasts. When the first British settlers arrived, they initially made clearings and established settlements from which the land was gradually divested of its dense woodlands.

The only portion of the ancient Forest of Brocéliande that has survived is known as the Forest (Forét) de Paimpont and it is rich in legends about King Arthur and his knights, with their memories living on in the place names.

It would appear that the key figure who promoted the Arthurian legend in the Forest of Brocéliande was Raoul II de Gael Montfort, who was once the owner of this part of Brittany. Born in Hereford in 1040, he was the son of Raoul I, who was the most prominent Breton residing in England during the reign of King Edward the Confessor. He was given the title 'staller' which signified that he was one who had a seat and special duties in the king's hall and palace. He entered the king's service in 1050 and died in 1069.

The son of Raoul I was also named Raoul or Ralph, and, at the age of 26, fought on the Norman side at the Battle of Hastings (1066) and was present at the court of William the Conqueror with his father in 1068. The following year he routed a force of Norsemen, who had invaded Norfolk and occupied Norwich. In recognition of this achievement, William created him Earl of East Anglia.

In 1075 Raoul II married Emma, the only daughter of William Fitz Osbern, 1st Earl of Hereford, and his first wife Adelissa, the daughter of Roger I de Toeny, at Exning in Cambridgeshire. However, because King William would not recognise this marriage, Raoul took part in the ill-conceived revolt of the earls which was thwarted. He fled back to his base in Norfolk and then sailed to Brittany. In due course, he was joined by his wife Emma and they retired to their Breton lands.

Raoul, in 1096, accompanied by his wife and under the command of Robert Curthouse, went on a Crusade and he was one of the Breton leaders who took part in the siege of Nicaea. He then joined Bohemund I's division of the army but, with his wife Emma, died on the road to Palestine during the course of the First Crusade.

It is relevant that a claim made at the Chateau de Comper and in the French Guide Bleu states that when Raoul I de Gael Montfort, one of the owners of the Forest de Paimpont in the eleventh century, took part in the Norman Conquest of England he became fascinated by the Arthurian tales that he heard there. It would seem that on his return to Brittany, in order to enhance the prestige of his own family and domaine, he encouraged storytellers to set Arthurian tales in his Forest of Brocéliande.

Furthermore, Chrétien de Troyes (c.1135–90), was an honorary citizen of the Forest of Brocéliande. His writings are both an indispensable prelude and a complement to any visit to the Forest of Brocéliande.

Robert Wace was the first writer to introduce Celtic material into French literature in the middle of the twelfth century and he describes Barenton in his poem 'Le Roman de Rou'. It was here that Lancelot was said to have been born and Merlin was bewitched by the enchantress Vivienne. The remains of a neolithic burial site have become the place where Merlin was entombed alive, and the fountain of Barenton is a spring where Merlin is said to have first met Vivienne.

The Chateau de Comper, a castle in Paimpont Forest that has been rebuilt as a chateau, is home to the Centre de l'Imaginaire Arthurien (Arthurian Legend Centre). It houses an exhibition of Brittany's legends of King Arthur and is an ideal starting point for a tour of Arthurian sites in Brocéliande.

These romantic traditions were summed up by Wace, author of the twelfth-century verse called 'Le Roman de Brut', who on hearing of the Brocéliande tales, travelled there to see for himself. He later wrote: 'I saw the forest and I saw the land. A fool I returned; a fool I went.'

Important Connections

Riwal Mawr, the son of Emyr Llydaw, was the traditional founder of the Breton kingdom of Domnonia (which was named after the Domnonian peninsula of Devon and Cornwall).[1] Riwal was killed in 524 in the Battle of Langres, fighting alongside his cousin Arthur, against Clodomir, the Frankish King of Orléans. Riwal was succeeded by his son Deroch who died in 535 and was succeeded by his son Jonas, who was assassinated on the order of Marcus Conomorus, Count of Poher, in 549.

Jonas's son and heir Judwal had to flee for his life to the court of the Frankish king Childebert at Paris. In 555 the combined forces of Samson, Judwal and Arthur defeated Conomorus in a battle fought over three days at the foot of the Arée Mountains. Judwal then became King of Breton Domnonia, which he ruled until his death in 580.

Judwal was succeeded by his son Juthael, who married Pritella, the daughter of Ausoch, who was grandson of Count Gwythyr (Withur) of Léon and had eventually succeeded to the principality of Léon upon the retirement of Arthur. Juthael was succeeded by his son Judicael, King of Breton Domnonia, 612–58. The residence of this saintking was at Gael, a small village situated 4 miles south of Saint-Méen-Le-Grande, and it was once the ancient capital of Breton Domnonia.

It is of great significance that Gael is also traditionally associated with King Arthur. In his *Tristan le Voyageur ou la Francais aue Xlme Sieche* (1825), Marchangy refers to the ruins of Chateau de Gael as the sumptious former residence of King Arthur.

The Church of Saint-Méen-Le-Grande was founded in the sixth century by St Mewan, the nephew of St Samson, and the benefactor was St Judicael.[2] According to Ingomar's eleventh-century *Life of St Judicael*, it was here that he finished his days in monastic habit. The former Abbey of Saint-Méen-de-Gael was re-established by Hinguethan, Abbot of Saint-Jacut-de-la-Mer in Cotes d'Armor (on the orders of Alan III, Duke of Brittany 1008–40), on a new site at Saint-Méen-Le-Grand in Ille-et-Vilaine. Inside this very fine monastery is an exhibition of the famous Breton saints, and their banners, including St Armel, the renowned soldier-saint of Broceliande.

Judicael is said to have founded the Priory of Paimpont in about 640. In the sacristy of the present-day Church of Paimpont is a silver reliquary of the arm of St Judicael. After his death he was buried near his abbot St Méen and declared a saint.

The tomb of St Onenne, the sister of King Judicael, used to be inside the nearby Church of Trehorenteuc, which was restored between 1942 and 1962 by the parish priest Henri Gillard. The stained glass windows of the choir depict the Arthurian quest for the Holy Grail. Above the sacristy door is a painting showing twenty-one knights and kings at the Round Table with the Grail, a golden chalice appearing before them.[3]

It is probable that the Forest of Brocéliande takes its name from Brocelidon, an area of woodland in Caledonia, and this is another example of the transfer of place names by the early immigrants. They also planted the old tales of the *Mabinogion* here, such as 'The Lady of the Fountain', and likewise the stories of Merlin were transferred from the Caledonian Forest of Scotland where his prototype, Myrddin Wyllt, once belonged.

The Forest of Brocéliande was thus substituted for that of Caledonia and a sacred spring at Barenton became associated with Myrddin (Merlin). Freshly located in Brittany these ancient traditions have caused much confusion.

Locations Associated with St Armel (Arthur)
The name Armel is a combination of the words Arz (bear) and Mael which means prince. Parish churches dedicated to St Armel include Plouarzel, Ploërmel and St Armel.[4] In addition, there are dedications to him at Loutehel, Ergue-Armel, Languedias and Langoet. He also had chapels at Bruz,

Fougeray, Lantic, Radebac, St Jouan de l'Isle, St Glen, Sarzeau and Dinan.

Ploërmel (Plou-Armel) was once known as Lann Arthmael, and it is situated on rising ground near the lake called Létang du Lac, just south of the Forest of Paimpont at the junction of roads from Rennes, Vannes and Dinion. The present church was rebuilt between 1511 and 1602 with a square tower added at the beginning of the eighteenth century. A window in the north chapel tells the story of St Armel in stained glass of the fifteenth century. He is depicted as follows: (1) Armel arriving from Britain; (2) With his company, he receives the ambassadors of King Childebert, summoning him to court; (3) St Armel curing lepers and lame men in the court of King Childebert; (4) King Childebert, at the door of his palace, bidding farewell to St Armel, who has undertaken to deal with a dragon, which symbolises the tyrant Marcus Conomorus; (5) St Armel meets the dragon and puts his stole about it; (6) He leads the dragon away and casts it into the River Seiche; (7) St Armel dies and is depicted lying in a grave while an angel bears a legend in the sky.

Arthur established his settlement at **Plouarzel**, a small village a couple of kilometres away from the cliffs where he had landed with his companions at Lyonesse, near a haven called Aber-Benniguel. Here, according to the 'Legendarium of Plouarzel', came the silver bier bearing the wounded Arthur, or Arzur as he is called locally.

In the Church of **St Sauveur at Dinan**, St Armel is represented in a late sixteenth-century stained glass window. He is depicted wearing the habit of an ecclesiastic with an armice over his shoulder and a cap on his head. A green dragon lies at his feet, bound by a stole.

At **St Armel-des-Boshaux** and at **Languedias** seventeenth-century statues showing St Armel as an abbot, trampling on a dragon, can also be seen. This again is a symbolic way of remembering how St Armel vanquished the tyrant Marcus Conomorus.

Le Camp D'Artus (Arthur's Camp) is an Iron Age hill fort situated in the Huelgoat Forest, on the top of a hill, about 13 miles north-west of Carhaix Plouguer in Finistère. The ramparts rise to a considerable height, and at one end is a mound, on which may be traced the remains of a stone building. The name Huelgoat reminds one of Arthur's ally Hoel (Riwal) Mawr and it could mean Hoel's Wood. There is indeed a local tradition that this fort was used by Arthur and his followers. This forest is now part of the Armorique Regional Nature Park, and it is a fascinating area of rocks and grottoes cut deeply by sunken watercourses.

The **Forest of Paimpont**, between Rennes and Ploërmel, was once part of the vast Forest of Brocéliande which extended over much of central

Brittany. This, even more than our own West Country, is the centre of surviving traditions of King Arthur and his knights. Many of the place names in this area have associations with Arthur, since Brocéliande was one of the places where he is said to have held sway and where his memory still lingers.

Examples of Celtic Saints Who Ended their Days in Armorica
Armorica became a place of sanctuary for a large number of Britons fleeing from the Saxon menace and the threat of the 'Yellow Pestilence', which was a form of bubonic plague. However, many noblemen also came here for religious reasons, and this is demonstrated by the fact that, just like Wales and Cornwall, most of the Breton place names have originated from the missionary saints of the Arthurian period.

St Brioc, born in west Wales, became the patron saint of St Breoke near Wadebridge in Cornwall. He later sailed to Armorica with eighty-four companions and established a monastery at the place now called St Brieuc, capital of the department of Côtes-du-Nord. It occupies a pleasant site on a plateau 100m above sea level, and is known as the gateway to western and southern Brittany. St Brioc died in 530 at the age of 90.

St Curig, who founded several churches in Wales, spent his final days in Armorica. He arrived there during the reign of Childebert I, when Deroch was King of Domnonia (520–35) and went to Lanmeur in Finistére, where he founded a monastery at Locquirec on the coast. He later retreated to Ploudaniel in Léon, where he built a chapel in a valley surrounded by dense woods at Traoun-Guevroc. While visiting Landernau, he fell sick and died there on 17 February 550. His body was taken by his followers to his monastery at Locquirec for burial.

St Leonore, the son of Hywel Mawr and Alma Pompeia, trained at the monastery of St Illtud, and then crossed the sea to Armorica where he founded the monastery of St Lunaire, nearly 4 miles west of St Malo. He went to Paris and was well-received by the Frankish King Childebert, who gave him security over the land where he had settled. St Leonore died at the age of 51 years and was buried at his monastery.

St Malo, a sixth-century monk from Britain, became Bishop of Aleth, now part of St Servan. He later retired to a monastery, which he founded on a rocky island that bears his name.

St Mewan, a disciple of St Samson, established the Church of St Mewan in Cornwall and later settled in Armorica, where he set up a monastery in the Forest of Brocéliande. He later founded St Méen, near Rennes, where he died in about 550.

St Non, the mother of St David, patron saint of Wales, ended her days at Dirnion in Finistére (about 4 miles from Plougastel). The church here contains a chapel dedicated to her and, while her tomb is no earlier than fifteenth century, her bones are contained in a reliquary of an earlier date. At the front of the church can be seen a statue of St Non and there are stained glass windows illustrating events in her life. Near the church can be seen her holy well, which is enclosed by walls and surrounded by benches. The spring itself flows under an arched structure erected in 1632 and it contains a statue of St Non. The water flows into three basins in succession. A miracle-play representing the story of St Non used to be performed locally.

St Tudwal was the son of Alma Pompeia and Riwal Mawr, who founded Domnonia. On becoming a widow Pompeia left Gwent and crossed the sea to Armorica with her sons Tudwal (Tugdual) and Leonore. Her white marble tomb can be seen at Langoat (the Church in the Wood). There is a recumbent effigy, carved in 1370, depicting her with feet resting on a rabbit. Also, in the church is a statue of her son St Tudwal, who is habited and wears a triple crown. He is best known as the founder of a large monastery called Val Trechor which stood on the site of Tréguier Cathedral. He died there in 559. Brittany has nine cathedrals and it is significant that seven of them were founded by holy men from Wales and Cornwall.

St Tysilio, the son of Brochwel Ysgythrog, ruler of Powys, fled to Armorica with a small band of monks after his father was defeated in the Battle of Chester (613) by Aethelfrith of Northumbria. They sailed up the estuary of the Rance and landed in a small creek where they established a monastery. St Tysilio died there in about 630.

The Tyrant Marcus Conomorus

Count Marcus Conomorus (Hound of the Sea), who is remembered in legend as King Mark, left British Dumnonia and settled in Armorica. He declared himself Count of Poher, a rich agricultural area between two ranges of hills. His stronghold was on a lofty hill at Cairhaix, the old Roman Vorganium. He also made claim to a large part of Léon and took the title Count of Léon, but he was still not satisfied and decided to take over Domnonia as well. Riwal Mawr, the ruler of this kingdom, had died in 524 and was succeeded by his son Deroch, who was followed by his son Jonas. It would seem that Conomorus arranged for Jonas to be assassinated, whereupon he married his widow and became regent of Domnonia during the minority of her son Judwal. In fear of his life, Judwal fled to St Lunaire's monastery, from where he was sent to the court of Childebert, King of the Franks (511–58), at Paris and sought his protection. Judwal grew up in the Frankish court and when he reached adulthood he was encouraged by St Samson to return to Domnonia and claim his inheritance.

St Armel, who had long been at odds with Conomorus, subsequently went to Paris, where he did his utmost to persuade Childebert to raise an army to overthrow Conomorus and restore Judwal as rightful ruler of Domnonia, but Armel's efforts were in vain. It took the intervention of his nephew St Samson, who headed a deputation of clerics, including Paul Aurelian and Bishop Albinus of Angers, and journeyed to Paris, to persuade Childebert to release Judwal and give support to a military campaign to overcome the tyrant Conomorus.

The Battle of Brank Aleg

Armel (Arthur) was by this time quite elderly, but he agreed without hesitation when his nephew Samson asked him to join forces with Judwal and himself to overthrow Conomorus and restore the rightful heir to the throne of Domnonia.[5] They assembled a large force, which included reinforcements provided by King Childebert, and set off to deal with Marcus Conomorus.

Strengthened by reinforcements (German barbarians) who landed at Ille de Tristan in the bay of Douarnenez on the west coast, Conomorus then marched north to meet his enemies at Brank Aleg near the foot of the Arée Mountains. Over a period of three days several battles were fought. On the evening of the third day, Prince Judwal struck Conomorus with a javelin. He fell from his horse and was trampled to death in the press of the charge. They buried the tyrant nearby and a large slab of rock known as Menbeg Konmor, standing above the village of Mengluez, not far from Brank Aleg, is said to mark his grave.[6]

St Armel was rewarded for his help in restoring Judwal to the throne of Dumnonia with a grant of land on which to found a church beside the River Seiche in the district now called Ille et Vilaine. It was here at the Church of St Armel-des-Boschaux, just south of Rennes, that St Armel was buried on 16 August 562, if we accept the date given by Albert Le Grand.

The Bones of King Arthur

It is not known for certain where St Armel died for the former *Breviary of Rennes* gives no information on the matter. Neither does Albert Le Grand or Dom Labineau. Chanonine Thomas believed that St Armel was returning from time to time to his church at the Boschaux, but died at Plöermel. A twelfth-century text (Morice, Preuves 1742) states that Armel's remains were lying in Ploërmel: '*Sanctus Armaleus, . . . cujus corpus . . . apud castrum quad dictur Ploasmel quie scit*'.

While Ploërmel never claimed to have his burial place, the church at St Armel-des-Boschaux proudly displays a stone sarcophagus which once contained his bones. It would seem that St Armel died at Ploërmel and his body was taken to St Armel-des-Boschaux for burial.

The old monastery at St Armel-des-Boschaux was destroyed during the Norman invasion in the tenth century, but the monks had prudently removed the relics of their founding saint to a safe location. When the present church was built, St Armel's coffin was set beneath an impressive archway, but it no longer contained his bones.

It would seem that St Armel's bones had been transferred to Ploërmel, for in 1645, the rector of Loutehel Church obtained from M. Tyart, rector of Plöermel, some relics of St Armel. Some of them were placed by rector Pierre Barre in a new reliquary at Loutehel in 1685. Other bones of St Armel held at Ploërmel were distributed to various churches in the area but the cranium was retained.

The skull kept at Ploërmel is not complete for Guiioux, Archbishop of Port-au-Prince, placed bits of it in the Church of Taupont's funeral monument, when he consecrated that church in 1784.

During the French Revolution, the constitutional priest Berruyer had actually claimed St Armel's skull as his own property. On 12 April 1794, he was arrested, in spite of pledges he gave the Revolution, but before he was thrown into gaol he gave the skull to Lady Le Gascombe, whose house adjoined the church. After the Revolution, she returned the skull to the clergy of Ploërmel and official recognition of this holy relic took place in 1810. In 1920, the rector of St Armel-des-Boschaux obtained from the priest of Plöermel the lower jaw, with permission of Bishop Gouraud of Vannes.

There are other relics of St Armel in existence, such as one kept by the parish of Plouharnel. It is made of bones from the lower arm – the radius and the cubitus. At Chateau-Revand in the Orléans area there are five fragments of his bones.

Contemporaries of St Armel Who Also Died in Armorica

St Samson, the son of Amwn Ddu and Anna (daughter of Meurig ap Tewdrig), was born in about 490 and just like his uncle Arthmael (Arthur), was educated at Llanilltud Fawr in Glamorgan.[7] He was ordained by St Dubricius who also consecrated him bishop on the Festival of St Peter's Chair, 22 February 521.

219

After periods on the island of Caldey and in Cornwall, Samson sailed to Armorica, where he settled at Dol to spend the greater part of his life.

St Samson can be accurately dated for he attended the third Council of Paris in 557 and signed his name among the bishops: 'Samson, peccator episcopus' ('Sinful Bishop Samson'). This was a conventional humble title.

He died on 28 July 565 and was buried at Dol. Much revered, he is recognised as the patron saint of Brittany. His body was interred in the sanctuary of his cathedral in the Gospel side of the altar. Samson was succeeded as episcopal abbot at Dol by his cousin St Maglorius, who had also been a disciple of St Illtud at Llanilltud Fawr.

Dol was too close to Normandy to know any peace in the tenth and eleventh centuries, though it did not fall to William the Conqueror, thanks to Philip I of France. Less than a hundred years later, it was taken by Henry II of England, and in 1203 the original cathedral was set on fire by King John. It was rebuilt in granite in the finest Norman Gothic style soon after and this is the building that can be seen today.

Lighting the apse is a fourteenth-century stained glass window, which depicts seven out of the nine Breton dioceses, each with its own bishop. The whole story of Samson, Dol's patron saint, is colourfully recorded.

In the 930s, King Aethelstan of Wessex acquired some of St Samson's relics, including an arm and his crozier. These were proudly displayed in Milton Abbey (Dorset) until the Reformation.

St Gildas, the son of Caw, was born in the district of Arecluta, which takes its name from the River Clut (Clyde), between Greenock and Glasgow. When his family found it necessary to seek refuge from the Picts and Scots they came to live in Mona (Anglesey), where Cadwallon Lawhir granted them land at Twrcelyn (the name of a commote in the north-east of the island).

Gildas was educated at Llanilltud Fawr and his fellow students were Arthmael, St Samson and St Paul Aurelian. Afterwards he became a disciple of St Catwg and then his confessor while residing at Llancarfan Monastery.

At a later stage in his life, Gildas left Britain and settled in Armorica where in about 530 he established a monastery on the rocky peninsula of Rhuys in Morbihan. Rhuys or Roe-is signifies royal, and the peninsula which is about 20 miles long and 6 miles across was always the property of the reigning duke, whose right of seignory extended over the whole area, with the exception of that held by the abbot and monks of St Gildas. He also spent time in St Nicholas des Eaux, a picturesque place on the River Blavet and founded a colony of monks in what is now the hamlet of Castannec.

In about 540 Gildas wrote a document known as *De Excidio et Conquesta Britanniae* (*Concerning the Ruin and Conquest of Britain*).[8] It is sometimes called the *Liber Querolus*, or *Book of Complaints*. Gildas weeps over the ruin of his country, the destruction of the Church and the slaughter and captivity of his countrymen.

Then follows his *Epistle* in which he makes scathing comments on five petty kings who were ruling in Britain at that time. It was an open letter of rebuke to the secular and ecclesiastical rulers of 'Britannia', which in a curious detached fashion he describes as *patria* ('fatherland') and its inhabitants as *cives*, citizens. By Britannia he does not mean the whole of the island of Britain, but just the portion that includes the Christian areas of Wales and the West Country. He addresses (by name) five kings, all of whom can be identified and located. They are Constantine of Dumnonia (Devon and Cornwall); Aurelius Caninus (who ruled in the lower Severn, in an area that included parts of Herefordshire and Monmouthshire); Vortiporius of Dyfed; Cuneglassus of Dinerth (near Llandudno in Rhos); and Maglocunus of Anglesey (Maelgwyn Gwynedd the Island Dragon).

Gildas accused Aurelius Caninus of murder, fornication, adultery and for having a thirst for civil war and constant plunder. He describes Vortiporius as being 'Like a leopard in manners and motley wickedness; though thy head has become grey, thou art seated upon a throne full of wickedness, defiled by murders and evil passions; thou worthless son of a good king!'

He refers to Cuneglassus as *ursus* (bear) and insults him by saying that he was 'a rough unmannerly person'. This may be interpreted as a description of Cuneglassus as an unmannerly bear, imitating Arthur, and that he was a poor ruler when compared to Arthur, the ruler of a strong Britain.

Maelgwyn Gwynedd is described as 'dragon of the island, you who have removed many tyrants from their country and even their life. You are last on my list, but first in evil, mightier than many both in power and in malice.'

Gildas, now living far away across the water, was able to look back at his homeland objectively and no doubt felt free to speak his mind. He obviously felt angry and frustrated for he wrote with heavy and bitter sarcasm, and expressed his concern for the future of Britain. Such strong invective against these rulers would have made it impossible for Gildas to return to Britain.

King Arthur is not mentioned in the manuscript which is surprising for he was a contemporary of St Gildas.[9] However, there would have been no need for Gildas to mention Arthur, for he was writing his epistle after Arthur had abdicated and was now residing just a short distance away. Gildas was criticising the tyrant kings and praising the good old days (in the lifetime of

Arthur), when there was peace and stability following the Battle of Badon. He is lashing out at the kings who succeeded Arthur after his abdication.

The *Annales Cambriae* record the death of Gildas at his monastery of St Gildas du Rhuys on 29 January 570. His death is also mentioned in the *Annals of Tigernach* and the *Annals of Ulster*, no doubt because he was highly regarded in Ireland as a religious leader.

St Paul Aurelian (St Pol de Léon) was born in Penychen (Caput Bovium = Head of the Oxen), Glywysing, in about 480. He was the son of Porphyrius Aurelianus who was descended from the family of Ambrosius Aurelianus. Porphyrius Aurelianus married a daughter of Meurig ap Tewdrig and was thus the brother-in-law of Arthmael (Arthur). After spending most of his life in Wales, where he founded churches at Llanddeusant and Llangorse, he travelled to Cornwall and then sailed to Armorica where he landed at Porz Ejenned (Port of the Oxen) on the island of Ouessant. Here, he erected a church at the place called Lampaul. He later crossed to the mainland and founded the church known as Lampaul Ploudalmezau. From there he went to Roscoff and on to the island of Batz, where he met his cousin Count Gwythyr, the ruler of Léon. The Count gave the island of Batz to Paul and he established a monastery at the eastern end where a Romanesque chapel now stands.

Paul then moved back to the mainland and founded a monastery in the ruined town of Ocsimor, which is now the city of St Pol-de-Léon. Here he ruled as a true saint-prince over an ecclesiastical principality conterminous in later times with the diocese of Léon. On the death of Count Gwythyr (Withur) in 530 without a male heir his principality was absorbed into Domnonia, with the exception of the portion that Paul had claimed and received as his right of kinship to the count.

Living to a great age, Paul was said to be so thin and wasted that the sunlight passed through his hand as if it was dull glass. He died in 573 at the age of 86 and was buried in his monastery beneath a black marble slab at the foot of the high altar. In the north side of the choir is the chapel of St Pol de Léon where there is a reliquary containing his skull, a finger bone and an arm bone. There is also a hammered bronze bell, which he is said to have owned and is reputed to have miraculous powers.

We possess an early *Life of St Pol de Léon* written by a monk named Wrmonoc before the destruction of the Breton monasteries by the Northmen in the tenth century. When the monasteries around the coast of Brittany were in danger, some of their treasures were taken inland, and Wrmonoc's *Life of St Pol de Léon* was taken to the great Abbey of Fleury, a few miles from

Orléans. The *Life* is in the handwriting of the ninth century and is now preserved in the public library at Orléans.

Of particular significance is the fact that Wrmonoc states that he received information directly from people arriving in Brittany from over the seas, from Cornwall and south Wales in particular. He mentions that St Paul Aurelian took with him from south-east Wales a party of twelve Presbyters to the court of King Mark (Marcus Conomorus) in Cornwall and they then proceeded on their way to Brittany. In that country he settled at Kastell Paol (now St Pol-de-Léon) from where his cult spread to many parts of north-western Brittany.

In the story of St Pol de Léon we have evidence of direct contact between early Christians and some of the leading Arthurian characters. The subsequent transference of much of this background to Brittany is the basis on which the French Arthurian Romances of the Middle Ages rests.

Summary

562 Death of St Armel (Arthur) at the age of 80 at Ploërmel. He was buried at St Armel-des-Boschaux, south of Rennes. His stone sarcophagus can still be seen and his jaw bone is kept in a gilded casket.

565 Death of St Samson (Arthur's nephew) at his monastery in Dol (now a cathedral), where his shrine used to attract large numbers of pilgrims.

570 Death of St Gildas at the age of 94 in his monastery at St Gildas du Rhuys, where his tomb and a reliquary containing some bones can be seen.

573 Death of St Paul Aurelian (cousin of Arthur) at his monastery where the Cathedral of St Pol-de-Léon now stands. His tomb is beneath a black marble slab at the foot of the high altar. During the Scandinavian invasions, his relics were transferred to the Fleury-on-Lovre monastery (Monastery of St Florent) in 954, where they were destroyed by the Huguenots in the sixteenth century (about 1567). Only part of his arm is preserved at of St Pol-de-Léon.

St Samson's Pillar at Llanilltud Fawr

It would seem that after the battle at Brank Aleg, in which Marcus Conomorus was defeated, St Samson returned to Glamorgan and commemorated the victory by erecting a stone cross at Llanilltud Fawr. It is known as the pillar of Abbot Samson and is a quadrangular cross shaft bearing decorated panels and a Latin inscription:

KING ARTHUR

IN NOM/INE DI SU/MMIINCI/
PITCRU/X SAL/UATO/RISQUA/
EPREPA/RAUIT/SAMSO/NI APA/
TIPRO/AMIMA/SVA & T P/ROANI/
MAIU/THAHE/LOREX
E/ART/MALIE/TECANI

In the name of the MOST HIGH GOD
was begun the cross of the Saviour which
Abbot Samson prepared for his own soul
and for the soul of King Iuthahel,
and for Artmal and Tecan

'TECANI', the last word, has been translated as Dean but according to Dr Peter Clement Bartrum, in *A Welsh Classical Dictionary* (1993), Tecan is identical with Bishop Tyrchan, who was present as a clerical witness to grants of land made by both Morgan ap Athrwys and Ithel ap Athrwys (see J. Gwenogvryn Evans and John Rhys, *The Text of the Book of Llan Dav* (1893), pp. 148 and 157).

Thomas Wakeman, a leading light of the Monmouthshire Antiquarian Association, examined the Samson Cross in 1848, and asserted that it was of the same period as the Hywel Cross because the individuals named can be identified in ninth-century Llandaff Charters. He identifies King Ithael who was killed in c.846, and either Arthmail, the grandfather of Hywel ap Rhys, or Arthmail a brother of Hywel.

In collaboration with Octavius Morgan, Wakeman suggested the date of the Samson Cross as c.850, some 300 years later than Iolo Morganwg (Edward Williams). This perceptive note by Thomas Wakeman, providing a chronological benchmark, was to have an effect on the dating of many early medieval crosses in Wales (Thomas Wakeman, 'On the age of some of the inscribed stones', *Archaeologiae Cambrensis*, 4 (1849), 18–20).

The appearance of the name Tecan on the Samson Cross gives it a sixth-century dating, as put forward by Edward Williams and the inscription testifies that St Samson made the cross for his own soul and for those of Iuthael (Judwal), the king, and Artmal (Arthmael = Arthur) and Tecan. It is confirmation of a successful campaign in Brittany organised by a band of soldiersaints to defeat the tyrant Marcus Conomorus.

CHAPTER 21

Henry VII, 'Son of Prophecy'

During the research for this book it became evident that Henry VII knew that King Arthur was synonymous with the great soldier-saint Arthmael (Armel). Through his own descent from the ancient British kings he saw himself as the successor of King Arthur and he believed that in defeating Richard III, to become King of England, he had fulfilled an ancient prophecy.

Although only partly Welsh, Henry was Celtic in appearance and temperament. He had been born in Pembroke Castle and had spent his early years there and in Brittany, which enabled him to become immersed in the ancient traditions of the Celtic people.

Henry was the son of Edmund Tudor and Lady Margaret Beaufort, the heiress of John of Gaunt. While fighting for the Lancastrian cause, Edmund Tudor died in his twenties of an epidemic disease at Carmarthen Castle three months before the birth of his son. His pregnant wife was just 13 years old and she sought the protection of her brother-in-law Jasper Tudor, who was constable of Pembroke Castle for the Lancastrians. She gave birth to Henry, the future King of England, in one of the rooms above the castle portcullis chamber on 28 January 1457. Henry spent his first years here, but when Pembroke Castle was captured by Lord William Herbert, a Yorkist, on 30 September 1462, he was taken to Raglan Castle in Gwent.

While living in the household of one of the two foremost Welsh bardic patrons of the age, it is quite likely that Henry Tudor was instructed in the history and culture of Wales. The young prince was brought up as a member of the Herbert family and he seems to have remained at Raglan for the next nine years.

After the death of Sir William Herbert, 1st Earl of Pembroke, at the Battle of Edgecote in 1469, his widow Anne Devereux, the sister of Sir Walter Devereux, 1st Baron Ferrers of Chartley, took Henry Tudor to the Devereux family home at Weobley. His time there must have been happy for Anne Devereux kept Henry Tudor's affections even after the death of her brother, fighting for the Yorkists at the Battle of Bosworth in 1485.

Henry now came back into the care of his father's brother Jasper, who was to be the crucial influence in his nephew's life for many years to come. In 1471, Jasper realised the increased importance of Henry as the possible Lancastrian claimant to the throne. He decided to take him abroad for safety and they set sail from Tenby, with the assistance of John White, a merchant from that town.

Jasper's original intention had been to sail to France, where he hoped to gain help from Louis XI, King of France, but the two exiles were blown off course to the little port of Le Conquet in Brittany. At this time, Brittany was an independent duchy ruled over by Duke Francis II. He proved to be a friendly and well-disposed host and gave them political asylum for fifteen years.

Initially, Henry and Jasper resided in the Chateau de l'Hermine, near Vannes, but were subsequently moved to the Chateau de Suscinio, on the Rhuys Peninsula, which encloses the Gulf of Morbihan. It was used as a summer residence by the dukes of Brittany and stands near the Abbey of St Gildas.

Henry and Jasper were separated two years later, with Jasper being sent to live in the fortress of Josselin, about 20 miles from Vannes. Henry was taken to the Chateau of Langöet where he lived in a tall octagonal tower known as the Tour d'Elven. It was owned by Jean de Rieux, the marshall of Brittany and councillor of Francis II.

During his long years of exile in Brittany, living among the descendants of the British emigrants who had sailed there in the fifth and sixth centuries, Henry would no doubt have listened to Breton versions of the story of King Arthur. He would also have recalled his childhood days in Wales, when he used to listen to the old bards proclaiming the ancient prophecy that a Welshman would one day yet again wear the Crown of Britain.

By 1483, Edward IV had died and he was succeeded by Richard III. Prince Henry was now about 28 years of age and he decided that the time had come to make a determined attempt to overthrow Richard and seize his crown. He came to the conclusion that the only way to obtain the support that he needed was to take full advantage of his Welsh ancestry. On Christmas day in 1483 Henry swore an oath in Rennes Cathedral that when he became King of England he would marry Princess Elizabeth, heiress of the House of York (eldest daughter of Edward IV). Through the Mortimers she was descended from a daughter of Llywellyn the Great and was truly a Celtic princess admirably suited to be his queen.

Henry decided to return to Wales and seek assistance from his countrymen, in the hope that he could persuade them to rise under the standard of the Red Dragon to fulfil the old dream and place him on the English throne.[1]

On landing secretly in Pembrokeshire, Henry made his way to the home of Richard ap Howell of Mostyn and pleaded his cause. However, his intentions had already been leaked to King Richard, whose soldiers marched from Flint Castle to Mostyn Hall. Hammering on the door, they demanded that Henry be handed over to them in the name of the king. Meanwhile, the young prince was being assisted out of a window at the rear of the building and he fled on horseback to a safe place in the Welsh mountains.

He then returned to France where he succeeded in mustering an army, leaving Sir John Bourchier, 2nd Baron Berners, and the Marquis of Dorset as security for the money he had borrowed. Henry and his army embarked at Harfleur and the flotilla emerged slowly from the shelter of the Seine.

On 7 August 1485, he landed at Milford Haven in west Wales with 2,000 men. They consisted largely of criminals, but in addition he brought over 2,000 exiles, men who like himself had fled to France for fear of death at the hands of King Richard. One observer described them as 'the worst rabble one could find'. Henry's uncle Earl Jasper had also come with him with the intention of persuading the men of his earldom to join them in their fight against the king.

Henry was also relying on his countrymen to give assistance and this was the very reason why he landed in Wales. It was his hope that the Cymry would rally to his standard in sufficient numbers for them to overthrow Richard. Owain Glyndwr had raised the Red Dragon, about eighty-five years previously, when he proclaimed himself Prince of Wales, and Henry now marched under the same banner. He was convinced in his own mind that his destiny was not only to free Wales from English domination, but also to seize for himself, as one of the descendants of the great Cunedda Wledig, the Crown of England which the Normans had wrested from the English at Hastings in 1066. Henry's slender claim to the English throne was through his mother Margaret, who married Edmund Tudor, Earl of Richmond, a half-brother of Henry VI. On this Welsh side of his family, Henry Tudor's great-grandfather Mareddud ap Tudor was a first cousin of the great Welsh hero Owain Glyndwr, who had made a bid for Welsh independence in 1400. It can be said that Henry VII, the first Tudor monarch, was one-quarter Welsh, one-quarter French and half English.

Since Owain Glyndwr had broken their power, the Norman Lords Marcher had nearly disappeared and had been replaced by Welsh chieftains who still listened to the songs of the bards and believed in the ancient prophecies. They had grown up under the spell of the old beliefs and their bards never ceased to sing of the times when the Crown of Britain had belonged to the Cymry. Word quickly spread that Henry, a prince born in Wales, had arrived on the scene and every bard was acclaiming him Mab y Darogan – 'Son of prophecy'. So, with very little persuasion the men of Wales took up arms and rallied to Henry's cause.

The subsequent battle was fought to the south-west of Market Bosworth, virtually in the heart of England, and it resulted in the death of King Richard III, the last Norman king. Once he had fallen, all his men fled from the scene and the Battle of Bosworth was over. The dead king's crown was picked out of a hawthorn bush and solemnly placed on the head of Henry Tudor. At last the old prophecy was fulfilled, for the Crown of Britain had now returned to a Welshman.

To the Welsh, Henry Tudor was the combination of a new Owain Glyndwr and the return of their ancient hero King Arthur. The Welshmen who helped him to regain his crown were well rewarded. His uncle Jasper became Duke of Bedford and Justicar of South Wales, and was later made Lord of Glamorgan. Rhys ap Thomas was knighted and appointed Constable of Brecknock, Chamberlain of Carmarthen and Cardigan and Steward of the Lordship of Builth. William Gruffydd was made Chamberlain of North Wales.

The Royal Commission
The Denbighshire historian David Powell (*History of Cambria* (1584)) states that Henry VII appointed a commission to chronicle his descent from the Welsh princes and British kings. The Abbot of Valle Crucis, Dr Owen Pool, Canon of Hereford and John King, an English herald, were empowered to make an inquisition concerning Henry's grandfather, Owen Tudor. These commissioners enlisted the aid of Sir John Leyaf, Gruffydd ab Llewellyn ab Evan Vychan and Guttyn Owain, historian and herald bard to the abbeys of Basingwerk and Strata Florida.

They diligently sought and studied the ancient genealogies in search of the British or Welsh books of pedigrees, out of which to draw Henry's perfect genealogy from the ancient kings of Britain and princes of Wales. Their findings were supported by Bernard André, a cleric historian who was later to write a history of Henry's reign, detailing his royal descent from Cadwaladr on his father's side, and from John of Gaunt on his mother's side of the family. It was emphasised that the ancient prophecies contained in the writings of Geoffrey of Monmouth had at last been fulfilled.

Arthur, Prince of Wales

Henry became so obsessed with the traditions of King Arthur that he even decided that his first born son should be named Arthur so that he would one day fulfil the ancient prophecy that Arthur should return to rule his people.

Though not unknown among English royal family personal names, Arthur was certainly unprecedented as a name for the heir to the throne on whom so much depended. The Welsh poets were delighted and prophesied a great future for the young prince.

It was considered appropriate that the child should be born in Winchester Castle, for it had been identified as Camelot by Malory and it was there that King Arthur's Round Table was kept. In late August 1486, King Henry and Queen Elizabeth set off with a large entourage to Winchester and on 20 September Elizabeth gave birth to a son whom they named Arthur, 'in honour of the British race'. The infant prince was christened 'Arthur – Arthurus Secondus' in Winchester Cathedral a few days later.

He was given the dormant title of Prince of Wales in November 1489 and betrothed to Lady Catherine, fourth daughter of Ferdinand II, King of Aragon, and Isabella of Castille. Twelve years later on 4 October 1501, Lady Catherine, now aged 18, arrived at Plymouth and she was married to 15-year-old Arthur, Prince of Wales, on 14 November of that year in St Paul's Cathedral. Her father gave her a dowry of 200,000 ducats, and her jointure was the third part of the principality of Wales, and of the earldom of Chester, and of the dukedom of Cornwall.

The young couple were sent to Ludlow Castle to set up court and to govern Wales with the assistance of a body of councillors. This was appropriate for a Council of the Marches had been established at Ludlow under Edward IV to administer Wales.

However, the dream was not to be fulfilled for Prince Arthur only lived to be 16 and died of influenza at Ludlow Castle on 2 April 1502. The young couple had lived at Ludlow for just four-and-a-half months.

Arthur's heart was removed and sealed in a silver box which was placed in the chancel of St Laurence's Church at Ludlow. His body was taken from the castle to Worcester Cathedral and laid in a tomb within a chantry chapel, which King Henry had constructed for his son on the south side of the high altar.

His death at such an early age changed the course of history for it meant that his brother Henry was now heir to the throne. Less than a year later young Henry was created Prince of Wales, a title that obviously meant little to him for it would seem that he never actually set foot in Wales. Henry in due course married his brother's widow, Catherine of Aragon, who became the first of his famous six wives.

Margaret, the daughter of Henry VII, became the wife of James IV of Scotland and in 1509 she named her second son Arthur but he died within a year. It is interesting that the name Arthur was also popular with royalty in later times. For example, in 1850 Queen Victoria's third son was christened Arthur and he became Duke of Connaught. King George VI had Arthur as one of his names and his grandson Charles, the present Prince of Wales, was given the name Arthur when he was christened in 1948. His eldest son William, the next in line to the throne, also bears the name Arthur.

The Ancient Order of Prince Arthur

In his preface to Sir Thomas Malory's *Le Morte d'Arthur*, William Caxton writes: 'In the Abbey of Westminster, at St. Edward's Shrine, remaineth the print of his seal in red wax closed in beryl, in which is written *"Patricius Arthurus, Britannie, Gallie, Germanie, Dacie, Imperator"'*. The name Arthur is given to St Edward in the same way as William of Malmesbury, speaking of Ambrosius Aurelianus, calls this man, having quite another name, '*Arthurus*'. It is significant that Latin writers always refer to Arthur as Arthurus, never as Artorius. The name is used as a synonym for a certain type of hero. It was a title given to those who honoured and fought for the continuity of the evolution of the island kingdom in such a way that the progress and evolution of other nations were included. It was many years after his death that St Edward received the title 'Patricius Arthurus' and it was sealed on his tomb. Those who did this must have had powerful authority behind them to have obtained the necessary permission. This shows that a Society of Knights must have existed closely connected with the royal house. The name of Arthur was used by this society because they worked for the historical continuity of the best traditions of Britain.

The description of the founding of such a secret knightly society in England, using the name of Arthur, may belong to a time a hundred years earlier than its publication in book form. In the British Museum there is a book entitled *The Ancient Order, Society and Unity Laudable of Prince Arthur and Knightly Armoury of the Round Table*, by Richard Robertson, printed by John Wolf and published in London in 1583. It is dedicated to the chief custom official of the Port of London and to the Society of Archers.

The book demonstrates that the Tudors established some kind of society, which centred in England, included in its membership men of other countries, some of them having been rulers of importance in Europe as, for example, the Holy Roman Emperor Maximilian I, who, one year after the publication of *Le Morte d'Arthur*, was elected Holy Roman Emperor. On his monument in the Royal Chapel of Innsbruck, the design of which had been made during his lifetime, there are twenty-eight figures as torch bearers, one of whom is King Arthur of Britain. This great monument was begun in 1509 and finished in 1583, the same year as the publication of Robertson's book *The Ancient Order, Society and Unity Laudable of Prince Arthur and Knightly Armoury of the Round Table*. Maximilian was counted as the last knight, and there is no doubt that he was fully acquainted with the knowledge of the Arthurian traditions. It was no accident that Maximilian I erected a statue of King Arthur in the Innsbruck court chapel. On the contrary, it is evident that the attempt to revive the Arthurian legend was not only in line with the dynastic interests of the English royal family but, beyond that, was of concern to members of the nobility in general.

The Devereux Connection
The Devereux family traced their descent from Robert d'Evereux, a companion of William I of Normandy. Richard, 3rd Count of Evreux in Eure, Normandy, who died in 1067, first married Helena, a princess of the House of Léon, the same house into which Arthmael (Arthur) had married over 500 years earlier.

During the residence of Prince Arthur at Ludlow Castle, a member of the Devereux family was present and the connection of this family with the Tudors is of special interest. Anne Devereux, the sister of Sir Walter Devereux, following the death of her husband Sir William Herbert, at the Battle of Edgecote in 1469, took young Henry Tudor with her to the Devereux family home at Weobley for safe keeping during the Wars of the Roses.

Sir Walter Devereux, 1st Baron Ferrers of Chartley, met his death while fighting for Richard III at the Battle of Bosworth on 22 August 1485.[2] It was a grandson of Sir Walter Devereux, of the same name, who was appointed in 1513, as a member of the Council of Wales and the Marches which had its headquarters at Ludlow Castle. In 1532 Sir Walter Devereux purchased Merevale Manor from the Crown.

The Merevale Window
At Merevale Church, near Atherstone in Warwickshire, can be seen a very fine sixteenth-century stained glass window that depicts St Arthmael. He is shown wearing a large cape fastened by a morse at the neck and open in front, disclosing a complete suit of armour consisting of a breast-plate and taces,

beneath which a skirt of mail appears. The legs are in plate armour and the feet are enclosed in broad-toed sabbatons. The left hand holds a crozier and on the head is a mitre. He holds a book in his right hand, suspended from which is a stole that is wrapped around the dragon like a halter. The armour is of early sixteenth-century style and the window glass is of a similar date. It is the only window in England that depicts St Arthmael.

Merevale Church was originally the gate chapel of Merevale Abbey and dates back to 1240. It is the only Cistercian gate chapel in Britain that is still in use throughout the year. It is of interest that Henry Tudor stayed at Merevale Abbey the night before the Battle of Bosworth on 22 August 1485. He returned to Merevale eight years later, in September 1503, and compensated the parish for damage to crops caused when his soldiers marched to the battlefield. It is possible that he also at that time arranged for the Arthmael window to be installed to commemorate his victory.

In the eighteenth century Merevale Abbey became a seat of the Dugdale family and one of their ancestors was Sir William Dugdale (1605–86), a celebrated antiquary and genealogist, who was the author of the *Monasticon Anglicanum*, a collection of records relating to monastic foundations. He compiled it in collaboration with Roger Dodsworth and it was subsequently published in three separate volumes in 1655, 1661 and 1673. On p. 190 of Vol. III it is stated that in the ancient register of the Cathedral Church of Llandaff is the only instance which occurs, in that register, of the name ARTHUR, so spelled, as the King of Gwent, son of Mouric, King of Morgannwg, and father of Morcant. Elsewhere, he is uniformly called Athruis and identified as a contemporary of Comergwynus, a bishop of the see of Llandaff.

It would seem that Sir William Dugdale knew the true identity of King Arthur and it is a remarkable coincidence that St Arthmael is portrayed in the Church of St Mary at Merevale, the seat of the Dugdales.

The Chapel of King Henry VII
Inside Westminster Abbey is a magnificent chapel in which the tomb of Henry VII and his wife Elizabeth of York is situated behind the altar. Henry died at his new palace of Richmond on 21 April 1509, aged 52, having suffered for some time with gout, asthma and general respiratory problems.

Confirmation that Henry knew that Arthmael was synonymous with King Arthur can be found in the third bay of the south triforium, where a statuette of a bearded man vested in a chasuble can be seen. It is a representation of St Arthmael. His hands are enclosed in plated gauntlets and with one he holds a stole in which a dragon is bound.[3] He is also depicted in a statuette positioned at the east end of the north aisle and is shown mailed beneath his habit, confirming that he was a soldier-saint, and is trampling on a dragon, symbolically destroying evil forces.

It is explained by the fact that it was believed that the great soldier-saint Arthmael, who delivered his people from tyranny, is synonymous with King Arthur. Henry Tudor undoubtedly believed that in overthrowing Richard III, he was fulfilling the prophecy of Merlin which foretold the return of King Arthur.

Further evidence for the obession of Henry VII with the cult of St Armel (Arthmael) can even be found in certain prayer books of this period which contain the name and picture of this soldier-saint.

The tomb of Cardinal Morton in the crypt of Canterbury Cathedral is decorated with a series of saintly figures. Unfortunately, they are all headless and mutilated, but the lowest figure on the east side has been identified as St Armel. It is relevant that John Morton in his younger days was imprisoned by Richard of Gloucester, but he escaped and joined Henry Tudor in Brittany. He continued to enjoy Henry's confidence after the Battle of Bosworth and served as his Lord Chancellor for thirteen years, until his death in 1500. As Henry Tudor's companion in exile and his later chancellor and confidant, it would certainly seem appropriate for a statue of St Armel to be carved on his tomb.

The Publication of Malory's *Le Morte d'Arthur*

It is perhaps more than coincidence that Sir Thomas Malory's *Le Morte d'Arthur* was published in the same year that Henry Tudor won the Battle of Bosworth and was crowned Henry VII. The identity of the author of this fifteenth century masterpiece has been open to question for there were several people named Thomas Malory around at the time when the book was being written, but it is generally accepted that the strongest candidate is Sir Thomas Malory of Newbold Revel in Warwickshire.

The manuscript was completed in the ninth year of the reign of Edward IV in 1470, and Sir Thomas Malory died the following year. He was buried at the church of the monastery of the Grey Friars, near Newgate prison, in which he had served a long-term sentence. The nearby monastery had a well-stocked library which may have provided the sources from which he wrote. These involved at least nine principal works, including the best known French Arthurian romances, and he also drew upon a number of English ones as well.

It is relevant that Henry Tudor's mother, Margaret Beaufort, patroness of the universities of Oxford and Cambridge, employed Sir Thomas Malory at her own expense to write a book about King Arthur. She firmly believed that her son was lineally descended from the famous British king and that such a book would help his cause to overthrow Richard III.

Malory was instructed to collect, sift and compile material from Welsh manuscripts then extant, various traditions in Wales and Cornwall, and all historical data that he could find relating to the story of King Arthur.

The final result was a cycle of Arthurian romances, coordinated and welded into a book of literature which the author described as 'The whole book of King Arthur and his Knights of the Round Table'. In his work there is little trace of Arthur's Celtic origins; he is presented as the rightful king of England, a realm that would not even have existed in Arthur's time.

Malory's patron was Richard Beauchamp, Earl of Warwick, whom he had followed to France in 1436. Malory fought in the War of the Roses, initially on the Yorkist side, and then largely on the Lancastrian side when Warwick made his final bid for power.

Malory would quite naturally have been influenced by the fact that 'King Arthur's Round Table' could be seen in the Great Hall of Winchester and this famous artefact ensured that he sited Arthur's court of Camelot in that place ('Camelot that is called in English Winchester'). He would have seen the table before it was repainted in green and white (1592) on the orders of Henry VIII in order to impress the visiting Emperor Charles V.

While he managed to complete his 383,000-word masterpiece, Malory did not live to see it in print, for he died at Newgate and was buried at Greyfriars Church on 14 March 1471, which was fourteen years before the book was published.

The publisher was William Caxton, who brought the art of printing to England in 1485, when he set up his press in the almonry of Westminster Abbey. Margaret Beaufort, who was residing at Westminster, took a personal interest in the printing of this book which Caxton named *Le Morte d'Arthur*. It came out on 31 July 1485, the day before Henry Tudor sailed from Harfleur and three weeks before the Battle of Bosworth. This book contained a whole cycle of Arthurian romances welded together into a work of literature. Only one copy of the first edition of the book has survived and this is held in the Morgan Library, New York, but in 1934 a manuscript found in the Fellows' Library of Winchester College was identified as a fifteenth-century copy of Malory's works. It had probably been written during the 1470s, after Malory's death but before the version printed by William Caxton.

APPENDIX I

Chronology

383	Magnus Maximus leads Roman legions out of Britain
388	Magnus Maximus dies
c.400	Hadrian's Wall is abandoned
410	Alaric the Goth sacks Rome and the Emperor Honorius tells Britons to look to their own defence
c.420	Death of Coel Hen, probably the last Roman *Dux Brittanniarum*
425	Vortigern's reign begins
c.428	Hengist and Horsa traditionally land, having been invited over by Vortigern
429	St Germanus of Auxerre visits Britain
446	Britons appeal to Aetius, Roman Governor of Gaul, for military assistance in their struggle against the Picts and the Irish/Scots; no help could be sent for Aetius is fighting off Attila the Hun
447	Saxons come to Britain as treaty troops
455	Hengist and Horsa fight Vortimer and Catigern at the Battle of Aylesford
457	Jutes defeat Britons at Crayford
c.460–75	Britons led by Ambrosius Aurelianus
c.469	Western Roman Emperor Anthemius appeals to the Britons for military help against the Visigoths. Riothamus takes a force of 12,000 to Gaul and is defeated in battle
477	Aelle, the Saxon chieftain, comes to Britain
c.480	Death of King Glywys of Glywysing whose kingdom is divided into Gwynllwg, Penychen, Gorfenedd, Edeligion, etc.
482	Birth of Arthur at Boverton
497	The death of Ambrosius coincides with the appearance of a comet which is described by Geoffrey of Monmouth. Arthur is crowned leader of the Britons at Caer Vudei (Woodchester)
508	The Gewissei and their Jutish allies make a piratical raid up the

235

Severn Sea. Their advance is checked by the western Britons led by Geraint Llyngesog. He is slain in the Battle of Llongborth and buried at Merthyr Gerein (Martyrium of Geraint) on the Gwent shore of the Severn Estuary

510   Arthur gives assistance to his kinsman Riwal Mawr in Armorica against an invasion of the Visigoths

512   Uthyr Pendragon comes out of retirement to fight a battle against the Teutonic alliance and avenge the death of his nephew Geraint at Llongborth. The *Anglo-Saxon Chronicle* tells us that a British Pendragon is killed at Dragon Hill (near Uffington) with 5,000 thousand of his men

Arthur takes over as battle commander and fights a series of twelve battles. Of these, five are fought to subjugate the settlements of the Middle and East Angles. Another is fought against the northern Angles, followed by one against the Picts. The remaining five battles are fought in south-west Britain against the Gewissei and their allies

517   Death of King Cadwallon Lawhir of Gwynedd and his son Maelgwyn takes the throne

518   The final battle is fought at Mount Badon, just outside Bath, and Arthur's decisive victory results in a long period of peace for the Britons and enables them to become a united nation

521   St Samson is consecrated a bishop by St Dyfrig

522   St Dyfrig resigns his see and retires to Bardsey Island

524   Riwal Mawr, the cousin of Arthur, is killed in battle and is said to be buried at Llanilltud Fawr

530   Count Gwythyr, the father of Gwenhwyfar (Guinevere), dies and she inherits his estates. Her husband Arthur thus gains control of the principality of Léon in Armorica (Brittany). Léon is absorbed into the Armorican kingdom of Domnonia under the joint rule of Arthur and Riwal Mawr's son and successsor Deroch (King of Armorican Domnonia, 524–35)

533   Deroch requests help against an invasion of the Visigoths, and Arthur, as a result, is away from his own kingdom for four years. Medraut seizes Arthur's realm and queen

c.535   Death of St Illtud, Abbot of Llanilltud Fawr

537   News of the uprising reaches Arthur, who is in Ireland fighting Llwch Llawinawg. He returns with all that survives of his army and lands at a little harbour (now called Cadlan – 'Place of

Battle') on the Llyyn Peninsula, where the family of Medraut have territory. After fighting his way ashore, he pursues Medraut to a location near Dinas Mawddwy, where the Battle of Camlann is fought. Medraut is slain and Arthur is critically injured. He is taken by boat, possibly sailing from Arthog, to a monastery on Ynys Afallach (Bardsey Island) to have his wounds tended. After recovering from his injuries, he abdicates, handing over his crown to Constantine, the son of Cadwy. Following the fall of Arthur, the great confederacy of British kingdoms disintegrates into its component parts

544	St David dies, aged 82, in his monastery at Mynyw (Menevia), where the impressive Cathedral of St David's now stands
546	Death of St Dyfrig in retirement on Bardsey Island
547	Maelgwyn Gwynedd dies of bubonic plague
549	Marcus Conomorus (King Mark), who has now settled in Armorica, assassinates Jonas, the son of Deroch. In order to obtain the regency. Conomorus marries Jonas's widow, and Judwal, the rightful heir, is forced to flee for his life to the court of the Frankish King Childebert in Paris
c.550	The Drustunus Stone is erected to commemorate Tristan, son of Marcus Conomorus
554	Arthur quarrels with the usurper Marcus Conomorus and goes to Paris where he endeavours to persuade Childebert to displace Conomorus and restore Judwal. Arthur's nephew Samson, arrives and together they manage to break down Childebert's opposition. They then return to Armorica to organise an insurrection on behalf of Judwal
555	The combined forces of Samson, Judwal and Arthur, together with reinforcements provided by King Childebert, meet the forces of Conomorus near Brank Aleg at the foot of the Arée Mountains and fight three battles over three days. Finally, Judwal runs Conomorus through with a javelin. He falls from his horse and is trampled to death in the press of the charge
	Judwal, now King of Armorican Domnonia, rewards Arthur for his services by granting him land on the River Seiche, where today stands the village of St Armel-des-Boschaux. Here he establishes a monastery. It is significant that the whole region of the Ille et Villaine, which was granted to St Armel (Arthur) by Judwal, is the area in Brittany most associated with the legends

	of King Arthur and his Knights of the Round Table and here their memory still lingers
562	Death of St Armel (Arthur), at the age of 80, possibly at Ploërmel. He is buried at St Armel-des-Boschaux in a stone sarcophagus
565	Death of St Samson, the nephew of Arthur, at his monastery in Dol, Armorica, where his shrine used to attract large numbers of pilgrims
570	Death of St Gildas, aged 94, at St Gildas du Rhuys, where his tomb and bones in a casket can be seen
573	Death of St Paul Aurelian at the age of 86 (who like Arthur was born at Boverton in Glamorgan), at his monastery, St Pol-de-Léon, in Armorica
586	Death of King Rhun Hir of Gwynedd
589	Death of King Constantine of Dumnonia
597	Death of St Columba
625	King Cadfan of Gwynedd dies and is buried at Llangadwaladr where his memorial stone can be seen. His son King Cadwallon succeeds to the throne
c.626	King Cadwallon is defeated in battle by King Edwin of Deira and flees to Brittany
632	King Cadwallon defeats and kills King Edwin of Deira in the Battle of Hatfield Chase
633	King Cadwallon of Gwynedd kills King Eanfrith of Bernicia and King Osric of Deira but is subsequently killed by King Oswald of Northumbria at the Battle of Heavenfield (Hexham). He is succeeded by Cadafael ap Cynfedw
654	Cadafael Cadomedd flees after deserting Penda at the Battle of the Winwaed. He is disgraced and resigns the throne to Cadwaladr ap Cadwallon
664	Death of King Cadwaldr Fendigaid of Gwynedd
665	Second Battle of Badon in which Morgan Morgannwg is killed
c.731	King Elisedd (Eliseg) of Powys expels the Mercians from his kingdom
754	Death of King Rhodri Molwynog of Gwynedd
c.784	Construction of Offa's Dyke by King Offa of Mercia
c.850	Cyngen, King of Powys, erects the Pillar of Eliseg as a memorial to his great-grandfather King Elisedd (or Eliseg)
854	Cyngen dies while on a pilgrimage to Rome and Rhodri Mawr of Gwynedd becomes King of Powys

APPENDIX I

871–99	The *Anglo-Saxon Chronicle* is compiled from early monastic records on the orders of Alfred the Great
c.960	The *Annales Cambriae* are compiled
c.990	The *Mabinogion* story of 'Culhwch and Olwen' is composed
c.1080	Lifris writes the *Life of St Cadoc*, which mentions Arthur
1125	William of Malmesbury writes the *Gesta Regum Anglorum* in which he refers to Arthur
1136	Geoffrey of Monmouth compiles the *Historia Regum Britanniae* Henry of Huntingdon writes the *Historia Anglorum* which includes a list of Arthur's battles taken from Nennius
1140	Caradoc of Llancarfan writes a *Life of Gildas* in which he mentions Arthur
1148	Geoffrey of Monmouth composes his poem *Vita Merlini*
c.1160	The *Mabinogion* story entitled 'The Dream of Rhonabwy' is composed
1191	The monks of Glastonbury Abbey claim to discover the grave of King Arthur and Queen Guinevere
1247	The monks of Glastonbury Abbey produce a revised edition of William of Malmesbury's *Gesta Regum Anglorum*
c.1250	The *Black Book of Carmarthen*, the oldest surviving manuscript to contain Welsh poems mentioning Arthur, is compiled
1265	The *Book of Aneurin*, containing the surviving copy of *Y Gododdin*, is compiled
1325	The *White Book of Rhydderch*, containing the earliest section from 'Culhwch and Olwen', is compiled
1400	The *Red Book of Hergest* is compiled. It contains 'The Dream of Rhonabwy', the tale of 'Culhwch and Olwen' and the 'Canu Llywarch Hen'
1470	Sir Thomas Malory completes *Le Morte D'Arthur*

The Positive Identification of King Arthur

Present-day academic historians refuse to accept Athrwys ap Meurig as the basis for Arthur because they insist on placing him in the seventh century and not the sixth century. He is made out to be a petty king of south-east Wales who was outlived by his father and never became king over a large area.

Arguments for identifying Arthur with Arthmael and Arthmael with Athrwys ap Meurig

1. Arthur was known as 'The Bear' after the Celtic bear deity and signifying a powerful leader of men. Arthmael means 'Bear Prince'. Therefore, Arthmael was like Arthur a royal prince who was also a powerful leader of men.

2. The *Vita Cadoci* (*Life of St Cadoc*), compiled by Lifris, mentions a grant of land, now known as Cadoxton-juxta-Neath, to St Cadoc (Catwg) by King Arthmael in c.530:

> When the islands became unsafe [Flatholm and Steepholm in the Bristol Channel], owing to the pirates who infested the estuary of the Severn making landing-places, St Cadoc was obliged to look for some other place of retreat. He found one on the banks of the River Neath. He sent gifts to King Arthmael, who thereupon made a grant of this spot, now known as Cadoxton-Juxta-Neath to St Cadoc.

According to the genealogy contained in the *Book of Llandaff*, the king who was reigning over Morgannwg and Gwent at this time was Athrwys ap Meurig ap Tewdrig. Lifris thus provides us with evidence that Athrwys and Arthmael are one and the same person.

APPENDIX II

3. According to the *Life of St Dubricius*, contained in the *Book of Llandaff*, St Dubricius crowned Arthur king when he was 15 years old. St Arthmael was born in 482 and would therefore have been 15 in 497 at the time of the death of Ambrosius Aurelianus, who had nominated Arthur his successor.

4. St Dubricius was a contemporary of St Samson, Bishop of Dol, whom he ordained on 21 February 521 and who attended the Council of Paris in 557, where he signed his name 'Samson peccator episcopus' among the bishops. St Samson was a contemporary kinsman of St Arthmael. Thus, Arthmael may be positively dated.

5. Arthur is depicted as a mighty warrior in the early manuscripts. In Nennius's *Historia Brittonum* and the *Welsh Annals* he is depicted not only as a military but also a religious leader. In Nennius's *Historia Brittonum* he is referred to as Arturus Miles (Arthur the Warrior) and in the *Life of St Efflam*, his contemporary, as Arturus Fortissimus (Arthur the Mighty). Arthmael is portrayed wearing armour in his designation of 'Miles Fortissimus ('Mighty Warrior') in the *Breviary of Léon* (1516), and the *Rennes Prose* (1492), in which he is invoked as the *armigere* (armour-bearer) against the enemies of our salvation. Therefore, Arthmael was a military and religious leader.

6. In his *Early Welsh Genealogical Tracts* (1966), P.C. Bartrum says that if we suppose that Arthur was born c.480 (Arthmael was born in 482!) and Eudaf Hen c.300, we should expect six generations between Arthur and Eudaf.

   482 - 300 divided by 6 = 30.3 years

   It should be borne in mind that Eudaf Hen was the brother of Meurig ap Caradog ap Bran, and that his daughter was Elen Luyddog, who was the wife of Macsen Wledig, who died in 388.

   Meurig, the brother of Eudaf Hen
   1. Erbig
   2. Erb
   3. Peibio Clavorauc
   4. Cynfyn
   5. Gwrgant Mawr
   6. Onbrawst, who married Meurig ap Tewdrig

7. Athrwys, known also as Arthmael (Arthur)

7. Arthmael or Armel, as he is known in Brittany, has church dedications around Vannes where Arthur and his cousin Riwal Mawr repelled a seabourne attack at Baden c.510.

8. Arthmael's tomb is in a church in the region of Brittany which is most associated with the legends of King Arthur.

Positive Dating of Athrwys ap Meurig

It is generally accepted that King Gwynllyw who gave his name to Gwynllywg, lived in the fifth/sixth century. His son St Catwg was thus a contemporary of Arthur and of St Illtud, who taught St Samson. The latter can be accurately dated as Bishop of Dol in Brittany from 547 to 565. Samson in 557 attended the Council of Paris and signed the decrees 'Samson peccator episcopus'. This council of bishops was concerned with the organisation of the Church in Brittany. Samson died in 565 and was buried in his monastery at Dol.

How the Identity of Arthur has been Obscured by Hugh Thomas of Brecon

Hugh Thomas (1673–1720) was the Deputy Herald to the Garter King of Arms. His great-grandfather Thomas ap John was keenly interested in antiquities and to him belongs the credit for having written the first history of Brecknockshire in about the time of Queen Elizabeth I.

According to Edward Owen (Catalogue of Welsh MSS in the British Museum, II, p. 460), this is the document in the Harleian Collection No. 6108, which is entitled *The History of Brecon from the time of Meurick, King of Britain, until the year of redemption, 1606*. There is no doubt that this was the document that first stirred Hugh Thomas's imagination and made him want to delve into Brecon's past history and to improve upon his great-grandfather's efforts by writing *An Essay towards the History of Brecknockshire* in 1698. Hugh's chief love was genealogy and his work in this field and his co-operation with William Lewes of Llwynderw, forms the basis of the *Golden Grove Book of Pedigrees*. In 1703, the Garter King of Arms appointed him his deputy with the sole right of recording genealogies in Wales, except Cardiganshire and Radnorshire.

In 1710 Hugh Thomas compiled a late and fictitious pedigree of the kings of Morgannwg (Harleian MS 4181), which he bequeathed to Lord Oxford.

It was derived from the *Book of Sir Richard Wynn of Gwydir*, whose source for the pedigree was the *Registrum Prioratus de Brecknock*.

This pedigree included Arthmael but in a genealogically and chronologically impossible position. Consequently, Hugh Thomas was responsible for losing Arthur in terms of historical fact. He took Arthfael, Gwrgan Frych and Meurig from the *Life of St Cadoc* and Meirchion from the *Life of St Illtud* and inserted them into his fictitious pedigree:

1. Bran
2. Caradog
3. Cyllin
4. Owain
5. Meirchion Fawdfilwr
6. Goruc
7. Gwrddwfn
8. Einudd
9. Arthfael
10. Gwrgan Frych
11. Meirchion
12. Meurig
13. Creirwy
14. Edric
15. Urban
16. Nynnio
17. Teithfalch
18. Tewdrig

Observations

8. Einudd ap Gwrddwfn, father of 9. Arthfael, may be identified with Einudd ap Morgan.

9. Arthfael ap Einudd is named in the pedigree as the father of Gwrgan Frych, but he may be identified with the Arthfael who appears as King of Gwlad Morgan in the *Life of St Cadoc* and who grants to the saint the land that became known as Cadoxton-juxta-Neath, i.e. Llangatwg (Glyn) Nedd.

10. Gwrgan Frych is named as the father of Meirchion and has been taken from the *Life of St Cadoc* and foisted into this fictitious pedigree in a chronologically impossible position. According to the *Life of St Cadoc*, Gwrgan Frych, the Welsh equivalent used by the Revd Arthur Wade-Evans for the name of Wrgannus Varius, King of Gwlad Morgan, was given a sword

243

by St Cadoc which the saint had received from Rhun ap Maelgwyn. In return St Cadoc received the right to half the fish of the River Usk. St Cadoc also gave Gwrgan a horse with all its trappings for one half of the fish of the River Neath. It has been suggested that this Gwrgan was the same as Gwrgan Mawr ap Cynfyn, King of Erging. This is somewhat corroborated by the fact that the Titus MS of the *Life of St Cadoc* gives the name as Wrganus Vawr.

Inabwy, Gwrddogwy, Elhaearn and Gwernabwy, who were all disciples of St Dyfrig, witness deeds in the time of Comereg. In two charters in the *Book of Llandaff* Comereg is described as of 'Mochros' and 'Abbas Mochros' respectively, while the bishop is Inabwy and the king is named as **Gwrgan**. This is certainly **Gwrgan ap Cynfyn, King of Erging**. Mochros is now Moccas in Herefordshire. In another charter Comereg is named as bishop and the king is **Athrwys ap Meurig**, King of Gwent.

11. Meirchion ap Gwrgan Frych was the father of Meurig but may be identified with the Meirchion Wyllt (the Wild) or Vesanus (the Mad), who appears as King of Gwlad Morgan in the *Life of St Illtud*.

12. Meurig ap Meirchion is named in the pedigree as the father of Creirwy but may be identified with the Meurig ap Enhinti who appears in the *Life of St Cadoc*.

Hugh Thomas, in foisting Einudd, Arthfael, Gwrgan Frych, Meirchion and Meurig into his fictitious pedigree in chronologically impossible positions, has lost Arthmael in terms of historical fact.

Hugh Thomas died in 1720 and in his will bequeathed all his manuscripts and historical collection to Robert Harley, Earl of Oxford. Eventually, his manuscripts found their way into the British Museum as part of the Harleian Collection.

The Missing Century

A major problem was initially created by the compiler of the *Book of Llandaff*, for he failed to realise that there was a gap of approximately a hundred years in the ancient charters. This gap may be due to the loss of a document, possibly a book of the Gospels, which contained memoranda covering the entire seventh century.

Furthermore, the compiler was no doubt misled by the *Welsh Annals*, which give the death of St Dyfrig as 612 and the death of Morgan Mwynfawr as 665. St Dyfrig was in fact born c.450 and retired to Bardsey Isle about twenty years before his death (at the age of 96) in 546.

Confusion between two Morgans has caused a mistake in the dating of Morgan Mwynfawr's death. The Revd Arthur Wade-Evans, on studying the

APPENDIX II

Llancarfan Charters, clarifies this problem as follows:

There was ruling in Wlatmorgan a king called Gwrgan Frych (the Freckled), to whom St Cadoc gave gifts in exchange for half of the fish of the River Usk that he might have Lenten food at Llancarfan and for half part of the fish of the River Neath that he might have Lenten food at Llanmaes.

This Wrgannus Uarius of the Vespasian MS is called Wrganus Vawr in the Titus MS. He is the Gwrgant Mawr (the Great) of the Book of Llandaff. It is evident that Gwrgant Frych, otherwise Gwrgant Mawr, was an important man in his time and place, filling the interval between the dynasty of Glywys and that of Morgan Mwynfawr. He had a son, Morgan, who seems to have been confounded and well nigh lost in the Morgans of the sixth and seventh centuries respectively.

(The Revd Arthur Wade-Evans, 'The Llancarfan Charters', *Archaeologiae Cambrensis*, Vol. LXXXVII (1932), 151–65)

The compiler of the Book of Llandaff made one 'King Morgan' out of two men bearing the same name. The first was Morgan Mwynfawr ('the Courteous') ap Athrwys and the second was Morgan Morgannwg, who re-united the kingdom and died fighting the second Battle of Mons Badonicus, which is recorded in 665.

This confusion led the compiler of the *Book of Llandaff* to post-date the early kings of Erging and Gwent and consequently the genealogists have stretched the pedigrees in order to accommodate Morgan Morgannwg, who died in 665, but as soon as the two Morgans are separated by a century the chronological difficulty disappears.

Such confusion no doubt caused Professor Hector Munro Chadwick, when he was constructing his genealogy of the dynasty of Gwent, to misplace Meurig ap Tewdrig, King of Glamorgan and Gwent, creating an anomaly which post-dated his son Athrwys by more than a hundred years, thus pushing him into the seventh century. Another error was caused by the late John Morris, who had Athrwys's son Morgan Mwynfawr fighting the second Mons Badonicus in 665 instead of Morgan Morgannwg.

The comment has been made that as Meurig's reign was exceptionally long, his son Athrwys must have died early in his reign. However, Athrwys did not die young and he no doubt spent considerable time away from Wales, fighting battles, while Caradog Freichfras ruled Gwent, during Meurig's semi-retirement. It is certainly true that Meurig was still the nominal King of Gwent and was still making grants.

Mistakes are so easily made when there is a duplication of names and it can be shown that that two Morgans and two Meurigs have been confused, this being yet another factor that led to Athrwys ap Meurig ap Tewdrig being placed in the seventh instead of the sixth century.

The Revd Sabine Baring-Gould and John Fisher, in *The Lives of the British Saints* (1907–13), were convinced that there were two princes of Morgannwg and Gwent named Meurig and two named Morgan and that the compiler of the *Book of Llandaff* had confounded them. This view was also supported by the Revd Arthur Wade-Evans in 'The Llancarfan Charters' (1932). He proved that the Morgan who witnessed the grants of Meurig ap Tewdrig was not his grandson Morgan Mwynfawr, but his brother-in-law Morgan, the son of Gwrgant Mawr, while the later grants attributed to Meurig ap Tewdrig were in actual fact made by Meurig the son of Caradoc Freichfras.

The confounding of two Meurigs and two Morgans has helped to stretch the chronology of the early charters contained in the *Book of Llandaff*. A prime example is a grant made to Oudoceus by Meurig the king, and Judic son of Nud, witnessed by Morgan the king. This Morgan can hardly be the grandfather of Morgan Mwynfawr. There can be only one logical explanation. There were no less than three Morgans making and witnessing grants in the sixth and seventh centuries. They were Morgan ap Gwrgant Mawr, Morgan ap Athrwys ap Meurig and Morgan Morgannwg, who, according to the *Welsh Annals*, died in 665.

The Wrong Arthur
It can be shown that the compiler of the *Book of Llandaff* made the mistake of confounding Arthur ap Pedr, King of Dyfed, with Arthur ap Meurig, King of Gwent. In the grant of Llan Cinmarch by King Athrwys ap Meurig of Gwent to Bishop Comereg (BLD 165), one of the principal witnesses is Gwernabwy, Prior of Llangystennin Garth Benni, but Gwernabwy also appears as a witness to the grant of Pennalun (Penally in Dyfed) by Nowy ap Arthur to St Dyfrig.

Arthur ap Pedr ap Cyngar ap Gwerthefyr (Vortiporix) cannot be considered as a candidate for the historical King Arthur because his great-grandfather Gwerthefyr (Vortiporix) flourished in c.550. Arthur ap Pedr was therefore three generations too late for the time of the historical Arthur. He must have lived in the middle of the seventh century. This is yet another example of the compiler of the *Book of Landaff* having failed to notice the hundred-year gap in the charters.

It is possible that this gap in the charters contained in the *Book of Llandaff* may be due to the loss of a document, possibly a book of the Gospels, which contained memoranda covering the entire seventh century, and which disappeared in a series of calamities which are hinted at on p. 196 of the *Book of Llandaff*.

Origins of the Arthmael = Arthur Theory

c.530   The grant of Cadoxton-juxta-Neath by King Arthmael to
          St Cadoc (Catwg)

c.1073–86 The *Vita Cadoci* (*Life of St Cadoc*), written by Lifris, attached
          to which are the Llancarfan Charters. Mention is made of the
          grant of Cadoxton-juxta-Neath to St Cadoc by King Arthmael
          in c.530:

> When the islands became unsafe [Flatholm and
> Steepholm in the Bristol Channel], owing to the pirates
> who infested the estuary of the Severn making landing-
> places, St Cadoc was obliged to look for some other place
> of retreat. He found one on the banks of the River Neath.
> He sent gifts to King Arthmael, who thereupon made a
> grant of this spot, now known as Cadoxton-juxta-Neath,
> to St Cadoc.

The eleventh-century stone found buried in the floor of Ogmore
Castle mentions a grant of land by King Arthmael to Glywys,
Nertat and Bishop Fili, who all belong to the sixth century. The
inscription reads: '*Sciendum est omnibus quot dedit Arthmail
agrum do et Gligws et Nertat et Fili epi.*' – 'Be it known to all
that Arthmael has given this field to God and to Glywys and to
Nertat and to Bishop Fili.' The particular usage of '*Sciendum est
quod*' is rare elsewhere and it is extremely significant that it can
also be found in the charters attached to the *Vita Cadoci* from
Llancarfan
The fifteenth-century *Register of Neath*, the cartulary of Neath
Abbey, contains an early history of Morgannwg (Glamorgan)

and mentions King Arthur as ruling over the 'Land of Morgan' in the sixth century

c.1560 Llywelyn ap Rhisiart (Lewys Morgannwg), who flourished 1520–65, mentions Arthur as the king of the warlike land of Morgan. Lewys Morgannwg had cultural connections with Lleision Tomas, the last abbot of Neath Abbey, which was dissolved in 1539. The chief patron of Neath abbey was Sir Edward Stradling (d.1535) of St Donat's Castle, who was also the first patron of Lewys Morgannwg

1572–91 Llywelyn Sion of Llangewydd (1540–1615), in *Llyma Enwau a Hiliogaeth Brenhinoedd Morgannwg* ('These be the names and genealogies of the Kings of Glamorgan'), mentions Morgan succeeding to the twelve hundreds of Gwent Essyllt in the principalities of Arthur. Elsewhere he records that Adras ap Meurig was a very heroic sovereign who frequently put the Saxons to flight.

Adras = Athrwys = Arthmael = Arthur

1578—84 Rhys Meurig (1520–87), in *A Book of Glamorganshire Antiquities*, refers directly to the Register of Neath, which was held in the library of St Donat's Castle, and names Morgan as the son of Adras ap Meurig (Adras = Athrwys = Arthur)

1591 Sir Edward Mansel of Margam, in *Another Account of the Coming of the Normans*, mentions Morgan as the prince who lived in the time of King Arthur and was his son as some would have it

1673 Sir William Dugdale, in *Monasticon Anglicanum* (Vol. III, p. 190), mentions Arthur as the son of Meurig. He also used as a principal source the *Book of Llandaff*

1747 Thomas Carte, in *A General History of England* (1947, Vol. I, Bk III, p. 202) says that there is little room to doubt that the Arthruis, King of Gwent, who granted the land of St Kinmark to Bishop Comereg, was the Arthur in question

1759 Lewis's *Dictionary of Wales* states: 'Meurig ap Tewdrig, a man of great valour and wisdom, was the father of that Arthur who is now regarded by Welsh writers as that hero whose exploits form so distinguished a feature of the British Annals and who succeeded Meurig in his dominion.'

APPENDIX II

1775   The Revd John Whitaker, in his *History of Manchester* (1775, Vol. 11, p. 34), names Arthur as King of Gwent: 'Arthur was the Arthuir, great man, or Sovereign of the Proper Silures and therefore the denominated king of Gwent, the Venta Silurum of the Romans, and British metropolis of the nation.'

1796   David Williams, in *The History of Monmouthshire* (1796), states: 'Athrwys or Athruis, the son of Meurig ap Tewdrig, King of Gwent, assumed the appellation of Arthwyr, or the Bear Exalted. In 506, Arthwyr was elected by the states of Britain to exercise sovereign authority . . .'

1803   William Owen Pughe, in *The Cambrian Biography* (1803), states: 'About the year 517, Arthur was elected by the states of Britain to exercise sovereign authority . . . having been from 510 till then only a chieftain of the Silurian Britons, being the son of Meurig ap Tewdrig'

1834   John H. Parry, in *The Cambrian Plutarch* (1834), states: 'Arthur was the son of Meurig ap Tewdrig, a prince of the Silurian Britons at the commencement of the sixth century . . .'.

The Royal Imperial Pedigree of King Arthur

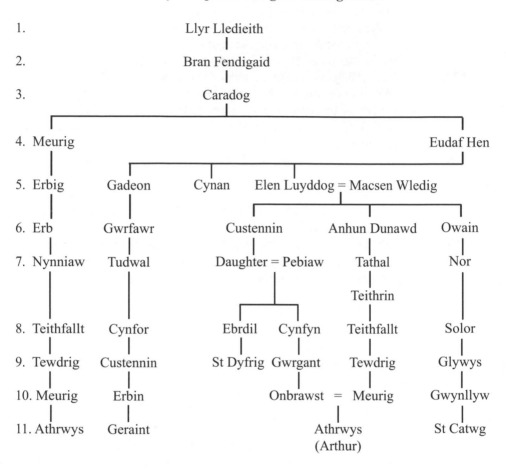

1.   Llyr Lledieith
2.   Bran Fendigaid
3.   Caradog

4. Meurig   Eudaf Hen

5. Erbig   Gadeon   Cynan   Elen Luyddog = Macsen Wledig

6. Erb   Gwrfawr   Custennin   Anhun Dunawd   Owain

7. Nynniaw   Tudwal   Daughter = Pebiaw   Tathal   Nor

                                                Teithrin

8. Teithfallt   Cynfor   Ebrdil   Cynfyn   Teithfallt   Solor

9. Tewdrig   Custennin   St Dyfrig   Gwrgant   Tewdrig   Glywys

10. Meurig   Erbin   Onbrawst = Meurig   Gwynllyw

11. Athrwys   Geraint   Athrwys   St Catwg
                                              (Arthur)

The above genealogical table illustrates that Athrwys belonged to the eleventh generation from Llyr Lledieith. He descended from Eudaf Hen's brother Meurig ap Caradog ap Bran. The grandfather of Athrwys was Tewdrig Fendigaid, who was also the grandfather of Brychan Brycheiniog. Tewdrig's daughter Marchell was the mother of Brychan. Both the Harleian MS 6108 and MS 7017 pedigrees name Meurig ap Tewdrig as the father of Athrwys and the Harleian MS 2414 pedigree names Eurbrawst, the daughter of Meurig, as the wife of Brychan. In view of the fact that Brychan was born c.480, Athrwys ap Meurig can be firmly dated.

Notes

Chapter One

1. Artur is mentioned in Book I, chapter 9 of Adomnan's *Vita Columbae* (*Life of St Columba*), written c.700. Aedan asks Columba which of his eight sons will succeed him. Columba seems to have prophetic powers for he predicts Aedan's successor and the fates of his sons, including Artur.

2. Adomnan (c.628–704) was the ninth abbot of Iona Monastery and a descendant of St Columba. He wrote the *Vita Columbae* in 691. There was an earlier *Life* written by Cummene Ailbe, the seventh abbot of Iona, who died ten years before Adomnan succeeded to the abbacy. Dorblene, the scribe of the earliest surviving Adomnan manuscript, inserted an extract from this *liber de vertutibus sancti Columbae* into Adomnan's text, but no manuscript of the Cummene work has survived.

3. Artur is called 'Arturus' in Adomnan's *Life of St Columbanus* and this is the earliest Latin documented form of the name.

4. Artur's death is also mentioned in the *Annals of Tigernach*, which date from c.1088.

5. Richard Barber (*The Figure of Arthur*, 1972) has argued a case for accepting Artur mac Aedan as the original hero. Likewise, David F. Carroll (*Artorius – A Quest for Camelot*, 1996) has also argued that Artur mac Aedan was the real Arthur, ruling Manau Guotodin from Camelon in Stirlingshire. Manau Guotodin was the area between the wall of Trajan and that of Antonine. It was the territory of the tribes of the Odeni and Votadini. The kingdom of Gododdin which controlled the region around the Firth of Forth until 638 was divided into two main regions: Manau, north of the Firth, around modern Stirling; and the large region of Lothian, on the south coast of the Firth, containing the capital of Caer Eden (Edinburgh).

6. The Scots came from a kingdom in Ireland that was known as Dalriada and was the equivalent in modern terms of County Antrim in northern Ireland. In about AD 500 the people of Dalriada led by Fergus Mor mac Erca crossed the water to Kintyre and in due course established a kingdom around Argyll.

7. Aneurin was the son of Caw (thus a brother of Gildas), who was lord of Cwm Cawlwyd, a region in north Britain. He does not appear to have been present at Catraeth in any other capacity than that of a Herald Bard. Although Aneurin survived this battle to celebrate the memory of his less fortunate

countrymen, he also met with a violent death. The Welsh Triads relate that he was killed by the blow of an axe, inflicted upon his head by Eidden son of Einigan. The poem *Y Gododdin* takes its name from the Latin appellation of the Votadini. It is the oldest poem in the Welsh language and is a description of a great battle fought in 570 at a place called Catraeth (believed to be the modern Catterick), where the confederate Cymry suffered a disastrous defeat. They fought with desperate valour, but only 3 out of the 363 chieftains who fought at the head of their clans survived. Aneurin was one of the survivors and he was taken prisoner, loaded with chains and thrown into a dungeon, from which he was subsequently released by Ceneu, a son of Llywarch Hen. The reference to the heroism of a certain Gwawrddur 'although he is not Arthur' is only in the B version and its antiquity is therefore uncertain.

8. Artur mac Petuir is named in the eighth-century Irish genealogy of the immigrant tribe of the Deisi. He appears as Arthur map Pedr in the Harleian genealogy of Dyfed.

9. The *Comes Britanniae* ('Count of Britain') was the supreme military authority, with a roving commission to defend the country against foreign invasion. As the commander of a mobile cavalry force he was able to move quickly to deal with any new threat.

10. The oldest reference to Athrwys ap Meurig is in the Harleian MSS 3859 as Atroys. Later manuscripts spell his name as Adroes, Athrawes, Arthues, Athraws, Arthraws, Athrwys and Adros.

11. Alternative names for the same person were not unusual in the sixth century. For example Catwg was also known as Cadmael. It is also of interest that the word mael (prince) entered into the composition of many Celtic names such as Maelgwyn, Maelog, Maelrhys and Dogmael.

Chapter Two

1. In his *Historia Regum Britanniae*, Geoffrey gives himself the Latinised Norman name 'Galfridus Monemutensis' and he accordingly became known as Geoffrey of Monmouth. He also describes himself as *pudibundus Britto*, 'a modest Briton'.

2. The *Vita Merlini* (*Life of Merlin*) appeared in 1151 and today only one complete version of the manuscript exists, with six extracts of varying length. It is dedicated to Robert, Bishop of Lincoln.

3. Acton Griscom, writing in 1929, suggests that the term 'Liber Vetustissimus' is a reference to the Welsh chronicles which Geoffrey of Monmouth translated and incorporated into parts of his *Historia Regum*

Britanniae. He comments: 'The spelling and pronunciation of Welsh names are notoriously almost impossible in the Anglo-Saxon or Latin. Latin scribes make nothing of these strange Welsh spellings of the names of early British characters or places, and it is obvious that they were modified to accommodate Latin modes of speech.'

4. William of Newburgh must have been aware that such a person as King Arthur had existed for he is mentioned by William of Malmesbury in his History *De Regibus Angliae*, which appeared in 1143, four years before the publication of Geoffrey of Monmouth's chronicle. Therefore, he merely means to reject the fabulous part of Geoffrey's work and not to deny the rest.

5. Robert, Earl of Gloucester, died at Bristol in October 1147 and was buried in the Priory of St James, his own foundation. His effigy, carved in wood (probably not quite of contemporary date), can be seen in the choir.

6. The *Book of Llandaff* has been twice published. It was first edited by W.J. Rees in 1840, but this was from the transcripts as the editor did not have access to the original. A far superior edition is that of Drs J. Gwenogfryn Evans and J. Rhys, a diplomatic reproduction from the twelfth-century original, published at Oxford in 1893.

7. The *Book of Chad*, also known as the *Lichfield Gospels* and the *Book of Teilo*, is a Latin manuscript containing texts of the Gospels of St Matthew and St Mark and part of that of St Luke. It was probably written during the first half of the eighth century.

Chapter Three

1. Segontium was the north-western termination of Watling Street and situated in a district called Venedotia. It was founded in about AD 80 and was an auxiliary fortress, connected with the legionary headquarters at Deva (Chester).

2. There are other places in Wales associated with Macsen and Elen, such as Cadair Macsen and Sarn Elen near Caerfyrddin (Carmarthen), which was one of three forts given to Elen in the *Mabinogion* story. In addition, there are churches throughout Wales dedicated to members of Macsen's family.

3. Eudaf Hen was the son of Caradog ap Bran. He married the daughter of Carausius II and their daughter was Elen Luyddog.

4. The archaeologist Mortimer Wheeler observes that at Segontium 'Intensive occupation ceased between 380 and 385'. It was in 383 that Maximus crossed to Gaul with his army.

5. After the death of her husband in 388, Elen returned to Wales and was regarded there as a saint and several churches are dedicated to her, including

Llanelen in Gwent, Llanelen near Llanrhidian in Western Gower and Bletherston in Pembrokeshire. There was formerly a Capel Elen in the parish of Penrhos llugwy in Anglesey.

6. Cunedda Wledig is credited with being the ruler of Manau Guotodin, a wide district from Carlisle to Wearmouth, which he administered from his court at Carlisle. His grandfather was called Paternus of the Red Tunic, which suggests that he held office under the Romans and wore the Roman purple. There is a tradition that Cunedda had nine sons, who were named Tybion, Ysfael, Rhufon, Dunod, Ceredig, Afloeg, Einion, Yrth, Dogfael and Edern. The eldest son, Tybion, had died, so he was represented in the warband by his son Meirion.

7. Caernarfon was known as Caer Gystennin in 1110 and it is referred to by this name in the *Historia Gruffydd ap Cynan*.

8. Vortigern appears in the oldest Welsh records as Guorthigern and later as Gwrtheyrn. Bede, writing in Latin, gives the name as Vertigernus and Uurtigernus. *Vor* means 'over' and *tigern* means 'king' or 'chieftain'. The title thus means 'High King' or 'Overlord'. Similar examples are Kentigern (Cunotigernos – 'Hound-like Lord'), Catigern (Catutigernus – 'Battle-Lord') and Vortimer (Wortamorix – 'Highest King'), as in Vortiporix of Demetae (Dyfed).

9. Geoffrey had learnt that Ambrosius was the son of Constantine and that Constantine was the son of Helena. He could only think of one Constantine, son of Helena, and that was Constantine the Great. He therefore concluded that Ambrosius was the son of Constantine the Great, instead of Constantine the son of Magnus Maximus.

10. As a gwledig, Emrys (Ambrosius) may be ranked with Macsen, Cunedda and Ceredig, who all bore this title, and can be shown to be representatives of Romano-British rule. Custennin Fendigaid and his son Emrys Wledig were connecting links between the Roman Empire and an independent Britain.

11. Aurelian was a Roman emperor who ruled from AD 270–5. He was Lucius Domitius Aurelianus.

12. Maes Elletus would appear to be named after Allectus, a lieutenant of Carausius, who in 287 became ruler in Britain. Carausius was made Caesar, but in 293 was assassinated by Allectus, who thereupon assumed the title of Emperor. Three years later Allectus was himself killed by Asciepiodotus, a general of Constantius, who likewise assumed the Imperial dignity. It is possible that he fought a battle at Maes Allectus which thereafter bore his name.

13. St Germanus was born at Auxerre, south of Paris, in 380. He was

appointed *dux* of Armorica with military responsibilities for the Channel coast of Gaul. This military experience was later to enable him to give good service to Britain as a warrior-bishop. In 418 he was made Bishop of Autessodurum (Auxerre). He sailed for Britain in 429 accompanied by Lupus (or Bleiddian), Bishop of Augustobona Tricassium (Troyes). They had been dispatched by the Gallic Church, under orders from Pope Celestine I as missionaries against the Pelagian heresy, which at that time was making headway in Britain.

Chapter Four

1. According to the record in the *Book of Llandaff* Tewdrig was brought from Tintern '*donec ad locum unum venerunt juxta pratum unum versus Savernam*', that is 'until they came to a place near a meadow towards the Severn'. This seems so absurd a description that it is possible that the transcriber made an error, and that for *pratum* we should read *portum*; and also, as a matter of conjecture, *unum* should read *isceuin*. With these alterations the text would read, 'until they came to a place near Port Iscoed leading to Severn', which would exactly describe the position of Mathern Church near the head of St Pierre Pill.

2. The *Book of Llandaff* gives a list of grants reputed to have been given by Tewdrig's son Meurig and his son Brochmael to Bishop Oudoceus of Llandaff in commemoration of Tewdrig. Dedications to Celtic saints are sometimes associated with the word Merthyr, as at Merthyr Tydfil in Glamorgan or Merthyr Cynog in Powys. Merthyr used in this respect is equivalent in meaning to 'memorial'; a memorial to the saint thus named. The word Merthyr in Welsh place names such as Merthyr Tydfil derives from the Latin *martyrium*, but does not necessarily have anything to do with martyrdom in the sense of one killed for his or her faith. *Martyrium* can also mean a 'monastic retreat'.

3. Francis Godwin was the son of a Bishop of Bath and Wells. He was a keen antiquarian and a close friend of the famous scholar William Camden. In 1617 Godwin moved to Herefordshire and lived at Whitbourne Manor until his death in 1633.

4. Miles Sally became Bishop of Llandaff on 12 May, 1500. In his last will, which is preserved in Leland's Collection (Vol. 6, p. 194), 'He bequeathed his body to be buried on the north side of Our Lady's Chapel, before the image of St Andrew, in St Mark's Church, Bristol, and his heart and bowels to be deposited at the high altar at Matherne, before the image of Theoderic, his mitre to be willed and deposited at Llandaff, and he appointed a solemn mass and dirigi to be kept for his soul at the convent of Evesham.'

5. It has been suggested that King Tewdrig of Gwent was named after King Theodoric the Great of the Ostrogoths and that he was a contemporary of King Theodric of Bernicia. This prompted John Morris to date the reign of Tewdrig's son Meurig as 580–615. However, it is more likely that Tewdrig, whose alternative Welsh name is Tewdws (from which the name Tudor originates), was named after the Roman Emperor Theodosius and that he was a contemporary of King Theodoric of the Ostrogoths. Tewdrig's grandson Athrwys would, therefore, have been a contemporary of Theodoric's grandson Athalaric, but **not** Aethelric of Bernicia. It is this confusion that has led some chronologists to post-date Athrwys ap Meurig by at least two generations.

6. It has been suggested that Meurig ap Tewdrig was named after Mauricius, Eastern Roman Emperor. The Latin equivalent of Meurig is certainly Mauricius but it should be borne in mind that the Roman Republic of the Silures lasted over three-hundred years and one would expect a certain amount of inter-marriage between the Romans and the Britons. It therefore follows that the name Meurig (Mauricius) was quite common during this period. There was an earlier Meurig, for example, who was the brother of Eudaf Hen and the great-grandfather of Pebiau, King of Erging. This Meurig was certainly not named after the Eastern Roman Emperor Mauricius.

7. It is of interest that the *Flores Flistoriam*, written by Roger of Wendover in 1235, contains some Arthurian material. He refers to Guinevere by the Celtic name of Guenhumara.

8. There are some interesting connections with Gwythyr and his son Gwythian in Wales and Cornwall. There is a Werthyr in the parish of Llangian in the Llyyn Peninsula and Eglwys Wythyr (Church of Gwythyr) is the Welsh name for Monington in Pembrokeshire. In Cornwall the name Withur is found in Trewether, north-east of St Winnow, and it means the hamlet of Withur. To the north-east is Llanwithian, formerly known as Langwythian and dedicated to St Gwythian or Gwythiel, son of Count Gwythyr.

9. W.A.S. Hewins, in his book *The Royal Saints of Britain from the Latter Days of the Roman Empire* (1929), makes an interesting statement: 'At this period, the Count of Leon, according to the *Life of St Pol de Léon*, and other authorities, was Withur. He is also called Ider, the son of Yvain, clearly the same as Uther or Withur (Victor). We may also compare Yetr or Uther in the pedigrees of the Welsh princes. It simply means a ruler or director. This Withur was related to St Paul Aurelian and was ruler when the latter arrived. St Paul Aurelian received from him the Ille de Batz and founded a monastery there in about 530.'

10. It is of interest that Amhyr appears as a personal name in the *Book of Llandaff* and in the same manuscript Amir and Humir or Humri appear as the names of two rivers, one is the Gamber and the other a stream near Caerleon-on-Usk. Also near Caerleon is a small rivulet called the Lechou, which rises in Caer Wood on Maendy Farm and falls into the Usk near the site of the old St Julian's House.

Chapter Five

1. Tintagel was named as Arthur's place of conception in editions of Geoffrey's *Historia* dating from the early 1140s. He wrote his original version in 1136 and it is possible that it did not include the story concerning Tintagel. In the nineteenth century it was the poet Tennyson who revived interest in Tintagel as the 'birthplace' of Arthur.
2. The name Tintagel in not mentioned in the Domesday Book, but no doubt it was the 'duncheine' of that record, and Tintaioel, Dindagel, Tindagel developed into Tintagel.
3. The Dukedom of Cornwall was the first Dukedom in the history of this country. It was created in 1337 by Edward III for his son, the Black Prince. Under the terms of the charter that created it, the title is always held by the son and heir of the reigning sovereign. When Princess Elizabeth succeeded to the throne, her eldest son Prince Charles became Duke of Cornwall.
4. King Henry II was granted possession of Tintagel Castle in 1155. A grandson was born to him in 1188, and he was named Arthur in the expectation that he would accede to the throne as King Arthur II. However, his uncle, King John, removed him, and tradition has it that the infant Arthur was murdered during a visit to France.
5. Mark, King of Cornwall, is mentioned as ruling from Tintagel in the two French romances *Tristan* and *Le Roman de Tristan et Iseut* by Béroul.
6. The *Saxon Chronicle*, written in 1154, talks of the 'Battle of Gafulford' (Camelford) in which Egbert was victorious.
7. According to Radford and Alcock, the lettering on the cross is of tenth- or eleventh-century style, which indicates that it was either made during the time of St Dunstan, or more likely it was a clever fake made when the monks carried out their excavation. The wording on it refers to 'Insula Avalonia' which seems to indicate the influence of the writings of Geoffrey of Monmouth. In particular, the word 'inclitis' (renowned) appeared on the cross and it is significant that Geoffrey also used this term. There was a copy of Geoffrey's *Historia* at Glastonbury from c.1170 and the wording on the cross is most likely derived from that source. The cross supposedly found inside

the grave of King Arthur **should** have read: '*Hic iacet sepulcum inclitis regis Arturi*' – 'Here lies the tomb of the renowned King Arthur'.

8. Henry de Sully (Soilli) was Abbot of Glastonbury from 1189 to the autumn of 1193. He was put in charge of the rebuilding works after the fire and he also gave the order for the excavation to find Arthur's remains. Soon afterwards, he was consecrated Bishop of Worcester on 12 December 1193. This fixes the date of Gerald's visit to Glastonbury as not later than the summer of 1193.

9. John Leland was librarian, chaplain and later antiquary to Henry VIII. In 1536, the king commissioned him to travel through England and Wales with the purpose of making inquiries into the antiquities of the two countries. He finished his labours in 1542 and returned to London with the extensive records of his research. When he died in 1552, his work was far from finished. His notes were taken over by the Bodleian Library at Oxford and, in 1710, his *Itinerary* was finally published under the editorship of Thomas Hearne.

10. The tradition is that King Arviragus in the first century AD bestowed 12 hides of land or 1,440 acres of land upon 12 early Christian missionaries, led by Joseph of Arimathea. It is significant that these rights were confirmed in successive charters by British, Saxon and Norman kings, including the pagan Caedwalla, King of Wessex, in the seventh century. The area known as the Twelve Hides of Glaston was subject only to divine law and was administered by priestly rulers. This grant of XII hides of land tax free is recorded in the Domesday Book, 'This land has never paid tax' (Domesday Survey, folio p.249b). The Twelve Hides of Glastonbury is a theme that recurs frequently in medieval records.

11. Domesday Survey, folio p.2249b.

12. The genealogy of the descendants of Cunedda Wledig shows a series of great political and religious leaders, who always reverted to their ancestral possessions in Glastonbury. St Gwytherin (Victorinus) founded a community house there which became known as Ynys Witherin, which in the passage of time was reduced to Ynys Witrin. The name Ynyswitrin occurs in William of Malmesbury's *History of the Kings of England*, as well as in a note at the end of the life of Gildas.

13. In the amplified text of William of Malmesbury the eponym Glast is said to have been a descendant of Cunedda Wledig named Glastening, who travelled from the west of Britain through the territory of the Middle Angles to the site of Glastonbury. There he settled, and the isle became the permanent home of his posterity. Welsh genealogies give his name in the more correct

form of Glast, and reveal faint vestiges of a tradition that Glast and his followers came from the vicinity of Lichfield.

14. The charter of the abbey, signed by King Ine in the old wattle church, is still in existence, one of the oldest charters in England.

Chapter Six

1. The late British name of this part of Britain was Cornouia, which was Latinised as Cornubia, and in the tenth century this became Kernow in Cornish and Cernyw in Welsh.

2. Cybi or Kebius was born in Tregonny, the son of Salevan, a Celtic form of Solomon which has been corrupted into the place name of St Levan. Cybi was related to Dewi (St David) for St Non, the mother of Dewi, was his aunt.

3. Two lives of Petroc, written in the Middle Ages, have survived. A translation of the text of the *Vita Petroci*, written in the twelfth century, was published in 1930 by Canon G.H. Doble, called *St Petroc, Abbot and Confessor*. St Petroc's father Glywys ap Gwynlliw also spent time in Cornwall and the parish church at Penrhyn is dedicated to 'St Gluvias'. He was known as Glywys Cerniw or 'Gluvias the Cornishman' and when he first settled in Cornwall his son Petroc probably came with him.

4. The Welsh form of the Breton Chenmarchoc or Kenmarhuc is Cinmarchus (Kynmarch) and is found in Ecclesia Cynmarchi or Lann Cinmarch, later known as St Kinemark's Church, near Chepstow.

5. Included in this grant is Campus Malochu, which can be none other than Mais Mail Lochou (the Plain or Field of Prince Llacheu). It would appear that March's territory was granted by King Arthur first to his son Llacheu and, upon the death of Llacheu, to his brother Comereg.

6. Cunomorus is the Latin form for the British Cynvawr and it is significant that in the tenth-century *Life of St Paul Aurelian*, written by the Breton monk Wrmonoc (who spent time in Cornwall), it is stated that Cynfawr was also called Mark. He was Marcus Conomorus who was referred to as King Mark of Cornwall in the love story of Tristan and Iseult. Wrmonoc's biography of St Paul Aurelian tells us that Drustanus had a quarrel with a king of Cornwall named Quonomorius. He also refers to this person as Marcus dictus Quonomorius, which translates as 'Mark called Cunomorius'.

7. The romance story states that Tristan was a nephew of King Mark, and Iseult was an Irish princess who was betrothed to King Mark. The king sent Tristan to fetch Iseult, and on the journey back to Mark's palace she and Tristan fell in love. In due course the lovers were discovered in compromising circumstances. Tristan then fled to Armorica, where he married the daughter

of a local chief, but could not forget his first love. In the medieval romance stories Drustanus was turned into Tristan and then Tristram (Sir Tristram).

Chapter Seven

1. *The Birth of Arthur*, edited and translated by J.H. Davies, appeared in *Y Cymmroder*, Vol. 24 (1900), 249–64.
2. In the *Dingestow Brut*, Igerna is claimed to be a daughter of Amlawdd Wledig, a first cousin of Custennin Fendigaid, and he is supposed to have ruled the borderlands with Herefordshire.
3. Penychen was one of five ancient cantrefs of Morgannwg and an explanation for the name can be found in Wrmonoc's ninth-century *Life of St Pol de Léon*. It states that 'Pen-Ohen, which means the head of an ox, because the inhabitants of that place followed the example of country people and in antiquity used to worship the head of an ox as a god.' In the Celtic regions of Britain there are numerous examples of place names with the compound of 'penn' or 'cenn' and that of an animal.
4. Porphyra means purple, according to *Webster's Dictionary*, and its use in association with a person's name may indicate a son born after the accession of his father to the throne, i.e. one born to the purple. St Paul Aurelian, for example, was the son of Porphyrius Aurelianus of the family of Ambrosius Aurelianus.
5. The Revd Arthur Wade-Evans has pointed out that a Welsh personal name of Erb or Erbin is found for Paul Aurelian's father Count Porphyrius Aurelianus. Llandough-juxta-Cardiff, variously called Bangor Cyngar and Bangor Dochau. Cyngar is also called Docwin and Dochau was the brother of Iestin, Selyf, Caw and Cadwy. Their father was Geraint the son of Erbin.
6. Details of the excavation of Cae Mead by the Cardiff Naturalists' Society in 1888 are to be found in the *Report and Transactions of the Cardiff Naturalists' Society*, Vol. XX, Part II (1888).

Chapter Eight

1. Archenfeld, in the *Anglo-Saxon Chronicle* of 915, is Ircingafeldes and variously Yrcingafeld and Iercinafeld. In the Domesday Book it is Arcenefelde, and in 1316 Ircinfeld. Leland in the sixteenth century rendered it Herchinfeld. Feld is early English for 'open country/land'.
2. The nickname 'Clavorauc' really means 'leprous', though the Welsh word for 'drivel' (*glafoer*) is not unlike it. King Peibio may have been a leper who was known after his death as 'Pepiau the Leprous'.
3. A fourteenth-century spelling of Llanfrother is 'Hendresroude' which

translates as 'the old place of the brethren'. Its modern name means 'the old sacred enclosure of the monks'.

4. Hen-lan ('The Old Lan') is a common name in Wales and Cornwall and it signifies the site of a church or monastery that has been abandoned in favour of a new site. It may well have been that Hentland was considered to be too close to the Saxon border for safety, and a more remote site was chosen.

5. The name Campus Malochu seems to have survived in that of Mawfield Farm in the parish of Allensmore, the church of which is about 3½ miles south-east of Madley Church. It is significant that Arclestone, now Arkstone Court, close to Allensmore, belonged to the bishops of Llandaff all through the Middle Ages, the sole remnant of all the St Dubricius land grants in Herefordshire claimed by the *Book of Llandaff*.

6. Lann Custenhin (Welsh Bicknor) is constantly mentioned in the *Book of Llandaff* and was evidently a place of special importance. It bore the name of Custenhin or Constantine and one charter mentions 'King Constantine's *Jaculum*' (apparently a ferry across the Wye). King Constantine was the original donor or founder of Lann Custenhin, which was consequently named after him. Welsh Bicknor, on the Wye, was on a prominent Roman trade route and a very early Christian foundation. It was not far from the old Roman town of Ariconium (now Weston-under-Penyard), the great iron centre of Roman Britain.

7. Constantine's property is given as being 'beyond the Wye'. As most of the land granted to Dubricius is the peninsula within the loop of the Wye that faces Lower Lydbrook, it follows that Constantine was an owner of land within the Forest of Dean on the other side of the Wye.

8. Dubricius is mentioned seven times in the *Vita Sancti Samsonis*. The three ordinations of Samson by Dubricius mentioned in the *Life*, pp. 9 20 and 43 6, G.H. Doble, *Lives of the Welsh Saints*, ed D. Simon Evans (1971).

9. There may well have been a gravestone there at that time or records of his burial in the monastery on Bardsey.

10. At Llandaff Dubricius is named as the first bishop, not the founder of the see. Teilo is named as the second bishop, although it was not a bishopric until the tenth century.

11. The archbishopric of the City of the Legions is entirely a creation of Geoffrey's fancy. Dubricius was certainly a bishop but archbishops did not exist in his day. However, they were being created in the twelfth century and the Book of Llandaff was part of a scheme to create a metropolitan Archbishop of Llandaff. The term 'Archbishop' in this instance should be

seen as signifying a 'chief bishop', who supervised a number of other bishops.

12. Wormelow Tump was beside the Roman Road known as Watling Street which starting from the coast of Kent, passed through London and St Albans to Viriconium near Shrewsbury. Turning south it passed through Church Stretton, Leintwardine and Hereford, past Wormelow Tump and St Weonards to reach the station of Blestium on the Trothy at Monmouth.

13. H.P.R. Finberg, *The Early Charters of the West Midlands*, Studies in Early English History (1961).

Chapter Nine

1. In the *Book of Llandaff* the school is called 'Ilduti' twenty-nine times, 'Lannildut' three times and 'Lanniltut' once; 'Sancti Ilduti' four times, 'Ecclesia S. Ilduti' three times and 'Podum S. Ilduti' once. In the latter parts of the book, written in the fourteenth century, it is spelt 'Lanyltwyt'. In the *Vita S. Gildae* it is 'Lanna Hilduti'.

2. In the *Horae Britannicae* it is recorded that the monastic college comprised 7 halls and 400 houses. Another account states that the establishment comprised 7 churches, each with 7 companies and 7 colleges in each company, having 7 students in each college, making a total of 2,401 students. Latin name: Samsonius, English name: Sampson.

3. Illtud died between 527 and 537 aged between 77 and 87.

4. Wrmonoc's *Life of St Pol de Léon* was written at Landévennec in Brittany but compiled from an earlier Life of the saint. The manuscript is now preserved in the public library at Orleans. See Albert Le Grand, *Les Vies des Saintes de la Bretagne Armorique* (1901), pp. 98–115.

5. Paul's father Porphyrius of Bovium was the younger brother of Aurelius Ambrosius. Paul's grandfather was Constantine Fendigaid. Paul's father was a brother of Uther Pendragon and Paul himself was first cousin to Arthur.

6. The *Vita Sancti Samsonis* was composed around the years 610–15 (possibly re-edited in the ninth century). Amon of Dyfed is given as the father of St Samson, but this must be an error, in view of the fact that Samson's father was Amwn Ddu (Annun the Black). This can be confirmed by the fact that the *Vita Sancti Samsonis* names Umbrafel, who was undoubtedly the brother of Amwn Ddu, as the uncle of Samson. Significantly, Afrella is the Welsh form of Aurelia.

7. The *Vita Sancti Samsonis* gives Anna of Gwent as the mother of St Samson. There can be no doubt that this Anna was the daughter of Meurig ap Tewdrig,

who was the father of Athrwys. Therefore, St Samson was the nephew of Athrwys ap Meurig (Arthur).

8. According to Count Nikolai Tolstoy, in *The Quest for Merlin*, it is clear that St Samson's encounter with these worshippers was a factual account of the celebration of the 'Feast of the god Lugh at the Festival of Lughansa', which took place on 1 August. The ritual encountered by St Samson was a British version of the Irish Festival of Lughansa, when the god Lugh brought fertility to the land and prosperity to the kingdom.

Chapter Ten

1. The reference to Dubricius as Archbishop was merely a device employed by Geoffrey to enhance the dignity of Arthur's capital. He exalted Dubricius to that imaginary honour. The term may also be misunderstood in modern times, being regarded as involving a primacy over other diocesan bishops, whereas it meant only the primacy of the episcopal abbot of the archmonastery over the episcopal abbots of subordinate monasteries.

2. Silchester was called Calleva Atrebatum by the Romans and it was the capital of the government district known as Civitas Atrebatum. The meaning of Calleva Atrebatum is 'the woodland town of the Atrebates', a Belgic tribe from Arras, who settled south of the Thames after the conquest of Gaul by the Romans in 57 BC.

Chapter Eleven

1. The Welsh Triads list Arfderydd (Arthuret) as one of the 'Three Futile Battles in the Isle of Britain'. It was a battle between different branches of the dynasty of Coel Hen. The kings of York combined with Dunaut of the Pennines to destroy their cousin Gwenddoleu, who ruled in the Carlisle region. Myrddin Wyllt was Gwenddoleu's bard.

2. Celyddon is a Brythonic or Welsh form of Caledonia, a term now relating to the whole of Scotland. Caledonia is the old Roman name for the country north of Stirlingshire, with its heartland between the Grampian Mountains and Strathhearn.

3. It is likely that during the seventh or eighth centuries this theme of the Wild Man of the Woods spread from the Welsh-speaking kingdoms of southern Scotland to Wales, where it was told at the courts of the Welsh princes.

4. The ancient town of Winchester was the tribal capital of the Belgae and the Romans named it Venta Belgarum. It became Winchester, the capital of Wessex, under Alfred the Great, and remained England's chief city until after

the Norman invasion. In the fine cathedral are buried many of the Saxon and Norman kings of England.

5. In the foreign accounts of Henry VIII it appears that the sum of £66 16*s* and 11*d* was expended in the repair of the 'Aula regis infra Castrum de Wynchestre et le Round Tabyll Ibidem'.

Chapter Twelve

1. In his book *Celtic Folklore* (1891), Sir John Rhys suggests that Aust Cliff in Gloucestershire is the location of 'Penrhyn Austin yn Kernyw'. He also makes the point that this implies the use of the name Kernyw in its ancient sense to denote the whole of the Domnonian Peninsula (see Vol. II, p. 506).

2. The word 'Gelli' or 'Celli' means a wood, a copse. The simpler form 'cell' means a grove, and the Irish 'coill' has an identical meaning. 'Cell ysgaw' means an ' elder grove'. The natives of Scotland were called 'Caeolii daoin' which meant 'the people of the wood'; the Romans changed the name to Caledonia.

3. The mouth of the Wye is mentioned in Nennius under the name Metambala, a cult site connected with apples. I.A. Richmond and C.G.S Crawford, in 'The Ravenna Cosmography' (*Archaeologia* XCIII, 1–50 (1949)), under Metambala, equate this place with the site of a miraculous apple growing on an ash tree, recorded by Nennius. They suggest that the name is a corruption of Nemetabala, the Sacred Grove of Apple Trees.

4. The *Genealogy of the Saints* records that Urien of Gorre was instrumental with the sons of Ceredig ap Cunedda in expelling the Gwyddelians (Irish Goidels), who had gained a footing in Gower from about the time of Macsen Wledig. Several charters in the *Book of Llandaff* refer to Gwrgant the Great who ruled Gower in the sixth century.

5. Gwrgant Mawr is otherwise known as Wrgannius Uarius and can be none other than 'Urbgennius (Urianus) of Caer Badon', mentioned by Geoffrey of Monmouth as one of Arthur's 'nobiles consules'.

6. *Y Seint Greal* is one of the gems of the Hengwrt MSS. It was originally written in about 1200 and was translated into English by the Revd Robert Williams MA in 1876.

7. Bledri Latimer ('the Interpreter'), also known as Bleheris, the first known story-teller of Arthurian themes on the Continent, seems to have frequented the court of the first known Troubadour, Guilhem IX Count of Poitou and VIII Duke of Aquitaine (1071–1127). In his second continuator of the Conte del Graal, Chrétien de Troyes cites as his authority Bleheris, who was born and bred in Wales and told the story to the Count of Poitou. Bledri's home

was in the district of Carmarthen. He was able to speak both Welsh and French and was described as *latemeri* (latimer or interpreter) in Latin documents which record his patronage of the priory at Carmarthen.

8. The existence of a British king named Arviragus is proved by the Roman satirist Juvenal, who makes one of his characters ask a pale nervous looking man: 'What is the matter with you? Have you seen the chariot-driven British king Arviragus? A mighty omen this you have received of some great and noble triumph. Some captive king you'll take, or Arviragus will be hurled from his British chariot. For the monster is a foreign one. Do you see the sharp fins bristling on his back like spears?'

9. Colchester has been successively the capital of the British chieftain Cunobelinus, a Roman colony founded by the Emperor Claudius; the traditional birthplace of Constantine the Great; a Saxon fortress razed by the Danes; and one of the chief centres of the Norman tenure of East Anglia.

10. Cunobelinus was the son of Cassivellaunus, King of the Belgic Catuvellauni of Hertfordshire, who fought the great Caesar with determination and resource and continued his own conquest of neighbouring tribes after the departure of Caesar. Cunobelinus was the greatest of the Belgic kings and he had a long reign of almost forty years, during which he gained control of most of south-eastern Britain. The Roman historian Suetonius refers to Cunobelinus as 'King of the Britons'. When he died, his kingdom was divided between his sons Togodumnus and Caratacus and they began a programme of aggression and enlargement. Togodumnus was killed in battle with the Romans in AD 43. His brother Caratacus made his way through the territory of the Dobunni to take refuge with the Silures and became their battle leader.

Chapter Thirteen

1. Both Nennius and Gildas use the name Saxon as a collective term for all the tribes invading from the Continent: Saxons, Angles, Jutes and others.

2. The *Anglo-Saxon Chronicle* was written by order of King Alfred the Great, the ninth-century Saxon ruler. The compilers when writing the entries for the fifth and sixth centuries made use of Bede and thus his errors were repeated.

3. Alis Ronwen is regarded as the progenitress of the English nation. Her name Rhonwen is derived from the Welsh Rhawngwen, meaning 'white horse hair', signifying a woman of the Teutonic race.

4. Vortimer did not support his father's policy of hiring federates, and when they revolted in 455, he and his brother Catigern (Cateyrn) conducted a sharp campaign against them. They are said to have fought four battles against the

Saxons in or near an area known as Danet, which has been identified as the Isle of Thanet in Kent. It would make much more sense if this location was closer to the territory of Vortigern and his family. This misidentification may be explained by the fact that the Forest of Dean was sometimes referred to as Llwyn Danet. Dean is derived from the Saxon word *denu* meaning 'valley'. Place names in that area are predominately Anglo Saxon in origin. It is possible that Nennius's story of Vortimer's three blockades of the Isle of Thanet is based upon battles fought against the federates near the lower reaches of the Wye in Gwent and western Gloucestershire. It would make a great deal of sense if the Saxon invaders from Germany had settled in the Forest of Dean for it would explain why in about 470 they crossed the Wye to invade the territory of King Tewdrig.

5. The 'Long Knives' affair, according to Nennius, took place some time before 473. This incident is not mentioned by Gildas, but, according to Geoffrey of Monmouth, 300 of the counsellors and officers of Vortigern were killed.

6. In Triad 21 Vortigern is one of 'the three arrant traitors of the Island of Britain'.

7. The Harleian Pedigree 4181 gives Edric, King of Glamorgan, as having married Henwen, the daughter of Kynmarch ap Meirchion, and Geoffrey of Monmouth gives Henwinus the title of *Dux* Cornubiae (*Historia Regum Britanniae*). As no Edric is mentioned in the Welsh genealogies as reigning over Morgannwg and Gwent at this time, then perhaps Cerdic of the Gewissei is intended here. If this is the case then Cerdic, by right of marriage, could lay claims to territories in Glamorgan and Gwent, and these same territories would have been sought after by his descendants.

8. Oesc appears in the *Anglo-Saxon Chronicle* under the spelling Aesc. He is said to have become co-ruler with Hengist in 455 after the death of Horsa. In 488 Aesc succeeded to the kingdom and reigned as King of Kent for twenty-four years.

9. Octha appears in various manuscripts as Octha, Octa and Osla.

10. Wrmonoc's *Life of St Pol de Léon* identifies Marcus son of Marcianus with Marcus Conomorus, who usurped rule in Armorican Domnonia. F. Lot, in his *Romania* (1896), noted that the name Conomorus is identical with the name that appears on the sixth-century inscribed stone near Castle Dore, Fowey in Cornwall. This is confirmation of a Glamorgan prince who held sway in Cornwall and Brittany.

11. The name Cinmarchus (Kynmarch) is found in Ecclesia Cynmarchi or Lann Cinmarch (now St Kinemark's) at Chepstow in Gwent. Chinmarchocus

(Marchocus) has a name similar to the Cornish place name Chenmark found in the *Exchequer Domesday Book I* (p.124b), which must be identical with the Cheinmerc found in the *Exeter Domesday Book* (p.263b). This has been identified with Kilmarth (Mark's Retreat), near Fowey, in the *Domesday Gazetteer* by H.C. Darby and G.R. Versey (1975).

Chapter Fourteen

1. Llywarch Hen's elegy represents Geraint, the martyr of Llongborth, and Arthur as contemporaries, while the episode relating to 'Geraint ap Erbin', contained in the *Mabinogion*, tells us that Arthur was a cousin of Geraint and the nephew of Erbin. During the wars, the Dumnonian forces obviously accepted Arthur as emperor and superior ruler over their own leader Geraint. Following the death of Geraint at Llongborth, it would seem that Arthur continued to be accepted as a joint ruler with Cadwy, the son of Geraint.
2. Geraint ap Erbin features in Triad 25 Series II (*Y Cymmrodor*, Vol. III, p. 127), as one of the 'Three Fleet Owners of the Island of Britain'. The other two were March ap Meirchion (Marcus son of Marcianus) and Gwenwynyn ap Naw. Geraint and March were both rulers in south-western Britain and, as fleet owners, they maintained contact by sea with Armorica (Brittany). Traditions of Geraint and March were certainly known in Brittany as early as the ninth century and both were rulers in Dumnonia, which may be assumed to have maintained some kind of connection with the Breton kingdom of the same name during the early period.
3. The name Twrc (or the 'Boar') is not uncommon in south Wales as the name of streams with deeply eroded channels, such as this has in Wentwood.
4. Merthir Gerin is recorded in the *Book of Llandaff*, p. 234, line 10 and also a Marthergeryn, p. 323.8. 'This chapel, 'De ecclesia de Marthergeryn', stood near Upper Grange Farm in the parish of Magor, but its remains were removed many years ago. See J. Gwenogvryn Evans and John Rhys, *The Text of the Book of Llan Dav* (1893).
5. In 1964 Canon Gilbert H. Doble came to the same conclusion. He commented in his book *The Saints of Cornwall Vol. II: 'St Gerein (Geraint) was honoured at Merthir Gerein (Martyrdom of Geraint), a place in the parish of Magor in Gwent, which is mentioned in the Book of Llandaff* (1840 edn), p. 224.

Chapter Fifteen

1. Geoffrey of Monmouth differs from Nennius in that he assigns only one battle, instead of four, to the River Douglas.

2. Riwal Mawr held the title of *Dux Britanniarum* and was subordinate to Arthur, who held the higher office of *Comes Britanniae*. The last person to have held the title before Arthur would have been Magnus Maximus as he was the successor of Count Theodosius the Elder. Arthur went one step further and took the supreme title of Amherawdyr, meaning Emperor.

3. The medieval romances of Arthur's knights of the Round Table represent a genuine folk memory of a mounted war band led by Arthur. The Romans had certainly made use of cavalry and two units served in Britain during the fourth century. It would appear that Arthur established a similar mobile force a century later. The best description we have of a sixth century war band riding to battle is contained in Aneurin's epic poem *Y Gododdin*.

4. Geoffrey of Monmouth ignores the Battle of Bassas and sends Arthur pursuing the Saxons to the Caledonian Wood.

5. To the south of Bassaleg, near the route of the Via Julia leading to Cardiff, is Maes Arthur (Arthur's Field) and a short distance away is Craig-y-Saeson (Rock of the Saxons) and this suggests another possible location for the Battle of Bassas. The dedication of Bassaleg Church to St Basil of Cappadocia is a medieval bad guess from the place name.

6. The *Chronicle of the Kings of Britain* contained in *Collectanea Cambrica*, translated by the Revd Peter Roberts (1811). Geoffrey of Monmouth makes a guess that the British 'Kaerluitcoit' is Lincoln while it is really Wall-by-Lichfield, situated on Watling Street, the Roman road that ran from the south-east of London for nearly 300 miles to Segontium (Caernarfon) in north-west Wales. This road was intersected at Wall-by-Ryknild Street, which ran north-east to York.

7. The name Letocetum represents the Celtic toponym *letocaiton*, from which evolved the form *luitcoit*. Both words mean 'grey wood' and reflect the wooded character of the area. The name Lichfield is a compound of the Celtic *luitcoit* and the Anglo-Saxon *feld*. Caer luit coit was also known as Caer Lwytcoed and is listed as such in the *Historia Brittonum* as one of the twenty-eight cities of Britain. 'Caer' means a fortified place and 'Luit' or 'Lwyt' is derived from Llwyd meaning grey and 'coed' from aroes, meaning a wood. The modern name 'Wall' is derived from a long stretch of masonry which could be seen at least up until 1817 in a field known as Castle Croft.

8. Castellum Guinnion implies a fairly significant fortification such as an old Roman camp or an Iron Age hill fort. Castellum comes from the Latin *Castella* while Guinnion is a Latinised form of the Celtic word Gwynion, meaning 'white place' or even 'holy place'. Arthur's image of the Virgin

Mary on his shield may be compared with Constantine the Great's troops painting the Christian sign of the Chi-Rho on their shields.

9. Cair Guorthegirn (the castle or fort of Vortigern) was mentioned by Nennius. If the Battle of Guinnion was fought on this hill (Little Doward) then it could explain the naming of Arthur's Cave and the folk memory of a battle fought in the river valley below this ancient British fortress, where a field beside the Wye is marked on the Ordnance Survey map as 'The Slaughter'. This would tie in with the statement by Nennius that in this battle 'the pagans were put to flight that day and there was a great slaughter upon them'. Folk memories of such events have often been found to be based on an element of truth

10. Oesc appears in the *Anglo-Saxon Chronicle* as Aesc and is said to have become a co-ruler with Hengist in 455, after the death of Horsa: 'In 488 Aesc succeeded to the kingdom and was ruler of Kent for twenty four years.' According to the ninth-century Cotton Vespasian MS, which contains a list of Dark Age kings, Hengist was the father of Oesc, the father of Octha.

11. St Curig's Chapel at Cat's Ash was once known as 'Capella Sancti Ciriaci' and is mentioned as such in the *Book of Llandaff*. From 1113 it came under the jurisdiction of the Benedictine priory at Goldcliff.

12. The *Black Book of Carmarthen* contains a poem written in Welsh which tells of one of Arthur's companions who came back from 'Tryvrwd' with a broken shield. It also refers to 'the shores of Tryvrwd' and suggests that this was a battle involving a river crossing.

13. To the Celt the boar represented strength and ferocity and boar images were often displayed on shields.

14. The River Troggy which flows through this area, once known as Cerniw, was originally called the Twrc. The Romans knew it as Taracos and this name has been anglicised to Troggy. It seems significant that Twrc means boar and in the early charters its source is mentioned as Pen Tyrch, 'the Head of the Boar'.

15. The name Severn Bore is derived from the Scandinavian word *bara* meaning billow, wave or swell. Generally, maximum bores occur on one to three days after a new or full moon. They are always seen at specified times between 7am and noon, 7pm and midnight, with the largest between 9 and 11, morning and evening.

Chapter Sixteen

1.The specific name 'Badonicus' must have been of Welsh origin, since it was first mentioned by Gildas, and it must have been derived either from 'baddon' or some very similar word.

2. Because Gildas does not mention Arthur, some historians have even suggested that he did not exist as a historical person. However, it is significant that in reference to battles, with the exception of Ambrosius, Gildas does not mention by name a single British chieftain. Yet, the fact that he fails to provide the name of a leader in connection with such an important event as the Battle of Badon is most surprising. We can only surmise that it did not suit his purpose to celebrate the names and virtues of the British princes.

3. The achievements of Arthur's army are being attributed to its commander. In a similar way the *Anglo-Saxon Chronicle* refers to the Battle of Chester when it tells how 'Aethelfrith led his armies to Chester and there slew a countless number of Britons.'

4. It is important to consider that a Celtic town of these times would most likely have been within the ramparts of a hill fort, e.g., on Solsbury Hill. In the valley below, by the river, where the hot springs bubbled, there might well have been a grove and a shrine where offerings were made to Sul.

5. The Hwiccas were a British and Christian people with whom the Anglo-Saxon settlers later intermingled. Their territory was portioned out into the shires of Hereford, Gloucester, Worcester, part of Warwick and the district between the Wye and Severn known as Rhwng Gwy a Hafren (between Wye and Severn) and which included the Forest of Dean.

6. The body of Cerdic is said to have been taken by the retreating Gewissei and buried at Stoke near Hurstborne priory in north-west Hampshire.

7. The *Anglo-Saxon Chronicle* tells of the capture of Bath in 577 and refers to the place as Badanceaster, the 'City of Badan.' At that time it had been the site of the court of King Farinmael, who was defeated by the Saxons at the Battle of Deorham (Dyrham), a few miles to the north of Bath. Also killed in this battle were King Condidan, whose court was at Caer-Ceri (Cirencester), and Conmael of Caer-Gloui (Gloucester). Condidan may be derived from the Roman name Candidianus, and if this is the case then Condidan can be none other than Aurelius Candidianus, the son of Aurelius Caninus. Thus, the last of the Aureli died fighting at the Battle of Deorham in 577.

8. One of the Welsh Triads makes Gelliwig one of the three archbishoprics of Britain over which Bedwini presided as archbishop. We also find Bedwini's name again in two of the *Mabinogian* tales. In 'Culhwch and Olwen' he is mentioned as the one 'who blessed Arthur's meat and drink' and in 'The Dream of Rhonabwy', as we have already described. Unfortunately, there are no churches dedicated to St Bedwini, nor is he celebrated in a saintly festival.

NOTES

Chapter Seventeen

1. Under the Roman Empire the Carnutes had the priviliged status of *Civitas Foederata*. Cenabum was made an independent *civitas* by the Roman Emperor Aurelian in AD 275, and named Urbs Aurelianesis (whence Orleans).

2. Riothamus is a Latinised form of the Celtic word 'Rigotamos', meaning perhaps 'supreme king', and was used as a title for the High King who also had a personal name.

3. In 469 we find in the letters of Sidonius Apollinaris (*Epistolae*, i.7) the statement that one Arvandus had been accused of treason before the Emperor Anthemius, for having incited the Visigoths to attack 'the Britons situated beyond the Loire'. In the same year we find that Anthemius solicited aid from these Britons and that their King Riothamus came to join the imperial army with a force of 12,000 men. This number, even if exaggerated, shows that there was a large colony already established in Armorica. Riothamus reached Bourges, and was apparently at that city for some time, as Sidonius wrote several letters to him, complaining of the conduct of his soldiers, who had been tempting away the slaves of the neighbouring Gallic proprietors. The Visigoths finally came up against Riothamus and defeated him at Deols in the department of the Indre, so that he was forced to take flight. He thereupon disappears from history, but his countrymen remain seated in Armorica.

4. Riatham, son of Deroch, appears in the genealogy of St Judicael, given in the *Life* of that saint by Ingomar (eleventh century) and quoted by Pierre le Baud in his *Histoire de Bretagne* (1638), pp. 64–82, but actually written c.1508. (S. Baring-Gould and J. Fisher, *The Lives of the British Saints*, Vol. I, p. 298). According to this he was the son of Deroch and father of Jonas, princes of Breton Domnonia. Arthur de La Borderie, in his *Histoire de Bretagne* (1891), says that Deroch was succeeded by Jonas and the insertion of Riotham into the pedigree is absolutely impossible. He concluded that Jonas was the son of Deroch, and that Riotham was perhaps another son of Deroch who died young. (See Peter Clement Bartrum, *A Welsh Classical Dictionary* (1993), p. 570.)

Chapter Eighteen

1. Geoffrey of Monmouth says that the Battle of Camlann took place in 542 but the *Annales Cambriae* give the date as 537. They antedate the Battle of Badon by four years so it is possible that they are five years too early in this case. The *Irish Annals of Tigernach* give the date 541.

2. Medraut is named in the *Annales Cambriae* ('the Battle of Camlann, where Arthur and Medraut fell'), but the later romance stories give him the Cornish

name Mordred or Modred and refer to him as an incestuous son who seizes power while his father is fighting a war on the Continent. The idea that Arthur had an illegitimate son may have stemmed from the fact that one of King Brychan's sons was named Artgen, which means 'the Bear begotten'. It is possible that Arthur (known as the Bear) begot a son, who was named Artgen, upon Rhybrawst, the first wife of Brychan Brycheiniog.

3. 'The Dream of Rhonabwy' mentions that Iddawc Cord Prydein (the Hammer or Agitator of Britain) betrayed Arthur by divulging his plans to Medraut. The meeting between Iddawc and Medraut took place in Nant Gwynant in Gwynedd, before the Battle of Camlann and it is spoken of in the Welsh Triads as one of the 'Three Traitorous Meetings of the Island of Britain'.

4. St Henwyn was educated at the College of St Illtud in Llanilltud Fawr. He later joined St Cadfan on Bardsey as confessor to the community of monks and is said to be buried on the island. His church at Aberdaron is the only one dedicated to him in Wales and the original wooden oratory was replaced in the twelfth century by the existing stone church.

5. This tradition was first mentioned by Thomas Davies (Tegwyn) who wrote a book entitled *Dinas Mawddwy a'i Hamgylchoedd*, which won him an Eisteddfod prize in 1893.

6. There was certainly a battle fought near here during the Civil War in 1644 or 1645 between some detachments of the Parliamentarians and the Royalist forces. A bridge named Pont y Clefion ('the bridge of the sick or wounded') possibly provides a folk memory of casualties from this battle being carried across it.

7. Laurence Main, *In the Footsteps of King Arthur* (Western Mail & Echo, Cardiff, 1995).

Chapter Nineteen

1. James Bonwick, *Irish Druids and Old Irish Religions* (1894; republished New York: Dorset Press, 1986), p. 294.

2. Archdruid Owen 'Morien' Morgan, *The Royal Winged Son of Stonehenge and Avebury* (London: Whittaker & Co., 1900), p. 1. The revised title is *Mabin of the Mabinogion* (London: Research into Lost Knowledge Organisation, 1984).

3. According to P.C. Bartrum, *Early Welsh Genealogical Tracts*, pp. 43–91, the Afallach who was the father of Gwalltwen, the concubine of Maelgwyn Hir of Gwynedd and mother of his son Rhun, is the same man who appears in Troedd Ynys Prydein (No. 70) as the father of Modron, who was the wife

of Urien of Gorre and the mother of Owain and Morfudd.

4. Lady Charlotte Guest, in her notes for the *Mabinogion*, points out that the Welsh counterpart of Morgan is Modron. The name Modron is a regular Welsh development of the great Celtic All-Mother Goddess, Matriona, worshiped by the Celts from Cisalpine Gaul to the Lower Rhine.

Chapter Twenty

1. The genealogy of Riwal, the founder of the Breton kingdom of Domnonia, came originally from the Abbey of St Méen de Gael and was inserted at the beginning of the *Life* of St Winnoc, the son of St Judicael, by a monk of Bergues in the eleventh century. It is significant that the genealogy includes the names of Gwythyr, Erbin, Geraint and Cadwy. This is confirmation that Riwal was a member of the ruling elite of south-eastern Wales and mainland Dumnonia, in view of the fact that Geraint held lands in both south-east Wales and Dumnonia.

2. St Méen (or Mewan), who founded the monastery and town that still bears his name, was a native of Erging. He died in about 617.

3. The Grail makes its first appearance in 'Perceval', a French Poem of the late twelfth century by Chrétien de Troyes, the greatest of all the medieval romancers.

4. The principal Breton authorities for the *Life of St Armel*, pp. 383–7 are the *Breviaries* of Rennes (1492), Léon (1516), St Malo (1537), Vannes (1589), and Folgoet (date unknown). Gaps in the *Life* can be filled by material gathered from the 'lives' of his kinsmen Paul Aurelian and Samson. Albert Le Grand, who is usually very reliable, gives the *Life* from the *Breviaries* of Léon and Folgoet, and the 'Legendarium' of Plouarzel.

5. According to the *Life of St Pol de Léon*, pp. 98–115, Samson was the cousin of Judwal, which helps to explain why he assisted the young prince to overthrow the tyrant Marcus Conomorus.

6. Dr John Morris mentions this battle in his book *The Age of Arthur* (1973), p. 258, but fails to identify St Armel as the abdicated King Arthur. He states that the body of Marcus Conomorus was taken from the battlefield and buried at Castle Dore, but tradition is strong in Brittany that Conomorus was laid to rest at the place where he fell and that it is marked by a large stone.

7. The seventh-century *Vita Sancti Samsonis* gives Amon of Dyfed as the father of St Samson. However, this must be an error in view of the fact that Samson's father was Amwn Ddu (Annun the Black). This can be confirmed by the fact that the *Vita Sancti Samsonis* names Umbrafel, who was undoubtedly the brother of Amwn Ddu, as the uncle of Samson. The *Vita*

Sancti Samsonis gives Anna of Gwent as the mother of St Samson. There can be no doubt that this Anna was the daughter of Meurig ap Tewdrig, who was the father of Athrwys. Therefore, St Samson was the nephew of Athrwys ap Meurig (also known as Arthmael/Armel and Arthur).

8. *De Excidio et Conquesta Britanniae* is the fountain-head of the story of the supposed Anglo-Saxon Conquest of Britain.

9. The fact that Arthur is not mentioned by name in the writings of Gildas has been much discussed by historians. In some ways it is not surprising really for Gildas also fails to mention Vortigern, Germanus and Hengist. In fact, the only two names that occur in the fifth-century portion of the *De Excidio et Conquesta Britanniae* are those of Aetius ('Agitus' as Gildas prefers to call him) and Ambrosius Aurelianus.

Chapter Twenty-One

1.The Denbighshire historian David Powell, in his *History of Cambria* (1584), states that Henry appointed a commission to chronicle his descent from the Welsh princes and British kings. It is significant that Henry adopted the Red Dragon of Cadwaladr as one of the supporters of his arms to stress his claimed descent from the ancient kings of Britain. A history of Henry VII's reign was written by Bernard André, a cleric historian, detailing Henry's descent from Cadwaladr on his father's side and from John of Gaunt on his mother's side of the family.

2. When Sir Walter Devereux was created 1st Baron Ferrers of Chartley in 1461, Chartley Castle passed to him in that year. It had been built by Ranulph II, Earl of Chester, in 1153, and he had also founded Basingwerk Monastery in Clwyd twenty-two years earlier. Originally, Basingwerk was affiliated to the Order of Savigny but joined the Cistercians in 1147. It is of interest that the *Black Book of Basingwerk* contains *Ystoria Dared*, an early version of the *Historia Regum Britanniae*. The Cistercian monks were interested in all matters relating to King Arthur and the Holy Grail.

3. According to *Webster's Dictionary*, an armill is an ecclesiastical stole used in the British coronation ceremony. With the purpose of signifying the quasi-priestly character of the anointed king, it was placed on his shoulders by the Dean of Westminster, as one of the 'garments of salvation'. It would seem likely that the word armill is derived from Armel and, thanks to the influence of King Henry VII and his involvement with Westminster, it preserves a memory of the illustrious King Arthur, the Defender of the Faith! Armel = Arthmael = Arthur.

Select Bibliography

Alcock, Leslie. *Arthur's Britain*, The Penguin Press, London, 1971.
Ashe, Geoffrey. *From Caesar to Arthur*, Collins, London, 1960.
——. *Camelot and the Vision of Albion*, Heinemann, London, 1971.
——. *Kings and Queens of Early Britain*, Methuen (London) Ltd, 1982.
——. *A Guidebook to Arthurian Britain*, Aquarian Press, Wellingborough, 1983.
——. *The Discovery of King Arthur*, Debrett's Peerage Ltd, London, 1985.
Ashley, Mike. *A Brief History of King Arthur*, Constable & Robinson Ltd, London, 2010.
Barber, Chris and Pykitt, David, *Journey to Avalon*, Blorenge Books, Llanfoist, 1993.
——. *The Legacy of King Arthur*, Blorenge Books, Llanfoist, 2005.
Barber, Richard, *The Figure of King Arthur*, Longman, London, 1975.
Baring-Gould, Sabine. *The Lives of the Saints*, John C. Nimmo, London, 1898.
——. *A Book of the West-Cornwall*, Methuen & Co., London, 1899.
——. *A Book of Brittany*, Methuen & Co., London, 1901.
Baring-Gould, Sabine and Fisher, John, *The Lives of the British Saints*, The Honourable Society of Cymmrodorion, London, 1907–13.
Bartrum, P.C. *Early Welsh Genealogical Tracts*, University of Wales Press, Cardiff, 1966.
——. *Welsh Genealogies AD 300–1400*, University of Wales Press, Cardiff, 1974.
——. *A Welsh Classical Dictionary*, The National Library of Wales, Aberystwyth, 1993.
Bede. *A History of the English Church and People*, Penguin Books, Harmondsworth, 1968.
Bowen, Emrys George. *The Settlements of the Celtic Saints in Wales*, University of Wales Press, Cardiff, 1956.
——. *Britain and the Western Seaways*, Thames & Hudson, London, 1972.
Bromwich, Rachel. *Troedd Ynys Prydein (The Welsh Triads)*, University of Wales Press, Cardiff, 1978.
——. *The Arthur of the Welsh*, University of Wales Press, Cardiff, 1991.
Butler, Alban. *Lives of the Saints*, Burns, Oates & Washbourne, Tunbridge Wells, 1936.

Camden, William, *Britannia*, John Stockdale, London, 1806.
Carroll, D.F. *Arturius – A Quest for Camelot*, D.F. Caroll, Goxhill, 1996.
Carte, Thomas. *General History of England*, Vol. I, Thomas Carte, London, 1947.
Chadwick, Nora Kershaw. *Studies in Early British History*, Cambridge University Press, 1954.
——. *Studies in the Early British Church*, Cambridge University Press, Cambridge, 1958.
——. *Early Brittany*, University of Wales Press, Cardiff, 1969.
Chambers, E.K. *Arthur of Britain*, Sidgwick & Jackson, London, 1947.
Clark, George Thomas. 'The Land of Morgan', *Journal of the Archaeological Institute*, London, 1883.
Coxe, William. *An Historical Tour of Monmouthshire*, Merton Priory Press, Cardiff, 1995.
Dark, Ken. *Britain and the End of the Roman Empire*, Tempus Publishing Ltd, Stroud, 2000.
Davies, Wendy. *The Llandaff Charters*, The National Library of Wales, 1979.
——. *Annales de Bretagne*, Rennes, 1892.
Doble, Gilbert H. *The Saints of Cornwall*, The Holywell Press, Oxford, 1964–70.
——. *Lives of the Welsh Saints*, ed. D. Simon Evans, University of Wales Press, Cardiff, 1971.
Dugdale, William. *Monasticon Anglicanum*, Vol. III, 1673.
——. *The Antiquities of Warwickshire*, John Jones, Coventry, 1765.
Edwards, Alfred George. *Landmarks in the History of the Welsh Church*, John Murray, London, 1913.
Ellis, Peter Berresford. *Celtic Inheritance*, Frederic Muller, London, 1985.
Evans, J. Gwenogvryn and Rhys, John. *The Text of the Book of Llan Dav*, Oxford at the Clarendon Press, Oxford, 1893.
Evans, Gwynfor. *Land of My Fathers*, John Penry Press, Swansea, 1978.
——. *Magnus Maximus and the Birth of Wales the Nation*, John Penry Press, Swansea, 1983.
Fife, Graeme. *Arthur the King*, BBC Books, London, 1990.
Fleuriot, Leon. *Les Origines de la Bretagne*, Payot, Paris, 1980.
Foakes-Jackson, F.J. *The History of the Christian Church from the Earliest Times to AD 461*, George Allen & Unwin, London, 1914.
Foord, Edward. *The Last Age of Roman Britain*, George Harrap & Co., London, 1925.
Frere, Sheppard. *Britannia*, Routledge, London, 1967.

Galliou, Patrick and Jones, Michael. *The Bretons*, Basil Blackwell, Oxford, 1991.

Gantz, Jeffrey. *The Mabinogion*, Dorset Press, New York, 1985.

Garmondsway, G.N. *The Anglo-Saxon Chronicle*, J.M. Dent & Sons, London, 1973.

Geoffrey of Monmouth. *The History of the Kings of Britain*, Penguin Books Ltd, Harmondsworth, 1966.

Gerald of Wales. *The Journey through Wales and The Description of Wales*, Penguin Books, Harmondsworth, 1978.

Gidlow, Christopher. *The Reign of Arthur*, Sutton Publishing, Stroud, 2004.

Gillingham, John. 'The Context and Purpose of Geoffrey of Monmouth's History of the Kings of Britain', *Anglo-Norman Studies*, XIII (1990).

Giot, Pierre-Roland, Guigon, Philippe, and Merdrignac, Bernard. *The British Settlement of Brittany*, Tempus Publishing Ltd, Stroud, 2003.

Green, A.R. 'The Romsey Painted Wooden Reredos with a short account of St. Armel', *Archaeological Journal*, XC (1933).

Griscom, Acton. *The Historia Regum Britanniae of Geoffrey of Monmouth*, Longmans, Green & Co., London, 1929.

Guest, Charlotte. *The Mabinogion*, J.M. Dent & Sons Ltd, London, 1906.

Hewins, W.A.S. *The Royal Saints of Britain from the Latter Days of the Roman Empire*, Chiswick Press, London, 1929.

Holmes, Michael. *King Arthur, A Military History*, Blandford Press, London, 1996.

Hooke, Della. *The Landscape of Anglo-Saxon Staffordshire: The Charter Evidence*, University of Keele, Keele, 1983.

Issac, David Lloyd. *Siluriana*, W. Christopher, Newport, 1859.

James, J.W. 'Chronology in the Book of Llan Dav 500—900', *The National Library of Wales Journal*, XVI (1969/70).

——. 'The Book of Llan Dav and Canon G.H. Doble', *The National Library of Wales Journal*, XVIII (1973).

Johnstone, Paul Karlsson. 'The Riothamus Riot', *Pendragon, Journal of the Pendragon Society*, Vol. XVI, No. 2 (Spring, 1983).

Jones, T. Thornley. *Saints, Knights and Llannau*, J.D. Lewis & Sons Ltd, Gomer Press, Llandysul, 1975.

Knight, Jeremy. *South Wales from the Romans to the Normans*, Amberley Publishing, Stroud, 2013.

de La Borderie, Arthur. *Histoire de Bretagne*, Paris, 1891.

Lacy, Norris. *The Arthurian Encyclopedia*, The Boydell Press, Woodbridge, 1986.

Le Braz, Anatole. *Annales de Bretagne*, 1895.

Le Grand, Albert. *Les Vies des Saints de la Bretagne Armorique*, Quimper, 1901.

Lempriere, J. *Classical Dictionary of Proper Names mentioned by Ancient Authors*, Routledge & Kegan Paul Ltd, London, 1978.

Lewis, Henry. *Brut Dingestow*, University of Wales Press, Cardiff, 1942.

Lewis, Lionel Smithett. *Glastonbury, 'Mother of Saint's' – Her Saints AD 37–1539*, A.R. Mowbray & Co. Ltd, London, 1925.

——. *St. Joseph of Arimathea at Glastonbury or The Apostolic Church of Britain*, A.R. Mowbray & Co. Ltd, London, 1937.

Lindsay, Jack. *Arthur and His Times – Britain in the Dark Ages*, Frederick Muller Ltd, London, 1958.

Lloyd, John Edward. *A History of Wales from the Earliest Times to the Edwardian Conquest*, Vol. I, Longmans, Green & Co. Ltd, London, 1911.

Loomis, R.S. *Wales and the Arthurian Legend*, University of Wales Press, Cardiff, 1956.

Maitre, Leon and de Berthou, Paul. *Cartulaire de l'Abbaye de Saint-Croix de Quimerle*, Paris, 1886.

Malory, Sir Thomas. *Le Morte d'Arthur*, Caxton's Text, 2 Vols, Penguin, Harmondsworth, 1969.

Markale, Jean. *Celtic Civilization*, Gordon & Cremonesi Ltd, London, 1977.

——. *King Arthur: King of Kings*, trans. Christine Hauch, Gordon & Cremonesi Ltd, London, 1977.

Matthews, Caitlin. *Arthur and the Sovereignty of Britain*, Arkana, London, 1989.

Matthews, John. *An Arthurian Reader*, Aquarian Press, Wellingborough, 1988.

Matthews, Caitlin and John. *The Aquarian Guide to British and Irish Mythology*, Aquarian Press, Wellingborough, 1988.

——. *A Celtic Reader*, Aquarian Press, London, 1991.

——. *A Glastonbury Reader*, Aquarian Press, Wellingborough, 1991.

Mersey, Daniel. *Arthur, King of the Britons*, Summersdae, Chichester, 2004.

Millar, Ronald. *Will the Real King Arthur Please Stand Up*, Cassell, London, 1978.

Miller, Molly. *The Saints of Gwynedd*, The Boydell Press, Woodbridge, 1979.

Morganwg, Iolo (Edward Williams). *The Iolo Manuscripts*, The Welsh Manuscript Society, Longman & Co., Llandovery, 1848.

SELECT BIBLIOGRAPHY

Morice, Pierre Hyacinthe. *Memoires pour Servir de preuves a l'Histoire ecclesiastique et civile de Bretagne, Vol. I* , Charles Osmont, Paris, 1742.

Morris, John. *The Age of Arthur*, Weidenfield & Nicolson, London, 1973.

——. *Nennius's British History and the Welsh Annals*, Phillimore & Co. Ltd, Chichester, 1980.

Morris, Lewis. *Celtic Remains*, Cambrian Archaeological Association, 1878.

Mountney, Michael. *The Saints of Herefordshire*, Express Logic, Hereford, 1976.

Parry, John H. *The Cambrian Plutarch*, W. Simkin and R. Marshall, London, 1834.

Parry, J.J. *The Vita Merlini*, University of Illinois Press, 1925.

Powicke, F. Maurice and Fryde, E.B. *Handbook of British Chronology*, Offices of Royal Historical Society, London, 1961.

Probert, W. *The Triads of Britain*, Wildwood House Ltd, London, 1977.

Pughe, William Owen. *The Cambrian Biography*, Edward Williams, London, 1803.

Ratcliffe, Eric. *The Great Arthurian Timeslip*, Ore of Stevenage and Bungay, Stevenage, 1978.

Radford, C.A. *The Pillar of Eliseg*, H.M. Stationery Office, Edinburgh, 1980.

Redknap, Mark and Lewis, John M. *A Corpus of Early Medieval Inscribed Stones and Stone Sculpture in Wales – Vol. I – South-East Wales and the English Border*, University of Wales Press, Cardiff, 2007.

Reed, Trelawney Dayrell. *The Battle for Britain in the Fifth Century*, Methuen & Co., London, 1944.

Rees, Alwyn and Rees, Brinley. *Celtic Heritage*, Thames & Hudson, London, 1961.

Rees, David. *The Son of Prophecy – Henry Tudor's Road to Bosworth*, Black Raven Press, London, 1985.

Rees, Rice. *An Essay on the Welsh Saints*, Longman & Co., Llandovery, 1836.

Rees, William Jenkins. *The Liber Landavensis – The Ancient Register of the Cathedral Church of Llandaff*, Longman & Co., Llandovery, 1839.

——. *Lives of the Cambro-British Saints*, Longman & Co., London, 1853.

Reno, Frank. *Historic Figures of the Arthurian Era*, MacFarland & Company, London, 1937.

Rhys, John. *Celtic Britain*, Society for Promoting Christian Knowledge, London 1884.

——. *Celtic Folklore*, Oxford at the Clarendon Press, 1891.

——. *Studies in the Arthurian Legend*, Oxford at the Clarendon Press, Oxford, 1891.

Ritson, Joseph. *The Life of King Arthur from Ancient Historians and Authentic Documents*, William Nicol, St James's, London, 1825.

Roberts, Brynley F. *Brut y Brenhinedd (The Chronicle of the Kings)*, The Dublin Institute of Advanced Studies, 1971.

Roberts, Peter. *Sketch on the Early History of the Cymry or Ancient Britons from 700 BC to AD 400*, Edward Williams, London, 1803.

——. *The Chronicle of the Kings of Britain*, Edward Williams, London, 1811.

Skene, W.F. *Four Ancient Books of Wales*, Edmonton & Douglas, Edinburgh, 1868.

Spence, Keith. *Nicholson's Guide to Brittany*, Robert Nicholson Publications Ltd, London, 1985.

Squire, Charles. *Celtic Myth and Legend*, Newcastle Publishing Co. Inc., 1975.

Stanford, S.C. *The Archaeology of the Welsh Marches*, Collins, London, 1980.

Stein, Walter Johannes. *The Death of Merlin – Arthurian Myth and Alchemy*, Floris Books, Edinburgh, 1990.

Stephens, Meic. *The Oxford Companion to the Literature of Wales*, Oxford University Press, Oxford, 1986.

Stephens, Thomas. *The Literature of the Kymry*, Longmans, Green & Co., London, 1876.

——. *Welshmen – a Sketch in their History from the Earliest Times to the Death of Llywelin the Last*, Western Mail Ltd, Cardiff, 1901.

Stoker, Robert B. *The Legacy of Arthur's Chester*, Covenant Publishing Co. Ltd, London, 1965.

Tatlock, John Strong Perry. 'The Dates of the Arthurian Saints' Legends', *Speculum*, XIV (1939).

——. *The Legendary History of Britain – Geoffrey of Monmouth's 'Historia Regum Britanniae' and its Early Vernacular Versions*, University of California Press, Berkeley, CA, 1950.

Taylor, Thomas. *The Life of St. Samson of Dol*, Society for Promoting Christian Knowledge, London, 1925.

Thomas, Charles. *And Shall These Mute Stones Speak?*, University of Wales Press, Cardiff, 1994.

Thomas, Hugh. *An Essay towards the History of Brecknockshire*, 1698.

SELECT BIBLIOGRAPHY

Thorpe, Lewis. *Geoffrey of Monmouth's History of the Kings of Britain*, Penguin Books, Harmondsworth, 1966.

Tolstoy, Nikolai. *The Quest for Merlin*, Hamish Hamilton Ltd, London, 1985.

Trevelyan, Marie. *The Land of Arthur – Its Heroes and Heroines*, John Hogg, London, 1895.

Wade-Evans, the Revd Arthur W., 'The Brychan Documents', *Y Cymmrodor*, XIX (1906).

——. *The Life of St. David*, Society for Promoting Christian Knowledge, London, 1923.

——. 'The Llancarfan Charters', *Archaeologia Cambrensis*, LXXXVII (1932).

——. *Welsh Christian Origins*, The Alden Press, Oxford, 1934.

——. *Nennius's History of the Britons*, Society for Promoting Christian Knowledge, London, 1938.

—— *Vitae Sanctorum Britanniae et Genealogiae*, University of Wales Press, Cardiff, 1944.

Whitaker, John. *History of Manchester*, Joseph Johnson, London, 1775.

White, Richard. *King Arthur in Legend and History*, J.H. Dent, London, 1997.

——. *Britannia Prima – Britain's Last Roman Province*, Tempus Publishing Ltd, Stroud, 2007.

William of Malmesbury. *The Acts of the Kings of the English*, trans. as William of Malmesbury's *Chronicle* by John Sharpe; rev. by J.A. Giles, Bohn, London, 1947.

——. *The Kings before the Norman Conquest*, trans. Joseph Stephenson, Llanerch, 1989.

Williams, A.H. *An Introduction to the History of Wales, Vol. I, Prehistoric Times to AD 1063*, University of Wales Press Board, Cardiff, 1941.

Williams, David. *The History of Monmouthshire*, Tudor & Hall, Monmouth, 1796.

Williams, Gwyn. *When was Wales?*, Black Raven Press, London, 1985.

——. *Excalibur – The Search for Arthur*, BBC Books, London, 1994.

Williams, Ifor. *Breuddwyd Maxen*, Jarvis & Foster, Bangor, 1908.

——. *The Poems of Taliesin*, The Dublin Institute for Advanced Studies, 1975.

Williams, John. *The Ecclesiastical Antiquity of the Cymry*, W.J. Cleaves, London, 1844.

Williams-Nash, V.E. *The Early Christian Monuments of Wales*, University of Wales Press, Cardiff, 1950.

Williamson, David. *Debrett's Kings and Queens of Britain,* Webb & Bower Publishers Ltd, Exeter, 1986.

Winterbottom, Michael. *Gildas's 'The Ruin of Britain',* Phillimore & Co. Ltd, Chichester, 1978.

Wood, Eric, S. *Collins' Field Guide to Archaeology in Britain*, Collins, London, 1973.

Index

ancestors, 46–50; family, 55–72; crowning, 119–22; courts, 132–45; enemies, 159–61; the twelve battles, 170–80; Battle of Badon, 181–8; Battle of Camlann, 196–202; taken to Avalon, 203–6; alleged exhumation, 77–80; final years in Armorica, 214–23; bones of Arthur, 218–19; the positive identification of Arthur, 240–50

Arthur, Prince, son of Henry VII, 229

Arthwyr was a title, 17, 18

Artognov Stone, 75

Artur mac Aedan, 12, 13

Artur mac Bicoir, 13

Artur mac Conaing, 13

Arturus Fortissimus, 25

Arviragus, 81, 82, 83, 139

Ashe, Geoffrey, 163, 193

Athrwys ap Fferfael, 15

Athrwys ap Meurig, 15, 18, 22–4

Aulus Didius Gallus, 21

Aulus Plautius, 20, 21

Aurelius Caninus 17, 34, 221

Badon, Battle of (Mons Badonicus), 10, 37, 87, 181, 182, 183, 188

Bangor-is-Coed, Battle of, 157

Bannerdown Hill, 183

Bardsey Island, 105, 106, 125, 203, 204, 205

Baring-Gould, Revd Sabine, 60

Bartrum, Dr Peter Clement, 59, 94, 224

Bassaleg, 174

Bassas, Battle of, 83

Bat's Castle, 87

Bath, 183

Batz, Island of, 222

Bede, Venerable, 53, 151, 160, 182, 183

Bedwin Sands, 133

Bedwin, Bishop, 133, 188

z xBen Arthur, 13

Béroul, 90, 91

Bicanys, 64, 112

Black Book of Carmarthen, 16, 38, 71, 162, 178

Bledri ap Cydifor (Bledri Latimer), 137

Bochriw Carn, 33

Book of Chad, 41

Book of Llandaff, 41, 56, 57, 101–8, 161, 168, 169

Book of Taliesin, 160

Bosworth, Battle of, 228

Boverton, 90, 96, 98

Bovium, 98

Brank Aleg, Battle of, 218

Breviary of Rennes, 218

Briafel, 69

Brioc, St, 216

Brittannia, 80

Britu, 155, 159

Bro-Weroch, 211

Brochfael Ysgythrog, 29, 157

Brochmael ap Meurig, 57

Brut y Brenhinedd (Chronicle of the Kings) 29, 43, 44, 184

Brut Dingestow, 31

Brut Gryffydd ab Arthur, 29

Brut Tysilio, 29, 30, 119, 125, 134, 174, 178, 199, 200, 202 *see also Tysilio's Chronicle*

Brychan King, 33, 60, 65, 67, 69, 74, 78, 88, 147

INDEX

INDEX